HISTORY
OF RUSSIA

Sergei Mikhailovich Soloviev

The
Academic International Press
Edition
of
Sergei M. Soloviev

History of Russia

G. EDWARD ORCHARD
General Editor

Contributing Editors

HUGH F. GRAHAM

JOHN D. WINDHAUSEN

ALEXANDER V. MULLER

K.A. PAPMEHL

RICHARD HANTULA

WALTER J. GLEASON, JR.

WILLIAM H. HILL

G. EDWARD ORCHARD

LINDSEY A.J. HUGHES

NICKOLAS LUPININ

GEORGE E. MUNRO

DANIEL L. SCHLAFLY, JR.

ANTHONY L.H. RHINELANDER

PETER C. STUPPLES

SERGEI M. SOLOVIEV

History of Russia

Volume 41
Empress Elizabeth
Domestic Affairs and
the Seven Years War
1757–1761

Edited, Translated and With an
Introduction by

Peter C. Stupples

Academic International Press
1997

The Academic International Press Edition of S.M. Soloviev's
History of Russia From Earliest Times in fifty volumes.

Volume 41. *The Empress Elizabeth. Domestic Affairs and the
Seven Years War, 1757-1761.*
Unabridged translation of the text of Chapters II, III, IV, V and VI
of Volume 24 of S.M. Soloviev's *Istoriia Rossii s drevneishikh
vremen* as found in Volume XIII of this work published in Moscow
in 1965, with added annotation by Peter C. Stupples.

ISBN: 0-87569-183-8

Composition by Peggy P. Pope

Printed in the United States of America

A list of Academic International Press publications is found at
the end of this volume.

ACADEMIC INTERNATIONAL PRESS
Box 1111 • Gulf Breeze FL 32562-1111 • USA

CONTENTS

Todtleben's Treachery—Anglo-French Peace Talks Break
Down—Favorable Changes in the English Ministry—Sweden's
Desire for Peace—Strengthening of French Influence in Po-
land—Treaty between Turkey and Prussia—Danish Court Acts
Over the Holstein Affair—Frederick II's Desperate Plight—
Rumiantsev Captures Kolberg—Elizabeth's Illness and De-
mise—Significance of Elizabeth's Reign—Domestic Affairs in
the Last Year of Elizabeth's Reign

Illustrations and Map

WEIGHTS AND MEASURES

Linear and Surface Measures

Arshin: 16 vershoks, 28 in (diuims) 72.12 cm

Chetvert (quarter): 1/4 arshin, 1/2 desiatine, 1.35 acre (sometimes 1.5 desiatinas or ca 4.1 acres)

Desiatina: 2,400 square sazhens, 2.7 acres, 1.025 hectares

Diuim: 1 inch, 2.54 cm

Fut: 12 diuims, 1 foot, 30.48 cm

Obza (areal): c. 10 chetverts, 13–15 acres

Osmina: 1/4 desiatina, 600 sq. sazhens, .256 hectare

Sazhen: 3 arshins, 7 feet, 2.133 m

Vershok: 1.75 in, 4.445 cm, 1/16 arshin

Verst: 500 sazhens, 1,166 yards and 2 feet, .663 miles, 1.0668 km

Voloka (plowland): 19 desiatinas, 20 hectares, 49 acres

Liquid Measures

Bochka (barrel): 40 vedros, 121 gallons, 492 liters

Chetvert (quarter): 1.4 bochkas, 32.5 gallons

Kufa: 30 stofy

Stof: Kruzhka (cup), 1/10 vedro, c. 1.3 quarts, 1.23 liters

Vedro (pail): 3.25 gallons, 12.3 liters, 10 stofy

Weights

Berkovets: 361 lbs, 10 puds

Bezmen: c. 1 kg., 2.2 lbs

Chetverik (grain measure dating from 16th century): 1/8 chetvert, 15.8 lbs

Chetvert (grain measure): 1/4 rad, 3.5 puds, 126.39 lbs, c. 8 bushels

Funt: 96 zolotniks, .903 lbs, 14.4 ozs, 408.24 kg

Grivenka: 205 grams

Kad: 4 chetverts, 14 puds, 505.56 lbs

Kamen (stone): 32 funt

Korob (basket): 7 puds, 252 lbs

Osmina (eighth): 2 osmina to a chetvert (dry measure)

Polbezmen: c. 500 g, 1 lb

Polosmina (sixteenth): 1/2 osmina

Pud: 40 funts, 36.113 lbs (US), 40 lbs (Russian), 16.38 kg

Rad: 14 puds, 505.58 lb

Zolotnik: 1/96 lbs, 4.26 grams

Money

Altyn: 6 Muscovite dengas, 3 copecks

Chervonets (chervonny): gold coin of first half of 18th century worth c. 3 rubles

Chetvertak: silver coin equal to 25 copecks or 1/4 ruble (18–19th centuries)

Copeck: two Muscovite dengas

Denga: 1/2 copeck

Grivna: 20 Muscovite dengas, 100 grivnas equals 1 ruble, 10 copecks

Grosh: 10 peniaz

Grosh litovsky (Lithuanian grosh): 5 silver copecks

Kopa grosh: 60 groshas, one Muscovite poltina, 1/2 ruble

Moskovka: 1/2 copeck

Muscovite Denga: 200 equals 1 ruble

Novgorod Denga: 100 equals 1 ruble

Novgorodka: 1 copeck

Peniaz: 10 equals one grosh (Lithuania)

Poltina (poltinnik): 50 copecks, 100 dengas, 1 ruble

Poltora: 1 1/2 rubles

Polupoltina (-nik): 25 copecks, 50 dengas

Ruble: 100 copecks, 200 dengas

Shiroky grosh (large silver coin): 20 Muscovite copecks.

Foreign Denominations

Chervonnyi: c. 3 rubles

Ducat: c. 3 rubles

Efimok: c. 1 ruble, 1 chervonets or chervonnyi

Levok: Dutch silver lion dollar

Thaler (Joachimsthaler): c. 1 ruble, 1 chervonets or chervonnyi

Note: Weights and measures often changed values over time and sometimes held more than one value at the same time. For details consult Sergei G. Pushkarev, *Dictionary of Russian Historical Terms from the Eleventh Century to 1917* (Yale, 1970).

PREFACE

This book is an unabridged translation of Volume 24, Chapters 2-6, which are pp. 391-647 in Volume XII of the multi-volume edition of *Istoriia Rossii s drevneishikh vremen* (History of Russia From Earliest Times, 29 vols., St. Petersburg, 1851-1879) published from 1962 through 1966 in Moscow.

Soloviev's text presents a number of challenges to the translator. Whilst his own Russian is the standard literary language of the late nineteenth century he includes a considerable amount of archival material from the mid-eighteenth century that ranges in style from stilted officialese through the often contorted language of rescripts of the College of Foreign Affairs to the freer prose of some of the military commanders, whose use of Russian is often highly individualistic. For the purposes of this volume I have attempted to render the text in a uniform style of standard English that smooths the varied linguistic patterns of the original in the interests of clarity and plain, common sense. Much has been lost of the flavor of the original in the process. Both Soloviev and his sources use long sentences, sometimes punctuated with semi-colons but often not. The subject, and sometimes even the sense, frequently become lost to the reader. Again in the interests of clarity I have broken these sentences into smaller conceptual bites. Soloviev, like many more modern commentators, associates Prussia with the state of that name that developed from the mid-eighteenth century until the unification of Germany in the mid-nineteenth. In order to make it clear that he is talking about the original kingdom of Prussia, from which Frederick the Great took his title, Soloviev often, but by no means consistently, precedes it by the word East. Where Soloviev has not added the adjective and there is an element of ambiguity I have added "East" in the interests of clarity. Soloviev also, and this time consistently, refers to Great Britain as England, insensitive to the feelings of the Scots and the Welsh. I have retained this usage as it highlights even an educated Russian's lack of awareness of the importance of such matters in the outside world.

An effort has been made to find English-language equivalents for all the technical terms Soloviev employs (ranks, offices, titles, legal, administrative and so forth) in the belief that English is no less rich in such terms than other languages. This is intended to smooth the flow of the narrative for the reader and to avoid marring the pages with annoying untranslated words. The exceptions involves words which have become common in English such as cossack.

Most of the subtitles are based on the descriptive topic headings clustered at the beginnings of the chapters in the Russian edition. These headings have been moved into the body of the text as subtitles to mark, and to ease for the reader, the transition from one subject to another. Soloviev's arrangement of the material has been followed strictly.

Brief explanatory or interpretative materials have been added as footnotes to each chapter at the end of the book. Emphasized words or phrases in italics are the author's.

The general policy followed in annotating has been to identify prominent personalities at first mention and to give explanation and elucidations of less common or obscure terms and passages, assuming the typical reader to have relatively little familiarity with Russian history. These appear as numbered footnotes found at the back of the book by chapters. Most of the author's own notes are not included because their highly specialized archival, documentary and bibliographic nature is of value solely to specialists who will prefer to consult the original Russian text. In addition, most of the notes added by the editors of the edition published in the Soviet Union are technical in nature and fuller bibliographic citations than those in Soloviev's notes, and these have not been included. When the author's notes and those of the Soviet editors are included, they are so designated. All other notes are those of the present editor.

Russian personal names are preserved in their Russian form except for Alexander, Alexis, Michael, Nicholas, Catherine, Elizabeth and Peter, which English usage has made familiar with respect to Russian historical figures. This applies to prominent individuals; Russian forms usually are used for the less prominent. Certain other names and terms have been anglicized for the sake of clarity and because they are used widely— Danzig, Volhynia, Galicia, rubles and others.

The editors of the edition published in the USSR frequently have added patronymics and other names, and these have been retained without brackets; patronymics appearing in the original edition also have been included. Plural forms for names and terms which might be confusing have been anglicized. Most Slavic surnames show gender, and this has been preserved. Since an "-a" at the word end usually indicates a female,

Shuvalov would have a wife or daughter, Shuvalova. The final "-iia" in feminine personal names has been shortened to "-ia"—"Maria" instead of "Mariia".

Non-Russian names, locations, terms, ranks and so on are spelled according to the language native to the person or particular to the city, region or culture when this can be determined. Confusion arises at times because the text is not clear about nationalities. In such cases the context is the guide used and as a last resort the Russian spelling in the text is accepted. Individuals whose families were once non-Russian but had been in Russian service for generations are named by the original spelling of the family name. Turkish, Tatar, Persian and other names and terms are spelled in the original according to accepted forms in scholarly books. In some instances, if not otherwise ascertainable, they are transliterated from the Russian as given by Soloviev. The names of geographical locations conform to commonly accepted English usage—Moscow, St. Petersburg, Copenhagen, Saxony, and so forth.

Finally, with respect to transliteration, this translation follows a modified Library of Congress system omitting diacritical marks and ligatures, rendering the initial "Ia-" and "Iu-" as "Ya-" and "Yu-" ("Yasnaia" and Yury"), the suffixes "-ii", "-skii", "-skaia", and "-skoe" as "Dmitry Poliansky", "Polianskaia" and "Polianskoe", and the form "-oi" has been replaced by "-oy" ("Tolstoy" and not "Tolstoi") for certain family names familiar in this form in English. In some cases "-i-" has been inserted in place of hard and soft signs, or apostrophes indicating these signs. Hence Soloviev and not Solov'ev. The soft sign is not indicated by an apostrophe, as in some transliteration systems, but is dropped completely.

All the dates, as in the original, except where otherwise specified, are according to the Julian calendar ("Old Style"); that is, for the eighteenth century, eleven days behind the Gregorian calendar used in the West. A table of weights and measures is included at the front of this volume for the convenience of the reader.

In conclusion I would like to thank Edward Orchard, the general editor, for his patient and invaluable assistance and suggestions, as well as acknowledging the help of my colleagues Alexander Kruglov, Aleksei Vikulov and Sandra Bennett. Naturally I accept responsibility for any errors or inaccuracies in the translation.

Peter C. Stupples

INTRODUCTION

The last years of the reign of Empress Elizabeth were dominated by Russia's participation in the Seven Years War. Every diplomatic endeavor, every activity of central government and many considerations of changes to internal regulations were driven by Russia's war effort and the increasing financial and organizational burdens it placed upon government and the nation as a whole.

Russia became involved in the Seven Years War for two major reasons. The first followed from Elizabeth's own sense of mission as the daughter of Peter the Great. As early as 1753 she identified Frederick II, the king of Prussia, as her principal enemy, the major threat to Russian expansion in the Baltic region, to Russia's domination of Poland and as a dangerous potential ally of the Turks, thus also threatening Russian expansion towards the Crimea. As her father had defeated Sweden in order to open up the Baltic and Ukraine, so Elizabeth set her sights on weakening and even dismembering the state of Brandenburg-Prussia for the same reasons. To pursue this policy she needed suitable alliances, which led her into the complex web of diplomatic maneuvers that took place in Europe in the 1750s. It was Russia's obligations to these alliances that present the second major reason for its participation in the war.

Elizabeth's first natural ally in support of her intentions was Archduchess Maria Theresa of Austria whose possessions in Silesia and Glatz had been overrun by Frederick II in 1740-1741. Austria was at the time allied to Great Britain. When Britain asked Maria Theresa for assistance against Frederick in 1755, she declined until Russia could be induced to attack Frederick the moment he moved a single soldier across his borders. Britain, through its envoy Hanbury Williams, had been laboring for two years already to secure Russian agreement to this idea, in exchange for financial subsidies, in order to prevent Frederick from attacking Hanover, the German state inherited by the king of England. The Russian chancellor Alexis Bestuzhev-Riumin saw sense in this alliance with Britain and Austria against Frederick and the best way to secure Elizabeth's ambitions. In addition Bestuzhev considered France the second most troublesome power in Europe threatening Russia's intentions, in particular through France's anti-Russian policies in Poland and Sweden. Britain was the principal enemy of France and thus would be the natural ally of Russia.

It was Britain which in 1755 made the first move to unsettle this pattern of alliances by making overtures to the king of Prussia which were reciprocated. Though negotiations with Russia continued through Hanbury Williams it became increasingly clear that these were based upon a false premise—that Prussia and Britain were enemies and not allies. This was made manifest in January 1756 when Britain and Prussia signed the Convention of Westminster. Under its terms Britain secured the protection of Hanover in exchange for supporting Frederick with financial subsidies. France was outraged by this turn of events, which saw its ally Prussia now in alliance with its mortal foe Britain. Elizabeth also was outraged by such seeming duplicity, and Hanbury Williams found himself considerably weakened in the competition that then ensued with France for Russian sympathy. Austria now also saw its own advantages lying with France, an ancient adversary, rather than Britain. Thus the "old system" of alliances of Britain, Austria and Russia against France and Prussia was superseded by the "new system" of Russia, France and Austria against Britain and Prussia. The new alliance between France and Austria was established by the Treaty of Versailles of 1756 to which Russia adhered in 1757. Russia did not break off relations with Britain. Both valued their trading links with each other, and this cool but well regulated relationship was to prove valuable to all parties when the time came to press for a peace settlement at the end of the war. These events and changes in policy are admirably set out by Herbert Kaplan in his *Russia and the Outbreak of the Seven Years' War* (Berkeley, 1968).

The "old system" died slowly in the imagination of the participants, as many of its considerable advantages frequently made themselves obvious, and the disadvantages, particularly the alliance with France, irked Russia considerably. Elizabeth was not one to make sharp distinctions between past and present policies. Soloviev makes it clear that, while pursuing the "new" system, Elizabeth never lost sight of the advantages of the "old." She was driven by the ambition to expand Russian territory in the Baltic and during the years covered by this volume repeatedly made it plain to her allies that she expected to be rewarded for Russia's participation in the war in support of Austria by acquiring the kingdom of Prussia, often referred to as East Prussia, the hereditary lands of Frederick himself and the territory from which he derived his very title. Should he lose Prussia he would be obliged to revert to his secondary rank of elector of Brandenburg, losing his royal crown. East Prussia was a prize worth fighting for.

Elizabeth also stated her intention to exchange East Prussia for the duchy of Courland with Poland, but there is no evidence that she would have kept to this. Courland, to all intents and purposes, was already the gift of Russia, and possession of East Prussia would have secured a long and very useful seaboard for Russian commercial expansion in Europe.

These intentions of Elizabeth greatly alarmed Maria Theresa, who did not want to see a weakened Frederick replaced as a potential threat to Austria by a more powerful Elizabeth. Austria was also aware of Russian interest in the Balkans. Russia already was standing up for the rights of the adherents of the Orthodox church in Serbia and Croatia.

Though France was severely defeated by Britain in America, India and Africa in the early 1760s, Louis XV never came to terms with his country's permanently weakened position in Europe. France still behaved as if it were the major power on the continent. It freely interfered in Polish affairs, paying subsidies and bribes to its adherents in the corrupt Saxon-Polish court and to those Polish gentry opposed to Russian influence. In Sweden it also arrogantly meddled in domestic affairs, again supporting those interests opposed to Russia. Russia's new ally, then, acted more frequently in relation to Russia under the terms of the "old system" rather than the "new." With each British victory over France, Russia saw the wisdom of retaining good relations with Pitt and Newcastle.

Within court circles Elizabeth kept in office the adherents of both the "old" system and the "new". The chancellor Alexis Bestuzhev-Riumin was an anglophile and francophobe, a passionate advocate of the "old." Yet his position was constantly undermined by his deputy Mikhail Vorontsov, who was pro-French and supported in this sentiment by the powerful Shuvalov family. Elizabeth refused to side clearly with the one or the other until events at the end of 1757 forced her hand. On September 8 Elizabeth suffered a mild stroke from which she swiftly and fully recovered. On news of this event the Russian commander-in-chief Apraksin appeared to be about to move rapidly back to the vicinity of St. Petersburg but changed the velocity and direction of this return into a quest for winter quarters nearer his supply depots when Elizabeth's recovery became known to him. Apraksin was a close friend of Bestuzhev-Riumin and also of Grand Duchess Catherine. Bestuzhev-Riumin's enemies claimed that there was a plot, in which Apraksin was implicated, to secure the throne for Catherine on Elizabeth's demise. The participants were arrested in 1758, but no evidence of a plot was found.

Elizabeth did not pursue these rumors with total commitment. She had brought her nephew, Prince Peter of Schleswig-Holstein-Gottorp, a grandson of Peter the Great, to St. Petersburg as her designated heir, but he had proved scarcely worthy of the honor. He was an ardent admirer of Frederick the Great and the Prussian way of government. If he became tsar, the main thrust of Elizabeth's foreign policy would be reversed. Though his wife Catherine was also German, she could see that her advantage at the Russian court lay in opposing Frederick, either under the "old" or the "new" system. There would be a lot of sympathy for her to take the throne, despite her tenuous legitimacy to do so. She had no love for her husband, nor he for her. They clearly stood for opposing government policies.

Soloviev is always hesitant to display his own prejudices. Nevertheless the thrust of his historiography is to unfold the steady growth in power and territory of the Russian state. Peter the Great is an obvious hero. Soloviev emphasizes that Elizabeth followed in her father's footsteps. Bestuzhev-Riumin also followed Peter's policies. The implication is that Soloviev also had sympathies for the "old system" and those who supported it. Catherine certainly would have been more likely than her husband to pursue these policies, and therefore had there been a coup, as there was to be in 1762, Russia's interests would be served better by Catherine than by Peter. The commission which examined Bestuzhev did not ask the right or always the direct questions. Time was allowed to elapse before Bestuzhev's arrest to give him time to destroy evidence of a plot. Word was passed to Catherine in time for her to act in her own best interests. In other words, although Elizabeth was forced by the anti-Bestuzhev faction to act against the plotters, she did so in such a way that clear knowledge of a plot would be kept from her. By the standards of the time she dealt with the supposed plotters with great leniency.

Nevertheless Bestuzhev was removed from his post and Vorontsov elevated to the chancellorship, while the Shuvalovs became almost undisputed managers of the government. The "old system" clearly was defeated. Soloviev's anti-French sympathies find much to be regretted in this. In his assessment of Elizabeth's reign he remarks that Vorontsov found the strain of running foreign affairs, with all its intricacies and careful considerations, beyond his strength in contrast, the assumption is, to the ease and astuteness with which Bestuzhev handled this portfolio during his years in office. He also displays an admiration for Bestuzhev when recounting his witty and incisive replies to the investigating commission, using the opportunity less for a defense of himself than for an attack upon the policies of his enemies at the Russian court, attacks which Bestuzhev knew would be read and understood by the quick intelligence of the empress. There is little wonder she was lenient with the "plotters" who so demonstrably stood for the very policies she held so dear.

What Soloviev also makes clear is that under Bestuzhev the College of Foreign Affairs had become, in so short a time, a very sophisticated department of government. Russian ambassadors abroad were well-informed, meticulous in their reports, balanced in their judgments and highly professional. If most Western European nations still regarded Russia as barbaric and unworthy of their very company, nevertheless Russian diplomats such as Prince Alexander Golitsyn in London often were treated with great respect. In fifty years the Russian foreign service had transformed its operations from medieval practice into the sophisticated diplomatic discourse of its contemporaries. In Sweden Panin kept aloof from the intrigues indulged in by the French, while in Poland Volkonsky and Voeikov were very confident in navigating the diplomatic shoals that swept around the Polish-Saxon court and inter-magnate rivalries, even if they did so with the assurance of politicians who knew that their own forces easily and swiftly could silence any opposition to the ultimate will of their government. Poland was a diplomatic colony of Russia. The king owed his crown to Russian support, in exchange for which he had acknowledged Russian claims to Courland. Russia moved its troops through Poland to fight Prussia with little regard for local rights. Polish and Turkish interference in Ukraine was irksome, but ultimately manageable.

To the modern mind the Seven Years War is an example of that interdynastic rivalry that so characterizes European history before the nineteenth century. It was an archaic war. The armies fought for the Habsburgs, Bourbons, Hohenzollerns or the house of Hanover almost regardless of nationality or statehood. Officers of all nationalities offered their services to the best paymaster or the army with the greatest prestige. James Keith, for example, was a Scottish Jacobite who served in Russia in the 1730s, assisting the Irishman Lacy in the invasion of Poland in 1733, yet he later joined Frederick the Great, becoming a field marshal in the Prussian army. The Russian army employed a large number of German-speaking officers, some of whom were trained in Prussia or had fought with the Prussian army. These officers were invaluable to Russia, as they were more competent and better trained than their Russian counterparts.

As the war developed a number of younger Russian generals came to the fore, lessening the necessity of relying upon those whose loyalty sometimes may have been insecure. For example many Baltic Germans certainly would have preferred the victory of Frederick the Great and Prussian expansion into the Northern Baltic over Russian expansion to the south. Elizabeth's choice of Grand Duke Peter as her heir is another example of setting dynastic imperatives over those of the nation-state. Elizabeth's primary loyalty was to the memory of her late sister Anna of Holstein, and she elevated her sister's son to the throne despite his known antipathy to Russia and things Russian, and indeed to her own foreign policy.

Elizabeth set and maintained the direction of foreign policy initiatives, and particularly Russia's participation in the Seven Years War, yet her interest in the management of the war effort was almost non-existent and her grasp of the realities and cost of war unbelievably naïve. Her remark that if it came to it she would be prepared to sell her jewelry and gowns to pay Russia's way gives some sense of her comprehension. Russian scholars have pointed out that while Elizabeth made seven appearances at the Senate in 1742, she attended four times in each of the following two years, and only bothered to come three more times in the remaining seventeen years of her reign.

If the Seven Years War was archaic in the sense of its dynastic motivation, it was also a very modern war. Armaments were becoming more sophisticated. The carnage in battle was very high. The parties were very evenly balanced so that a swift solution was always unlikely. It was only Russia's second experience of the conditions of modern warfare but this time against the most formidable military machine in Europe. In these circumstances its army performed very creditably. The military background to the period is interestingly surveyed by Christopher Duffy in his two books *Russia's Military Way to the West. Origins and Nature of Russian Military Power, 1700-1800* (London, 1981) and *The Army of Frederick the Great* (Newton Abbot, 1974).

Soloviev's work is one of serious scholarship, very thorough, and expository in nature. It ranks with the classics of nineteenth-century historiography and laid the groundwork for the Russian historical writing that followed.

This reputation as a scholarly foundation piece is well deserved. Soloviev utilized an immense body of archival material previously untapped. This material is impressive, and in keeping with Soloviev's emphasis on the history of the Russian state, both political and diplomatic.

It may be instructive to note some of the vast array of sources: the Protocols of the Conference, the Journals and Protocols of the Senate, the Vorontsov Archives, the Shakhovskoy Archives, the Moscow Archives of the Ministry of Foreign Affairs, the diplomatic papers of Russian relations with Austria, Prussia, Sweden, Denmark, France, Turkey and Great Britain, materials published in *Sbornik Russkogo Istoricheskogo Obshchestva* (Collection of the Russian Historical Society) and contemporary Russian newspapers. He utilized the memoirs of Catherine the Great and A. T. Bolotov, as well as the collected works of Frederick II. He also made use of secondary sources such as A. Schaefer's *Geschichte des siebenjährigen Kriegs* (History of the Seven Years War), Ernst Hermann's *Geschichte der europäischen Staaten. Geschichte des russischen Staats* (History of the European States. History of the Russian State), F. Raumer's *Beiträge zur neueren Geschichte* (Essays on Recent History), and M. E. Boutaric *Correspondance secrète inédite de Louis XV* (Secret and Unedited Correspondence of Louis XV). This is truly an impressive list, especially when we consider that this is a partial one.

Inevitably Soloviev takes up a lot of space in recounting the events of the Seven Years War as they affected Russia. He naturally takes a very patriotic tone, but was not unaware of the fragile nature of the victory at Gross-Jägersdorf and the near defeat at Zorndorf. Neither was he indifferent to the poor leadership of the Russian forces, only Saltykov emerging with even the semblance of a reputable performance. Soloviev does not, however, take a broad look at Russian achievements and weaknesses. It was a monumental task of logistics to keep such a large and heterogeneous body of men as made up the Russian army on the road and in a forward direction in days of poor communication, unmetalled roads and moving through a generally hostile local population. The Russian commissary did a commendable job with little reward. The Prussians and Austrians were often fighting within or near their own frontiers. Their lines of communication were firm and short. The Russians were fighting often hundreds of miles from their border, with lines of communication frequently threatened and extended beyond the limits previously experienced by Russia in prolonged warfare. The Russian army was comparatively untrained and ill-equipped. It suffered from a debilitating inferiority complex when confronting a commander with the reputation of Frederick the Great. Foreign officers within its ranks, either as mercenaries or volunteers, were often contemptuous of their Russian companions and the Russian commanders-in-chief. Despite these real and imaginary weaknesses, Russia

and Austria were about to achieve a final victory when they were robbed
of its realization by the death of Elizabeth and the accession of the pro-
Prussian Peter III. Soloviev brings out the jealousy and lack of trust
between the Russians and Austrians. The Austrians were fearful of
Russian success, and the Russians convinced that it was they who were
taking the brunt of Frederick's aggression.

Soloviev is less successful in covering Russian domestic affairs.
Although he relates some decisions of the Conference and the Senate he
does little to analyze the relationship between these institutions and their
relative responsibility for managing the affairs of state. The Conference
was established on March 25, 1756 to administer the war effort against the
king of Prussia. The best discussion of this establishment and the early
activity of the Conference is to be found in Kaplan, but there is no such
scholarly treatment available for the last years of Elizabeth's reign. The
Conference had authority, through the empress, to issue decrees on any
matter relating to the war, which would have the power of law throughout
the Russian empire. The Senate, which carried out the daily routine
management of government policy through the various colleges subordinate to it, was obliged to accommodate the decisions of the Conference
within that daily management. The membership of the Conference and the
Senate overlapped. In the final years of Elizabeth's reign both institutions
were working inefficiently and were subject to the corroding corruption
common in Russian political circles in the eighteenth century. There were
too few men of talent or commitment to fill the highest managerial
positions. The same few families supplied ministers, ambassadors and
administrators. These families were now Russian rather than Baltic
German, but were short of the highly trained support they needed to run a
state machinery of swiftly growing complexity and responsibilities.

Soloviev pays no attention to Russia's cultural development. Here
Elizabeth's reign can be distinguished clearly from that of her predecessor.
There was respect for education, European education, in the circles of the
élite. Grand Duchess Catherine herself was proud of her own learning, and
Soloviev remarks on the fact that she had a copy of the French encyclopedia in her rooms. We learn of payments for Locatelli's opera company, yet
we must look elsewhere for the intriguing details of its existence in
barbaric Russia. We read of reports in newspapers, yet Soloviev makes no
mention of their influence, distribution, readership, of censorship and the
control of information. Of literature and poetry we learn nothing. He
certainly would have read about the acculturation of the middle nobility in
the writing of Andrei Bolotov, one of his sources.

Soloviev's tantalizing glimpses into the Russian provinces raise the common prejudices of Western Europeans. Bribery and corruption were the common stuff of daily life. Inefficiency and arbitrary rule, cruelty and lawlessness were everywhere. Yet in the absence of any analysis of the common realities of Russian life at the time, Soloviev presents a view of Russian history posited upon the evidence of notorious court cases, exceptions rather than rules. A cursory perusal of Boswell's journals of his Grand Tour is enough to convince the reader of the general primitiveness of Europe in the mid-eighteenth century. Russia was indeed by comparison a backwater, yet there was now a sense of political vigor and economic energy absent a century before. Mining and manufacturing were significant realities. International commerce was on the threshold, even though it is clear that banking methods, already well advanced in Britain, France, Holland and Germany, were almost unknown and the subject of suspicion and disbelief that they could assist Russia's economic development. The precarious nature of Russia's economic management, as demonstrated by Soloviev, nevertheless bears comparison with similar primitive economic instruments operating further to the West. In the whole of Europe the economy was there to serve the dynasty and its aristocratic supporting class rather than to assist the development of the nation-state. Only slowly over this period was popular sentiment given ear. In Britain Pitt was popular because his style of aggressive empire-building satisfied the prevalent ambitions of ordinary British citizens. In Brandenburg-Prussia and German-speaking Eastern Europe there was great popular enthusiasm for Frederick the Great, a leader standing up for German rights against the Hapsburgs and the surrounding non-German speakers. These sentiments did not yet cohere as nationalism. Soloviev gives no indication as to whether the Seven Years War was popular or not amongst ordinary Russians. No doubt it was seen by most soldiers of the line as just another burden that life placed so indifferently upon the backs of the unprivileged.

The reign of Elizabeth is little studied in Russia or the West by comparison with that of Peter the Great coming before it or of Catherine the Great that almost immediately follows. Marc Raeff's two books, *Imperial Russia 1682-1825. The Coming of Age of Modern Russia* (New York, 1971) and *Origins of the Russian Intelligentsia. The Eighteenth Century Nobility* (New York, 1966) are sound introductions to the period. Hans Rogger offers another general discussion in his book *National Consciousness in Eighteenth Century Russia* (Harvard, 1960). There are two lives of Elizabeth herself. Robert Nisbet Bain, *The Daughter of Peter the Great. A History of Russian Diplomacy under the Empress Elizabeth*

Petrovna 1741-1762 (London, 1899) has not been bettered as a general summary. Bain leans heavily on the work of Soloviev. Tamara Talbot Rice's *Elizabeth, Empress of Russia* (London, 1970), though more recent, offers few additions to the work of Bain. The detailed diplomatic history of Herbert Kaplan, *Russia at the Outbreak of the Seven Years War* (Berkeley, 1968), is one of the few substantial scholarly works on the period. A more recent work, Evgeny V. Anismov's *Empress Elizabeth. Her Reign and Her Russia, 1741-1761* (Gulf Breeze, Fla.: Academic International Press, 1993), offers dramatic and provocative glimpses of high politics, court intrigue, Elizabeth's *coup* and personality, eminent personages and lively court culture.

The life of Catherine the Great during the reign of Elizabeth is discussed in both John T. Alexander, *Catherine the Great. Life and Legend* (New York, 1989) and Isabel de Madariaga, *Russia in the Age of Catherine the Great* (London, 1981). Gerhard Ritter's book *Frederick the Great. An Historical Profile* (London, 1968) gives a useful summary of his reign, and the set of essays by Peter Paret, *Frederick the Great. A Profile* (New York, 1972) contain more detailed studies. The Polish background can be traced in Chapter 17 of the second volume of Norman Davies, *God's Playground* (Oxford, 1981). The political situation in Scandinavia is summarized succinctly in Chapters 12-13 of David Kirby, *Northern Europe in the Early Modern Period. The Baltic World 1492-1772* (London, 1990). Details of military matters in the eighteenth century can be found in the books of Christopher Duffy, *The Army of Frederick the Great* (Newton Abbot, 1974) and *Russia's Military Way to the West. Origins and Nature of Russia's Military Power 1700-1800* (London, 1981).

In a recent brief survey of the period, the second edition of Paul Dukes, *The Making of Russian Absolutism* (London, 1990), the author rather casually dismisses Elizabeth's government as scarcely more competent than that of her predecessor Empress Anna. Yet Soloviev is probably right to point out that the seeds of Catherine's success were sown in the reign of Elizabeth. Russia's participation in the Seven Years War marked a forward momentum upon which Catherine could build. The future partition of Poland was made possible by the growing power of Russia and the disarray of the Polish political state. The training of the aristocracy in statecraft and diplomacy was a resource that Catherine was able to utilize more consistently and more broadly than her immediate predecessor. As Soloviev (p. 289) rightly points out, "while giving our due to Catherine II we must not forget how much, both within Russia and without, was prepared for her by Elizabeth."

History of Russia

Volume 41

Empress Elizabeth

*Domestic Affairs and
the Seven Years War, 1757-1761*

I

OPENING OF THE SEVEN YEARS WAR, 1757

TREATY BETWEEN RUSSIA AND AUSTRIA

Winter interfered with the movement of the armed forces but not with diplomatic preparations for war. On January 22 a new treaty was concluded in St. Petersburg between Russia and Austria. The treaty of May 1746[1] was confirmed, in particular the separate and secret article of that treaty which formed the basis of the present agreement. Maria Theresa undertook to maintain not less than eighty thousand regular troops against Prussia for however long the war lasted. Elizabeth also would maintain eighty thousand troops, as well as between fifteen and twenty ships of the line and at least forty galleys. The treaty powers agreed to furnish each other with detailed and precise information on the state and condition of their forces, which was to be forwarded reciprocally by generals who had the right to be present and to vote on councils of war. There would be mutual agreement in respect to the general plan of military operations.

As the king of Prussia was currently using the greater part of his forces against the army of the empress-queen, the empress of All Russia undertook to move her forces into his territories as soon as possible. The empress-queen agreed to engage the Prussian forces in order to assist the operations of the Russians. Both sovereigns undertook to conclude neither peace nor an armistice with the common enemy, the king of Prussia, without mutual agreement. They would pursue the war until the empress-queen received undisputed possession of the whole of Silesia and the county of Glatz.[2] The peace of Europe could be established securely only when the king of Prussia lost the means to disturb it. Both empresses would use all the means at their disposal to render mankind this service, and they would communicate these intentions to all other powers inclined towards their policy. In separate articles the treaty powers committed themselves to summon other sovereigns to join their alliance, in the first place the king of France and then those of Sweden and Denmark, while Sweden must be compensated in keeping with its participation in the war. Russia and Austria were obliged to use every means at their disposal, not only for the return of Saxony to the king of Poland,[3] but also to furnish him, at the expense of Prussia, with appropriate compensation for his losses. In a separate and secret article Austria was obliged to pay Russia a million rubles a year. The treaty was written in French, but it was inserted into the agreement that this was not to be taken as a precedent. The treaty was signed by Count Alexis Bestuzhev-Riumin,[4] Count Mikhail Vorontsov[5] and Count Nicholas Esterhazy.[6]

In order to divert Grand Duke Peter Fedorovich's[7] attention from the king of Prussia, Maria Theresa considered it necessary to conclude a particular agreement with him, according to which the court of Vienna would pay him one hundred thousand florins. Kaunitz[8] was displeased, and said the empress was throwing this money out of the window, because the grand duke would not change in his feelings towards the king of Prussia. Maria Theresa could agree to the annual payment of a million rubles to Russia because by a new treaty, concluded with France on May 1, 1757, the king of France undertook to pay her ten million guilders. The king agreed to pay money to the empress-queen and to assist her with armed forces until she obtained Silesia, the county of Glatz and the principality of Crossen through a peace settlement with the king of Prussia. The elector of Saxony was to receive the duchy of Magdeburg. France would receive part of Austria's Netherlands possessions, while the other part would be awarded to the son-in-law of Louis XV, the Spanish Infante Philip.

The treaty between France and Austria determined what both powers would receive if they forced the king of Prussia to conclude peace. Yet when Russia, in a special declaration, wanted to assert its desire to obtain the province of East Prussia, to be bartered with Poland in exchange for Courland,[9] Maria Theresa strongly opposed such a declaration. Esterhazy explained to Vorontsov that the empress-queen was prepared to obtain for Russia not only East Prussia but even greater acquisitions. Moreover the word she had given would have greater force and action than an empty resolution concluded in general terms. Should this resolution and secret become known, France would suspect and distrust both courts. The king of Prussia, Poland and other powers would spread the voice of censure throughout the world.

The fact is that the court of Vienna already had let France know about the Russian demands, and from France came the advice to tell Russia that it was not yet time to make France a proposal about such matters. Moreover the French ambassador in Vienna received a warning from his court that Vienna would be making a mistake if it favored the expansion of Russia in the proximity of Germany, and the court in Vienna would perhaps be the first to repent.

"In my humble opinion," Vorontsov observed in his report to the empress concerning Esterhazy's advice, "in the present delicate and extremely complex circumstances it seems we may act upon this wish of the court of Vienna without criticism. When God gives His blessing to Russian arms, and East Prussia and the other territories of the king of Prussia are conquered, perhaps in a general peace treaty, according to the circumstances existing at the time, we can retain Courland or the city of Danzig, or receive some other benefits in compensation for our losses." The matter was set aside until a more propitious time.

TREATY BETWEEN RUSSIA AND FRANCE

We have seen that at the very end of 1756 Elizabeth acceded to the first Treaty of Versailles, but with a particular stipulation with respect to Turkey and England. Bekhteev[10] had to explain to the French ministry that Russia was slow in acceding to the Treaty of Versailles. It not only wanted to renew this sound agreement, but also to give it an unshakable foundation. Therefore it was concerned particularly with this problem, and not with the form alone. Were both England and Turkey excluded from the treaty, it would simply amount to a restoration of friendship,[11] as England in respect to France, and Turkey in respect to Russia, were the only powers that could be expected to violate the peace.

Bekhteev told Vorontsov that it was impossible to describe how this most secret declaration was a matter of regret to the French court. It considered the affair dishonorable, and suspected that the chancellor created it on purpose, wishing either to cause France to fall out with the Porte or to create coldness between France and Russia. Rouillé[12] expressed the fear that Bestuzhev on purpose had given instructions that the declaration should not be communicated to the Porte. "Vice Chancellor Vorontsov, as an honest man, would not have done this," said Rouillé. They were extremely irritated by Douglas,[13] putting all the blame on him. Rouillé even made up his mind to tell Bekhteev that if this was the way things were to be done, it was impossible to have any dealings with the Russian court.

LOUIS XV FAILS TO RATIFY SECRET RUSSIAN DECLARATION

Officially Bekhteev announced on February 8, 1757 that the deed of accession was ratified, but that the ratification of the declaration was not agreed. The king said that he "could not agree to this excellent secret deed, which Douglas had the stupidity to sign." Rouillé told Bekhteev flatly that political reasons and the particular interest of France would not permit the king to do so. In present circumstances the Porte must be held back from joining with England and the king of Prussia, in order not to lose influence with the Porte or destroy French trade in the Levant.

The Porte was greatly alarmed on hearing of the Treaty of Versailles and in particular of Russia's accession. Only one reassurance would calm the Porte, that it specifically be excluded in the deed of accession. This reassurance was given. After this it would have been contrary to the custom and conscience of the king to conclude at once two deeds about the same matter in direct contradiction one with the other, especially as in France no one was assured that secrets could be kept (it rarely happened that the most secret paragraph did not come out). Such conduct, however, would not be vindicated by reason of a secret. Therefore his majesty the king put his hopes in the known sincerity and perspicacity of the empress. The justice of the reasons preventing ratification of the declaration would not escape her. This incident, however, was regrettable to the French government.

"Indeed," wrote Bekhteev, "the French court has been thrown into great sorrow and confusion. On the one hand it is constrained by the reassurance given to the Porte, and on the other feels the unpleasant consequences of the denial of ratification. The ministry is seriously annoyed with Count Esterhazy, with Douglas and with Count Starhemberg;[14] at Esterhazy for forcing Douglas to sign the declaration, and at Count Starhemberg for failing to interpret sufficiently exactly the opinions of the French government, which counted on him in this matter. Rouillé spoke about Douglas with great displeasure. In conclusion Rouillé begged me to assure her imperial majesty that, in spite of this unpleasant incident, the king sincerely wanted the real affirmation of a friendship successfully renewed and gave an assurance that the unpleasantness that has occurred in no way would hinder him, together with Russia, from taking measures for the satisfaction of the courts in Vienna and Saxony with respect to the king of Prussia."

CONFLICTS BETWEEN RUSSIA AND FRANCE OVER POLAND

In addition to Turkey, Poland also gave considerable trouble, because France was afraid lest the Russian party in Poland become stronger following the entry of Russian forces into that country. The French court saw a clear sign of the strengthening of the Russian party, the party of the

Czartoryskis,[15] in the appointment of a nephew of the Czartoryskis, and a friend of Williams,[16] Stanislaw Poniatowski,[17] as Polish plenipotentiary in St. Petersburg. In vain August III[18] reassured the French court. In vain Bekhteev assured Rouillé that Poniatowski gave his word of honor to adhere to the present political system.[19] If his conduct proved to be in any way hostile, the king would recall him immediately. Rouillé kept repeating one thing, that Poniatowski was a friend of Williams. Rouillé handed Bekhteev a note stating that the king of France recognized the need for the passage of Russian troops through Poland but that it was necessary to anticipate any harmful consequences that might arise. There was no doubt that the Poles attached to Russia were planning a confederation.[20] They counted on being supported by the Russian generals commanding the forces in Poland and hoped that the presence of the Russian army, even if it took no part in Polish affairs, would give them greater strength. Their enemies, who had resort to the French court, would be forced to convoke their own confederation and would perhaps even want to forestall their enemies.

As the passage of Russian forces through Poland was designed to render assistance to the king of Poland as soon as possible by entering the territories of his enemy, the French court acknowledged, and would acknowledge as the best scenario, that Russian troops proceed to East Prussia from Courland, seizing a small part of Samogitia.[21] If both imperial courts believed it necessary for Russian forces to go through Poland by another route the French court, for the maintenance of peace in Poland and to soothe the Turks, would agree to this on one condition, that the Russian forces pass through Poland with all possible speed, observing the strictest discipline and paying for everything meticulously. Later the French court acknowledged that before Russian troops entered Poland the Russian ministers in Warsaw must let it be known, verbally and in writing, that on their passage through Poland the forces of the empress had no intention, under any pretext whatsoever, of interfering in the domestic affairs of the Commonwealth and that everything would be left as it was, in particular the prison regulations. Russia must use all its influence to restrain its adherents from forming a confederation and must not in any way intervene in the private disputes of the Polish grandees. The king of France for his part was prepared to make a similar declaration to the Poles, not to expect any help from him in sowing discord in the Commonwealth or in impeding the passage of Russian forces.

BEKHTEEV ON RELATIONS BETWEEN ALLIED COURTS

Bekhteev, on returning the note to Rouillé and thanking him for its prior communication, remarked there was no need to demand reassurances on such a matter as the maintenance of peace in Poland, which the empress herself desired more than anything else. This note would merely serve to prove that the perfidious interference of troublemakers trying to arouse distrust between the two courts had succeeded, and that the French court suspected that the empress intended to support some kind of confederation. Such a note would be disagreeable to the Russian court and might even confirm all those reports of the unfriendly acts and opinions of the French ministers in Warsaw and Constantinople, which thus far the empress had not believed. Not only was there no need for the formal declarations asked for, but the French court had not a single legitimate reason to demand them. It was inconsistent with the dignity of both courts to act so formally at the behest of some concerned Poles, whom it was in no way possible to satisfy. If the French court listened to them, similar declarations would have to be demanded often, whereas it was very easy to avoid any unpleasantness without any declarations at all. Simply let the ministers of the allied courts do their level best to maintain the Poles in a well-disposed system, while acting in accord on all matters.

"The guilty party in this whole affair," wrote Bekhteev, "is Count de Broglie,[22] the French ambassador in Warsaw, who has the reputation here of an expert on Polish affairs. The head of the French party in Poland is the crown hetman. Therefore the forces of the Commonwealth are under the control of this party, which is stronger than all the rest. If it knows that no one will stand up for the others, it will oppress them, and thus bring about unrest in the Commonwealth. Count de Broglie is a very restless man, loves to lay down the law and is forever changing his ideas. Through the natural sharpness and quickness of his mind he is always in a position to think up a multitude of ways to defend his ideas."

Bekhteev was sent to Paris to establish friendly relations between France and Russia, considered natural and necessary in consequence of the change in political circumstances. He did not allow himself to be carried away by his position, and appeared sober and cautious. "All power resides in the marquise de Pompadour[23] through the king's extraordinary kindness towards her and trust in her," he wrote to Vorontsov. "She undoubtedly possesses a very penetrating and remarkably cunning mind. Marshal de Belle-Isle,[24] in spite of his advanced age, has a fresh mind and memory.

In speeches brief rather than verbose his ideas are very clear, and he expresses them distinctly and coherently, so that it is very easy to understand his opinion. Only one fault can be attributed to him, a passion to add to his riches. Besides, he is thought a man able to give the appearance of sincerity to parasitism and hypocrisy. The abbé de Bernis[25] is astute and has a very lively imagination. In political matters he is considerably learned and knowledgeable, smooth-tongued, loves society and merry-making. He knew the marquise when she was Madame d'Étioles. In great poverty he wrote verses for her and was an accomplice in her merry-making. When things turned out well for her she promoted him little by little, that is to say from nothing to the rank of a minister of state. It could be said that he is her privy councillor.

"In foreign affairs these two ministers have the most power with great store set upon them by the marquise, which is why all the ministers from foreign countries address themselves to them. They are from time to time resented by Monsieur Rouillé, but he does not dare to be annoyed openly at this, being afraid of losing his position. It would seem in every way that it is impossible for courts to be more friendly than the one here with Vienna. The present particular concern of the court in Paris for the interests of Vienna may be ascribed to two principle causes, to the influence of the marquise and to the attraction of acquiring new territories. Only the marquise herself and the abbé de Bernis, as creators of this system, are trying to procure its advancement. Other ministers follow the same policy, and as long as these two individuals are in power, it will be followed.

"In general I must say that thus far the people themselves dislike the Austrians. There is a sense of obvious indignation that troops and their maintenance are being wasted on the relief of their ancient adversary. The court in Vienna thinks the court here has perceived much of what is going on. It appears that the ministry in Paris is not very discerning, but the machinery established in ancient times is so stable that it cannot be damaged easily. In fact France finds great profit in the present circumstances. Its view always has been to weaken the house of Austria and gradually to acquire the Netherlands. Perhaps France will acquire them and in exchange give Silesia to the Austrians, to whom it rightly belongs. Either way France will be the victor. Moreover France, though unwillingly, already sees the strength of the king of Prussia who, being of the Protestant faith, conceives of wielding power himself in Germany and of sharing France's influence. With time Prussia will be as much or even more dangerous perhaps to French interests than even the house of Austria, which France could at least restrain through the Turks.

"For all these reasons you will understand that it has been suggested to the ministry here that there is no benefit to France in relating to Russia other than on a basis of sound friendship. The ministry, however, through its own weakness, afraid of and wishing to please the marquise, who is rather inclined towards the court in Vienna, holds the same opinion on this matter. For this reason Count Starhemberg tried to conclude negotiations before the arrival of the ambassadors without the good offices of all the other courts, although their interests now have been discussed. Nothing was left to them but a common accession and acceptance. Russia could forgive the court at Vienna this policy. There was no need to express our disagreement. The matter common to us both demanded that France be brought seriously into play against the king of Prussia in whatever way possible, in order to bring that state back into its proper borders, and this is Russia's principal point of view. Now that France has been brought into play, Russia must of necessity take an active part at court here.

"All the powers at present railing against the king of Prussia for his victories are hopeful of success. Austria, as an unwarrantedly offended party, undoubtedly will take back Silesia, both by right of conquest and as a recovered possession. France will not dispute receiving the Netherlands as it was promised formally by treaty. Sweden also will take back from the enemy land which belonged to it and to which it still lays claim.[26] Moreover the three major allies have anticipated this and not only promised Sweden what was mentioned above, but even have bound themselves formally by treaty. So these three points between the allies have been decided beforehand. In any general conciliation no one will dispute this. The only difficulty will be for Russia alone to gain what it was promised from the present conflict, namely the acquisition of Courland, in addition to weakening the position of the king of Prussia. It is true this has been resolved with the court of Vienna but the other allies, who will be major powers in the peace-making, do not know about it. It is true that later they can say they have no right to dispose of the property of others and must not do so. Moreover, having obligations to Poland, they will deter Russia in every way possible. Russia can put forward the fact that it will cede East Prussia to Poland in exchange for Courland.

"The obvious reply is that Russia has no right to East Prussia, or annexation of territories belonging to the king of Prussia, because it made war as an auxiliary power, both because of its obligations to the house of Austria and to the house of Saxony. Everyone, growing tired of war and having obtained all they wanted, will then betray Russia. In the first place the court of Vienna will not want to stop the peace process for Russia's sake. On the contrary, should it persist in holding on to East Prussia, Russia will be abandoned by Austria. For political reasons we must understand that Sweden, which cannot be trusted fully, may declare explicitly against Russia. Moreover to that end Sweden can put pressure on Russia by being in a position to incite the Poles and Turks, merely suggesting to them that Russia, without any right, wants to take possession of Courland from the Commonwealth, to which it rightly belongs. First it is absolutely necessary that, if Russia is successful militarily, it declare war, for which there are legal grounds, on the king of Prussia. Second, to communicate with France and Sweden and formally declare that if Russia conquers Prussia (the province), then in any peace settlement it will be obliged to give East Prussia to Poland, and Russia must be compensated for the materials used and losses suffered in prosecuting the war. It remains for Russia to discuss this and come to an agreement with the Commonwealth."

BESTUZHEV-RIUMIN APPOINTED AMBASSADOR TO FRANCE

On June 10 Count Mikhail Petrovich Bestuzhev-Riumin[27] arrived at Versailles as Russian ambassador plenipotentiary. In 1755 the senile and infirm Bestuzhev was recalled to St. Petersburg from Dresden, where he left his wife in an advanced stage of consumption. Nevertheless in a letter to Vorontsov he volunteered to travel as ambassador to France. "Your excellency has been the worthy instrument of the peace settlement between our court and the French to which not a little of our glory and honor is attached. Moreover you are pleased to be the worthy instrument in the appointment of an ambassador there. This distinction will be a particular pleasure for me, and your standing with the French court will increase when your faithful friend and servant is appointed to the post there."

Bestuzhev was appointed and it is easy to understand how his brother the chancellor regarded this appointment. The brothers observed the outward civilities, visited each other. Mikhail Petrovich on one occasion dined with the chancellor, but Williams made a witty observation regarding this dinner. "You can imagine how merry and joyful this dinner was. Had there been milk on the table, it would have curdled from the sight of their faces."

Bestuzhev travelled to France by way of Warsaw and used the opportunity to write to the empress from there about Gross,[28] whom he found not to his liking. "On taking my leave from the local dignitaries and other officials, they said plainly and practically unanimously that the Russian court is losing a great deal in having Gross here as envoy. He is a most strange individual, who ruins all useful matters by his strange behavior. In particular he shows a lack of respect to the magnates, which is entirely inappropriate in the Commonwealth. We must treat everyone there in an outwardly friendly manner, and try to incline everyone to our point of view with solicitude. Moreover he does not comprehend the local system at all, and keeps only to the Princes Czartoryski, who are so angry with Count Brühl[29] that they no longer enjoy as much power as previously. They act in a manner hostile to the court, as the granting of rank and the receipt of estates for service does not depend upon their recommendation. They act in accord with Benoît,[30] the chargé d'affaires of the Prussian king in Warsaw, evidently communicating secretly with the Prussian court. Gross has attached himself blindly to their party and threatens their enemies with Russian protection, which the Czartoryskis enjoy. As a consequence the grand crown hetman and other great nobles adhere as one to the French, and the others to the Prussian party. Seeing Gross's incompetence and the lack of self-restraint in his speech, seeing that he cannot keep a secret, no one has the slightest trust in him. Everyone has an aversion to him and avoids his company. I cannot describe what degradation there is for Russia from this."

Bestuzhev was charged to win over the Polish gentry, so that Poland would declare war on Frederick II, taking the part of their king, but his efforts were in vain. "I have even come to hate the Poles myself," he wrote to Vorontsov, "and it is obvious that you do not like them. I have flaunted before them glory and honor, urging them in their own self-interest to assist their king, that in present circumstances they might obtain for themselves all the Prussias. I put before them the example of King Jan Sobieski,[31] when he marched against the Turks under the walls of Vienna. What glory and honor the Polish nation gained.

"I make no progress. They merely continue their malice between themselves. I also told them that when the king of Prussia achieves success in his objectives they will be the first to suffer. They reply that Russia will not allow such a thing to come to pass. They are a strange people. They are ready to indulge in any base behavior in their own interests, to throw their arms about your legs or to kiss your hand."

On the way Bestuzhev met his dying wife,[32] driven out of Saxony by the Prussian invasion and, sick himself, brought her to Paris to die. Notwithstanding these circumstances Bekhteev described the conduct of Bestuzhev at a reception by the king. "His excellency, in spite of many attempts by the embassy equerry, acted intelligently and with that dignity natural to his character in everything, not letting himself be deafened by the ceaseless local gossip. Rather it seemed to me that he proceeded to the audience and spoke more boldly than the others and with such bearing that he could not sufficiently take pleasure either to see or to hear the opinion of the French on this occasion."

At Versailles it was easier for Bestuzhev to talk about Polish affairs because he no longer had to treat with a Rouillé under the influence of de Broglie, but with a new minister, that abbé de Bernis with whom we are already familiar. Bestuzhev managed to persuade de Bernis that not all news coming out of Poland should be believed, because of the character of the Poles, as well as that of de Broglie. In present circumstances there must be no confusing the important with the unimportant, Prussian affairs with Polish. In St. Petersburg Douglas was told quite plainly that the declaration requested by his court was not in any way compatible with the dignity of the empress. The king himself would clearly perceive this were he to reject all the perfidious suggestions of restless people, and rely on the good faith of her imperial majesty.

DE L'HÔPITAL NAMED FRENCH AMBASSADOR IN ST. PETERSBURG

In conjunction with Bestuzhev's appointment the marquis de l'Hôpital[33] simultaneously was appointed ambassador to St. Petersburg. Bekhteev described him in the following manner. "He is a fine figure of a man, probably a little over fifty, very kindly. It seems that he asked for this appointment himself, and comes to us with enthusiasm." Bekhteev, in his response to Vorontsov, was not very complimentary about the nobles within the embassy. "When they were presented to me I did not know what to do. You cannot believe how little knowledge they have about us here. The reason is that few if any of their nobility have been to our country, and only those of a mean disposition, or at the very least the impoverished, not even excluding those who were ambassadors. Through vexation, or in justification of their bad deeds, they put mean opinions about us as much as possible. So that apart from scholars and those who know what is going on (and not even all of those), the other Frenchmen, especially those of exalted station, think the French must die of cold and hunger among us. It is difficult to drive out of their heads such a fixed opinion in the face of the luxuries in which the nobility here is immersed, and in light of the little understanding which it has in general about other countries."

OPENING OF HOSTILITIES

While the previously unthinkable union of the three great continental powers, Russia, Austria and France, was dragging its feet in Paris and St. Petersburg, the initiator of this union, the common enemy Frederick II, opened the campaign in April with the invasion by his army of Bohemia. After a bloody battle near Prague the losses in both armies were even. In a battle in June at Kolin, Frederick suffered a defeat, as a consequence of which he was obliged to evacuate Bohemia.

PRUSSIAN SPIES

The Austrians adhered to the treaty. They took on the main Prussian army. Now the Russians had to fulfill their obligation to enter Prussian domains at the same time. In February the Austrian general St. André, appointed by the treaty to be on the military council of the Russian forces with voting rights, arrived at Field Marshal Apraksin's[34] headquarters in Riga. "This new arrival," Apraksin wrote about St. André, "seems to be a man of tolerable sentiments, with no small knowledge of the military arts, a steadfast individual. He told me that because of the present condition of the enemy, we must attack him with all our might at any opportune moment. We must not in any circumstances divide the army lest he take the opportunity to make raids upon detachments in the first instance, as he is in the habit of doing, reducing the main army to impotence by defeating outlying detachments. He added, that with such a proud enemy we must not use stratagems (meaning dividing our forces), but either act with strength or do nothing."

Apraksin then learned that the proud enemy was using other means in addition to the defeat of separate detachments. At the general headquarters in Riga was an assessor for secret work, Veselitsky, a Montenegrin by birth, who analyzed the ciphered letters of Blom, a Livonian lieutenant colonel, who as a consequence was arrested and gave evidence that in 1753 he had wanted to transfer to Prussian service and in order to receive leave stated that he was expecting an inheritance in Prussia. He made a request to Frederick II, but was told that he could not be taken into Prussian service because of his age, as he was already seventy-three.

When he was preparing to leave Potsdam the well-known Manstein[35] came to see him and detained him. Later a Captain Winterfeldt made him a proposition not to leave Russian service, but to be a Prussian spy with a salary of one hundred and eighty chervontsy. His duties consisted of sending information about Russian regiments, about conscript levies, about the various movements of the forces. His letters were addressed to a Procurator Berens in Berlin and appeared to relate to litigation in connection with his inheritance, but Manstein received them and not Berens. When Blom was in Potsdam, Field Marshal Keith,[36] General Winterfeldt[37] and Manstein in particular called on him. Where is Prince Ivan?[38] Is he well and is he married? Was it true that Princess Anna[39] died, or was the body of some other woman put in her place? Was Biron alive and well?[40] Was Münnich alive?[41] Blom heard Keith, Winterfeldt, the king's adjutant Buddenbrock and Colonel Manstein read a letter written in French, which Keith had received from Russia, which said that profound disagreements existed between the most important people in St. Petersburg, that the chancellor's influence was greatly diminished. News about Colonel Olitz and the peasants also was added. Keith read the letter, concealing the signature with his hand. Keith, on Blom's assurance, received letters from Russia by almost every post with precise information about everything that was going on. In his correspondence Blom used a pre-arranged language. Fifty sheep stood for fifty thousand recruits, the cavalry was referred to as oxen, and so on.

ST. PETERSBURG'S DISPLEASURE AT APRAKSIN'S SLOWNESS

Even at the beginning of the year there was dismay over Apraksin's tardiness. This displeasure considerably perturbed Chancellor Bestuzhev, whose influence was in decline. He was surrounded by strong and exultant enemies. Apraksin remained his only friend of any importance. His success in the war was extremely important for Bestuzhev. Apraksin's failure would deprive the chancellor of his last support. Moreover the chancellor was afraid that his enemies would ascribe Apraksin's tardiness to him. All this forced Bestuzhev to hurry Apraksin, who became angry. Apraksin was a good man but no longer young (he was fifty-four). The "pacific field marshal," although he seemed much more bellicose than the other two pacific field marshals, Razumovsky[42] and Trubetskoy,[43] preferred to live on a friendly footing with everybody, in comfort, in merriment and in luxury, so that generally he did not want to hurry the campaign. He had reason to hope that the affair would not get to the point of actual warfare, that it would be limited to a campaign similar to other western campaigns of Russian auxiliary detachments under Empress Anna and recently under Elizabeth, outings to excite fear and to hasten peace. Moreover the young court was against war, and to go counter to the heir to the throne and his wife[44] was far from Apraksin's mind. Moreover his clever friend the chancellor was on the side of the young court, and on his departure said that the campaign should not take place until everything was ready. Apraksin thought everything still far from ready, that a great deal of preparation must be done over a long period in order to fight successfully against the most significant military commander of the age and his exemplary organized forces.

It was good that the Austrians were able to hold Frederick back. Should he turn against the Russian troops with his main forces, would the Austrians help? Their slowness was legendary, and were they advancing now? What gave the chancellor the idea to hurry the Russian forces to commence a campaign in winter without waiting to see what would happen between the king of Prussia and the Austrians?

On February 17 Apraksin wrote to Bestuzhev in great agitation, saying that he would resign from command of the forces. He complained about the Austrians and concluded with a question. He asked if the chancellor had changed his mind, because in St. Petersburg Apraksin had been privy to Bestuzhev's opinions, and on all issues they agreed with his own. Apraksin sent this letter with a trustworthy fellow, Quartermaster General Weymarn,[45] so that he could ascertain from the chancellor what the problem was, and why he was being so hurried. Bestuzhev answered through Weymarn that Apraksin, in his opinion, had no cause whatsoever for displeasure. "Up until now not one of your representations has been refused. There have been, it is true, several and at times severely compelling reasons not to accept them, but your excellency may have noticed that even these always have been entrusted to your final consideration and decision. Whenever you have put forward the difficulties and impossibilities against a proposal, immediately you have received our agreement. It is true that from here we cannot see everything as well as your excellency, but none the less we must let you know our opinions.

"It is true that no one here has such influence, where their opinions and representations always receive such swift approbation. Similarly we cannot complain about our allies. They ask us like beggars for alms. Yes, and truth to tell, their situation is very pitiful. If only we were in their position and had the same reassurances from them as they received in the presence of your excellency, I would dare say that we already would have quarrelled with them. On the contrary, their silence speaks to our conscience even more, and so lamentably that with this silence they give us no cause either to express our opinion or to justify ourselves. Yet in truth we have nothing to offer.

"On another matter I do not have to express anything other than my extreme regret that your excellency should doubt my sentiments. They have not changed, and upon my life they will not change. Put them to the test. I shall bear any difficulty to maintain your friendship, which is most valuable to me. Meanwhile I shall not have any peace until I am assured that your excellency is confident of the true diligence and devotion I have towards you."

With this letter Bestuzhev sent another letter from the grand duchess, in which she also begged Apraksin to delay no longer. Weymarn was instructed to tell the field marshal that the grand duchess's letter was genuine, so that he should not have any doubts. Apraksin was extremely angry. He had hoped he would receive through Weymarn a statement from Bestuzhev agreeing to his wish to stall, but was deceived. The letter from Catherine took away his last hope. Yet a man parts with hope with difficulty. "These are all the chancellor's tricks (ideas)," he said in a fit of temper and took from a box another, earlier letter of Catherine and checked one against the other. They were by the same hand! There was nothing more to be done. In his reply to the chancellor he dismissed the misunderstanding, which proceeded from the use at that time of the foreign word sentiment, which meant both opinion and feeling. In his previous letter Apraksin had understood by the chancellor's change of sentiments a change of opinion or point of view, but Bestuzhev considered this a reproach, an alteration in their friendly feelings.

It was not until May 17 that Apraksin crossed the Lithuanian border from Courland into Samogitia and on the twentieth was in Szawly. On the eighteenth General Vasily Abramovich Lopukhin entered Lithuania. The cavalry was under the command of General Lieven and Count Rumiantsev.[46] On June 4 the forces entered Kovno and stayed there until the sixteenth, as the number of the sick significantly increased because of the heat. Besides, wrote the field marshal, because of difficult and narrow roads a considerable amount of reorganization of the transports had to be done, and to a certain extent the previous dispositions changed. On the nineteenth almost all the army was beyond the Nieman. On the twentieth the field marshal himself crossed the river.

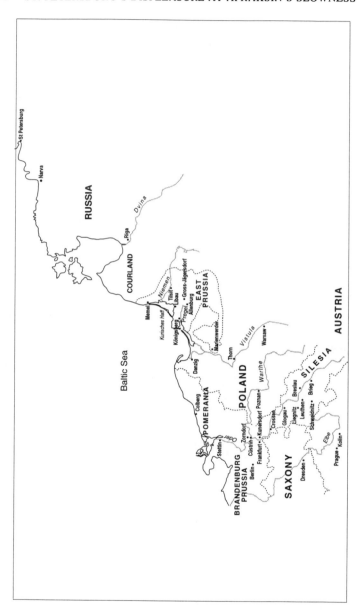

The Theater of the Seven Years War in Europe

In the meanwhile on June 18, General Fermor,[47] leaving Libau, where regiments were brought to join him by sea, crossed the East Prussian border and made his way towards Memel. He began to bombard the city on the twentieth. On the twenty-fourth Memel surrendered on condition that the garrison be released with their arms.

The taking of Memel was celebrated at Tsarskoe Selo on July 6. A service of thanksgiving was held "for the blessing of the Most High at the very beginning of this armed conflict." This blessing was sent to a detachment of the forces, whereas the main army with Field Marshal Apraksin had yet to cross the border. On July 15 Bestuzhev again had to write to Apraksin. "My unbounded candor with your excellency will not permit me to conceal from you how very much generally it is regretted here that a lack of provisioning has hampered your excellency's advance into enemy territory and your expedition of the matter in hand up until now. Mr. Lehwaldt (the Prussian field marshal), making use of this circumstance, already has begun to withdraw. This regret is multiplied even more by the fear that, in the meantime, he should leave East Prussia completely. That would be a considerable loss, which could not be rewarded by the conquest of Königsberg and the whole of East Prussia, from which God knows what interpretations will be made. My total diligence in support of your excellency forbids me to conceal the fact that at an evening reception on the day of the Conference[48] her imperial majesty, coming out into the hall in the absence of others expressed her displeasure to myself, to Prince Nikita Yurievich (Trubetskoy), Alexander Borisovich (Buturlin)[49] and to Prince Mikhail Mikhailovich (Golitsyn)[50] that your excellency was lingering so long in Poland."

On July 18 there was a new letter from the chancellor to the field marshal. "The duties of a sincerely devoted friend, with extreme regret and in the utmost confidence, do not permit me to hide the fact that, in spite of all the strong measures of an edict prohibiting [loose talk] among the people issued in your interests, the sluggishness of your march, and consequently of the military operations, is beginning to produce all around the city here very reprehensible talk with respect to your excellency, some even extending so far as to promise a reward to the one who can find the missing Russian army. It is true that such false commentaries proceed from an ignorance of the difficulties experienced by your excellency in this affair. As these things always do harm and are able to do harm to your excellency, I would advise you, in spite of calming sentiments in this matter sometimes proffered to you from another quarter, that you overcome as far as possible all the difficulties you are experiencing and hasten your march and operations, and so cut short the opinions expressed above and shut everybody's mouth."

RUSSIAN FORCES CROSS THE BORDER

On July 19 news was received at last from the main army that on the fourteenth it was only half a mile from the Prussian border, near Wierzbolowka. It was awaiting the other forces which had been unable to move with them because of the narrowness of the roads. The causes of the slow movement of the forces was appended to the announcement of this news. "The great obstacles and difficulties which slowed our campaign as far as Kovno in no way can be compared with those we have had to overcome from Kovno to the present. Reserve stores were well maintained up to Kovno. Prudence and the proximity of Prussian forces did not permit us to stage those forward. Intolerable hot days, which in themselves have caused difficulties in the campaign, deprived us of the means of receiving stores and forage by water, for the rivers became so shallow that boats no longer could get through. We had to bring stores to the army on local carts that demanded as much time as it did labor."

On July 20 the main army crossed the East Prussian border and immediately began minor skirmishes with the enemy. In the meantime Fermor occupied Tilsit from Memel, and was moving to join with the field marshal. Russian troops crossing the Prussian borders, according to the roll, numbered up to one hundred and thirty-five thousand in all, but in reality this number was considerably less.

BATTLE OF GROSS-JÄGERSDORF

At last on August 28 the inhabitants of St. Petersburg were woken at four in the morning by a one hundred and one gun salute. At nine the previous evening a courier, Major General Peter Ivanovich Panin,[51] with trumpeting heralds, galloped into Tsarskoe Selo where the empress was staying, bringing news of a major victory gained on August 19 by Russian forces over the Prussian field marshal Lehwaldt on the banks of the Pregel, near the village of Gross-Jägersdorf. Apraksin described the affair in the following manner.

On the seventeenth the enemy occupied the forest not more than a mile from the Russian army with the aim of hindering further movement of the

Russians, and for three days running gave every appearance of intending to attack them. On the nineteenth at five in the morning, when the Russians began to move and were passing through the forest, the enemy also began to leave the forest and to approach the Russian regiments in good order, under cover of strong artillery fire. In half an hour, approaching the Russian front, they attacked "with such fury at first on the left flank, and then on the right, that it would be impossible to describe it." Fire from small arms continued without interruption from both sides for about three hours. "I must confess," wrote Apraksin, "that in all this time, in spite of the courage and bravery both of the generals, staff and senior officers, as well as of all the soldiers and the great work of the secret howitzers newly devised by Count Shuvalov (which are of such value that, of course, he merits your imperial majesty's favor and rewards for such good work), it was impossible to foresee anything decisive regarding victory. This was particularly so because the renowned forces of your imperial majesty, being on the march, could not be deployed or utilized with such flair as I would have wanted and would have arranged, because of the great number of baggage carts."[52]

In spite of this the enemy was broken, scattered and driven off by light forces across the Pregel river to its previous camp near Wehlau. There had not been such a brutal battle in Europe before, according to the evidence of foreign volunteers, in particular the Austrian lieutenant field marshal St. André. From our side the losses were not yet known. Counted among the dead were the general commanding the left flank, General Vasily Lopukhin, whom Apraksin was unable to recall without tears, Lieutenant General Zybin and Brigadier Kapnist. Lieutenant Generals Yury and Matvey Lieven and Matvey Tolstoy were wounded, as were Major Generals Debosquet, Villebois, Manteuffel, Weymarn and Brigadier Plemiannikov, but all without grave harm. The enemy lost eight cannon, three howitzers and eighteen field guns. More than six hundred prisoners were taken, amongst whom were eight senior officers. Deserters were put at more than three hundred.

Apraksin wrote that Major General Panin, who carried news of the victory, was the orderly general under his command throughout the campaign. He shouldered a great deal of hard work and had helped the field marshal a great deal during the engagement. Where the field marshal himself could not make his way, he sent Panin in order to persuade people and to approve their actions, so that he was under the heaviest fire.

"Certainly with time," added Apraksin, "through daring and bravery he may be a great general. In a word all subjects of your imperial majesty in the army entrusted to me in this battle, each according to his rank, conducted themselves as the natural duties of service to their sovereign demand. The volunteers, in particular Prince Repnin,[53] Count Bruce and Apraksin, fervently and fearlessly distinguished themselves. All the general staff, in particular the young generals, acted very bravely and were under such fire that two horses were killed or wounded under some. Major General Villebois, although wounded in the head, to the very end of the engagement never dismounted from his horse. Lieutenant Nadasdy,[54] in the Holstein service of his imperial majesty, who is serving as a volunteer under me, is daring and brave and has such an eagerness to serve. He was not only to be found in all parties, even in the advance guard, but acted everywhere superbly and fearlessly. I entrust all staff, senior officers and all the troops, prostrating themselves at the feet of your imperial majesty, to your most imperial maternal generosity. The foreign volunteers, first of all General Field Marshal Lieutenant of the Holy Roman Empire Baron St. André particularly distinguished himself, together with the staff and senior officers serving under him. The French regimental commanders Fitingof, in particular L'Hôpital, and the Saxon regimental commander Lamsdorf, with their officers, also deserve not a little praise for their brave deeds.

"As regards myself I confess to your majesty, as before God, that at first I was most unhappy when the enemy attacked us on the march with such fury and in such good order. As I was behind the baggage carts, I suddenly realized that I could not move everywhere as I would have wished. I was exposed to such fire that somewhere near me Sergeant of the Guards Kursel was killed and two grenadiers were wounded, a sergeant-major of hussars was killed and several officers and a hussar also were wounded, as was the horse under me. In a word I was in such danger that only God's right hand preserved me, for I wanted rather to seal my loyalty with my blood than to witness failure."

Because of the nature of this work we are unable to enter into details of the military action, but we cannot overlook the account of an eyewitness, Bolotov, in which the report of the commander-in-chief is both clarified and expanded.[55] We must not forget here that we are dealing with the story of a nineteen-year-old lieutenant, written under the influence of Apraksin's subsequent actions. "I confess before you that all the circumstances were unknown to me at the time in detail, although I was present myself and saw everything with my own eyes. How could such an insignificant fellow, as I then was, know all the details of what took place in the army? Being a company commander at the time, I could not absent myself even a step from my place and from my company. The army on the march cannot be compared to anything but a great and heavily populated city, in which someone who finds himself in one corner naturally cannot know every detail of what is taking place in another."

Despite his acknowledgment that an insignificant fellow could not see and know everything, Bolotov willingly repeated antagonistic gossip and rumors about Apraksin. Moreover he generally looked with hostility upon almost all the commanders. One of the generals-in-chief, Georgy Lieven, appears in a particularly bad light. "Lieven did not command any forces, but was in the field marshal's suite. He gave him advice, even authoritatively, like a tutor. A strange example indeed! He took a great part, however, in all the military operations. We would not have covered ourselves with such shame before the world, had we not had this genius and sham philosopher with us."

In agreement with the report, Bolotov related how the Russian army set out upon a further march because there was no other hope of forcing the enemy to engage in battle. The Prussians took advantage of this movement of the Russians and the disorder associated with it, caused by the transports and unevenness of the ground. They attacked unexpectedly, not giving the Russians time to form up. The enemy, said Bolotov, had incomparably greater advantages. Their attack was carried out in good order, by the best regiments and troops, and by dispositions made in advance and correctly observed. Their artillery acted as it was supposed to, and their whole rear was open and reinforced with a second line and reserves. Nothing prevented them immediately from reinforcing their positions with replacements to make good losses in the front fighting line. They had a similar ability to supply their soldiers with the necessary munitions and powder. As far as our own men were concerned, first no dispositions were made beforehand, and in any case there was no time to do so. Second, we had far fewer men on our side. The enemy fought with a complete line, while we could deploy only eleven regiments. Unfortunately even these few men were bound hand and foot. First of all we did not have any artillery, except for a few regimental cannon and Shuvalov's howitzers. What could be done with these when less than half of their boxes and shells could be brought from the forest? Second, they were so pressed up against the forest that they had no space behind them. Third, there was nowhere to gain assistance or to replace those killed with reinforcements. Most of the army was not in action but stood behind the wood, from which it was impossible to reach them.

In spite of all these disadvantages the Russian regiments stood as firm as a wall. For two whole hours they kept back the enemy onslaught. At length a great number were killed or wounded. The lines held. There were practically no officers left alive, and no powder remaining. In this desperate situation they were pressed closer to the forest and matters became even more desperate. The enemy thought they were retreating and rushed upon them with redoubled ardor. However much the general-in-chief Vasily Abramovich Lopukhin urged the soldiers to valiant defense, he could do nothing. He fell, severely wounded, into the hands of the Prussian grenadiers, but the Russian grenadiers rushed forward and seized their commander, only to see him die amongst his own. Then the Russian regiments situated behind the wood, tired of standing idle at the very moment when their comrades were perishing, took it into their heads "or, possibly, were sent" to force their way through the wood as best they could to come to the aid of their comrades. The wood was so dense that the men could only force their way through singly and with the greatest difficulty. In spite of this the regiments, abandoning their troublesome cannons and boxes of ammunition, rushed towards the cry of their dying comrades. Then the situation changed. The fresh regiments, firing a volley, with a shout rushed with fixed bayonets at the enemy, who wavered, tried to form themselves into better order, but there was no longer any time. The Russians fell upon their neck, to use Bolotov's phrase, and did not pause. The Prussians at first conducted an orderly retreat, but soon were fleeing in disorder.

Bolotov reproached Apraksin because the field marshal praised only the volunteers and the foreigners and was silent about Colonel Yazykov, a man who conducted himself particularly heroically. Despite his wounds, Yazykov and his regiment endured all the fire and held on to an extremely important position, beating off the enemy. We have seen that Apraksin particularly commended General Peter Ivanovich Panin. There is a curious passage in Bolotov's story where he describes how several regiments made their way through the wood to the aid of their comrades, who no longer could withstand the enemy onslaught, and put the Prussians to flight. In

Bolotov's account we meet the strange phrase "the regiments took it into their heads or, perhaps, were sent." Was it really not possible to find out the most important fact, namely who first took it into his head, who made the first move? If the author said reluctantly "or, perhaps, were sent," why did he not finish by saying that their general Count Rumiantsev must have sent them and gone with them. To say that, evidently, was very hard for an "insignificant man," who very imprudently revealed his attempt to take away from the *commanders* any part in the success of the affair. "The battle was so tightly fought and confused," he explained, "that not one of the commanders could do anything." Yet one commander was killed carrying out his duty, and another, by moving fresh regiments through the wood, ensured victory. Is it possible that Bolotov, enquiring about the details of the battle, did not made enquiries about one thing, the whereabouts of General Rumiantsev at the time his regiments were winning the victory of Gross-Jägersdorf?

It is curious that Bolotov, reproaching the Prussians for inaccurate accounts of the battle, praised only King Frederick II who, in his own words "speaks more fairly than all the others and describes the battle almost exactly as it took place," apart from reducing the losses suffered by the Prussian and revealing the number of troops under Lehwaldt. Frederick II says the following in his notes concerning the battle of Gross-Jägersdorf. "Lehwaldt attacked the wood where the Russian grenadiers were situated. These grenadiers were vanquished and almost destroyed. Rumiantsev moved twenty battalions of the second Russian line to their aid. They struck at the flank and the rear of the Prussian infantry, which was forced to retreat."

Apraksin concluded his report of the victory with the words, "Nothing now remains but to try my diligent best to make the greatest progress for the attainment of your majesty's objectives." Everyone in St. Petersburg awaited news from him about this great progress.

APRAKSIN'S RETREAT AFTER VICTORY

On September 13 the College of Foreign Affairs received the following edict. "After the victory gained over Prussian forces on the nineteenth day of last month our army continued its march. It approached Allenburg with the intention of giving further battle but the enemy, in spite of his very advantageous and very strong position beyond the Alle river, did not have the courage to wait for an attack. Rather swiftly it withdrew under the

guns of Königsberg, leaving signs everywhere of an extreme and unex-
ampled rage with its own subjects, depriving them of their last sustenance. That is why there are inadequate victuals and forage for our victorious army in any further forward progress, and why the transport of
supplies has become so difficult. In these circumstances General Field
Marshal Apraksin considered it necessary, instead of exposing the army
to certain hunger through a further advance into land that has been destroyed, to turn for the time being closer to the supply depots on the Nieman. There he could leave the sick and other distracting burdens of the
campaign, and so continue his operations afresh with greater success, as
soon would be apparent. The College of Foreign Affairs should make
plain the current state of affairs in East Prussia, both to those courts allied to us as well as wherever else it needs to be made known, so that of
course a totally different interpretation will not be left to be given to these
events from the Prussian side."

On September 25 there was another edict. "Naturally we hoped that
General Field Marshal Apraksin would not delay the renewal of operations. We later confirmed, in terms as strong as possible, that he should
indeed hasten to do so. To our extreme regret we received a new dispatch
from him reporting that, despite the fact that our army furnished itself
with supplies for two weeks when it arrived at Tilsit, our poor field marshal felt himself constrained nevertheless to cross the Nieman in order to
be nearer to where the army could be stationed more comfortably in winter quarters. The causes prompting this new objective are so significant
that they cannot go unacknowledged. Our army, having just experienced
incessant periods of hot weather, the like of which has never been experienced before in this local climate, suddenly once again was subject to
unceasing prolonged rain for about four weeks in very low land. In these
circumstances you can easily imagine how diseases could not but greatly
increase, and the number of sick rise sharply.

"The cavalry, brought from Ukraine and other distant places at the
beginning of spring, completed a march of which there can be no comparable example elsewhere, and was exhausted on account of this alone.
Unfortunately the insufficiency of forage this year, which was fairly general even in Poland, became so much greater on entering East Prussia that
often nothing could be found at all by the foragers, who often were sent
distances greater than twenty versts. It is therefore easy to understand the
condition of the poor cavalry and that its further sojourn in this exhausted

land could only lead to certain ruin to no useful purpose. In addition, although there is no insufficiency in the supply depots, yet by virtue of the army's distance from them transportation is becoming extremely difficult or even impossible. In these circumstances our field marshal could reason justifiably that not only for us, but also for our allies, it would be incomparably more useful to preserve a fairly large army for a future campaign rather than expose it in vain to such dangers, which neither bravery nor courage, nor human effort would be able to avert.

"We know that from the Prussian point of view another interpretation could be put upon all of this and, perhaps, to which we normally would not appear to be totally indifferent, namely that a victorious army was leaving the defeated enemy the land it had conquered. Knowing, on the contrary, that the principal cause is lack of forage and the extreme difficulty in feeding the army, and that the enemy has been left no quarter whence it may interfere and enter its land once more, we may be quite content, whatever view is taken by the Prussian side, the more so as we are also sure that our allies will not doubt the inflexibility of our objectives and our firm desire to further them. Our generosity and real concern for the interests of our allies exceed all the aforementioned esteem. So as soon as we received the latest unwelcome information that our field marshal intended to cross the Nieman, we ordered him once more to use every possible means to remain in Prussia and, whenever the opportunity presents itself, to attack the enemy."

This order was not carried out. A military council was held in the army on September 28 at which it was decided to retreat beyond the Nieman. When Apraksin sent the minutes of the military council to St. Petersburg he wrote on September 30, "The severity of the season and lack of stores and forage in the vicinity, as well as a quite exhausted cavalry and a weary infantry, are the main reasons motivating me to take the resolution to cross the Nieman and move closer to our own frontier for the maintenance of the army entrusted to me. This in itself has created an impediment to the further progress of the defeated enemy. Following a stratagem made by me, he withdrew out of sight at the Alle river to the left hand towards Allenburg, without waiting either for the crossing of the river by the army, nor an attack, but he did not run away completely. He simply made this withdrawal in order to occupy the best and strongest position. Thus he could hinder my passage more effectively, fearing my movement towards Königsberg by way of Allenburg, by one of several routes previously prepared by him from the Alle river to Königsberg. By this withdrawal he actually gave notice of the fortified positions on the way to Königsberg, which would cost a great many lives to take. The scarcity of reserve stores made itself apparent, in addition to which there is a lack of forage in the land laid waste by the enemy, as in Königsberg a bushel of flour is being sold for seven thalers. Hence a turn was made towards Tilsit with the common agreement of the senior generals with the clear intention, having once put our house in order there, of making an advance.

"Finding in Tilsit many major and, to the mind of man, insuperable obstacles caused by foul weather and frosts, premature in relation to the local climate, and not willing to defy the will of God, to my most profound grief and that of all the senior generals, I was obliged to act at variance with the objectives of your imperial highness and contrary to our sincere desire. We were obliged particularly to choose this move towards the frontier as the best way of preserving the army. To hold on to Tilsit and the Nieman river and to maintain the army in this conquered part of Prussia it would have to be split to preserve the conquered territory, and because of the shortage of stores and forage this would have caused the ultimate destruction of the forces. Although there are sufficient stores in Memel, they cannot be delivered to the army either by the Kurisches Haff or by dry land. You can fit no more than one thousand five hundred quarters on ten galleys and the other shallow draft vessels which have been found capable of navigating the Kurisches Haff, that could be brought together in all that district. This is not to mention the difficulty that each galley has to be unloaded and lifted across the Schwarzer-Ort because of the shoals. We cannot transport anything in the autumn by land, because of the terribly churned-up roads at this time of the year locally and in Samogitia. The Nieman itself is very dangerous because of its winding course and many shoals. For this reason we have to sail upstream and adhere for the most part to the hostile bank.

"As far as the willingness of the local inhabitants to become the subjects of your majesty is concerned, any move made by them must be considered enforced. That is how it has turned out in reality. Many who recently took the oath to protect themselves immediately took up arms against us. We cannot expect anything else. Their obligations naturally draw them to their natural sovereign. Moreover, the authorities have given instructions to all inhabitants, especially those living in the towns, not to expose themselves to ruin and to submit to your armed force. Besides they have been told that an oath undertaken under such extreme duress always may be broken without violation of conscience."

The vehement outcries of the French and Austrian ambassadors against Apraksin, the complaints against him by General St. André, forced Elizabeth to send him threatening edicts. "The more I read your imperial edict that I received yesterday, madam," Apraksin wrote to the empress on October 6, "the more trepidation and despair multiplied within me. In the light of the edict I dared to suggest to all the senior generals assembled for council today that if they feel I am a real hindrance to the presentation of their free opinions in council or a cause of the non-performance of your esteemed orders to me, they should be prepared to take the senior command away from me, and I would also hand over to them my sword of office. They did not find me guilty of any crime and declined my offer."

In the meantime an instruction was sent to Memel for General Fermor, who was trusted more than any other, to reply frankly and point by point regarding the condition of the army and the behavior of the field marshal. "I shall report in all servility to your imperial majesty, as before God, in complete truth to the points instructed by you in a letter written by my own hand," Fermor replied on October 14. "Over the twelve days before the battle I found the army in good condition, but the horses of the cavalry and artillery, and those with regimental demands made upon them, were in a weak condition. They arrived looking extremely emaciated because of the rain that set in and the considerable mud day after day. They even collapsed on arrival at the Alle river. For the most part the men are at present terribly weak because of the long and difficult march and the inclement weather, and the horses are quite worthless. For that reason we cannot carry out military operations with the desired success. The cause of the army's retreat to its supply depots is the lack of subsistence for man and horse. Without having any ready supplies, even if the enemy were defeated a second time and Königsberg taken, there would be no way of provisioning the troops. If in such disagreeable circumstances the blockade of the city were to continue under cover of the Prussian troops, the army would be forced to retreat because of insufficient provisions and in this way it would diminish the reputation it has gained. There is no way that the stationing of the army in winter quarters on enemy soil can be contemplated until the enemy army is completely defeated and driven off, apart for those means already undertaken by virtue of the high wisdom of the senior staff."

APRAKSIN REPLACED BY FERMOR AS CHIEF OF STAFF

The outcries of the French and Austrian ambassadors against Apraksin continued unabated. Despite Fermor's explanations it was decided to replace the field marshal and to give the overall command to Fermor himself, who had borne witness to his participation in and agreement with Apraksin's orders, carried out with the common agreement of all the senior staff. A decree of the College of Foreign Affairs was issued on October 16 to be communicated to the ambassadors of the allied courts. "The withdrawal by our General Field Marshal Apraksin, undertaken without authority, has led to unpleasant consequences that we could not foresee and therefore prevent. The severe and almost extreme winter season that has now set in so much earlier than in any previous year makes fruitless all our efforts to improve these circumstances quickly. Naturally, over and above our great sorrow to see such an undertaking delayed and, for a time, even brought to a complete standstill, an undertaking which, it seemed, could not but have achieved the success we all so much desired, we feel even more distress that the operation of our army in general is not in keeping with our wishes. It is not in keeping either with those declarations and reassurances we made to our allies to endow the retarded conclusion of the campaign with the speed and forcefulness of military action. Relying upon the report of our field marshal we told the world that our army returned to its supply depots only temporarily, and that operations would begin anew with better success. By our decree of the twenty-fifth of last month we again gave our allies the hope that our army would try as much as possible to maintain itself in Prussia and, if the occasion arose, to attack the enemy. It appears that neither the one nor the other could have taken place. Nevertheless our intention is no less firm and steadfast. We shall not in any way depart from the measures agreed. In this respect we intend most particularly to investigate the direct causes as to why our army's campaign was at first slow to get started, and then why it also was particularly compelled to withdraw. In order to be able to take these necessary measures the more reliably we considered it necessary to remove command of the army from Field Marshal Apraksin and to entrust it to General Fermor, and to recall Apraksin here to answer these questions."

ORTHODOX CHRISTIANS IN AUSTRIAN PROVINCES

This statement was intended to calm the court at Vienna. Yet at the end of the year Keyserling[56] had another unpleasant interview with Kaunitz.

In November Keyserling received a rescript from the empress instructing him to communicate to the Austrian government complaints of the Orthodox Serbs of persecution on account of their faith. Keyserling began his conversation with Kaunitz by saying that although the Russian empress always refrained from interference in the domestic affairs of other states, she could not but intercede on behalf of coreligionists suffering want and oppression. She was sure that the empress-queen did not know about the matter, and therefore Keyserling was obliged to tell the chancellor.

In 1754, in Croatia and other provinces it was proclaimed that all those professing the Greek rite must abandon it for the Roman Catholic faith, or else be condemned to be hanged and quartered. The Greek rite and those professing it were reviled in the most dishonorable manner. They were called infidels and apostates. Yet only pagans are described in this way, not those believing in Christ and his Apostles. Count Petacy, the commander in Croatia, Dalmatia and Transylvania, took the monastery of the Archangel Michael away from Orthodox parishioners. As a consequence the Serbs were deprived of confession and holy communion and were forced to live in despair. Lack of respect for the most holy objects had gone so far that during the consecration of the Holy Eucharist some Catholics climbed onto the altar, where they committed every indecency and placed foul-smelling objects into the censers. They often stopped the holy service, came into church with loaded arms, fired them and in this way forced the parishioners to abandon their places of worship. They defiled the churches, permitting themselves to perpetrate there such acts as would not be permitted even in legal matrimony. They attempted by every means to draw the Orthodox to accept union. Those who were steadfast in their faith were forced to leave their wives, children and property, or were subjected to capital punishment like state criminals.

Kaunitz answered this in writing. "The opinion of the ambassador that complaints about the oppression of people of the Greek confession have not reached the throne of our sovereign is quite justified. For this very reason the aforementioned complaints are suspect, because with the holy union between sovereign and subjects it would be more in concordance with our policy that those who are aggrieved first of all resort to their natural sovereign and expect from her an end to their troubles. The empress-queen ordered the matter to be investigated. The complaints turned out to be entirely false, so much so that the Greek clergy itself was both amazed and angry. The All-Russian empress has been distressed with these complaints by troublemakers simply in order to excite disobedience and unrest in the hereditary lands of the empress-queen and, if possible, to upset the close union between the two imperial courts."

RELATIONS WITH ENGLAND, SWEDEN AND POLAND

At the beginning of the year the English ministry was still asking why Russia could not be a mediator between Austria and Prussia. The Russian envoy Prince Alexander Golitsyn[57] told his court of a conversation with the earl of Holderness.[58] "I cannot but marvel," began Holderness, "at the fact that your court has reacted so unfavorably to the proposal to take upon itself mediation between the courts of Vienna and Berlin. You know such a step cannot signify anything other than full confidence in your empress." "If her imperial majesty has already announced," answered Golitsyn, "that she intends exactly and faithfully to carry out her obligations concluded with the empress-queen, then the renewal of the proposal by Sir Charles [Hanbury Williams] must undoubtedly appear at our court as somewhat more strange than the refusal to mediate must appear at yours. It is clear that such a proposal proceeds not out of friendly confidence in the king of Prussia, but out of the desire to gain time and somehow to stir distrust between the allied courts. Moreover a threat has even been made that if this mediation does not take place, the king of Prussia will attack the Russian forces immediately. Such unseemly threats are quite astonishing if you take into account, on one hand the fortunate position of the Russian empire and on the other that these threats were received through the British ambassador."

At this point Holderness interrupted Golitsyn. "On this last point," he said, "I am in complete agreement with you. I may add that Williams acted in this way not only without instructions from here, but in his last despatches denies he ever conveyed any threats. Nevertheless every court can judge its ambassadors only by their own testimony, and as Williams is in poor health and the St. Petersburg climate is positively harmful, it would be inhuman to keep him any longer at the Russian court."

Golitsyn was instructed to let the cruelties the Prussian forces permitted themselves in Saxony become known at any favorable opportunity, and to add that Frederick II may repent of this with time. "With his plundering he has already justified in advance what may happen in his own territories from Russian irregulars. Nevertheless, whatever happens, the cossacks and Kalmyks can hardly be compared with the Prussian soldiers in savagery." In respect of these injunctions Golitsyn wrote to St. Petersburg,

"Without doubt they will not be surprised here if the Russian irregulars do anything in Prussia contrary to military discipline. The public here is unconcerned with the destruction of the Prussian provinces, provided that the king of Prussia has success against the Austrians, protects Hanover and finally can act against France. For Prussian military success it is much more important for the king to maintain his forces at the expense of Saxony than to preserve some of his own provinces from destruction."

Golitsyn wrote to his court in May that the successes of the Prussian king strengthened the pride of the English people and reassured the English court, which was beginning to consider itself fortunate to have entered into such a close alliance with Frederick II and to have exchanged its previous allies for him. They hoped that, safe from Austria, he would also act with similar success against France. Those who were loyal and impartial regretted that blind fortune made the English court give credence to such guesswork. Nevertheless it was considered necessary in England to maintain friendly relations with Russia. In conformity with a directive from his court Prince Golitsyn gave Holderness to understand that, although the empress never made a complaint against Ambassador Williams, she would not hide the fact that she was glad to be informed of the king's intention to recall him. When instead of his expected departure Williams gave the impression that he wanted to stay in St. Petersburg for another year, it became impossible for the empress to hide the fact that his further sojourn at the imperial court would not contribute either to her pleasure or to any success of the king's affairs. The conclusion of the trade agreement would be set aside for a long time as a consequence of her unwillingness to have any dealings with such an ambassador, who inopportunely preferred to demonstrate his dexterity rather than assist the matter with straightforwardness and firmness, and maintain the agreement between the courts.

In conclusion Golitsyn added that no matter whom the king sent in place of Williams, and whatever the character of the ambassador, anyone would give equal pleasure to the empress. Holderness answered that there was no doubt at his court concerning the unwholesome disposition of the empress towards Williams when it was found that the conduct of matters relating to the trade agreement had been entrusted to Baron Wolff[59] instead of to him. Therefore for this reason, as well as because of his poor health, it was decided to recall Williams from St. Petersburg. Since thus far a worthy successor could not be found, he had been ordered to postpone his departure from St. Petersburg lest the empress's court be without an English ambassador. If Prince Golitsyn had an instruction, and even without an instruction the simple suggestion was made, that the presence of Williams brought no pleasure to the empress, an instruction immediately would be sent him from London to hasten his departure from St. Petersburg. Having informed Golitsyn that an instruction already had been sent to Williams concerning his immediate departure from St. Petersburg, Holderness assured him in the name of the king that his majesty sincerely wished to maintain the empress's friendship, even though circumstances had forced the two courts in different directions.

In June Golitsyn received the following declaration from Holderness. "The threats made at a number of courts against the king of Prussia by the empress of All Russia have caused his majesty the king of Great Britain considerable regret. The empress need not doubt the king's sincere friendship. His britannic majesty reiterates his strongest trust in this friendship, of which he hopes to give new proof by a friendly statement with regard to the consequences which the unfriendly actions of Russia against Prussia will have. His majesty hopes that, before embarking upon unfriendly actions, the empress will pay attention to his obligation to defend the trade of his subjects in the Baltic Sea and to carry out the obligations into which he entered with the king of Prussia. The obligations consist in that England and Prussia are to join their forces to prevent any power whatsoever bringing its troops into Germany."

In June Frederick II suffered a setback,[60] and England experienced considerable anxiety. Golitsyn wrote that there was nothing to be feared concerning the conjunction of English forces with the Prussian, for the simple reason that the English had no forces there. The English fleet scarcely had appeared in the Baltic Sea, even though rumors were in circulation. The company of merchants trading with Russia sent a deputation to the earl of Holderness stating that sending a fleet to the Baltic Sea was not in conformity with the interests of the English people. It could set them at variance with Russia, causing grave harm to English trade, which the new allies of England were not in a position to compensate. Holderness replied that his thinking was in complete agreement with theirs. The king was very anxious to maintain friendship with Russia and intended to send Keith,[61] presently ambassador in Vienna, to St. Petersburg to replace Williams. In respect to rumors relating to the sending of naval squadrons to the Baltic Sea, the king had not taken a final decision about this matter.

In the meantime the declaration handed by Holderness to Golitsyn concerning English obligations to Prussia gave rise to a rescript of the empress, sent to the College of Foreign Affairs on June 30. "The declaration given to our ambassador, Prince Golitsyn, surprised us more by its form than its content. Not very long ago the earl of Holderness told Prince Golitsyn that although the English court indeed would assist the king of Prussia, it would not be against Russia. There is no need for us to examine the causes of such a sudden change and the incoherent blend of assurances of sincere friendship and threats, which we are least of all accustomed to suffering. If the English court permitted itself these threats, priding itself on the victory gained by the king of Prussia at Prague,[62] perhaps now it is repenting with knowledge of the change of fortune in Bohemia and Westphalia. If by this declaration it hoped not exactly to frighten us but to bring about a certain reflection, it is deceived. The English court evidently will communicate its action to the king of Prussia and he will exaggerate its significance and use it to his advantage. We therefore enjoin you to instruct Prince Golitsyn to reply to the English ministry to the effect that after the recent assurances of friendship from the English government we expected quite a different manifestation of this friendship, not at all this declaration. If before the beginning of war his britannic majesty had made an effort equal to our own to prevent it, perhaps now there would be no need to refer to the consequences which the declaration threatens and which always will be attributed to the king of Prussia as instigator of the present confusion in Germany. We are merely fulfilling our obligations, and if they are now extended, this has been well justified beforehand by the danger to all neighbors from the enterprise of the king of Prussia. We have instructed our forces to operate on land and sea against the forces and provinces of the king of Prussia, for no alternative means remained to render assistance to allies subjected to unwarranted attack. To blockade by sea those places which it has been determined to besiege by land is in accordance with the rules of war and is utilized universally. So we do not see why his britannic majesty considers it his duty to defend the navigation of his subjects in the Baltic Sea, when he has been reassured formally for our part that we have every intention of protecting their trade in particular.

"In respect to the undertaking by England and Prussia to oppose foreign troops entering Germany, such an assertion least of all can either restrain us from fulfilling our obligations or justify anything which might be carried out against such an action by the English. The main purpose of the agreement concluded between England and Prussia lay in maintaining the general peace in Germany, but this has not been carried out by one of the parties to the agreement. The king of Prussia was the first to begin the war, and England did not try to restrain him. As this central and most significant point has been disregarded, it is not clear by what means they are attempting to introduce a new right to oppose the entry of foreign troops into Germany in order to make it possible for the strongest party to arrange matters in an arbitrary manner and to oppress the weak who would be devoid of any assistance.

"We shall not change anything in respect to our intentions, and will state our point of view plainly. Until now we have earnestly tried, and are trying, to separate English from Prussian interests. We therefore hope that England will not subscribe to the unkind desires of the king of Prussia against us. Otherwise, and particularly if from the English side there is committed in any way even the smallest act against our forces or fleet, we shall take this as a violation of all treaties hitherto existing between us and England, and as a clear breach of the peace on England's part, in consequence of which we shall not refrain from taking measures in respect to our honor and dignity." When this declaration was conveyed by Golitsyn to Holderness, the secretary stated that as it served as a reply to the English declaration, there was no need to make answer at this time.[63] The king hoped that the empress would remain on such a basis of friendship with him as he felt towards her.

England could not do anything for its new ally.[64] Nor could anything be done in Sweden, which Austria, France and Russia persuaded to join in the war against Prussia. On the instructions of his court Panin[65] told Senator Höpken[66] that the empress heard with particular pleasure of the success of the negotiations of the Austrian and French ambassadors in Stockholm, and that the king of Sweden[67] could not in any way strengthen further his friendship with Russia and reinforce on a more stable basis of equilibrium the broken peace of the North other than by his agreement to those measures which might be proposed by the courts mentioned above. To induce Sweden to agree to these measures the empress not only permitted the export of ten thousand quarters of grain from Russia to Sweden, but also made a gift of this grain to the king, which was of particular importance, as several Swedish provinces were suffering from famine.

This act made a quite different impression in Stockholm to that expected in St. Petersburg. Senator Höpken told the king that although the

Russian gift was made to his majesty, the Senate could not hide the fact that such a gift would make the king a debtor to the empress, and would be a burden on Sweden, which was not in a position equally to show its gratitude to Russia. In such a situation it was necessary to follow the example of Portugal, which returned a monetary gift sent it from the English court after an earthquake[68] and paid cash for the food supplies sent by the same court. The Senate would season his majesty's refusal to accept the gift with such compliments that the empress could not take offence. The king let Panin know this through one of his friends, pledging the envoy on his word of honor not to give away the fact that he had been told in order not to put in jeopardy even more the king's relations with the Senate. Höpken asked Panin whether he would like to obtain an audience with the king in order to inform him of the gift.

Panin understood that the Senate wanted to place all the blame on the king for the refusal and therefore he replied to Höpken, "I cannot hide my astonishment on hearing how you separate the king from the crown. It is improper for me to be concerned with your domestic regulations in respect to the power of the king. Every free nation has its statutes, but sovereigns demand equal rights and privileges in respect to each other. In your country it is laid down that all public affairs, and in particular those relating to foreign countries, are carried out in the sovereign's name alone. Were it otherwise, you can easily understand what unfortunate difficulties would follow. England presents us with a similar example. Its government is constituted in just the same manner as the Swedish, but there is not a single foreign court that wishes to offend it by distinguishing between the king and the crown. That is why my most gracious sovereign is sending her gift to the king as head of state for distribution to the Swedish poor, in no way distinguishing the king from the Swedish crown. I have no right to demand an audience, as my court made the gift known directly to Baron Posse, the Swedish envoy in St. Petersburg, about which I have been informed recently." Höpken, having listened to all of this with a sullen expression, answered, "All that you say is true, but remember that in many documents the phrase is used 'the king and the crown of Sweden,' but in the present case the note communicating the particular sign of the sovereign's friendship in the form of assistance to a neighboring people does not have sufficient status as a public document." Having said this, he changed the subject.

Two days after this conversation Höpken told the king that the Senate could not consider the matter of the Russian gift, as it was made strictly to the king, and therefore it depended entirely upon the will of the king to accept or reject it. At this point the king gave him a note written in his own hand for submission to the Senate stating that, having in mind the severe shortage of grain in the realm, the king considered it his duty to accept the gift with gratitude. He conveyed this opinion for debate in the Senate and would abide by what the majority in the Senate decided. News from the provinces of famine and demands for help from the government forced the Senate to agree to accept the gift. The king invited Panin to his chambers and told him, "I accept the gift of her imperial majesty with complete gratitude. I am delighted that Mr. Höpken has not thought fit to come here. Evidently in his opinion the Swedish crown is taking no part in my gratitude. You already know that any methods are used, on this as on other occasions, to promote coolness between the empress and myself. They tried to lay upon me the unpleasant task of refusal. I told Mr. Höpken plainly that I would not take upon myself the decision to refuse without formal resolution of the Senate. They then had a change of heart and understood how unpleasant it would be for the empress should they so distort her good will towards the Swedish people in sowing dissension between myself and the government. The empress would never recognize this difference, of that I am confident, having had the most demonstrative experience of her maternal care for me."

Afterwards Höpken replied to Panin about his suggestion with respect to acceptance by Sweden of the French and Austrian proposals. "The Swedish court," said Höpken, "sincerely wishes the common undertaking success, and would assist it willingly. At present, however, the king and the Senate consider it impossible to take an active part at this time without exposing our Pomeranian possessions to obvious danger. Being as you well know without defences, there is no physical possibility at present of even transferring troops overseas for the defence of Pomerania, even if millions were expended. As soon as Sweden dares take part in the war and tells the German diet, the king of Prussia, through his standing and disposition, immediately would take possession of Pomerania and subject it to the same fate as Saxony." After this Höpken expanded on his dislike of Prussia. "I was never a Prussian," he said. "I regard Frederick II as the most dangerous of all present and past European sovereigns. His way of thinking is well known to everyone, the extreme of military principles, inhuman and terrible rules of domestic administration and a barbaric interpretation of international law must rouse the whole of Europe against him."

It was not difficult for Russian envoys to act against Frederick II. They were used to this. Yet it was very difficult to enter into friendly relations with the French court, which for some time the envoys had not been used to distinguishing from the Prussian court in hostility to Russia. Panin, like Korff, did not imagine policy had changed so abruptly in St. Petersburg. Being used to adapt to the chancellor's views, he wrote that the declaration of France on its obligation to preserve the guarantee of the Peace of Westphalia[69] would make war general. Resolution of these matters in itself would pass into the hands of France, which would achieve the predominant position as a consequence of the weakening of the maritime powers, which no longer could maintain the balance.

In answer Panin received an angry rescript, corrected by the hand of Vorontsov. "We cannot hide the fact," it read, "that your spontaneous reasoning seemed very strange to us, when you have been notified of the renewal of good relations between ourselves and France, as well as our intentions in the present circumstances. Our highest pleasure and precise instruction to you is that, by your humble office, henceforth you think and act with the greatest care and in conformity with our intentions in these matters." With respect to this the chancellor wrote to Panin, "I have already warned your excellency that in your communiqués you should cut down your reasoning as much as possible and report only the fulfillment of the rescript sent to you. In the present changed condition of affairs it may easily happen that an ambassador through his own commentary, which may sometimes seem in opposition to the measures taken here, will earn himself a serious reprimand instead of the anticipated approbation. This indeed happened recently with Baron Korff. Expatiating in his text on the old system, and praising those who still adhere to it, he was sent a rescript with such a severe reprimand for what he had said, that it would be almost impossible to write one more brutal. At the Conference, which I did not attend because of illness, a resolution was passed to issue you a reprimand similar to that sent to Baron Korff. I tried as hard as I could to stave it off completely but was quite unable to prevent it. In the end it was written in a much lighter tone. In these circumstances, to avoid similar reprimands for a commentary that proceeds solely from zeal, there is no better remedy than to fulfil the rescript exactly as sent, and to make a report about it without entering into extensive commentary. It is true that in this way a zealous ambassador and faithful son of the fatherland cannot express his most diligent sentiments, and in this way clear his

conscience before God and his sovereign, but in my opinion it is the saf-
est method. When circumstances demand, when important issues come
into your head from time to time, you may describe them in every detail
in your communiqué without a moment's hesitation, only give the appearance that they originate from a third party. In this way not only is your conscience clear but the danger of a reprimand will have been avoided, even
though the reported analysis does not receive approbation here."

Panin replied to Bestuzhev with complaints about his bitter and straitened circumstances. "I do not know how to begin. I am afraid of going
out of my mind. Can I preserve my resolution and resist a failing of spirit,
when regrettable consequences come before my eyes and domestic destruction already threatens loss of honor? All of this is taking place when
I see snares about me from the whole college, and there is no doubt that
they have made up their minds to eradicate me. I swear by my conscience
that I would have considered myself fortunate had the opportunity presented itself to deliver myself from their hands by an honorable death."

Panin again was instructed to further Austro-French talks with Sweden with respect to dispatch Swedish troops into Pomerania for action
against the Prussians. As a consequence, in July Panin recommended to
Höpken the necessity of Sweden commencing military operations that
very autumn. One consequence would be taking Prussian Pomerania, for
Frederick II was busy with the Austrians, and Field Marshal Lehwaldt
could not help Pomerania without placing himself between two fires,
between the Swedish and Russian forces. Höpken replied that Sweden
was only waiting, before commencing military operations, for final news
from the courts of Vienna and Versailles regarding subsidies, without
which Sweden could not conduct the war. At the beginning of August
Panin reported that agreement on the commencement of war by the Swedes
was completed, dispositions were made in agreement with the operations
of Field Marshal Apraksin, and the Prussian envoy Solms[70] had left Stockholm. On this matter Chancellor Bestuzhev wrote to Panin asking why he
did not report the opinions of the king and queen regarding these events,
as they were very anxious to know about this in St. Petersburg, in particular the views of the queen,[71] how she felt about the change of policy,
about war against her brother.

"I would advise you," wrote Bestuzhev, "to find out as much as possible about it, and to report directly in your communiqués. Avoid as much
as possible foreign words, that are criticized here by some." "Nothing

now remains of the royal prerogative of the king of Sweden," Panin replied, "except the name, and in public even the name 'majesty' is scarcely left to him. His wife is disfranchised in exactly the same way. Furthermore it must be admitted that fortune has scarcely played with anyone more than with her. Over a number of years this queen has endured an inner struggle between the interests of her husband and her hereditary Prussian attachments. These came together in their prejudice in favor of France, suggested to her by Count Tessin[72] and his friends. No sooner had she disavowed France and Prussian interests, and made firm intention to support in Sweden the restoration of the previous system of maritime powers, than her brother flung himself in the same direction. This once more aroused tender feelings towards her brother. The more Frederick II has become cold towards France, her hatred towards that country has reached unprecedented heights. Thanks to France, enmity between the Swedish nobility and the crown has been driven to extremes. The strength and power of the senators among the people are now sustained by France. The French ambassador was a friend of the grandees and the scourge of the court. It is impossible to describe the uncouth manner in which senators conduct themselves in respect to the queen. It is enough to say that from the time of the Riksdag they have not entered her rooms. Since that time also the wives of Senators Tessin and Höpken have stopped going to court. Last winter in the Senate it was agreed that all the other senators' wives should follow their example, so that only two ladies of rank go to court, Countesses Bonde and Söderkrys. It is true that the queen gave occasion for this by her cold reception of several of them or, more accurately, a change in her attention to them when they and their husbands rose up against her.

"Yet can she really be blamed? There is no nonsense they would not trumpet in public about her. They regard the king as completely incapable and his name, except in a formal sense, is nowhere heard in affairs of state. This is a true portrayal of the court here. To be infected with the bias of others and, without explaining the underlying causes, to report the words of the queen, either those provoked by her inflexible pride or those obviously invented by her enemies, would that not be a mean, unforgivable act for a kind man, and would that not damage the honor of a faithful servant? In particular it would be unforgivable when the king and queen show particular respect toward her imperial majesty, and our policies do not interfere with those of others. The changes in Europe, and through them the strengthened significance of their personal persecutors, they ascribe solely to their own misfortune, the fury of the king of Prussia, the subtleties of French politics and the impatient desire of the court in Vienna.

"Besides, my own security demands that, as far as honor and conscience will allow, my reports are in agreement or at least do not contradict the news which may easily come to their notice from the direction of the French ambassador here, Marquis d'Havrincourt,[73] and the Austrian Count Goëss. From Havrincourt I cannot expect any kind disposition towards me. His letter to Douglas, which was sent on to me from the Austrian court, may serve as proof. I make bold to assure you that he wished merely to set a trap for me which happily I would have avoided. Let anyone say, if they have any quality of nobility, that Count Goëss is not a flatterer and not a coward, neither is he filled with that pride characteristic of an imperial count of miserly upbringing. For some time he has sought by might and main the favor of the French ambassador, and now has become so attached to him that if the court in Vienna kept a copy clerk here, even he would not be able to fawn upon him more. Because of this the French ambassador now treats all of us unbearably arrogantly, so that the Spanish ambassador, being always an adherent of the French system, was obliged recently to point out to him that his dictatorial voice offends the representatives of other powers."

In what *sentiments*, in the expression of the time, Panin found himself in respect to the new system is evident from his next letter to the chancellor. "By planting the French ambassador with us, the court in Vienna has lured us away from the general system natural to us. Time will show how long Count Esterhazy will enjoy any significance in light of [the French ambassador's] presence amongst us, and whether he will not himself in the end become a petitioner to [the French ambassador] for the affairs of his own court. The blindness of the Viennese court is truly incomprehensible. It cannot see that England's decline under the might of France will be more distressing than the loss of Silesia. After the miserable success of its latest attempt to destroy a German corps,[74] France has hastened to attack by every manner of insult that supreme power [Britain], by whom all France's efforts have been turned to nought, and without which it will be easier for [France] to overwhelm the house of Austria, even with the addition of Silesia, than now without it."[75]

The Russian ambassador in Poland was in a similarly difficult position in respect to the French ambassador, the more so as Gross, like Korff and

Panin, was accustomed to the previous anti-French policy. The government asked Gross to carry out an exceedingly difficult task, that is, to do his utmost to reconcile the Polish parties of large landowners. Durand,[76] the French resident, acted more simply and easily. He stood for his own set of grandees against the Czartoryskis, declaring that any change in the Ostrog affair[77] would be very unpleasant for the opponents of the Czartoryskis, and that this would give occasion to the Turks to interfere in Polish affairs. The Princes Czartoryski for their part could never be reconciled with the court if the Ostrog affair was not settled in their favor. "From this you will understand," wrote Gross, "in what a difficult position the king finds himself trying to reach an agreement on these matters, and how my exhortations to compromise and moderation can be to his liking."

At this time Gross was more alarmed by the letters about which the postmaster at Lvov told him in secret. The Ukrainian emigrants, followers of Mazepa,[78] the Nakhimovskys, the Miroviches, the Orliks,[79] suffering from the general malaise of emigration, still dreamed that at some time fortune would smile upon them again, that Ukraine would be freed from the yoke of the Muscovites. Arriving in Jassy from the Crimea, Nakhimovsky wrote to the young Orlik, a brigadier in the French army, dignifying him with the title of count. "The matter of our fatherland is beginning to come right because the cossack camp with the Zaporozhian Host[80] has sent a courier disguised as a merchant secretly to the khan of the Crimea.[81] He has been living in the Crimea for more than two months. He has visited us nearly every day at Bakhchisaray and on oath has confirmed the matter of the Zaporozhian Camp. The khan would have agreed to acceptance of the camp at Aleshki, where it was before, but he has not yet announced a final decision. Evidently he has told the Porte about this matter. Together with Lord Mirovich I recommended to the Zaporozhian envoy that the Russian frontier go as far as Sevsk, not as far as Ingul and Ingulets.[82] I suggested to him that more than anything else they begin to restore the small fortress on Mikita's Horn, on actual Zaporozhets land given by the kings of Poland, from whom the Zaporozhians were granted the privileges of freedom and their own laws, which the Muscovites have taken away and have surrounded you, the Zaporozhians, with peasant settlers. They keep you under guard through the fortress they have built among the cossacks.[83] We made many other suggestions about Russia, setting out a number of examples to show that it has never spared any rights in its treachery."

From another direction the Prussian resident in Warsaw, Benoît, was also a cause for alarm. He boasted that his king had reliable information from St. Petersburg that Russian forces would not act against Prussia earlier than halfway through July, and that before that time he, the king, would perhaps have compelled the Austrians to seek peace. The same postmaster from Lvov, having received three hundred chervontsy from Gross for his services, told him that Benoît sent him various Prussian declarations, manifestoes and similar short prose pieces, for distribution among the Polish gentry, but that he, the postmaster, had kept his hands on all these pieces and had not distributed them.

On the return of Hetman Branicki[84] from Bialystok in May, Durand had a conversation with Gross. "What does it mean," Gross asked, "when the adherents of the French in Poland are still maintaining intrigues with the Porte against the passage of Russian troops across Poland? They well know that the state of European affairs is completely transformed, that Russian troops are on the move solely to assist the Polish sovereign. These so-called French partisans are equally supported both from the French as well as from the Prussian side, while Benoît dignifies them with the name of true sons of the fatherland!" "All the local magnates," replied Durand, "are so used to intrigues and underhand plotting that now you cannot break them of the habit. We must induce them to this end by gentle means. I went to Bialystok for a purpose, to suggest other ideas to the hetman and those around him, which I hope will have a beneficial effect."

That May Gross told Brühl of the agreement of both imperial houses to deliver to the king of Poland the city of Magdeburg and its environs, as well as the Saale river district, and if possible even more in compensation for the losses suffered in Saxony. Brühl replied that the king could not find words to express his gratitude. He begged leave to convey to the attention of the empress a request from the king, whether it might not be possible to deliver to him, in addition to Magdeburg and the Saale district, also that part of Silesia which separates Saxony from Poland, which must assist the attainment of the empress's well-known objectives.

In June Warsaw was greatly alarmed by the transit of the Prussian general Lomut who, after staying two days with Benoît and seeing no one else, set off for Breslau. It was decided that the general had visited to examine the road from Silesia to Prussia through Poland. The theater of war would be transferred to Poland, where there would be great to do. It would be impossible for the king of Poland to remain in Warsaw. Together with the Austrian and French ministers, Gross persuaded Brühl to think in good time as to where, in such a situation, the king should move. Grodno, protected by the Russian army, was suggested, Lvov or Seypusch on the Hungarian frontier. The king's position was in such danger that on Brühl's admission the court did not know which of the important Poles could be trusted. If the Princes Czartoryski and their friends were dissatisfied by the Ostrog affair, so too by the predominance of Count Mniszech,[85] Hetman Branicki and his advisers considered themselves also insulted because not everything had been done to their satisfaction. Others, such as Potocki[86] the palatine of Bielz, who had nothing to lose, fished in muddy waters for the sake of trouble.

A cause of considerable talk was the foreign journey of the young Prince Czartoryski, son of the Russian military governor, a journey through Danzig, Berlin and Holland to England. Gross suggested to the governor that such a journey was untimely. The governor replied that rumors put about by his enemies would not compel him to change any plan for the education of his son, whom long ago he had thought of sending to England as a cure for his empty-headed behavior. Besides everyone knew that neither he nor his friends would commit themselves to Prussia. Gross assured his court that it was not in keeping with the character and interests of Czartoryski, as the richest man in Poland, to raise anxiety in the country. Brühl suggested to Gross that, to save Poland from impending misfortune, Field Marshal Apraksin hasten his operations and drive Lehwaldt out of East Prussia, for the king of Prussia had written to his mother saying that in six weeks he hoped to take possession of Bohemia and overcome the Austrian army.

In the summer General Major Mikhail Nikitich Volkonsky,[87] a nephew of Bestuzhev (son of the celebrated Princess Agrafena Petrovna Volkonskaia),[88] arrived in Warsaw also in the capacity of ambassador plenipotentiary. Gross stayed on with him in his previous capacity. Volkonsky's instructions maintained that he was sent in consequence of requests from Count Malachowski, the Princes Czartoryski and other loyal patriots, not only the better to divert and to prevent any disaster, but also for the restoration of the previous system which Peter the Great had proposed as the basis of peace in the Commonwealth, and in the general interests of Russia and Poland. First of all Volkonsky was to attempt a reconciliation of the opposing parties, bringing together all large landowners with those loyal to the cause, that is with those of the Russian party. This was an extraordinarily difficult matter, the more so as France, according to its well-known principle, would not cease to support its adherents strongly, and the king of Prussia, in particular in his present great round of activity, naturally would try to arouse any form of trouble throughout Poland and Lithuania. Volkonsky must try to gain such influence with the Poles that they would always act, particularly during an interregnum, in the interests of her majesty, and that her patronage, more than that of the other powers, holds firm, and that they give greater satisfaction in respect to our coreligionists in Poland, as well as to frontier matters and extradition of runaways.

In 1755 Chancellor Count Malachowski gave his views in confidence to the Russian court, namely that until now they did not have a clear understanding of Russia. To the gentry Russia was nothing more than a scourge used to punish the willful. The name of Russia was used by France in this way. Thus France increased the number of its friends and made Russia hated. Therefore an ambassador was needed in Poland who could refute boldly negative suggestions about Russia, such as being likened to a scourge. This ambassador must not adhere to any one party, but must be an intermediary and conciliator, just as peace was restored in 1717 by the mediation of Peter the Great. The hetmen were to oversee the troops at the frontiers, but now the hetmen had greatly strengthened their authority and did just as they liked, while the gentry did not dare to say anything. It was impossible to set this right without a Russian intermediary.

As all these opinions of Count Malachowski were well-founded, Volkonsky had to make sure that any disorder and violation of law and liberties in Poland were nipped in the bud. He had to ensure that no impediments were created to the prime authority of the crown in the discharge of its office, and that the illegal power of the hetmen be subordinated to the crown and Lithuanian chancellors. He was to see that there were no violations of laws or established customs and procedures at the district and national Sejms and the major tribunals. He was to calm any passions raised by the "ordination" of the Ostrog estates as soon as possible. Should anyone suggest that a foreign power not interfere in the domestic affairs of the Commonwealth he was to reply that there would be interference if Russia took a hand in deciding the [Ostrog] matter, declaring to whom the properties of ordination belonged. Russia, in leaving the decision to the king and Commonwealth, insisted merely on the speedy and satisfactory conclusion of an affair giving occasion to great enmity and discord.

In prompting the king's court to curtail dissension between the families Volkonsky was to give credit for this cessation to the king, and he himself simply was to urge everyone to compliance and moderation. He must also, when justified, support the old Russian well-wishers. Several of these loyal large landowners, and in particular the Princes Czar-toryski, would make a considerable fuss about financial assistance. It would certainly be impossible to manage without it in the case of an inter-regnum. It would be superfluous to give financial assistance now, because some magnates already were receiving annual pensions, namely Primate Komarowski at five thousand rubles a year, Crown Chancellor Count Malachowski seven thousand rubles, the Lithuanian Chief Equerry Prince Radziwill one thousand rubles, and the Lithuanian chancellor Prince Czartoryski was supplied with a significant sum. So when they visited the ambassador with their requests he could reassure them in general terms of imperial favor which would never be abandoned in significant and essential circumstances.

In respect to the most important point, the election of the king, measures had to be taken at this point and in good time, because the present king was unreliable, by reason of his advanced age and the loss of his inherited lands. As the king wished to secure the election of his son, and as her majesty had told him of her agreement through Ambassador Gross in the strictest confidence, Volkonsky must cautiously, and at the same time also fervently, suggest this to the most distinguished Poles and solicit their agreement, as Russian interest required raising a Saxon prince to the Polish throne. Volkonsky was to try extremely hard to prevent the matter of freeing Biron being raised.

By the ninth article of the Treaty of "Perpetual Peace" between Russia and Poland[89] it was stipulated that the four bishops of the Greco-Rus rite, those of Luck, Przemysl, Lvov and Belorussia, the monasteries, archimandrites, abbots, brotherhoods and all people living in Poland and Lithuania, had the right to free exercise of their Greco-Rus faith without any oppression or any coercion to adopt the faith of Rome or the Uniates.[90] In spite of this the first three dioceses for some time had been drawn into the Uniate church by the Poles, and now only the White Russian diocese remained, together with several monasteries. Even this last diocese endured incessant cruel injury. The clergy were taken through the civil courts. Others were beaten. The churches were locked and generally taken out of use. Those that became dilapidated were not allowed to be repaired, nor could new churches be built. All representations from the imperial court were unsuccessful. On Volkonsky was laid the task of lodging at the Polish court, verbally and in writing, the strongest complaints about all of these injuries, both old and new. Everything transferred to the Uniate church must be returned to the Orthodox. The repair of old and the construction of new churches must be permitted. There was to be a ban on forced proselytizing to the Uniate church, without accepting any excuses. The frontiers between Russia and Poland were as yet undefined, but it appeared that the Poles had seized 988 square versts of Russian land. Volkonsky was to demand the appointment of commissioners to define the borders.

Prince Volkonsky at first could comfort himself with the hope that he had arrived in Warsaw at an opportune time. News arrived of Apraksin's victory at Gross-Jägersdorf and to celebrate the king conferred on Volkonsky the Order of the White Eagle. Then news arrived of the withdrawal of the Russian forces, and in the meantime French relations presented considerable difficulties. The Poles of the French party conveyed to the French ambassador in Warsaw their complaints at the burden entailed by the passage of Russian troops. The French ambassador in Warsaw conveyed these complaints to the French ambassador in St. Petersburg, the marquis de l'Hôpital, who presented them to the Russian ministry.

Such mediation strongly offended the court at St. Petersburg. Volkonsky was to make an effort to bring it to an end, but this was difficult. Chancellor Malachowski told Volkonsky and Gross in confidence that a note was being composed by the French ambassador in which all complaints of the Poles at Russia for the past forty years were to be set down. Volkonsky noticed in this regard that the best way to lessen French influence was to end the argument over the Ostrog estates in favor of the Russian party. Malachowski replied that the withdrawal of Russian forces made it impossible to expect such a step. The court of Saxony was dependent upon the French, anticipating from them, as the most significant benefit of that dependence, the liberation of its hereditary possessions. The measure proposed would give great offence to the French court.

Volkonsky and Gross then turned directly to Count Brühl with the suggestion that the conduct of the French ministers de Broglie and Durand, and the Polish government's connivance, could bring about mistrust among the allied courts and destroy the agreement reached between Russia and France. Brühl confessed that indeed de Broglie eagerly seized any opportunity to make Russia hated, but what could he do about it? It was necessary to spare the French ambassadors at that time, after Russian forces had retreated from Prussia completely. The Austrians also had let slip the opportunity to take Breslau. Only the French could rescue the Saxon lands from the Prussians.

From the assurances of the man in charge of foreign affairs in France, the abbé de Bernis, it seemed evident that the French ambassadors in Warsaw were not acting on the order of Louis XV, but without authority. Therefore it would not have been a bad idea for the empress to deal directly to the king of France, with a request to give better directions to his ministers or to ask for their recall. When Volkonsky remarked on the necessity of settling the dispute over the Ostrog estates in the favor of the Russian party, Brühl replied that the time was inopportune. Volkonsky suggested he begin reconciliation of the Czartoryşkis with the court party by the following transaction. At the death of Crown Marshal Bie-linski to make Count Mniszech marshal in his place, and in place of the previous marshal of the court to appoint Prince Lubomirski, son-in-law of the Russian governor Prince Czartoryski. Brühl did not hold out much hope for such a settlement.

Malachowski and Czartoryski told Volkonsky that the French ambassador de Broglie had forced Count Brühl to petition the king for the rank of clerk of Braclaw for the nobleman Bogatko, who had no right to this office. At his first meeting with Brühl, Volkonsky reproached him for such a breach of good order. He replied that he was forced to do this not without some regret. What could he do about it when with the withdrawal of the Russian forces the king's sole hope lay with France, and he must please the French in everything?

In respect to this conversation with Brühl, Volkonsky wrote to St. Petersburg, "In order to gain influence here I must either distribute more money or have at my disposal at court vacant offices and positions in the local administration. France controls the distribution of offices, but does not hesitate to make use of money either, and in this way greatly reinforces its party. Not being satisfied even with this, the French ambassadors even make use of a third method, particularly damaging to the Russian interests, of gathering and falsely interpreting all complaints of the Poles against Russia. By taking their part the French make themselves agreeable, and us hated.

"Thus Count de Broglie in the presence of Counts Brühl and Sternberg (the Austrian ambassador), as well as in the presence of Gross, spoke with extreme indignation against the winter quarters occupied by the Russian forces. He claimed that the inhabitants of Lithuania, even as it was, were ruined by the passage of the Russian forces, from buying up of food supplies for the Russian supply depots, the prolonged stay of ships on the Nieman and requisitioning of transports. Count Brühl remarked that her majesty had made clear her intention of appointing commissioners for the examination and satisfaction of all these complaints. Gross added that so far no complaints had reached either himself or anybody else. Zabiello, in the company of Field Marshal Apraksin, attested to both that all complaints referred to him had been satisfied. In spite of this de Broglie continued to maintain that he had received a great many complaints, and moreover that the commission promised by your majesty would not convene for some time, because your instructions are not being carried out. De Broglie enlarged upon the complaints of Potocki, governor of Kiev, and Prince Jablonowski, the military governor of Braclaw. Gross objected that Potocki's complaints had been investigated and responded to. As to Jablonowski's complaints about Chigirin,[91] there could be no dispute in this case because the boundaries of the Chigirin prefecture were settled by the treaty of 1686. Gross added that there was no necessity for a third party to interfere in border disputes between Russia and Poland, as there were special commissioners appointed from both sides to settle such matters. It was not in accordance with the dignity of a foreign power to intervene in all such trifles as may take place from time to time on the frontiers of another distant state.

"De Broglie became excited and said that in standing up for the Poles he was acting in accord with the instructions of his court. It was not at all surprising that the Poles, not receiving satisfaction from Russia, sought the protection of an allied power. There was an agreement between the allies that during the passage of Russian forces through Poland there must be no losses to the inhabitants. He, de Broglie, had every right to stand up for all the complaints of the Poles, lest as a consequence of their dissatisfaction the peace of the country be violated. Without his efforts and those of Durand, disturbances would have taken place long ago." Volkonsky and Gross ended their report of October 19 with the news that Count Poniatowski had been recalled from St. Petersburg in consequence of a letter from the king of France. In their opinion this was proof of the absolute authority which France enjoyed over the Polish court.

Volkonsky and Gross received a most unexpected reply from their court to this report. "We recognize that these days the Polish court expects to receive everything for Saxony from the bounty of the court of France. The Polish court might suggest to the French that, however great its gratitude, nevertheless it trusts that the king of France will never demand that this gratitude take the form of an infringement of the rights of the Polish crown and blind indulgence of the requests of all those who, perhaps without having demonstrated any services to the fatherland and without furthering an agreement between the courts, have only the art of pleasing personally Count de Broglie or the resident Durand. Do not neglect to let our opinion be known to the king through Count Brühl.

"It is true that those who have offices and senior local administrative posts at their disposal at court may put together a large party, but there is no reason to be concerned. The gratitude of the Poles is well known. As soon as it is no longer the French ambassador but someone else who has offices at his disposal, the French ambassador will be forgotten completely. The Princes Czartoryski were raised from nothing by the court and, with offices at their disposal, took pride of place in Poland. Now they have lost their significance because they do not have offices at their disposal.

"Everybody has his time. We must wait, and when our time comes, we must make use of it. As to the distribution of money to the Poles, we have pointed out that we do not observe any great value in this. We only grow tired, you know, of hearing frequent reminders of this from all our ambassadors, whoever has been sent there, and we never see any benefit. It is well known that we can acquire 'friends' for money, but we cannot be restricted simply to that use, taking our money. Four thousand chervontsy were sent to Poland with Weymarn at the particular request of Prince Czartoryski, the Lithuanian chancellor. This money brought no benefit whatsoever, and this rich magnate accepted the money without due respect, as if it had been thrust upon him. If France really is distributing money in Poland, it may receive some benefit, being situated at such a distance, not being in a position either to assist or to oppress Poland directly. Without the distribution of money, France would be completely insignificant in Poland. With us it is a completely different matter. We must keep an eye on French movements but need not imitate them in every particular."

At the end of the year Volkonsky and Gross reported that de Broglie and Durand were beginning to conduct themselves better, maintaining merely a coldness, an unwillingness to enter into conversation. The change in the conduct of the French ambassadors proceeded from the fact that it was impossible to laugh at Apraksin's withdrawal for long. After a detachment of Austrians under the command of General Hadik[92] seized Berlin and rapidly abandoned it, merely taking from the inhabitants one hundred and eighty-five thousand thalers indemnity, the French forces in

October suffered a defeat by Frederick II at Rossbach, and the Austrians in November at Leuthen. The Swedish forces, having invaded Prussian Pomerania, were thrown back by that same Lehwaldt who did not have the same luck at Gross-Jägersdorf. Frederick II triumphed over the formidable coalition. A long and difficult war was anticipated, for which both troops and finances had to be prepared.

THE FORCES AND FINANCE

In March the Senate ordered a report from the War College asking how many soldiers were due for retirement or assignment to civil duties, because from various quarters there were requests for them to mount guard and other duties, as there were now no regular troops in these places, and the couriers had been taken into military service. The war also threatened to become a naval one, since an English squadron was expected to enter the Baltic Sea, and therefore the fleet demanded as much attention as the land forces. It was decided to divide in half the number of those not of adult age who were entered for the Cadet Corps, both for the land forces and the navy, so that these services could be filled evenly.

At the end of the year the War College issued a report about conscription. It turned out that the last conscription drive brought in 43,088, of which 41,374 were handed over to the officers. Of these 37,675 were dispatched, but in fact only 23,571 arrived at their regiments. The Senate ordered the college to tell them what happened to these 19,517 men. A little earlier the Senate heard an extract from a protocol of the Conference, on a motion of Prince Peter Shuvalov, to carry out an annual conscription drive, not over the whole state but only in one part, dividing the whole of Russia for this purpose into five conscription districts. The same Shuvalov pointed out the damaging slowness of the mail in times of war. A report from a commander of the First Regiment of Musketeers sent on September 26 was received only on November 14, taking a month and twenty days to get from Smolensk to St. Petersburg.

We have mentioned already the conflict between Shuvalov and Chief of the Commissary Prince Yakov Shakhovskoy.[93] From Shakhovskoy's notes we know what happened to the 19,517 recruits about whom the Senate asked the College of War. In the period under discussion Shakhovskoy was in Moscow with the Main Commissariat. "At that time, towards the end of winter," said Shakhovskoy, "when I had covered half of my journey to the military hospital, I was met by several wood-sledges full of soldiers and conscripts lying down. I stopped and asked where they were being taken. A junior officer with them told me that they were being sent to the staff hospital for the treatment of dangerous illnesses. It refused to accept them because of the danger, and ordered them to be taken back to their commander. Seeing the pitiful condition of these unfortunates, amongst whom several already seemed to be half-dead, I ordered them to be taken back with me to the military hospital, reassuring them that I would accommodate them there. When I arrived with these patients at the hospital building, I saw a number of other patients lying on wood-sledges by the main steps. As soon as I got out of my carriage both a doctor and a member of the commissariat immediately hastened to tell to me not to walk further than the steps. Over the three days since I was last there an extraordinary number of soldiers and recruits from a number of military commands were brought in sick, for the most part with acute temperatures and infectious fevers. There were already more than nine hundred in the infirmary. Not only were all the rooms on the lower and upper floors filled to capacity, even the entrance halls were jammed. A terrible stuffy heat resulted from their close crowding, but the windows could not be opened because of the cold weather. Not only were they infecting each other, but also the healthy caring for them and serving them were falling sick. The numbers were growing almost without pause, as more were being sent. They had to be sent back to their barracks.

"For that reason it was intended to send those lying on the wood-sledges back to their barracks, lest they add to the number of dead to be buried at the expense of the hospital. Then the junior officers sent with the sick begged me to take them in, pointing out that of those on the road several already were dead and others were in an extremely pitiful condition, shivering in the severe cold. I collected my ideas together as to how I could find some relief for these patients, searching in all directions whether I could find any buildings in the vicinity which could be used as more spacious housing for them. I asked a member of the commissariat and the doctor who was living in these buildings. They pointed out those in the vicinity in which various members of the hospital staff lived. I ordered them to move out into rented apartments and to place the sick in their rooms. The doctor and the member of the commissariat told me that the day before they already had taken such a step, but could not find a way.

There were no rented flats in the vicinity and even for far around. Because a rumor already got around about our sick soldiers, nobody would let their premises at any price to the hospital department. At the same time I found out that not very far away was a cavalry department with several empty rooms. I also heard of a large wooden building not very far away at all from the hospital behind the Palace Gardens on the banks of the Yauza river. I was told that it was the brewery of a department of the Palace Chancellery and at present, in the absence of her majesty, was quite empty. Only a member of the commissariat lived there, whose task was to look after it. Others also told me what an unpleasant place it was, that it was very dilapidated, that it had been decided to remove this building to another site further from the garden, and tenders for these operations had been called for by an advertisement in the newspapers."

Shakhovskoy decided to remove the hospital staff to this brewery and place the sick in their apartments. He did this without waiting for permission from the Palace Chancellery in St. Petersburg. Knowing that he might stir up displeasure by such initiatives, he wrote a letter to the favorite Ivan Ivanovich Shuvalov[94] asking for his protection should those ill-disposed towards him in his absence say things against him. Ivan Ivanovich Shuvalov, amongst the nobility of that period, was distinguished by his gentleness, the humanity of his treatment of others, trying above all to preserve good relations with everybody, especially with those distinguished by their service and abilities. He tried to appear quite impartial, free of the opinions of his relatives the Counts Peter[95] and Alexander Shuvalov,[96] tried "with noble courtesy" and service to make his favor a pleasure and something to be desired. In his reply Ivan Ivanovich Shuvalov praised Shakhovskoy's philanthropic act, and assured him of his protection.

At the same time Shakhovskoy described the affair to his friend Major of Guards Nashchokin, who informed him that in the distinguished households of Shakhovskoy's enemies he had heard remarks against him by members of the Palace Chancellery. There was talk about the unheard-of impertinence of a general of the Commissary of War who had the effrontery, without leave, to assign the sick with infectious diseases to the very place where, when the court is in residence, beer is brewed and sauerkraut soup made for the personal use of her majesty. The Senate requested an explanation from Shakhovskoy. On what basis had he occupied the court brewery without permission from the Palace Chancellery? The procurator general[97] sent him a friendly letter, congratulating him for the fact that his enemies, "unable to find any justifiable reasons by which they could injure you, incline towards reconciliation, because yesterday, at the Conference, Count Peter Ivanovich Shuvalov, knowing that I have great regard for you, approached me and said to everyone aloud that he deplored those arguments and the nonsensical talk to which your initiative gave rise, and now, having found out to his satisfaction that your stubbornness was generally for a practical reason, he was dropping all his complaints and would think no more of them."

In his letter Nashchokin confirmed, as before, that Shakhovskoy should be careful. The complaints of the Palace Chancellery were growing all the time. Nashchokin was right. One day a Guards officer came to Shakhovskoy from St. Petersburg and handed him a paper from the head of the terrible Secret Chancellery,[98] Count Alexander Ivanovich Shuvalov. "It has been made known to her imperial majesty that without authority you took possession of those rooms in the building of the court brewery in which bottles with beverages are poured and corked for her majesty's own use. You lodged laundresses in them, who wash linen with every sort of filth upon it from the sick. A special messenger, a lieutenant of the Guards, has been sent to you from the Secret Chancellery by order of her majesty, instructed to ascertain if there are patients and laundresses in those rooms, and to transfer all of them to live in your house immediately, not overlooking a single room in your palace, and certainly not your bedroom."

All this was correct. An assistant of Shakhovskoy in the management of the hospital, General Major Koming, and the manager of the hospital had ordered the lodging of the sick and the laundresses in the brewery unknown to the general of the Commissary of War. Later Shakhovskoy found out that the manager had dealings with an official of the Palace Chancellery from St. Petersburg and, as if on purpose, just before the arrival of the Guards officer, took the sick and the laundresses into the brewery. Nevertheless, the order was carried out, and Shakhovskoy had to support the sick and the laundresses in his house for two weeks, until a reply was received to his explanatory letter to the empress. Ivan Ivanovich Shuvalov wrote him a favorable letter with expressions of deep regret at what happened and assured him in the name of the empress, that "her majesty, recognizing Shakhovskoy's excuse, regrets what was done to him so peremptorily and imprudently."

When later Shakhovskoy went to St. Petersburg his friends told him how this indiscretion came about. According to them, members of the Palace Chancellery tried to take their revenge on Shakhovskoy with the assistance of the Counts Shuvalov, Peter and Alexander, who were angry with him for not agreeing to satisfy their demands for the troops under their command. "Count Peter Ivanovich Shuvalov," Shakhovskoy himself relates, "by his usual artfulness, through his wife Countess Maria Yegorovna, then in a position of great favor and trust with her majesty and living at the palace, just as he achieved other things he wanted, cleverly succeeded in obtaining that decision relating to me from her imperial majesty. To that end he used his servant, at that time at court and in her majesty's favor, the chief butler Bakhteev. In this way they began to play their roles at the first opportunity.

"When they were in the inner rooms in her majesty's presence, and she moved away to the window, they intentionally held a conversation with significant and astonished airs. Her majesty, noticing this, came up to them and asked what they were talking about so seriously. They both fell silent, giving the appearance that it would be dangerous for them to interfere in such matters and that they did not dare report it to her majesty. She took their modesty as something of great significance, demanded in an imperious manner that they tell her in detail all about it and what they, fearing her even more, were hiding. 'Oh, I am afraid, little mother,' Countess Shuvalova replied, 'that this man, lucky in all his enterprises, whom everyone generally fears and gives in to, reviles me through the mediation of others. If my husband acted in this way there would be a great many who would inform against him to your majesty, but no one dares against this dare-devil'. At this she pointed to the chief butler Bakhteev. 'Look he should report this to your majesty, but even he, you see, is afraid.'

"When she heard this, her majesty asked with even greater impatience and rising anger, 'What is this all about, and who is more to be feared by you than I?' Mr. Bakhteev (as I was told by someone who happened to be present during all this), gave the appearance of great timidity. He then gave an account, magnified as much as possible to my own disadvantage, of how I had taken over the brewery, lodged the sick with foul diseases, together with the laundresses who wash the linen taken from them, in the very rooms where they pour out and cork the bottles for her majesty's use. So these unscrupulously wicked and perfidious people feigned a virtuous heart to prepare a verdict against me. Her majesty said, 'Well,

I'll prove to you that you need not fear this dare-devil,' and called Count Alexander Ivanovich Shuvalov who, as if on purpose, was at that very moment nearby. She ordered him to send without delay an officer to me in Moscow as courier with her imperial command."

As a consequence of this whole story, an extension was ordered to be built to the Moscow military hospital. Shakhovskoy pointed out that the hospital was situated near the palace and further upstream on the Yauza, therefore sewage in the river might reach the palace, and a foul stench be brought by the wind. "Would it not be better to rebuild the stone block on the banks of the Moscow river, not far from the New Savior monastery or near the residence of the bishop of Krutitsa? Not only the sick non-commissioned officers and soldiers should be housed there, but also other officials, both military and civilian, suffering from incurable diseases and senility, as well as orphans and illegitimate children left by those killed in war. Should hospital income not suffice, maintenance should be paid from the income of the inherited synodal lands,[99] as well as anything left over after expenditure in the bishop's households and monasteries, as many decrees relating to the construction of hospitals and almshouses by monasteries have not been carried out. Although retired officers and soldiers were sent to monasteries for their sustenance, they have been kept there for the most part without proper care or the satisfaction of their needs. Frequent complaints of various incidents and disputes have been made by them against the monastic authorities, and by the authorities against them. The present military hospital may serve as a barracks for a company of the Life Guards or for other palace requirements."

When this suggestion was read to the Senate, Procurator General Prince Trubetskoy and Count Peter Ivanovich Shuvalov declared that the founding of houses for the disabled on such a basis as Shakhovskoy suggested was already at her majesty's pleasure. They gave instructions to accept Prince Shakhovskoy's recommendation. The Senate accepted that a site on the Moscow river near the Danilov monastery was suitable, and asked the architect Prince Ukhtomsky[100] to draw up a plan and put together an estimate.

There was little hope of carrying out such an extensive building program during wartime because of the financial situation. "There is no spare capital," Count Peter Shuvalov told the Conference. "Those millions acquired by the Treasury have been spent. An increase in the price of wine and salt has been made by regulation. Increased income is exhausted. A loan of a million received as a grant has gone. There is a reliable method of obtaining money. If every eight rubles of copeck coins is fixed at a pud of copper, 437,500 puds can be remade into half-copeck and copeck coins and tokens at sixteen rubles a pud. Instead of circulating amongst the public 7,397,910 rubles of copper money, by my plan 12,502,154 rubles can be circulated in the country. Our subjects will receive the advantage that they will not be burdened as at present by carrying sixteen rubles of coins weighing a pud. The previous coinage was set at such a low value with the aim of cutting imports from foreign countries, but this precaution is now considered superfluous. It is true that other methods of gathering a large capital sum will be put forward, following the example of foreign states, by the establishment of lotteries or a bank, for example. Such institutions are not suitable for us. A large-scale lottery to obtain six million can hardly be collected quickly, or even at all, particularly when the very idea of a lottery is unfamiliar to us. As regards a bank, the danger of counterfeiting bank notes and pieces of paper instead of money will seem to the public not only ridiculous, but credit itself will be quite damaged. When using bank notes in trading all sorts of lunacy and deceit may take place."

In the Senate Shuvalov stated that the Treasury had received an increase of more than fifteen million rubles (15,671,172 rubles 53 copecks) by his introduction of new methods between 1750 and the present day. The Gentry Bank[101] was established from receipts, but this very useful move might lead to the complete ruin of noble families, as only a three-year period was prescribed for repayment, and many members of the nobility are not able to pay off their loans in three years. There was nowhere the nobility, in particular those serving in the army, could borrow, and because of this their immovable property had been seized. The period for payment must be extended. The Senate agreed to increase the period for a further year. Two hundred and seventy-five thousand rubles were to be assigned from the Mint to the College of State Accounts in the form of a loan with the payment of customs efimoks [silver coins], which it was instructed to use quickly for recasting, so that an insufficiency of money would not follow at the Mint. The College of State Accounts was ordered be given 39,490 rubles from various other sources.

Apart from military expenditure, it was necessary to continue work at Kronstadt without interruption. After the canal, a commercial and secondary port was being built there, for which 97,000 rubles were assigned.

Ways of curtailing expenditure had been examined, and the endless number of commissions once again came to light. The procurator general stated that commissions were established in Yaroslavl concerning tavern and other matters, and in Novgorod over the illegal acts of authorized tax-collectors, but these were prolonged for a considerable period of time with arguments and the mutual distrust of the members. These problems should be apportioned to the appropriate institutions, to the Treasury and the College of Justice, and if they cannot resolve matters there, to the Senate, so that petty officials not receive their salary for nothing, nor the guilty remain unpunished. The Senate agreed.

As the administration of finances was concentrated in the Senate, lower institutions thought they must report to the Senate on every, even trivial, expenditure in the area of finance. The secretary of local government in Moscow reported that he had placed a fifty copeck rent on a warehouse built by the merchant Efimov for the pea trade. The Senate.ordered the secretary to ask him why he was bothering the Senate with such an irrelevant matter. No one found it an irrelevant matter that permission to open an inn or an hotel should lie within the jurisdiction of the Senate. There was an inn already in Moscow, kept by the Savoyard Berlir in the Foreign Settlement, and now permission was given to open another in the village of Pokrovskoe in Yelokhovo. That consent was granted to the St. Petersburg merchant Tsyginbein, who also had an inn in St. Petersburg. The Senate further gave permission for Moscow University to have a guest house or inn under its control for foreign professors, holders of a master's degree or for instructors. At the end of the year it was forbidden to have more than two thousand cab-drivers in St. Petersburg, on account of the high cost of forage.

PEASANT UNREST

As before, of all manifestations of provincial life, peasant unrest excited particular attention. Yevdokim Demidov again complained that an ensign with a military detachment was sent to pacify his peasants in the Aleksin and Likhvin districts. The peasants disobeyed the ensign. They refused permission for the detachment to go to the village of Rusanovo, threatening to fight it to the death. Two priests and the peasants said that they would not obey Demidov and his sons. Lieutenant Colonel Khatunsky was despatched against the rebellious peasants of the New Savior monastery, the villages of Spasskoe and Vvedenskoe in the Shatsk district. As a consequence of resistance by the Spasskoe peasants he was forced to use artillery and rifles and to enter the village by force. The peasants took to their heels. Later a search was made in the village and sixty-two people came forward, but in the village of Vvedenskoe only ten did so. As this uprising took place because of offences by the stewards and servants of the monastery, the matter was investigated by a joint commission established from members of the Senate and the Synodal offices.[102]

SITUATION IN THE UKRAINE

The Ukrainian hetman was finally and successfully sent on his way from St. Petersburg to Glukhov.[103] At every post-station along the way two hundred carts were ordered to be available. Following the example of the receptions of Hetman Skoropadsky,[104] Razumovsky was given 1,116 rubles and 52 copecks instead of a caftan and length of cloth, and the following gifts, instead of sables and lengths of damask, to those officials with him, to a chief justice, two hundred and fifty rubles and all others sixty rubles. The Zaporozhians as before constituted the main problem from the Ukrainian point of view. Here Ataman Shkura of the Minsk company and Ataman Kishensky of the Irkleevsk company stirred up the cossacks of a number of companies, took the kettle-drums by force and, beating them with cudgels, gathered a council together. More than three hundred cossacks joined them, raising a cry, seizing two maces, those of the camp commander and the judge's office, giving the first to Shkura and the second to Kishensky. Shkura became the commander and Kishensky the magistrate. Then the atamans met and appointed the old commander and lieutenant colonel of cossacks as before. The hetman ordered Shkura, Kishensky and other ringleaders placed under guard and brought to Glukhov. The decision of the atamans, as became clear, turned out to be unreliable. The old commander and lieutenant colonel thought it necessary to refuse their duties under the pretext of old age and new ones were selected. The hetman, when he learned of this, wrote to Zaporozhia that because of this the Camp certainly deserved to be put to the torture and made to pay a fine. So that they should not dare imperial anger in the future, they must themselves dismiss the commander and lieutenant colonel, and select replacements. The cossacks slandered the commander and lieutenant colonel for taking stolen goods from them as presents.

We have seen that Gross, the Russian ambassador in Warsaw, received information about the aspirations of the Ukrainian emigrants living in the

Crimea.[105] When this news was sent to St. Petersburg, naturally a document was sent from there to the hetman to redouble his attention to the problem. Razumovsky was afraid, but not by the plotting of the emigrants who were able to disturb the peace of the country entrusted to him, but that in St. Petersburg they were so scared by such a prospect that they would not let him leave Ukraine. In despair he wrote to Vice Chancellor Vorontsov, "I confide to your excellency as to my friend, that this matter is quite unbelievable and unfounded. I rather think it has been thought up by my well-known friends as if they were imaginary spies of the king of Prussia. They have the single object of making my presence here necessary, important and indispensable, so as to lodge in the mind of the sovereign the idea that there may be danger from this quarter, in order to confine me in this tedious place and to close off any means of returning to St. Petersburg, however much I may wish to do so."

The Ukrainian emigrants were real and not imaginary. It was for that reason Razumovsky invented a remedy against those able to hinder his visits to St. Petersburg. "The latest rescript," he wrote to Vorontsov, "has forced me to think how to destroy the channel from whence this news emanates, which disturbs those with whom these matters are entrusted. They blame this region for a lack of loyalty when no one here has such a shameless thought. On the contrary everyone has an unshakable loyalty to her imperial majesty, of which I firmly assure your excellency. It seems to me that the following method may be used to cut off this channel. Torture two or three of the ne'er-do-wells, who have been living in the Crimea for a very long time. Infected with ancient ideas, they write and think in the old manner and have forgotten the fact that after all this time Ukraine, it may be said, has been reborn. It does not in any way have the same form of government or the same rulers, nor, it seems to me, the same people and consequently not even the same ideas. For complete reassurance, I believe we can kidnap those rogues from there or destroy them in some way. I cannot in truth assure you of success, only that a very creditable attempt could be made. I beg you to let me know what you think of this."

"Although it would be very desirable," Vorontsov replied, "that the two scoundrels in Ukraine should somehow be exterminated or kidnapped, this method is very unreliable. Moreover it could bring unpleasant consequences in its wake. I think that it would be better to leave it completely alone, particularly as we may have no fear whatsoever from their chicanery. They are elderly men and will soon go to their grave."

Khorvat reported from New Serbia[106] that the population was growing fast. In three months, from January to April, 822 souls of both sexes arrived. Then reports began to come in about Khorvat, stating that he was settling New Serbia by illegal means. Hetman Razumovsky sent the Senate a copy of statements by Lieutenant Mochvan and Savransky, the settlement officer at the new Chernotashlyksk settlement. From these statements it appeared that Khorvat ordered Savransky to call together the Zaporozhian Cossack volunteers, to march with them into Poland to drive the local population by force to this side of the Bug and to place them in the settlement. Savransky went to Poland with the Zaporozhian Cossacks and from the village of Wierzbowiec, which belonged to Mniszech, drove thirty-five families into his settlement. Mochvan testified that Khorvat, in the presence of Lieutenant Bulatsel, ordered the cossack lieutenant Tabanets of the settlement of Dobrianka, who complained of insults from the Poles, to take volunteers from the Zaporozhian steppe to scare the Poles, only in secret, without letting it be known. Khorvat said that he would take responsibility for the raid, and gave Tabanets his hand. Tabanets also went to Poland, took more than three hundred horses from a market and murdered thirty people. The Senate ordered the hetman to take action against Tabanets and Savransky for their part in brigandage and border violations. He was not to believe the testimony of Khorvat, for this testimony was made by an accomplice.

Further to the east in Ukraine the resettlement of inhabitants proceeded by another method. At the end of the year the government learned that the peasants of a number of landowners from the Tambov and Kozlov districts were running off, taking their belongings and horses. Others confessed that these runaways gathered in Tsaritsyn and, crossing the Volga, dug mud huts for themselves. They were now living in these abodes and were willing in the future to accept other arrivals in their settlements. Some peasants ran away and declared explicitly that they were going to settle in Tsaritsyn and the state silk factory at Kamyshenka, where Major Parubuch was appointed to receive them.

From the Orenburg district of Ukraine came echoes of a struggle between the old inhabitants, the Bashkirs, and the Russians who arrived to exploit the ore riches of the country. The factory offices complained about the Bashkirs, who were making life difficult for the plant, stopping production. Moreover they lit fires around the factories. They directed magical smoke at the plant and mines, from which came fatal air so that at the

Avziano-Petrovsky works almost everyone was ill, and a considerable number even died. With their lies they also stopped the surveying of lots bought from the Bashkirs with forests and arable land. They drove off numerous horses belonging to the peasants living about the factories. In relation to these complaints Nepliuev[107] offered the following opinion. "In Orenburg, apart from this information, nothing can be foreseen that might give cause for Bashkir unrest. We cannot conduct a precise investigation into the fires and the rustling of horses, because no one has been caught. As far as the so-called magical smoke is concerned, it is clear that this was written out of superstition."

II

FALL OF BESTUZHEV-RIUMIN, 1758

FALL OF CHANCELLOR BESTUZHEV

The beginning of 1758 was marked by an important event, the overthrow of the Chancellor Count Alexis Petrovich Bestuzhev-Riumin, already in preparation for two years.

We have seen the difficult position in which the chancellor was placed by the change in European politics in 1756, by the Anglo-Prussian alliance on one hand, and the Austro-French on the other. Pride, an unwillingness to recognize mistakes, a system established in days gone by in which France, in consequence of the antithesis of its interests, could never be an ally of Russia, a deep-rooted hatred for France and dread of its ambassador, prevented Bestuzhev from changing his attitudes suddenly, from turning away from England and becoming a fervent champion of the French alliance. He defended England too explicitly, agreed to intimacy with France too unwillingly, and so became suspect in the eyes of the empress.

His influence declined. Vice Chancellor Vorontsov conducted the most important foreign relations without reference to him. The rapprochement with France proceeded through the latter whereas a French ambassador arrived in St. Petersburg was warned by his court to beware more than anything of the chancellor and his intrigues. Austria was hostile to Bestuzhev for his opposition to the alliance with France. Kaunitz, who considered this alliance his doing and who expected immense benefits, told

Count Bestuzhev-Riumin

1756 engraving by I.M. Bernigerot
after an original by K.G. Prenner

the French ambassador in Vienna that he would not forget the difficulties Bestuzhev was making for him. Consequently, apart from the Russian enemies Bestuzhev had in St. Petersburg, there were now two other powerful foreign enemies, Esterhazy and L'Hôpital, and he could expect no support from anywhere.

It is easy to understand how under such circumstances Bestuzhev had to act with caution. We have seen how he was worried by talk of Apraksin's tardiness, and how he tried to stir him to take the field as soon as possible. Apraksin's retreat after victory, which aroused a storm in St. Petersburg, must have concerned him even more. On September 13 the chancellor wrote to him, "I already had the honor, your excellency, through Count Peter Ivanovich Panin, to congratulate you on the victory gained over the enemy. At present I am unable to reply to your letter in any other way but to say that I regret extremely the fact that the army under the command of your excellency, which had an insufficiency of stores through almost all the summer, nevertheless in the end, even though it won the day, found it necessary to retreat despite being the victor. I commit to the personal and profound sagacity of your excellency what loss of honor may result, both for the army and also for your excellency, especially when you are abandoning enemy territory completely."

Nevertheless Apraksin withdrew, and the acrimony against him grew more and more intense. Rumors of a plot emanated from the French and Austrian embassies, and went all around Europe. On September 26 Bekhteev wrote to Vorontsov, "Through the whole of this week we have been extremely anxious. After August 19 we had no letters from St. Petersburg, but received the following news from Holland by two posts. You had only to begin thinking about it to be struck with horror. In a word, according to this news, all misfortunes were visited upon us. According to these news reports the army departed from Prussia in a great hurry. Apparently it was retreating and leaving behind a great many cannon. All the city was full of this ugly rumor."

A seizure suffered by the empress served as the foundation for this ugly rumor. On September 8, on the feast of the Nativity of the Virgin, Elizabeth, who was at that time resident at Tsarskoe Selo, went to mass in the parish church. At the beginning of the service she felt unwell and left the church alone, but before she could get to the palace she fell to the ground and for more than two hours lay unconscious. This event was connected by some with Apraksin's retreat. People grew suspicious and interpreted this event in the following way. Bestuzhev made this known to Apraksin and ordered his return to Russia with troops the chancellor needed to support his intentions with regard to the succession to the throne. Of course anyone capable of thinking the matter through calmly and thoroughly must have understood that this conjecture had no foundation. The empress's seizure occurred on September 8 and the withdrawal was decided at the military council on August 27. Had it been possible to stop and to advance, why was Apraksin unable to do so on receipt of so many strongly worded orders, and when he found out that the empress had recovered? Apraksin was doing nothing but carrying out the decision of the military council. Could it be supposed that of all the generals and regimental commanders who voted at the council there was not a single honest man or patriot, but they all demanded a withdrawal even when they knew the troops could advance without need of stores and forage? Yet were there any who could think the matter through thoroughly and, what is more important, calmly? It is well known how the crowd has a weakness for supposing that a plot or evil intention is at work with every significant and unpleasant event. In this case there were so many motives behind such suspicion. The foreign allies were embittered at Apraksin, whose withdrawal threw their plans into disarray. It made things easier for Frederick II, raised his spirits, freed him from the dread of a Russian invasion, gave Lehwaldt the possibility of demanding satisfaction from the Swedes, and the Russians repeated what was said by foreigners thanks to outraged patriotism.

Apraksin found a strong advocate, at the palace and in the Conference, in Count Peter Ivanovich Shuvalov. Chancellor Bestuzhev, however, attacked him most virulently of all, first out of desire to stop speculation at his own participation in the retreat, second out of hostile feelings towards Apraksin arising precisely as a consequence of Shuvalov's strong protection. It was clear to the chancellor that Apraksin was very close to and favored by Shuvalov. Consequently Shuvalov considered him completely faithful to him. Bestuzhev's enemies said that the chancellor was mixed up in the affair of the retreat, but Bestuzhev claimed that Shuvalov was responsible for everything. Shuvalov so defended Apraksin before the empress that the general was not afraid of being made responsible for anything, and did just what he liked.

Shuvalov, in spite of the strength of his position, could not save Apraksin, who had to give up command of the army to Fermor. We have seen that the new commander-in-chief totally vindicated his predecessor. There were many who were displeased with this appointment, saying that Fermor's poor advice was the reason behind Apraksin's withdrawal, and that it would have been much better to have given the high command to General Browne.[1] The appointment of Fermor was explained solely by the empress's particular favor. In addition to this favor there was another reason for this appointment. The first military successes, the occupation of Memel and Tilsit, were linked with the name of Fermor.

On October 18, 1757 Apraksin received an order to go to St. Petersburg, and he wrote to the empress that this order "gave him back once more his quite despairing life." At the beginning of November Apraksin arrived in Narva. He received through Lance Corporal Suvorov,[2] an orderly of the Life Guards Company, the imperial reassurance of the monarch's favor, while ordering him to hand over all letters in his possession. The reason for this seizure was the correspondence between Apraksin and the grand duchess, which came to light in this way. When Bestuzhev received letters from Catherine to send on to Apraksin, he showed them to Prasse,[3] councillor at the Saxon embassy, and to the Austrian general Bukkow, who had arrived in St. Petersburg, to reassure them of the young court's favorable disposition towards the common venture. In these letters Catherine urged Apraksin to hasten the campaign. Bukkow told Esterhazy about the letters and now, when they wanted to harm both Apraksin and Bestuzhev, Esterhazy told the empress herself about this correspondence between the grand duchess and Apraksin, and suggested that it was a very dangerous matter.

About six weeks passed after the seizure of the letters. Apraksin lived the whole of that time in Narva. On December 14 he decided to write a propitiatory letter to the empress. "In presenting the poverty of the condition in which I, the least of your slaves, a miserable creature, who have been here already for six weeks, have not only been quite deprived of my health but have lost my reason and memory, have to this day scarcely been able to preserve my failing spirits, and to this day I have hardly the use of my leg. I have the impertinence to beg your imperial and most merciful pardon. As before God I confess to your majesty that if I have sinned in any way, it is surely from complete ignorance and a total lack of understanding. Moreover I can also report that in the entire army there is not one who would not have wanted to give the last drop of his blood for the satisfaction of your imperial interests and in fulfillment of your majesty's will.

"Whenever a matter of great importance and circumstances demanded, the entire company of senior commanders was called together to all the councils. The general staff without exception made every endeavor for the benefit of the cause, and no comments were noticed by me to the contrary. It is true that before joining up with General Fermor that General Lieven, from his experienced knowledge of the art of war, was my most significant adviser on all councils. On joining up with General Fermor all major matters proceeded from that time through his particular kindness towards me, and he came to see me twice a day. Moreover through the particular favor and trust which I know your imperial majesty has towards him, I did nothing without talking it over and taking counsel beforehand with him, which caused considerable envy in many generals, which was true even when General Lopukhin was alive. Yet inasmuch as there was any good sense in my reasoning, I would moderate it to the extent that I would not allow it to go further, and not only did not meet with any arguments or displeasure, or even hear of any. I further take the liberty to report that the best proof is that, even in respect to our return from Allenburg, I first of all revealed my thoughts to General Fermor. On taking his advice and without revealing it to anyone else, I decided this matter in agreement with him alone. I summoned the military council, invited the regimental commanders and put the proposal. That is why, with the agreement of all parties, it was decided to turn towards Tilsit. In respect to all these matters I call to witness Fermor himself."

It is understandable that reference to Fermor served as the best justification for Apraksin. It was impossible to take away the title of commander-in-chief from one for the same reason for which another was elevated to that title. It was not necessary to ask Fermor if Apraksin was telling the truth about his agreement to the withdrawal. In his note of October 14 Fermor resolutely acknowledged that Apraksin's dispositions were essential, and those who spoke against Fermor's appointment were consistent. Yet there can be no point in talking about consistency. Apraksin was not subject to disfavor for the withdrawal. He was a scapegoat sacrificed to soothe the allies, to maintain the common enterprise. Naturally Apraksin would have been suitably recompensed for his role of scapegoat, had the matter consisted of nothing other than the withdrawal. But the matter now included the grand duchess's correspondence with Apraksin. The letters in themselves would not have been enough to incriminate either the writer or their recipient, but why such a relationship, such a correspondence? Were there not some other suggestions on Catherine's part?

The chancellor, the chancellor under suspicion, had acted as intermediary!

In January 1758 the head of the Secret Chancellery, Alexander Ivanovich Shuvalov, set out for Narva to talk with Apraksin about the correspondence. Evidently nothing in particular came from these conversations. A rumor was going the rounds that Apraksin made a sworn statement that he had given no promises to the young court, and it had received no intimations from him in favor of the king of Prussia. At this point the matter should have rested. The empress treated the grand duchess and the chancellor coldly.

Apart from the correspondence there were yet other causes of displeasure against Bestuzhev. The Polish-Saxon court, taking into consideration the empress's displeasure and the demands of France and Austria, decided to recall Poniatowski from St. Petersburg. Bestuzhev opposed this, and insisted on having his way on this point. In addition, after some trouble, Bestuzhev obtained the Polish Order of the White Eagle for Privy Counselor Stambke, who was in charge of Holstein affairs for the grand duke. It was known that Stambke was an agent of Bestuzhev. There was also much talk about the chancellor's scheme relating to the succession. It was said that the Conference secretary Volkov,[4] who had been Bestuzhev's agent for a long period, had revealed the existence of this scheme to the chancellor's enemies. Yet all these conjectures as to why Bestuzhev was holding on to Poniatowski, was trying to obtain the Order of the White Eagle for Stambke, the rumor that Bestuzhev had some plan relating to the succession, all this still could not have led to the chancellor's overthrow. It would have been all confined to irritation and unpleasant speculation.

It was England, having undermined the chancellor's importance in 1756 with the Prussian alliance, that probably gave cause for the final overthrow of its chief well-wisher in Russia. News arrived that England did not want to leave the court of St. Petersburg without a representative after the departure of Williams, and appointed Keith, formerly ambassador in Vienna. This news, of course, must greatly have alarmed the Austrian and particularly the French ambassadors in St. Petersburg. In the same way that Williams was agitated by the arrival of the French ambassador, so now L'Hôpital was agitated at Keith's arrival which there was no possibility of stopping since Russia had not severed relations with England.

The ground had to be prepared for a bitter struggle. This would not be so perilous if Keith were not to find a powerful ally in St. Petersburg in the great chancellor, the central figure in diplomatic relations. It was impossible to be free of Keith, yet Keith alone was not a danger. Bestuzhev must be banished, and the means were there. He was under suspicion. The empress no longer was favorably disposed towards him. He was surrounded by powerful enemies. The enemies themselves would not come out into open conflict because they did not feel they had sufficient weapons at their disposal for the certain defeat of their opponent. They had to be forced to forge such weapons. They had to be intimidated, compelled to act out of an instinct for self-preservation.

The attack was launched successfully because the weak spot was chosen. As soon as it was known in St. Petersburg that Keith was in Warsaw, L'Hôpital went to Vorontsov and presented to him the need to inflict the final blow on Bestuzhev. If Vorontsov did not want to take part, L'Hôpital would go straight to Bestuzhev and reveal everything to him, and would join him in Vorontsov's overthrow. According to Keith's report of these events to his court, a frightened Vorontsov agreed to cooperate, to support L'Hôpital's intimations against Bestuzhev before the empress.

There is other evidence, in essence no less contradictory than the first. According to this evidence L'Hôpital came to Vorontsov and said, " Count! Here is a dispatch I just received from my court. It states that if the grand chancellor is not replaced by you in fifteen days, I must turn to him and have no further relations with you." This information is more probable in the detail it gives. L'Hôpital found Vorontsov's most vulnerable spot, insisting on a matter that was most plain and comprehensible, without putting forward any personal considerations, but defending the dignity of his court, demanding for himself a way out of an awkward situation. Up to this point the French ambassador was obliged to deal with the vice chancellor and not with the chancellor, and this was unseemly, somehow clandestine. It might have been possible to agree to this temporarily, in expectation of a replacement of the chief minister as a consequence of a change of policy, but if everything remained as it was the French ambassador would have to deal with the chancellor. With respect to his threat to reveal everything (what "everything"?) to the chancellor, and to join him for Vorontsov's overthrow, this threat was too uncouth. According to the latter version Vorontsov, stung to the quick, went to Ivan Shuvalov, and together they suggested to the empress that her reputation was suffering from Bestuzhev's influence in Europe. More power and significance was attributed to the chancellor than to the empress herself. It is understandable that this suggestion, cunningly striking at Elizabeth's pride and confirmed by reference to the Poniatowski affair, would not have been enough by itself. Elizabeth must be convinced that there were significant suspicions against Bestuzhev. He could not be removed from affairs of state by a single suspicion. His guilt could be established only by his arrest, seizure of his papers and his trusted associates. It was decided to arrest the chancellor and to conduct an investigation into his affairs.

There is another item of information which shows the way in which Elizabeth was prepared for this decision, exasperated by Bestuzhev. Esterhazy reported to his court that the grand duke came to him with complaints against the chancellor. Esterhazy advised him to go directly to the empress. Elizabeth was very touched when her nephew turned to her as a member of the family, evidently with complete frankness and trust. She never was more affectionate with him, and Peter, repenting of his previous behavior, laid the blame on bad advice, and that bad adviser turned out to be Bestuzhev.

On the evening of Saturday February 14, Bestuzhev was arrested as he appeared at the Conference, and was conducted under guard to his house. The grand duchess when she awoke the following day received a note from Poniatowski. "Count Bestuzhev has been arrested, deprived of all offices and duties. Your diamond-jeweler Bernardi, Elagin[5] and Adadurov[6] have been arrested with him." Catherine's first thought on reading the note was that she would not escape misfortune. Bernardi, an intelligent, adroit Italian, had access to every household by virtue of his trade. Almost everybody was in some way beholden to him. He had rendered some small service for almost everyone. As he was constantly running from house to house, he was given errands. Notes sent through him arrived more quickly and reliably than when sent with a servant. He served the grand duchess as a go-between. Elagin was the old adjutant of Count Alexis Razumovsky, a friend of Poniatowski and very attached to the grand duchess, as also was Adadurov, who had taught her the Russian language. In the evening there were two society weddings. At the ball Catherine went up to Prince Nikita Trubetskoy. "What news do you have?" she asked him. "Have you found more crimes than criminals, or have you more criminals than crimes?" "We have done what we were ordered to do," Trubetskoy answered. "The crimes are still being investigated, so far without success." Then Catherine went up to Field Marshal Buturlin, who told her that Bestuzhev was arrested, and that they were now looking for the reason why.

The following day Stambke came to the grand duchess and said that he had received a note from Bestuzhev in which he was told to inform Catherine that she should not be afraid, everything had been burned. This related to the scheme regarding the succession. One of Bestuzhev's musicians had brought the note, and it was agreed that in future notes would be placed in a pile of bricks situated not far from the house of the former chancellor. On Bestuzhev's instructions Stambke was also to let Bernardi know that under questioning he should tell the absolute truth, and then let Bestuzhev know the substance of the interrogation. This correspondence of those arrested soon came to an end. After several days Stambke came to the grand duchess early one morning, pale, much changed, and told her that the correspondence was discovered, the musician seized and, in all probability, the latest letters were in the hands of those watching over Bestuzhev.

Stambke was not mistaken. The letters came into the hands of the investigating commission appointed for the Bestuzhev case. It consisted of three members, Field Marshals Prince Trubetskoy and Buturlin, and Count Alexander Shuvalov. Volkov acted as secretary. The inquiry against Bestuzhev is incomplete. Several responses of the accused are missing, as are the first examination and the responses to it. From this dossier it is clear that the examinations were completed on February 26. The empress remained dissatisfied with the former chancellor's evidence and so on the following day, February 27, Bestuzhev was told, "Her imperial majesty is so dissatisfied by the responses you made yesterday that she has given further instructions, and for the last time, that you be told clearly that if there is the slightest concealment and evasive clearing of your conscience and your behavior, she will order you to be taken to the fortress immediately and to be treated as if you were a common criminal." On the twenty-seventh Bestuzhev was asked why he preferred to seek the favor of the grand duchess rather than the grand duke, and had concealed from her imperial highness that correspondence (the exchange of letters between Catherine and Bestuzhev) about which he was obliged to report out of duty and loyalty. "I did not seek the favor of the grand duchess," he replied. "Moreover I tried to open her letters on the authority of her imperial majesty, for at that time the grand duchess was committed to the king of Prussia, Sweden and France according to the old system. A year or eighteen months from that time her highness completely changed her opinion and came to hate the king of Prussia and the Swedes, except for the king, her uncle, whom she loves very much. I tried not only to confirm her highness in this policy but even encouraged her to lead the grand duke towards opinions in agreement with those of her imperial majesty as well.

"The grand duchess indeed labored in this cause, but however much she talked to the grand duke, her efforts were in vain, adding the German expression, 'What I build, others destroy,'[7] recalling the roles, in particular, of Colonel Browne, that true Prussian, of Lord High Chamberlain Brockdorf and of other officers about the grand duke, about whom I even reported at that time to her imperial majesty." He did not refer to the fact that he knew all about this from the grand duchess.

The following question was formulated on the basis of the note sent to the grand duchess while Bestuzhev was under arrest. "You advised the grand duchess to act boldly and firmly and with good spirits, adding that suspicions can prove nothing. You cannot but admit that these last words in particular mean a very great deal, and have considerable significance. Therefore a candid explanation of these words is certainly required." "I advised the grand duchess to act boldly and firmly and with good spirits," Bestuzhev replied, "only because her letters to Field Marshal Apraksin contained nothing to which blame could attach."

A great deal was made in the interrogations of the chancellor's frequent and unusual conferences with Stambke and Poniatowski. Bestuzhev swore that such conferences never took place. Nevertheless they continued to interrogate him. "As Stambek [sic] and Poniatowski were in continual and exceptional conference with you, there must have been more participants and confidants. You must frankly tell us all of them. Do not conceal anything either, because all these meetings could not have taken place for no purpose whatsoever. So the question is, did you not agree upon and decide some plan, both for the present as well as for the future?" As no trace whatsoever was found in Bestuzhev's papers of his scheme for the succession, they wanted to force him to talk, emphasizing the frequent assignations with Stambke and Poniatowski. Bestuzhev stood firm, knowing that there was no evidence, and that with suspicions alone nothing can be proved. He replied even more directly than the question was put. "Neither with Stambek [sic], nor with Poniatowski or with any other confidant, of whom I had none, did I express my thoughts about any scheme whatsoever, either for the present or for the future, and moreover how could I consider such a question, for the succession has been affirmed already by the oaths of allegiance of the entire government."

Then they put a strange question. "Her imperial majesty knows for certain that when she happened to have conversation with ambassadors, you always encouraged the grand duke, and taught him whom to approach in order to hamper such conversations or to stop others. Her imperial majesty therefore simply would like to know what intention or motive you had for doing so." "As God is my witness", Bestuzhev replied, "no such idea ever entered my head. Perhaps I do not remember. Sometimes as the grand duke would move away, I would point out to him that such retirement was impolite, particularly when the grand duke shielded himself by entering into conversation with men of no importance."

These responses were naturally unsatisfactory. On March 4 the demand was repeated to Bestuzhev, in the name of the empress, that he confess sincerely. The previous threat also was repeated. The following question was put. "You have shown that you advised the grand duchess to act boldly and firmly and with good spirits, only because her letters to Field Marshal Apraksin did not contain anything to which blame could attach. Since you added to that the specific words that nothing can be proven by suspicions, it is clear that you place your hope in the fact that there will be no direct proof, or rather you confess you have given many causes for suspicion. You can therefore tell us precisely what it is not possible to prove by suspicion, as well as against whom you advised her to act boldly and firmly and with good spirits. Your statement, under oath, that you had no conferences either with Stambek [sic] or with Poniatowski at an unusual time, at night, excites, more *than anything else* the righteous indignation of her imperial majesty, and reveals your stubbornness. It is a prospect worthy of punishment to make amends for these crimes—cunning, perfidy and intrigue—for which already you are suffering. Her imperial majesty for a certainty knows that Poniatowski and Stambek [sic] were with you almost every day, and at every time of the day, and sat with you for a long time. She is not even asking you about this, but simply wishes you, without hesitation and without seeking any way around it, to say plainly what these conferences were about. There were no reports about them to her imperial majesty with the notes by which you always reported what took place in your room with other ministers. From whom did you know that the grand duchess had changed her ideas and come to hate the king of Prussia and the Swedes, except for the king, her uncle, whom she loves very much? What was the cause of such a sudden change? How was it that the grand duchess revealed so much to you, that she named to you all those who corrupt the grand duke, when you state that you never sought her favor?

"Her imperial majesty knows for a certainty that you sent many couriers from here to the hetman in the Ukraine. Therefore you can certainly tell us who these couriers were, how many there were in all, with what and when they were dispatched. It is known for a certainty by her imperial majesty that you obtained the Order of the White Eagle from the king of Poland for Stambken [sic], and so you are merely being asked through whose intervention you did that from here, and for what purpose.

"Apart from these letters, about which you already have confessed you received from the grand duchess through Bernardi, her imperial majesty knows that there were more of the same, both from her highness to yourself, as well as from you to her highness, carried by the same Bernardi. Therefore you are required to reveal the nature of this correspondence. Where are all these letters now? Why were they not sent through the direct channels but only in an impermissible manner? Why you did never report this to her imperial majesty? If they were burned, then why? You told his highness, the grand duke, that if he did not stop acting the way he was, you would take other measures against him. Clearly you can explain what changes you wanted to see in the grand duke, and what other measures you were contemplating."

Bestuzhev attempted to explain his relations with the Polish-Saxon court in as much detail as possible because a lack of sincerity in this respect *more than anything else* aroused the empress's anger. "Warned by Count Brühl about secret instructions given to the marquis de l'Hôpital to try to obtain my overthrow," he answered, "I sought through the Polish court to proffer better opinions about myself to the French and Viennese courts, and in that way to escape persecution from them. The ambassador Count Esterhazy revealed to Maltzahn, the late Danish ambassador in St. Petersburg, and to Count Horn, the former Swedish military attaché here, and they both told me that Esterhazy, through his influence and ideas, was instrumental in her imperial majesty deciding to establish the Conference at her court so that the chancellor no longer would exercise his previous power in matters of state. Apparently her imperial majesty did not give her approval to any important decisions without taking advice from the ambassador beforehand. Esterhazy suggested to her imperial majesty that the chancellor be excluded completely from future negotiations with France. As his mind could not be changed on this matter, she should be made aware of the fact that, because of his devotion to England, he would place any obstacles in the way of good relations with France. The Danish envoy Osten, what is more, found all this in the dispatches of his predecessor Maltzahn to the court, and informed Count Poniatowski. Poniatowski spoke about this to the ambassador Count Esterhazy. He asked why he was persecuting the chancellor in this way. Esterhazy refused to admit everything to Poniatowski and alleged, on the contrary, that her imperial majesty told him she wanted to exclude the chancellor from negotiations with France, but that he, Esterhazy, apparently was opposed, saying that of course the chancellor must be there to carry through all the negotiations required to secure firm establishment of the present system. Otherwise, he said, perhaps it would be better to dismiss him from all matters of state." They wanted more details, and Bestuzhev did not grudge giving them. These details would have been disagreeable only to Esterhazy, whom it was quite unnecessary for the former chancellor to spare.

There are no more of Bestuzhev's replies in the dossier. We already pointed out that the inquiry is incomplete. Subsequently, on the accession of Catherine II, when Bestuzhev once more found himself close to the throne, the inquiry was put in his hands, as the notes that remain in his handwriting indicate. So in respect to the question about sending letters to Hetman Razumovsky we read two notes. (1) "For a footnote and information. This secret could not have been known to anyone except Teplov.[8] He alone, angry with Elagin and Bestuzhev, was the secret informant." (2) "It is also worthy of note that, apart from Teplov, this was unknown to anybody. If he, as then, is to take part in a new secret council (which is still not known to the writer of this note) and to set everyone at variance then, not out of impertinence but from modesty, Adadurov would be superior, with his clean conscience and skills."

Yet the fact that the dossier of the inquiry was in Bestuzhev's hands later does not give us the right to suppose that some responses in the inquiry were destroyed by Bestuzhev himself. Rather we must think that they were omitted by the secretary Volkov, just as Bestuzhev complained later that Volkov disavowed noting many of Bestuzhev's responses which served as justification of his case, and would not accept them. This must have happened precisely with those responses which demonstrated the strange character of the questions. For example what could have been more strange than the question to "tell us what it is not possible to prove by suspicions, and against whom you advised the grand duchess to act boldly and firmly and with good spirits." Of course Bestuzhev must have replied triumphantly that the whole inquiry had been undertaken because of baseless suspicions with which it was impossible to prove anything, and that he advised the grand duchess to preserve her good spirits in order to avoid suspicion, and not against anybody at all. Another question was also curious, namely from whom did Bestuzhev find out that the grand duchess had changed her ideas, how did she reveal so much to him? The answer was obvious. He found out from her personally. She pointed out those hindering the right policy, wishing to attest to the fact that she was promoting this policy. Bestuzhev could have refused to answer such questions, and could have demanded they ask Catherine herself, not him, about her motives.

Those responses that gave rise to new questions in which they were repeated were not inserted also. On March 7 Bestuzhev was asked to respond to new questions. "In your reply on the fourth of this month you revealed that only one packet sent to you from the hetman's house was forwarded by you to him in Ukraine by post, but from Moscow. Her imperial majesty knows for certain that you sent him more, if not by special courier, then by regular mail. Besides you have also confessed you knew of the attempt made by the grand duchess to reconcile Apraksin with the hetman, so naturally you must tell us how many in all you sent the hetman. What was their content? From where were the packets brought to you for this purpose, through whom, and with what requests concerning their dispatch? Her imperial majesty is angered greatly by the fact that you continue to disavow your part in these affairs, a confession which will not lead to any consequences, and about which her imperial majesty is very well informed. You have testified that no one asked you, neither did you seek in Warsaw, the award of a knighthood of the White Eagle for Stambke. Her imperial majesty also knows that the rescript concerning the knighthood to which you refer, and which was shown to Poniatowski in St. Petersburg, was drawn up here by your instructions. Solely out of charity she desires, at least in this one point, merely to see your frank confession. Her imperial majesty commands that you explain in detail how Apraksin gained such favor with the grand duchess, and who encouraged him!"

The replies to these questions have not been preserved. Bestuzhev confessed to one thing, that he tried to retain Poniatowski in St. Petersburg. "In point of fact after Count Poniatowski received his recall," he replied, "I tried, through Councillor Prasse of the Saxon embassy, to keep

Poniatowski here. I did not write either to Count Brühl or to Prince Volkonsky about this. I proceeded only because, in view of my persecution by Count Esterhazy and Marquis de l'Hôpital, I wanted to have at least one ambassador favorable to myself, and no one more so than Count Poniatowski, who informed me of everything he heard from Count Esterhazy and L'Hôpital."

In the inquiry one question was struck out. "You know that at Tsarskoe Selo on September 8 last year her imperial majesty suffered a certain indisposition. Contrary to what you remember Apraksin, stationed at Tilsit, took it into his head to reinforce St. Petersburg. Suddenly on the night of the fourteenth and fifteenth he decided to abandon everything and to return hastily, giving just cause not only to suspect, but even to believe without any shadow of doubt, that naturally he had been informed of this indisposition. Therefore you can testify whether you informed him about it or at least whether you knew that someone else did." It is clear why Trubetskoy, Buturlin and Shuvalov did not permit Volkov to ask this question and instructed him to delete it from the inquiry. This would have meant casting suspicion upon, and bringing to trial, all the generals and regimental commanders who took part in the military councils, in particular the commander-in-chief Fermor, who directly testified to the necessity for the withdrawal.

The investigators complained to the empress about the absence of sincerity in Bestuzhev's testimony, at the fact that he disavowed everything on oath, and for final confirmation of the truth of his testimony took communion, after which further investigation was without purpose. They noted his offenses. (1) Before her imperial majesty he maligned their highnesses and at the same time tried to cause great distress of their highnesses against her imperial majesty. (2) For his own purposes not only did he fail to carry out decrees issued in the name of her imperial majesty, but opposed their implementation by underhand methods. (3) He offended against the state because he knew or saw that Apraksin was unwilling to leave Riga to take the field against the enemy. The Treasury and government were exhausted to no purpose, the glory of the monarchy suffered, because he did not report this to her imperial majesty. He has offended her majesty because, instead of the necessary report about this matter, he took it into his head that he could correct this better by himself and through involvement in impermissible correspondence with one who had no necessary part in these matters, through which he insensitively introduced into the autocratic government co-rulers, and even made himself a co-ruler. (4) While under arrest he revealed in writing secrets about which he was forbidden to speak under pain of death. For all these offenses the commission considered Bestuzhev worthy of capital punishment, but committed the case to the monarch's pleasure and charity.

The decision was not long delayed. In the meantime Bestuzhev was held under arrest in his home. On January 2, 1759 he was called before the commission that they might show him a gold snuff box with a portrait of the grand duchess and ask him how he obtained it. Bestuzhev answered directly that the grand duchess gave him the snuff box herself as a present at a reception in the palace, several months before his arrest. This was the last matter remaining to the commission. In April the case was concluded with the exile of Bestuzhev to one of his villages, Goretovo in the Mozhaisk district. All his landed property remained in his hands but he was made to answer for all financial debts.

Field Marshal Apraksin was transferred from Narva closer to St. Petersburg, to a place called Chernye Ruki, and here he was interrogated. It is understandable that we do not encounter questions relating to the reasons for returning towards the frontier after the battle of Gross-Jägersdorf in this interrogation. The matter was resolved finally by the explanations of the new commander-in-chief Fermor. The interrogation touched upon Apraksin's correspondence with Bestuzhev and the grand duchess. One thing came to light in his replies. Both the chancellor and the grand duchess had encouraged him to commence the campaign with greater speed, whereas formerly they had been of a different opinion in St. Petersburg. Apraksin was guilty of the fact that he had been unwilling to move from Riga, and had conducted an unauthorized correspondence with the grand duchess. Of course they were delighted with these two offenses, otherwise there would have been no justification for taking the command of the armed forces from him. Apraksin died suddenly on August 6, 1758. The others involved in the affair, Weymarn and Adadurov, were subjected to exile but without any further punishment. Weymarn was assigned to a Siberian military command. Adadurov was appointed deputy governor in Orenburg. Stambke was expelled. Bernardi was sent to reside in Kazan, Elagin to a village in the Kazan province.

RELATIONS OF GRAND DUCHESS CATHERINE WITH THE EMPRESS

Grand Duchess Catherine was seriously implicated in the inquiry. Apraksin's unauthorized correspondence with her, and forwarding of letters by

Bestuzhev, lay at the basis of interrogations both of the former chancellor and the former commander-in-chief. Although Catherine did not fear any serious indictment, because it was impossible to prove anything by mere suspicion, her position was nevertheless grave. Nothing could be proved by mere suspicion, but the suspicions could remain in the empress's mind. Even apart from suspicion, Catherine knew that she must have irritated Elizabeth by her interference in matters of state and by the importance she had acquired. The commander-in-chief, knowing the sovereign's definite intentions, hesitated, checked himself from carrying them out on account of the grand duchess's contrary wishes. The empress's anger, her acute anger, was not in doubt. Where might Catherine find shelter from this anger? Who could transform it into charity? Those devoted to her had fallen, declared state criminals. Her enemies were triumphant.

The grand duke was disposed to extreme hostility for which, according to Catherine's testimony, the Holsteiner Brockdorf, who had become close to Peter, was responsible. Brockdorf had said, speaking of Catherine, that "the serpent must be crushed." Esterhazy reported to his court that the grand duchess sent Stambke to him twice for advice and assistance, giving him to understand that all her misfortunes had befallen her as the result of diligence in the interests of Maria Theresa. "Because Empress Elizabeth bitterly complained to me about Catherine's behavior, and as a foreign ambassador, I must not interfere in the sovereign's domestic affairs," Esterhazy wrote. " I have deflected this matter away from myself. I gave instructions for her to be told that it would be best if she would turn to the mediation of her husband, who enjoyed the empress's full favor and trust."

It is easy to understand how Catherine must have regarded Esterhazy after this advice, akin to the most vicious mockery. Her future was somber indeed. There was only one way to get out of this grave situation, to turn directly to Elizabeth, who was very kind, who could not bear the sight of another's tears, who knew very well and understood Catherine's position. It was said that Ivan Ivanovich Shuvalov assured the grand duchess that the empress would soon see her. If, for her part, Catherine would show a little submissiveness, the entire matter would end very well. This information was very probably correct, because the favorite was trying to be a universal peace-maker. On the other hand there were rumors that the grand duchess would be expelled from Russia, rumors that were implausible because Elizabeth would never endure such a scandal for the sake of a few letters to Apraksin. Well and good, this threat from her enemies could be turned against them, defense turned into attack. They were forever insulting Catherine. Her life in Russia had become unbearable, so let them give her freedom to leave Russia. The grand duchess wrote a letter to the empress in which, describing her sorry situation and her consequent upset health, she begged to be given leave to undergo treatment at the waters and then to go on to her mother, because the grand duke's hatred and the empress's disfavor made it impossible for her to remain in Russia. After this letter the empress promised to have a word personally with the grand duchess. The mediation of the empress's confessor hastened this meeting.

The meeting took place after midnight. In the empress's room, besides herself and the grand duchess, there were also the grand duke and Count Alexander Shuvalov. When she caught sight of the empress, Catherine threw herself on her knees before her and implored her to send her to her relatives abroad. The empress tried to lift her from the ground, but Catherine would not get up. If Ivan Ivanovich Shuvalov advised her to show a little submissiveness, she made use of this powerful stratagem and the more quickly achieved her goal. Sorrow rather than anger was written on the empress's face, tears glistened in her eyes. "How can I let you go? Remember, you have children!"[9] she said to Catherine. The Grand Duchess artfully touched the other tender side of the human heart. "My children," she replied, "are in your hands and I could wish nothing better for them. I hope that you will not abandon them." "What should I say to others? What reason should I have for sending you away?" asked the empress. "Your imperial majesty," Catherine answered, "will outline the reasons why I have brought upon myself your disfavor and the hatred of the grand duke." "How," asked Elizabeth, "will you live at your relatives?" "As I lived before you brought me here," replied Catherine. Elizabeth once more bade her rise, and Catherine obeyed.

Elizabeth moved away from her, deep in thought. She felt that she was defeated by the woman kneeling before her. She needed to gather her strength for the attack. Yet this was difficult to do. The attack had been thrown into disarray and confusion. Elizabeth went up to the grand duchess full of reproaches. "God is my witness how I wept when on your arrival in Russia you were sick unto death. Later you did not wish to give me deference as you should, but considered yourself cleverer than everybody. You interfered in many matters of state which did not concern you.

Elizabeth Petronovna, 1754

engraving

I would never have dared do this in the days of Empress Anna. How, for example, could you have dared send orders to Field Marshal Apraksin?" "I...?" replied Catherine. "It never even entered my head to send him orders." "How," retorted the empress, "could you refuse to admit that you wrote to him? Your letters are there (she pointed to them on the dressing-table). You were, after all, forbidden to write such letters." "That is true," Catherine replied. "I have broken this injunction and ask you to forgive me, but as my letters are there, they can serve as witness that I never gave him any orders, but that in one letter I informed him of rumors about his conduct." "Why did you write to him about that?" the empress interrupted. "Because," Catherine answered, "I had a great regard for him. That is why I begged him to carry out your orders. The second letter contains congratulations on the birth of his son; the third, best wishes for the New Year." "Bestuzhev says that there were many other letters," said Elizabeth in reply. "If Bestuzhev says this, he is lying," replied Catherine. At this point Elizabeth made use of moral torment in order to extort an admission of guilt. "Good," she said. "If he is lying about you, I shall give orders for him to be tortured." Catherine was not afraid and replied, "You may do anything you consider necessary. I wrote only these three letters to Apraksin." Elizabeth said nothing in reply.

As was her habit she paced about the room, turning now to the grand duchess and now to the grand duke, but even more often to Shuvalov. This entire conversation, lasting an hour and a half, made a profound impression, but did not irritate her. The grand duke, on the contrary, expressed considerable animosity towards his wife. He even tried to make Elizabeth annoyed with her, but did not achieve his purpose because his words too harshly expressed his passion. At last the empress went up to Catherine and said to her gently, "I should have a lot to say to you but I cannot speak because I do not want to quarrel with you even more." "Neither can I say anything," replied Catherine, "however earnestly I want to open up to you my heart and soul." Elizabeth was very touched by these words. Tears welled up in her eyes, and so that others would not notice how she was moved, she let the grand duke and grand duchess go, saying that it was very late. It was indeed around three in the morning.

The empress sent Alexander Shuvalov after Catherine to tell her not to grieve, and that she would talk with her on another occasion, in private. In expectation of this conversation Catherine locked herself in her room under the pretext of ill-health. At this time she was reading the first five volumes of *The History of Travel*[10] with a map on the table. When she was tired of reading she turned the leaves of the first volumes of the French encyclopedia.[11] Soon she was able to give herself the pleasure of knowing how successfully she had acted when she demanded leave to depart Russia. Vice Chancellor Vorontsov came to see her, and on behalf of the empress begged her to give up the idea of leaving Russia, because this proposal was greatly saddening the empress and all good people, including Vorontsov himself. He also promised that the empress would have a second meeting with her. This promise was fulfilled. The empress demanded first of all that Catherine answer all her questions with the absolute truth. With the first question she asked whether Catherine wrote only the three known letters to Apraksin. Catherine swore that there were only three.

The conclusion of the business in the palace between the empress and the grand duchess also naturally had a fundamental influence on the case of Bestuzhev and his accomplices, although it did not save them from exile, honorable or dishonorable. Catherine's correspondence with Elagin, one of those banished, has come down to us. Catherine sent him money and consoled herself with the hope of his speedy release from exile. "Following the change that has now taken place," Catherine wrote, "I have no other object but to free you as soon as possible. In the meantime I am sending you three hundred chervontsy to use at the earliest opportunity. I hope to achieve a successful outcome but it is still impossible to mention the matter at present. *Homme d'or* (the golden man) is here, and there is a good reception for him. We never cease to mention you. Good health, and rest assured that your innocence and enthusiasm will not be forgotten for long." In another letter Catherine said, "I seldom see *the motionless one*, and there is practically no way of sending things. At the same time I shall not fail to remind him to make moves on all matters that might be of use to you."[12]

RELATIONS WITH AUSTRIA CONCERNING MILITARY OPERATIONS

Arrangements for the active prosecution of the war did not stop during these events at court. The failures suffered by Austria at the end of 1757 with the loss of Breslau[13] forced the court in Vienna to seek assurances in St. Petersburg that Russian forces would enter Prussia once more as soon as possible, or that a thirty-thousand-man detachment would be sent through Poland to assist the hereditary lands of the empress-queen. In this request Esterhazy was supported by the French ambassador L'Hôpital and the ministers of the Polish kingdom. It was decided at the Conference to reply that, instead of the one or the other, her majesty would fulfill both wishes of the empress-queen. General Fermor already was instructed to bring the forces into the field as soon as possible and in spite of the inclement season of the year was marching to take East Prussia. In addition an observation corps, consisting of the best picked men, was ordered to march through Poland under the command of General-in-chief Count Saltykov, with the commanders Lieutenant Generals Count Chernyshev and Prince Dolgoruky under him, of whom the first was chosen especially because the empress-queen favored him with her approval. "The Austrian court must inform the Conference as soon as possible where this allied corps should go, and take measures so that, before it joins the Austrian forces, it is not overtaken and defeated by the king of Prussia.

"As the king of Prussia will not await meekly the coming together of the Russian and Austrian forces, and the Russians, however they hasten, will not arrive at the chosen destination before the beginning of the campaign, perhaps it would be better to select a place where the Russian corps could make a diversion more painful to the king of Prussia and, consequently, more useful for the empress-queen. This may be done in Silesia or a little lower, at Frankfurt-on-Oder. If that were so, in the first place the march would be severely shortened and, second, the king of Prussia would not know until the last minute where the auxiliary corps was going. Third, General Fermor, having taken East Prussia, would extend his operations into Pomerania to support the operation of the Swedish army. General Browne, already ordered to move to the Vistula, may penetrate into Brandenburg itself rather earlier. If the third corps under Saltykov, heading for Breslau or Glogau, could be in line with them, the king of Prussia certainly would be put into an embarrassing situation." To attack the king of Prussia in such places with these three corps, each strong in its own right and situated at such a distance one from another, seemed a unique and most safe means of dividing the strength of the Prussian king and of forcing him to conduct a defensive rather than an offensive war.

Maria Theresa refused the offer of the auxiliary corps. In the meantime, on January 3, news was received that Fermor had taken the city of Tilsit, with the domains of Russ and Kukernezen. The Russian forces entered East Prussia in five columns under the command of the second general, Saltykov, Generals Riazanov, Count Rumiantsev, Prince Lubomirski, Panin and Leontiev. On the tenth, when Fermor was in the town of

Empress Maria Theresa

Jean Etienne Liotard, pastel, 83.5 x 65, Lvov Picture Gallery

Libau, deputies came to him from Königsberg, the major city of East Prussia, with a request to take them under the empress's protection with preservation of all privileges. The next day Russian forces entered Königsberg and were greeted by bells pealing throughout the whole city, with trumpets and kettledrums playing on the towers, the citizens standing in front and presenting arms. Fermor was appointed governor-general of the kingdom of Prussia. In Vienna there was great rejoicing at the taking of Prussian territory by Russian forces, but immediately disquiet was expressed. Esterhazy received instructions to demand that any further taking of Prussian territory be done in the name of the empress-queen, "in order not to give grounds in other courts for reflection, and also so that it might be possible to distinguish the side at war from the one rendering assistance." To this the following reply was given. "Our relations with the king of Prussia in no way, we believe, merit such precautions. His declaration, issued against us, is considered an indirect declaration of war only by those who do not wish to understand it directly. We have declared to all courts that there is no other way to furnish our allies appropriate assistance than to operate directly against the king of Prussia. Therefore we believe that all courts should be indifferent in whose name Prussian territory is taken. It is enough for us to believe that our allies, in particular the empress-queen, being cognizant of our feelings, will do us justice and not think that we, under the guise of assistance, have looked only to our own advantage. In respect to the oath which the inhabitants of the Prussian territories, made tributary to our arms, are being obliged to take, it immediately will be evident that both justice and necessity prove it necessary. We merely ask that the inhabitants not undertake anything reprehensible against us, either in secret or openly."

OCCUPATION OF EAST PRUSSIA BY RUSSIAN FORCES

May arrived, the time to take decisive action, and the court of Vienna sounded the alarm. "The common foes," Maria Theresa wrote to Esterhazy, "continue to reassure themselves with the belief that the Russian army will not undertake anything of consequence in the present campaign. It is short of personnel and suffers from such a shortage of money that it cannot consider establishment of supply depots, purchase of forage and supply of similar military necessities. Thus the best period for military operations will pass fruitlessly." In reply to these fears Esterhazy replied, "If circumstances have not yet allowed us to do as much as we would have liked to assist our allies, it may be said in all truth that we have done everything possible. The occupation of East Prussia proceeded at a time of the year, with such expense and exertion, that it has cost us no less than a full season's campaign. Moreover the requested corps of thirty thousand men was made ready here to send into the territories of the empress-queen. Indeed it was already on the march when it was countermanded at the request of her majesty. This corps is now near the remaining forces with whom it should join up. It is to be hoped that soon the whole army, which in any case is situated for the most part beyond the Vistula, will be on the march. It is impossible to consider the spring season in any way lost, for the future campaign demands endless preparation. Misfortunes have come together here, harvest failure of grain and forage and now, as a result of unusually dry and cold weather, the grass has not yet sprouted."

In June Maria Theresa once more hurried the Russian forces and wrote in her rescript to Esterhazy, "Now all is dependent upon the fact that the Russian forces no longer remain inactive but that they support and refresh by their speedy activity the allied movements. Friends and enemies await this impatiently. If the high hopes of her majesty the empress are to be fulfilled, the enemy will become seriously alarmed and abandon his ambitious plans. In this way both we and our allies will be encouraged. Russia has in its hands the opportunity to inflict a mortal blow on the common adversary, her dangerous enemy as much as ours, and to do so that much more easily and certainly, as the king of Prussia cannot gather a sufficient army to repulse the Russian forces, even if he is successful in Moravia. All this you must present to the court in St. Petersburg in the strongest terms. Its very honor, reputation and well-being now depend on its perfect or imperfect operations. What is let slip now will be impossible to recover later."

Fermor, the new commander-in-chief of the Russian army, through the sad experience of his predecessor knew that it was impossible to move quickly if there was poor organization of stores. He also knew that in the event of tardiness he would have great enemies in the Austrians, who would raise their voices against him in St. Petersburg and throughout Europe, and would lay the blame for their own failures upon the Russian forces. That is why, having taken command of the forces, Fermor secured patrons in St. Petersburg who would defend him in the hour of need. He wrote to Vorontsov, "Since this important post (of commander-in-chief) demands the considerable support of kind patrons, I make so bold as to beg your excellency to extend to me, and to the army entrusted to me, your gracious protection and to reward my imperfections with your wise instructions."

FERMOR ADVANCES TO THE ODER

On May 22 Fermor let it be known that he was ready to set out from East Prussia. On June 20 he was in Poznan and on July 1 he set out from that city directly to the west towards the frontier of Brandenburg, specifically to the small town of Meseritz, where the whole army arrived on the fifteenth. From there they wanted to go directly to Frankfurt-on-Oder, but a shortage of stores and forage, and damage to harness, the consequence of prolonged rain, obliged them to reconsider whether to continue the march in that direction. At the military council the Austrian general Baron St. André, as before attached to the Russian forces, was of the opinion that it would be better for the Austrian army to stay near Lusatia, while the Russian remained at Frankfurt-on-Oder or Crossen and there, whenever feasible, to try to cross the Oder to join up with the Austrians. Thus the enemy could not attack the Russians without exposing itself to the danger of being subject to an attack from the rear by the Austrians.

The commander-in-chief, Lieutenant General Saltykov, Prince Golitsyn[14] and Chernyshev objected that there was no forage whatsoever in the place appointed. The horses were in such bad condition that they could not bring up the stores. Therefore the Warthe river had to be crossed at Landsberg. Then, stopping at Küstrin, one corps was to be sent into the vicinity of Schwedt to establish a main supply depot as quickly as possible in Stargard, in the meantime allowing the horses to rest so that it would be possible to proceed to the vicinity of Frankfurt and render assistance to the Austrian army. Should Swedish forces also approach the town of Schwedt it would fall to the Russian forces to hasten to the Oder to secure the bridges and, linking with the Swedes, to move further into enemy territory to divert the king of Prussia from Silesia. St. André agreed with this opinion. Therefore the army set off towards the north and on twenty-eighth took up a position near Landsberg.

BOMBARDMENT OF KÜSTRIN

On August 4 the Russians approached Küstrin and set fire to the town with red-hot cannon balls, but the fortress did not surrender. It was protected by two rivers, the Warthe and the Oder, as well as by canals. To surround the town the Russians were obliged to extend their forces over a large area. Fermor could not bring himself to do so, being near the Prussian corps commanded by Count Dohna.

In reply to his report on the bombardment of Küstrin, Fermor received the following rescript. "The enterprise which you have prosecuted so successfully against Küstrin not only gains for you our praise and approval, and not only precisely corresponds to our instructions, our hopes for your military skill, for your diligence and zeal, but in part even exceeds our expectations. Even if the fortress of Küstrin is not taken, even if it is not forced to surrender by your crossing of the Oder and cutting its communications with the Prussian corps of Count Dohna, it is enough, and more than enough, that by the exemplary bravery of our troops the enemy forces have been frightened. The rural inhabitants, by the loss of their property that has been conveyed into the town, have been taught to rely more on our reassurances and to remain quietly in their homes rather than to rely on the protection of their forces. With the destruction of their vast supply depot, consisting of in excess of six hundred thousand quarters of grain, naturally a great impediment will have been created to the enemy's plans if the Prussians are forced to allow you to gain a foothold locally in secure winter quarters."

Fermor was sent another rescript dated August 24. "Now is the most critical period in which the present war, reputation and welfare of the government may be decided. On one hand Field Marshal Count Daun[15] is now deep in Lusatia, even if he has not entered Brandenburg. On the other hand the king of Prussia will make every effort to anticipate Count Daun and to stop you joining with him. It is impossible to guarantee that the king will not take a firm decision, whatever the consequences, to attack you and so defeat you that afterwards it will be easy for him to stand up to Count Daun alone. Finally, which is the least probable, might not the king take it into his head, on the example of that behavior of his which is amazing in all respects, to turn his attention to Poland, in order to create a diversion there to his advantage, and so remove the theater of war from his own territories? On all these three possibilities we cannot here and at this point give you extensive instructions. We trust that you will always be in a position to hold in check the enemy's aspirations and to become firmly established in Pomerania in winter quarters, in a word, to complete a splendid campaign. Simply try diligently to find out the enemy's movements; for that reason we approve of the fact that you have given Father Joseph Locke a commission to send out our spies once more."

BATTLE OF ZORNDORF

This hope was not realized. Frederick II was situated on Austrian territory when he heard of the Russian intrusion into Brandenburg. The Sudden King moved swiftly with his forces in defense of his home territories. In Frankfurt-on-Oder he heard the thunder of Russian cannon bombarding Küstrin and, unperceived by Fermor, in a single night crossed the Oder several versts below Küstrin, cutting Fermor off from Rumiantsev's corps situated lower down the Oder in the direction of Schwedt. Fermor got to know of the king's approach when a crowd of cossacks stumbled upon Prussian hussars. Twenty cossacks were taken prisoner.[16] The remainder galloped off and brought the news to headquarters that the Prussians were on our side of the Oder. Fermor quickly raised the siege of Küstrin and stationed his forces in an advantageous position near the village of Zorndorf. The Russian army was drawn up in the manner of Field Marshal Münnich, in a large square inside which were placed the transports and horse.

On August 14 at nine in the morning the battle began with an attack by the Prussians on the right flank of the Russian army. Here stood the so-called observer corps newly formed by Shuvalov, excellent men, but never under fire before. Even so they did not waver under Prussian fire and frustrated the attempts of the Prussian grenadiers, whom the Russian horse threw into confusion and forced to give way. Twenty-six enemy cannon were in Russian hands. The movement of the horse made a great deal of dust, which together with smoke, was carried by the wind onto the second Russian line, which could not distinguish anything and fired on its own cavalry from behind. The Prussian horse appeared from in front under the command of General Seydlitz.[17] The Russian horse was thrust back onto its infantry. In the dust and smoke the Russians got mixed up with the Prussians and a terrible carnage took place, in which the Russian soldiers surprised the enemy by their determination. When they had fired all their bullets they stood like rocks. They could be broken, but not put to flight. There was yet another unfortunate incident. Some of the soldiers threw themselves onto the sutlers' barrels of wine and looted them. When they got drunk they assaulted their own officers in their frenzy, wandering about without understanding anything and refusing to obey any order whatsoever. The midday sun shone brightly straight into the face of the Russians. The dust and smoke blinded them. All this led to the utter confusion of the right flank.

After one in the afternoon the king ordered his troops to advance against the Russian left flank. The attack was repulsed and the Prussians were put to flight. At this point Seydlitz appeared with his cavalry and came to the assistance of his own side, restoring the balance. The battle became desperate. Powder ran out on both sides. They fought with swords until darkness fell. Both forces, quite worn out, spent the night on the battlefield. Neither side could claim victory. The next day Fermor yielded first, and in this way gave the Prussians cause to claim victory. The losses on the Russian side were horrendous. There were more than twenty thousand casualties. More than a hundred cannon were lost, more than thirty standards. Lieutenant Generals Saltykov and Count Chernyshev, Major General Manteuffel and two brigadiers, Thiesenhausen and Sievers, were taken prisoner. The elderly general-in-chief Browne received more than seventeen wounds to the head. The casualties on the Prussian side were twelve thousand, and twenty six cannon were lost. The king was unable to pursue Fermor and retreated to Küstrin.

On August 25 Colonel Rozen arrived in St. Petersburg with the news of a "general and very intense battle" that had taken place on the fourteenth. "At nine in the morning," Fermor reported, "the battle commenced with ceaseless cannon fire, continuing for an hour and a half. Then small arms fire broke out, supported by cannon fire, which continued into the night, at which time, with several changes of fortune, one side dislodged the other and then refused to give ground. In the end, at ten, the Prussian army ceded the battlefield to the Russians. The Russians gathered themselves together through the night and not only spent that night in sight of the Prussians, but the next day, at full height, were able to gather their wounded and cannon, as many as the enemy would allow. The casualties among the senior generals, the staff and senior officers were considerable. Owing to shortage of time, however, I cannot indicate these exactly. I am not in a position to describe sufficiently to your majesty the actions of the senior generals, the staff and senior officers and soldiers. Moreover, had the soldiers obeyed their officers all the time and not drunk more than one cup of the wine, which was ordered to be distributed for encouragement, we could have gained a complete victory over the enemy as desired.

"So I must report that because of our great losses, the weakness of the men and the lack of bread, I must today (the fifteenth) set off seven versts to Gross-Kammin where our heavy transport and bread is located. Then on to Landsberg, where I hope to join up with the third division stationed at Schwedt and seek subsistence for the army along the Warthe river. Up to the present the financial resources are almost completely untouched. The papers of the secret despatch office, together with all cipher codes, have been burned. His excellency Prince Karl (of Saxony) and General St. André, without awaiting the complete conclusion of the battle, evidently inferring the worst, withdrew to Schwedt. In the face of this unsuccessful event I shall not fail to make use of every possible measure to fulfill my duty in your service."[18]

An event that began with the denunciation of a volunteer with the Russian army, the Polish gentleman Kaznowski, against Brigadier Stoianov may serve as a supplement to the news of the battle of Zorndorf. Kaznowski testified that on August 14, in the evening after the battle, he and Stoianov met each other on horseback. Stoianov said, "Some Lutheran, a general in command, placed the army in the face of the wind and destroyed it completely. At a favorable opportunity, I will ride up to him and shoot him. Where can we go now? The peasants will attack us. It would be better to find a trumpeter and ride to Küstrin." Major General Panin, together with Stoianov and many others, actually set off for Küstrin. Panin thought better of it and turned to Stoianov saying, "Let's go back together to the camp." "Go where you like," Stoianov replied, "but I will go my own way. It is a pity that night has fallen." Conversing in this way they all once more set off through the forest. At that moment a priest from a Georgian regiment earnestly begged them not to ride to Küstrin. From the forest they came out onto the former Russian camp near Küstrin. Then a certain lieutenant colonel of infantry said once more that as they had indeed come out by Küstrin they should beware of Prussian hussars. Panin immediately turned left from Küstrin and the others rode off with him. Slowing down a little, and seeing that no one was riding with him to Küstrin, Stoianov also set off after them. During the night they all arrived at the Russian transports.

Stoianov testified that he did not remember whether he made any improper remarks to Kaznowski about Fermor, but he never had any intention of killing him, or else he would not have defended Fermor from the enemy. When the Prussians began to outflank our army, at that point Stoianov was ordered to attack them with a Serbian regiment of hussars. This he did, and was in the very front rank of the enemy, but withdrew because of the enemy's superior strength and transferred to the right flank of the Russian army. Later again, with a Croatian regiment, he was sent to attack the enemy artillery, which he succeeded in doing before the start of the general battle, during which he was on the left flank. When the enemy intensified its efforts our front was broken and at first the right flank began to retreat. Because the whole army made for the forest, Stoianov also rode towards the forest.

At that very moment he saw enemy hussars and cuirassiers surrounding Fermor. He drove them off with a small number of his hussars, who saved the general from death or captivity. Later he rode along the line of battle where he caught sight of Panin with a number of officers. Panin, holding on to his stomach, said that he was badly wounded and that his brigade was quite finished. He begged Stoianov to find him somewhere to bind the wound. Stoianov led him into a village near the Russian right flank and, leaving him there, intended to ride in search of Fermor. Panin told him he could not remain in that spot, since there was danger from the enemy. Then Stoianov, becoming angry, said to him, purely as a joke, "What can I do with you? Let's go to Küstrin!" and they set off. Stoianov wanted to find a transport and to leave Panin there to bandage his wound. In the meantime night had fallen. "Where are we heading?" Panin asked. Stoianov, again as a joke, replied "To Küstrin." "It is too late to ride to Küstrin now," said Panin. "It would be better to ride into the forest." "It is no good in the forest," Stoianov replied, "the peasants will come and beat us with sticks." Panin said, "Look here is a trumpeter!" "Go ahead and sound your trumpet at Küstrin," Stoianov replied, joking, "and say that General Panin and Brigadier Stoianov are coming." While they were talking they arrived at the transports. Stoianov was absolved from any punishment because of lack of any evidence in the denunciation. Kaznowski was given two hundred chervontsy for his zeal.

Fermor received the following rescript from the empress in response to his communiqué about "this unsuccessful event." "The resistance made bravely for seven whole hours against an enemy superior in strength, the gaining of the field of battle and remaining on it also for a second day, so that the enemy, even when he showed himself and began firing cannon, was unable through all that day to do anything, not even to launch a direct attack, are great deeds which will remain in the eternal memory of all the world to the glory of our arms, to the particular praise of the general staff and to the renowned service of yourself as commander-in-chief. We acknowledge the great number of casualties suffered with due reverential acceptance of all God's Providence that works for the good. The results of this are in His holy power and with due unfailing thanks we will accept even the worst punishment from His beneficent hand if that is His will. We will always put our trust in His inexhaustible munificence, that would rather forgive us and, when we are grieving, would lift us up with joy, and when we are weakening would give us strength. So even in misfortune, should it come upon you, you must have a spirit of courage and fortitude equal to ours. Find a place for Him in the whole army under your command. Comfort the wounded with our maternal pity and warm wishes for their recovery, no less also to all and every one of those whose services will be with us in our eternal memory and will not remain without worthy reward. Publish this our decree throughout all the army so that all shall see how great is our mercy to those deserving, so that, seeing these favors, those who through faintheartedness or some other cause did not quite fulfill their duty feel how much they should try to set this to rights, and how much incomparably happier and envious is the lot of those who ended their lives with such glory and with eternal merit before their maker, than those who displayed disgraceful timidity."[19]

FERMOR'S ADVANCE INTO POMERANIA

At dawn on August 16, in full view of the enemy, the Russian army left the field of battle and marched seven versts in square formation. The soldiers carried off the artillery, both their own as well as that taken from the enemy, by any means at their disposal for want of sufficient harness. Cossacks carried the wounded in saddle-bow straps on their thoroughbred horses. The Prussian forces were not disturbed. At nine Fermor arrived safely at Gross-Kammin, where for several days he remained in a well-fortified camp. "On the eighteenth," Fermor reported, "a service of thanksgiving was sung to the Almighty for His merciful forgiveness. At its conclusion a cannonade was fired. The enemy also celebrated the victory. Their cannonade anticipated ours by a quarter of an hour." Then Fermor moved on towards Landsberg and joined Count Rumiantsev's detachment. At this point he had forty thousand troops, apart from hussars and cossacks. In St. Petersburg this move met with approval, as well as the decision of the military council not to consider a withdrawal, to act defensively until an opportunity arose to move over to the offensive.

CONFERENCE'S OBSERVATIONS ON FERMOR'S COMMAND

The empress had great and real concern, as her rescript mentioned. She could not see any planning for the future in Fermor's reports, although the late season demanded taking decisive measures. "We are greatly concerned by the fact," the rescript stated further on, "that, despite the enemy's close proximity you are almost in complete ignorance of his strength and position and that, before commencing any operation, you await our decrees based upon the reports sent by you after the battle. Because of distance these decrees must always arrive late. They can never give you any satisfaction because in the reports you sent after the battle there are only the briefest of references. Moreover you neither put forward your own opinion, nor do you give any description of your present circumstances, which would help us give orders reliably and soundly from here. We want as much as possible to give you an extensive and detailed explanation of our opinions in exchange for the extreme brevity of your reports.

"Had you attacked, Count Dohna's corps, though not completely broken, were weak until joined by the king's forces. Being thus weakened and disorganized, naturally the king of Prussia would not have had such an advantage in attacking you and would have had to bring up considerably more troops, thus relieving the Austrian field marshal Count Daun. This would have enabled Daun to join with you, or the king of Prussia would have had to return through Silesia to Bohemia in order to divert Daun in that direction. Likewise if the corps remaining against you now had been broken and driven across the Oder you would be completely free and secure. You could have at your disposal enemy territory on this side of the Oder to do with as you please.

"If, on the other hand, Count Dohna's corps remains opposed to you on this side of the river, you need to beware of still more ill-fated consequences. First of all the occupation of winter quarters will be subject to considerable difficulties. The enemy will stay in camp purposely for a long time, so as to exhaust our army during the bad weather. Second, and most important of all, should Count Dohna remain on this side of the Oder, the king may join him again and attack you with his united forces. Your declaration that your main concern is the occupation of winter quarters on enemy territory was very much to our liking. We shall not conceal, however, the fact that you refer lightly to such important matters, as if in passing, and this concerns us very much, even more so as the season is so advanced.

"As regards the plans you sent of the last battle, because of the brevity of the descriptions attached to them we can neither compose a detailed report, which everybody expects of us, nor even have any clear idea ourselves. The plan of last year's battle was much more detailed. There we were able to see which regiments took part in the fighting and when, and what happened afterwards. Even here we can see the disposition of the regiments, but their operations are passed over in silence. We recommended to you particularly not to keep us in ignorance about which regiments and whom out of the general staff distinguished themselves the most. When else should we expect such essential information, if not in respect to this great and rare event?

"On one of the plans we see that the advanced guard of the Prussian army is rather nearer to our forces than to its own. As it is altogether impossible to see what measures you were taking as a consequence of this circumstance, we are concerned by your quite inadequate information concerning the disposition of the enemy, in consequence of which you must always be afraid of unexpected attacks from him.

"We earnestly hope (1) that our army will take up winter or cantonment-quarters on the territory of Brandenburg and, if possible, along the Oder river. (2) That Kolberg, as a port essential for the sustenance of our army, will be taken as swiftly as possible. (3) That Count Dohna's corps not only will be driven beyond the Oder as quickly as possible, but will be completely broken also. Avoid such resolutions as have been adopted in all the military councils held in the present campaign and in particular the addition to every resolution of the words 'if time, circumstances and the enemy's movements allow.' Such resolutions serve merely to demonstrate indecisiveness. The real art of a general consists in taking measures which neither time, nor circumstances, nor the movements of the enemy can check."

VORONTSOV'S LETTER TO FERMOR

Apart from these uncompromising observations written in the Conference Fermor received from Vice Chancellor Count Vorontsov a translation from an article on the condition of the Russian forces, written by a foreigner during Apraksin's command. Vorontsov wrote that the author of the article patently must have been a spy in our army, and suggested to the commander-in-chief he examine the enclosed material. Perhaps, among the great number of false statements, he had put his finger on real deficiencies in the army, which we could make use of. "I cannot hide from your excellency," Vorontsov wrote, "that almost everyone considers lack of transports in our army our greatest deficiency, as well as the fact that we do not know how to make positive use of our irregular forces. It is true

that it is difficult to introduce new methods of operation in place of what
has been accepted and of customs observed over a long period.

"I understand that even your excellency is sometimes afraid to introduce anything new. When you consider what has been done even in the
present century, given the condition of our government, given our people,
it seems it is not so difficult to get anything done, and even more swiftly
than anywhere else. In ancient times we conquered the Turks with all
their superior strength. During the Swedish war, with hardly any regular
troops and being defeated at first, we succeeded in assimilating Swedish
methods, of learning the art of war from the enemy and, with their own
weapon as it were, defeated them. Now the king of Prussia has the same
significance for us as the Swedes once had. We have nothing to be ashamed
of, that we are not acquainted with some of the useful military formations
and methods which the enemy introduced. It would be unforgivable if we
disregard them after discovering their usefulness. We may compare our
men boldly, in respect of their strength and obedience legitimized by the
government, with the best material, capable of taking on any form required.

"As a friend I advise your excellency, together with your noble generals,
to analyze diligently where our faults lie, and what helpful institutions and
methods of the enemy's army we must employ as soon as possible. If there
is something you find impossible to do, point this out immediately and in
earnest."

The text that Vorontsov enclosed, *Letter of a Traveler from Riga*,[20]
stated that "the Russian infantry regiment carries practically nothing going into battle.[21] There is no army as free of excess baggage as the Russian. There are a great many attending to the transports. In each company
there are soldiers attached to the provision wagons, to the closed sleighs
carrying tents and the sick, to the carriages and ammunition vans. They
must feed the horses, as only a small number are put out to graze. Moreover a captain makes use of ten to twelve men for his own service in the
name of state business. They are very slow taking up positions. The first
column always remains kneeling. Loading fire-arms is very poor and
even when ordered to form up in preparation for battle it may take an
hour to put together an infantry regiment, and there will always be disorder. The soldiers march on parade at a great distance from each other,
in four columns, so that each man is a pace apart. Each regiment takes
many pointed stakes on special wagons to protect the whole battle position of the regiment. This is done as a precaution so that cavalry cannot
burst in upon the infantry.

"The main strength of the army consists of the grenadier regiments. Indeed all the grenadiers are strong, solidly built men, but they have no agility, no liveliness. The grenadier officers are also excellent men, but only of a Russian character. I have seen very many intelligent men in the grenadier regiments who have been in the service of other sovereigns. I asked why they have not introduced into their own forces what other armies have found useful. On this point a Captain Engelhardt replied that he would have attempted to put such things into effect in his company, but this would only bring down on him the wrath of the greater part of the officers of his regiment. Therefore he requested to be transferred to another regiment, which cost him more than one hundred rubles, in particular because Germans are held in little respect. The other infantry is extraordinarily poor. The senior and junior officers have only left-over arms. I cannot compare their infantry regiments with any similarly poor troops for there is scarcely a vulgar regiment in our army that does not carry out its training better than their infantry regiments brought from the Moscow district. Every regiment is equipped with pointed stakes, in which they put all their trust.

"In the Russian army a great many artillery pieces are carried under the command of Lieutenant General Tolstoy. I often happened to talk with him and I noticed that he was a skillful artillery officer. In firing at a target only two shots out of thirty failed to hit the mark. This general had not participated in a single battle, only having served at the siege of Ochakov as a captain under Field Marshal Münnich. Tolstoy in particular complained at the poor state of the artillery horses. There are six regiments of cuirassiers in all. Five must go to East Prussia and the sixth, called the Horse Guards, remains in St. Petersburg. The first two may still be considered regiments of horse. Their horses are mediocre, but are at least German. They have been brought up to strength on the march by men and horses in the cities of Riga, Reval, Narva and Dorpat, where horses were requisitioned from all citizens with a payment of sixty rubles for each, without regard to age or defects, as long as they measured seven hands and could amble. Horses are kept until they collapse on their feet. Their squadrons are formed very slowly and make an attack no more forcibly than at a trot. When the command is given to halt and to dress, in one place there will be in more than twelve columns and in another there will be such gaps that you could drive a whole platoon between them. Firing took place by whole columns, but in complete disorder. The whole regiment came together as a heap. Many horses stumbled and men were thrown from them. They do not understand precision in their exercises. Everything is all the same to them whether one rider goes to the right, another to the left, and a third looks straight ahead. It is the same story in the other three regiments, so that now they are only formed from dragoons. I became particularly friendly with the commander of one of these regiments, Schwanenburg, who told me that their horses were quite worthless, all of Russian breed, extremely timid, unbroken and more excitable than the mounts of the hussars. A rider does not even carry his cloak on his horse. Everything is carried on the wagons, and a cavalry regiment has even more wagons than an infantry regiment.

"There are twelve dragoon regiments in the army, which do not deserve to be called cavalry. Their officers are very simple, so that stupid Russian officers of other regiments have the saying "he is as stupid as an officer of dragoons." The main reason for the unpreparedness of these regiments is the fact that they have not been assembled for ten years, but have been posted perpetually on the Tatar, Turkish and Polish borders. The hussars constitute the best of the cavalry, although in general they lack good order, equal ability and equipment, liveliness and training. Their officers are hardly capable of mounting a patrol, reconnaissance or an ambush because they have not been taught any of these things. The Kalmyks are the best of the irregular forces. The cossacks serve only to annoy the enemy incessantly, to keep an eye on him and to intimidate him. The general in command never takes into consideration the number of such riffraff on a campaign. Among the cossacks, the Don are considered the best as far as skills and bravery are concerned. They place all their trust in their leader Brigadier Krasnoshchekov.[22] They say that he is a sorcerer. General-in-chief Lopukhin assured me of this. When I said that in Germany nobody believes in magicians, he replied, "Is it possible not to believe in something so real?" I have often had occasion to see and to speak with this famous Krasnoshchekov. All of his wisdom consists in the fact that he can hit the target on a cannon shot with a lance or an arrow and also in the fact that, in his own words, he will accept pardon from no one. His fame is rather on a par with that of Razumovsky.

"Field Marshal Apraksin concerns himself for the most part with having as much staff and equipment as possible. In my daily and prolonged conversations with him I noticed that he does not possess the necessary theoretical knowledge of a field marshal. He cannot have the necessary practical experience because, apart from Ochakov, he has not been anywhere. He is merely concerned with forcing his people to fight bravely.

He worries little about the care of men and horses. General Weymarn leads him on a string. He is a very skillful man and was always adjutant to General Keith. He has a wide general knowledge in the science of war and the Russians regard him, as well as General Lieven, as their oracles. General-in-chief Lopukhin is little skilled in military matters. His main areas of knowledge are in eating, drinking and cards. General-in-chief Lieven need scarcely be taken into account because serious illness prevents him being able to think rationally. Because of his long service the Russian treat him as their idol. He will never do anything really significant, which I noticed in his conversations with General St. André, who told him quite incredible nonsense and he believed everything. General-in-chief Browne has little spirit and has not served anywhere except in Russia.

Lieutenant General Prince Golitsyn has never given a thought to military matters. He has been at court from a young age and was later resident in Hamburg. Lieutenant General Lieven is considered very expert but he is not on good terms with Apraksin, with a relative of whom he quarrelled. Major General Dolgoruky has a reputation for great bravery, but has little expertise. General Villebois is young, but a very capable officer. Nevertheless he confessed to me himself that he is losing his enthusiasm in the present way of things. 'May the devil take them,' he told me. 'Here you must pretend to be as much of a fool as the rest, or else you will make enemies of them all.' Count Rumiantsev is also a young man. He has taken a lot of trouble to make himself fit for service, and indeed has a wide theoretical knowledge. In short, he is the most expert of the Russian generals. His greatest fault is his excessive enthusiasm. Major General Panin told me himself, 'Why did they make me a general? I did not ask to be one. I am content when I can instruct a regiment.' Prince Lubomirski is an empty braggart. The field marshal places all his trust in Colonel Bülow, who transferred to Russian service from the Saxon army. He is said to be unstable, but capable of setting all the inhabitants of the globe upon one another."

FERMOR'S RETREAT TOWARDS THE VISTULA

Letters were sent to Fermor suggesting he take up winter quarters on Brandenburg territory and take the offensive against Dohna. Even in August he had suggested to Vorontsov that he should make his way to winter quarters in the direction of Poland! "At present," he wrote on August 23 from near Landsberg, "the army consists of thirty-five, and with the lightly wounded, up to forty thousand men. In addition there is a great shortage of generals and staff officers. The best have become casualties. The field artillery is in good condition. We fall short of a full complement of ammunition. We are also very short of skilled officers, bombardiers and fusiliers. We cannot hope to receive further supplies because, on the crossing of the Oder by the Prussian army, both towns and the peasantry are unruly. They run away from their homes, and in the forests exchange fire with the cossacks. Consequently the same problem has arisen which occurred last year. We cannot possibly maintain the light cavalry because of the destruction of the land. The harness, both for the artillery and the transports, is wearing out with the onset of autumn weather. If we abandon the Warthe river, or move even further along it, but remain in one spot, we may have to kill off the horses, and what service can men perform without horses? There will be no means to move the artillery and ammunition. From this it charitably can be concluded that extreme necessity will force me and the whole general staff to make our way upstream along the Warthe or the Netze by short marches to our supply depots on the Vistula, and in that way we may preserve the army without abandoning the very many wounded into enemy hands."

At the military council held on September 7 it was decided that it was impossible to remain on Brandenburg territory. To go directly to the Vistula would be to incur the empress's anger. Therefore a middle way must be chosen, to go to Pomerania, to make camp at Stargard and send a detachment of troops to seize Kolberg, a coastal fortress important for the transport of troops and food supplies from Russia.

The council's decision was carried out. The army took up a position near Stargard. A military council was held there on September 23, at which Fermor put forward the following for discussion. As the month of October was approaching, severe autumn winds with rain were about to begin, there was no forest cover in the local open district, which is similar to the steppe, and nowhere to obtain firewood. Those staying in camp would suffer considerable deprivation and the horses would become physically exhausted from insufficient grazing. Therefore must the army absolutely remain in this district, and for how long? Would it not be better to move towards the Drage river, near which there was more chance of obtaining grazing and firewood?

It was decided to send all the heavy transport, the regular and irregular cavalry with horses in poor condition, the unmounted hussars and cossacks, together with the sick, towards the Vistula, but to maintain the army in its previous positions, as time and circumstances allowed. In respect to the demand from St. Petersburg that they take the field against Count Dohna, Fermor replied that it was impossible to attack an enemy who was always in impregnable camps, has excellent cavalry and artillery whose murderous deeds are still fresh in the memory, without subjecting the troops to extreme danger. Even if we managed to defeat Dohna, or with one forward movement press him back beyond the Oder, even then we would have to fall back on Pomerania because in the vicinity of the Oder, from Küstrin to Schwedt, no sustenance could be found. In respect to the reproach concerning the modest description of the battle of Zorndorf, Fermor replied that because of the dust and smoke he could not make out the movements of the regiments and disposition of the commanders. Regarding the brevity of the reports, he replied that there was not time to write in greater detail, owing to the army's constant movement, the poor weather and the demands of reconnaissance. Not a single sheet of paper left the chancellery without him seeing it, not a single incoming matter was unsealed by anyone without him being present.

At the beginning of October the insufficient grazing and firewood in the forest around Stargard forced Fermor to cross to the bank of the Drage river. From here the army moved further on towards the Vistula into winter quarters. The authorities in St. Petersburg had to reconcile themselves to this, although they expressed their regret that Dohna was not defeated, and therefore the campaign had ended without glory. They regretted even more that Kolberg was not taken. General Palmenbach, sent by Fermor, remained for a considerable period near the city, but was forced to return without success.[23]

In respect to winter quarters Fermor was instructed to set up a cordon from Thorn to Elbing, as in the previous year. To this instruction Fermor replied that he would not fail to carry it out. A firm decision was to have been taken to position the army as a cordon in Pomerania to preserve the reputation of Russian arms and to await the approach of the Swedish army. Pomerania was dreadfully exhausted from the presence there of two armies and Fermor, very soon after the battle of Zorndorf, concluded a contract with the Jew Baruch for the supply of twenty-five thousand quarters of grain along the Netze and Warthe rivers. To this latest information Fermor received the following reply. "Our regret is all the greater because your intentions are always revealed to us late. You always have

maintained that to stay in Pomerania was impossible; otherwise we would
have made every effort to facilitate you in any way in this undertaking."
Neither was St. Petersburg pleased by Fermor's instruction to buy grain
from Wernik, a merchant from Danzig. "We took the firm decision," the
rescript maintained, "to supply our army abroad with grain and oats from
our empire. However high the price might be here, and however expensive the transport abroad, the government has money to use for this purpose."

Despite this, on November 25, on the anniversary of Elizabeth's accession, Fermor received the Order of St. Andrew. Evidently no action
was taken in response to the criticism of foreigners. After the battle of
Zorndorf Prince Karl of Saxony sent Vorontsov a long letter with accusations against the commander-in-chief. The hussars and cossacks were
used improperly. They were kept with the army, whereas they should
have been sent out to keep an eye on the enemy and keep him in a state
of constant alarm. The transport was enormous, demanding thirty thousand wagons and taking more than four thousand soldiers from the army.
The rank and file were very hard-working and tireless, but poorly trained
in military matters and with little discipline. Fermor made a great mistake
in wasting much time near Küstrin to no purpose. He chose the worst
place for the battle, in spite Prince Karl's exhortation. After the battle he
set off too quickly for Landsberg, also against the advice of Prince Karl
and General St. André. Fermor did not know how to manage the establishment of supply depots, did not know how to be firm and decisive, was
too distrustful. His gravest misfortune consisted in the fact that he entrusted himself to a young man, Colonel Irman, acting as quartermaster
general.

General St. André also made a complaint against Fermor because he
was not invited to meetings of the military council. A Swedish major,
Baron Armfeld, described the battle of Zorndorf in such terms that, in
Fermor's words, it was not possible to imagine a more malevolent enemy.
"I beg most humbly," Fermor wrote, "that the army be delivered from this
malevolent gentleman, and if possible, from all the gentlemen volunteers,
who have done nothing during the past campaign but enjoy themselves
and go hunting. Our expenses would have been less, and so would the
spurious items of news. It may be better to believe more him to whom the
whole army is entrusted, and by whom a correct journal is kept. These
gentlemen have created so much anxiety for me with their empty-headed

escapades and conjectures that I did not know how to get away from them or how to keep any matters secret."

CAMPAIGN PLAN FOR FOLLOWING YEAR

On December 20 a plan of campaign for the following year was put together for Fermor. He was told to act aggressively in Pomerania and Brandenburg or the Neumark. The sooner he opened the campaign the better. He should hasten the occupation of Kolberg so that in spring, or in the first months of summer, there might be a sufficient supply of provisions and other necessities, eliminating any fear of shortage. He should persuade the Swedes to lay siege to Stettin, and give them every assistance. He should move along the Oder in order to cover this siege. If peace were not concluded he was to arrange future winter quarters along the Oder. He should occupy Berlin, if time and fortune allowed. It was most important to conceal this plan from the enemy.

"We simply have in mind rendering assistance to the allies and undermining the king of Prussia, not the conquest of Pomerania or Neumark. Therefore, should the enemy assemble his greatest army on the borders, it should be enough for us to approach him to keep him fearful of our intentions and not give him the freedom to turn in another direction. We must attack him only when he appears weak, or it is known that he is awaiting reinforcements and will then attack himself. We must begin the campaign early and swiftly in order to occupy the necessary positions before the Prussians arrive in strength. In this way we will distract the king of Prussia and relieve the court in Vienna if Frederick II has managed to defeat Field Marshal Daun at the beginning of the campaign. It is true that neither the court in Vienna nor Count Daun by his turn into Saxony last year, instead of the promised march towards Frankfurt-on-Oder or Berlin, deserves such consideration for his preservation. It must be confessed, however, that if the court in Vienna is weakened or forced into a unfavorable peace, our affairs and interests will lose as much as theirs, and all the losses and difficulties borne so far will have been in vain. We must consider the occupation of Kolberg the main objective of the entire campaign. Without that our army in Pomerania cannot receive reliable supplies, either to help the Swedes in taking Stettin or to occupy winter quarters there. It is the only port through which we can receive the necessary supplies."

RELATIONS WITH ALLIED COURTS

The campaign of 1758 ended unsuccessfully. In St. Petersburg it was impossible not to be annoyed with the Austrians, who did nothing for the Russian forces either before or after the battle of Zorndorf. The Russian court was displeased with the Viennese, who in turn placed all the blame on France. Esterhazy told Vorontsov of Maria Theresa's rescript of October 19, in which she said, "The difficulties that have beset us this season in our military affairs and our poor progress have been principally because France did not heed our sincerely offered advice. Instead of sending from thirty to forty thousand troops into our hereditary lands and keeping the German courts quiet with an army of observation on the Rhine, it became enmeshed in a war over Hanover. By this mistake it not only drained its finances, brought its fleet to the point of collapse and suffered major losses in America and Germany,[24] but also lost a considerable amount of its former standing within and outside of Europe, not to mention the fact that there is a certain timidity and weakness in the decisions of the French court. In these circumstances the French ministry believes that there remains little to gain. There is no hope whatsoever of obtaining what was anticipated through French aid. Trade and the fleet are exposed to the danger of complete destruction. It believes that when, for us, for Russia and for Saxony, the war ends successfully and each of the three powers can draw the thorn from its foot, France, on the contrary, will remain with its thorn and will receive no compensation for all its efforts and expense.

"For our part we find that such misgivings of the French court are not without foundation, and for our other allies this could have dangerous consequences. Since the beginning of the year France often has made the point that the burden of the war was becoming unsustainable, and therefore we must think about peace. We replied that the question was not about whether peace were necessary, but what sort of peace. As this reply cannot give any satisfaction to the French ministry, our primary obligation is to arrange with our loyal ally, the empress of Russia, ways of keeping the French court from premature thoughts of peace. The Prussian forces are not as close to Russia as they are to us. Still until they are reduced Russia will be in continual danger. This is especially so should Prussia take advantage of a Turkish war or destroy the present form of government in Sweden and conclude a close alliance with that power. Experience has shown that many, even great powers with their combined forces, can do nothing against Prussia. What success could be hoped for in single combat with that nation?

"Moreover it would be extremely unjust were Saxony not to be compensated in any way for the unprecedented disasters it has experienced. A reprehensible peace would deprive us and our allies of influence in the general system of political affairs, and even in a period of peace we would be obliged to maintain a large army. As the Russian court is a natural ally of our archducal house, we place our greatest trust in the advice of her imperial majesty and would like to be informed of her intentions with respect to any future peace negotiations."

"It is true that France has made a grave mistake," the Russian reply stated, "but it has tried to rectify it. It has declined to occupy Hanover, when such an occupation would have been very advantageous in any future peace negotiations with England. It was due to French efforts that Sweden went to war with Prussia. By agreement with the French court even Denmark put together a significant force in its German provinces. Besides, France has become even more involved in the war by its mistake than it intended previously. Her imperial majesty always believed, and still believes, that France agreed to assist in weakening of the king of Prussia because it was promised gains in the Netherlands, which balanced its support of the house of Austria. The empress-queen has sacrificed the Netherlands in order to get rid of a dangerous enemy, the king of Prussia, for ever. With that aim in mind the Russian empress agreed to increase support to the kingdom of Sweden. This purpose has been so well achieved that the more France had the forces and the influence to win over the Swedish and Danish courts, the more it was absolutely necessary for it to uphold its obligations to the empress-queen rather than to contemplate hasty peace negotiations.

"Even should France not take into account that, with the conclusion of an unfavorable peace, it would lose irrevocably the military expenditure it has made; even if it finds a means of excusing itself before the Swedish and Danish courts for the fact that it drew them into the war, it cannot but foresee that England will not agree to a peace settlement without the king of Prussia. It is easy to imagine what the English claims will be and how strong the king of Prussia will become, when the former allies of France, seeing its weakness, must cross over to Prussia's side and become its dependents. It is still impossible to conclude absolutely that France has the unequivocal intention of insisting on peace simply from the general assessment of the French court that the war is becoming burdensome and insupportable, and that therefore it must contemplate a speedy conclusion of peace.

"Nevertheless the empress through her particular friendship with the empress-queen, takes it upon herself to present in stronger terms to the French court the reasons why we must not hasten towards such a peace settlement. The empress's opinion is that we must continue the war started by the king of Prussia until such time as it pleases the Almighty to bless righteous arms with complete success, and without pride based upon self-esteem alone, to permit a worthy recompense to all the injured parties. As to military operations, we must observe that the side blessed with victory will be that which has tried to make good use of its successes, without glancing back to look at the other party. For however much the objectives of everyone are identical, circumstances can never be the same, and the king of Prussia takes advantage of that fact when he sees that one army, having gained a victory over him, waits for the other to do likewise."

In France at the beginning of the year Bestuzhev was obliged to listen to complaints about Apraksin's withdrawal. When he complained to Abbé Bernis at de Broglie's behavior in Warsaw, Bernis replied that Broglie would be leaving Poland and thus a stumbling-block would be removed. There was no need to think about such trifles any longer, but how the king of Prussia's progress could be stopped because the Austrians, having lost about forty-five thousand of their best troops in the last campaign, were no longer in a position to act against him. In short, Frederick II had become so powerful that he was dangerous, not only to the allies, but to the whole of Europe. In such circumstances, being very intelligent, fortunate and capable, he might easily conquer Bohemia and take the leading position in Germany. He might also make his brother king in Poland and dictate laws to everybody. It would not be difficult for him to deal with the Swedes. What then would it be like for the others? Therefore it is a very great pity that Field Marshal Apraksin without any legitimate reason withdrew hastily and gave Lehwaldt the opportunity to move into Pomerania. So much harm was occasioned to the general cause that it was impossible to set the matter right quickly.

From recriminations the allies had to switch to vindication. The Russian army moved into the field once more and occupied East Prussia proper, and the French retreated beyond the Weser. Louis XV considered it necessary to placate Elizabeth with a letter in his own hand. He also blamed this development on shortage of supplies. The king assured the empress that he was now still more intent on using all his forces to compel the transgressor of the general peace to respect the Imperial Statutes[25] and to establish a general peace on a firm and just foundation. He, the king, would never abandon the alliance. In November Abbé Bernis once more complained to Bestuzhev about the unsuccessful operations of the Russian generals. "I fail to understand," said the abbé, "how Kolberg could not have been taken. Is there any special reason apart from lack of skill and the blunders of the commanders? The forces besieging Kolberg never had enough ammunition. No more than three days' supply was sent to them, at the most five. A Swedish general wrote to Count Fermor that he was stationed at a distance of only two days' march away, and that he could obtain any supplies the Russian army needed. In spite of this Count Fermor moved further away from him. We clearly understand the sincere desire of the empress to render assistance to her allies. We can rely upon the bravery of the Russian soldiers, but it is a pity that the empress's orders are not always carried out as they should be."

This was the last statement of Abbé Bernis. At the end of the year he was replaced in the administration of foreign affairs by the duc de Choiseul.[26] The first act of the new foreign minister was to let Bestuzhev know that through the Danish court the English had been asked whether they were prepared to make peace with France without the king of Prussia, but received a definite refusal. "It is clear that there is a considerable shortage of money in the Treasury here," Bestuzhev reported. "Among the people the poverty is obvious. Commerce and the manufacturing industries are in decline. Seafaring is constrained. The people are grumbling vigorously. In spite of this there is always sympathy among the people for the needs of government." From St. Petersburg L'Hôpital told his court of Esterhazy's note regarding the French desire to conclude peace. Choiseul told Bestuzhev, on the order of the king, that his majesty would observe religiously and inviolably all obligations to his allies, and conclude peace only with common agreement. The Austrian ambassador, Count Starhemberg, assured Bestuzhev that Choiseul could be relied upon, because he was more disposed towards the continuation of the war than to the conclusion of any form of unfavorable peace.

RELATIONS WITH ENGLAND AND POLAND

In respect to England, no one in St. Petersburg had any hope that it would conclude a separate peace which excluded the king of Prussia. They were more concerned that an English squadron might appear in the Baltic Sea to assist Prussia against Russia and Sweden. At the beginning of the year

Golitsyn, reporting that the duke of Newcastle[27] was not very devoted to Prussia, added that at present in England it was difficult for the well-intentioned minister "to go against the flow of the fanatical passion of almost the whole nation for the king of Prussia." He also added that the basic rule of English politics is that France's enemy is England's friend, and that the present purpose of the English court is quite clear, to try to make Prussia the strongest power in Germany instead of Austria, the alliance with whom is abrogated. The English concern is not which power should be the strongest in Germany, merely that it be in close alliance with England against France. To this must be added also the chimerical title of defender of the Protestant religion conferred upon Frederick II.[28] Golitsyn was instructed to demand a direct reply from the court in London whether Russia was understood to be among the common enemies against whom the English court in its declaration promised always and intensively to assist the king of Prussia. The English ministry avoided such a reply under the pretext that it had not received a detailed report in respect to Russian relations from Keith, its ambassador in St. Petersburg. They were afraid to send a squadron, not wishing to harm trade by a decisive break with Russia, and moreover irritate Sweden and Denmark. On the other hand they did not want to say directly that they would not send a squadron, in order to keep Russia a little longer in fear of such an event, and in this way render assistance to Frederick II. The occupation by Russian forces of Prussia proper made an impression in London. It was suggested to the Danish envoy that his court should not look with indifference upon such an amplification of Russia's position.

Suggestions made in this vein to the Poles merely gave rise to talks. On January 27 Prince Volkonsky dined with the Crown Hetman Count Branicki. After dinner the host took his guest aside and said, "It is astonishing how much disorder the Russian forces stationed at present in the provinces of the Commonwealth have caused!" "If indeed some disorder has occurred," Volkonsky replied, "there is no point in the Poles complaining. The empress has promised repeatedly to appoint special commissioners, who together with Polish commissioners should investigate everything that has taken place and give real satisfaction to those injured."

Then Branicki enlarged upon complaints against his own government. "The court rules autocratically here in Poland," he said. "Although I have no intention of starting anything myself, yet we must be concerned lest an exasperated gentry form a confederation."[29] "If that is really so," Volkonsky answered, "you must demand from the court changes in behavior. In our capacities as ambassadors of the empress of All Russia by the guarantees of 1717[30] we will try in every possible way to support these just demands." The hetman was not pleased with this answer and said, "The father of the present empress was only an intermediary, not a guarantor. With the death of King August II the treaty of 1717 lost its validity." "If that is the case," retorted Volkonsky, "all your rights and freedoms affirmed by previous kings also have lost their validity." Branicki dropped this subject and went on to say, with some passion, that Russia was interfering in the domestic affairs of Poland in that the Russian chancellor had sent a letter to the Lithuanian hetman Radziwill regarding elections to the future tribunal. Volkonsky replied that the Polish statutes in no way would be broken if a neighboring and friendly power gave benevolent advice to any loyal magnate.

On February 7 Volkonsky and Gross were invited to a conference with Crown Marshal Count Bielinski, at which they found Crown Chancellor Malachowski, Hetman Branicki and Marshal of the Court Count Mniszech. Bielinski presented a list of grievances which Polish citizens had suffered at the hands of the Russians, in particular the inhabitants of Braclaw province. As these grievances were caused by Ukrainian cossacks, Volkonsky replied, "You, lord ministers, must admit yourselves that the Ukrainian cossack bands are made up of a variety of fugitives, principally of Polish subjects. Consequently the Poles themselves must look to see how to keep them from brigandage. It is easy for Ukrainian cossacks to plunder because Polish forces are positioned twenty miles from the border. Were they to be moved to the border itself, this would be a better way of stopping the raids."

The Poles had to admit that the Ukrainian cossack attacks were carried out not by Russian citizens alone. They complained that the Russian border commissioners avoided proceeding with these matters. Volkonsky objected that, on the contrary, the Lithuanian border courts had not brought any benefits whatsoever. Therefore it was not surprising if mutual complaints multiplied daily. The entire fault lay with the Polish commissioners who, neither in Lithuania nor in Poland, seriously came to grips with such matters. "What can we do?" the ministers replied. "The Lithuanian commissioners, not receiving any salary, cannot carry out their duties. Let us hope that the next Sejm will take place soon. There we shall make

every effort to take such measures as will put an end to all border disputes
once and for all."

KARL OF SAXONY RECEIVES THE DUCHY OF COURLAND

In spite of the fact that, following the fall of Chancellor Bestuzhev, Prince
Volkonsky received assurance that his uncle's crime in no way would
alter the empress's gracious favor to his nephew, unbeknown to him the
important matter of the election of the king's son Prince Karl to the duchy
of Courland was settled between the Russian and Polish courts. On July
17 Volkonsky and Gross wrote that they were surprised to receive news
from Mitau that Aloe, secretary to Chancellor Malachowski, was petition-
ing in that city for the election of Prince Karl to the duchy. Knowing Aloe
for a schemer, both ambassadors asked Count Brühl whether Aloe had
really been charged with such an important mission. Brühl answered directly that he had, and not without the knowledge and agreement of the
Russian court. Volkonsky and Gross wrote that they were instructed to
make sure that everything in Courland remain unchanged. Then they begged
to be furnished with a new most gracious instruction. This new candidate
for the duchy of Courland was the third son of King August. We have
seen him in the Russian army, read Fermor's report about his behavior
during the battle of Zorndorf and that of Karl himself about the Russian
army and its commander-in-chief.

Before his departure for the army Prince Karl travelled to St. Petersburg with the intention of eliciting the duchy of Courland from the empress. On May 24 he sent to Vorontsov to remind him of his request,
declaring, "I commit myself to the maternal care of her imperial majesty,
and await from her imperial munificence the foundation of my happiness,
in which I place all my trust. It is solely in the power of her imperial
majesty to bestow upon me the principality of Courland and to make
happy both myself and all my descendants."

Vorontsov gave the following opinion in respect to this request. "If we
directly refuse the prince at this point it will intensify the predicament of
the king of Poland. The Polish-Saxon court will be made more despon-
dent, and it will lessen their hope for favor. It has always been sustained
by the strong support and patronage of the empress. On the other hand it
is impossible to foresee how the present war will end. Perhaps we will
have to use Courland in a general peace settlement for the attainment of
some other useful goal."

The first consideration was given priority, the more so as the second did not have sufficient force behind it. In a general peace settlement St. Petersburg wanted to obtain East Prussia in order to exchange it with Poland for Courland. In this event Prince Karl would merely move from Mitau to Königsberg. On August 29 Volkonsky and Gross told the king that the empress had ordered Simolin, the present adviser to the chancellor in Mitau, to act in concert with Aloe to convey the duchy of Courland to Prince Karl. The king with joyful countenance replied that he could not find words to express his thanks, and that his son would bind himself to the empress with eternal gratitude.

This event brought serious dissatisfaction at the young court in St. Petersburg. The grand duke, because of his Prussian attachments, hated the house of Saxony in any case. Now he wrote to Volkonsky that the empress should concern herself rather about a prince from the house of Holstein, than about Prince Karl. His uncle twice-removed, Prince Georg Ludwig,[31] had more right to the patronage of the empress and therefore he, the grand duke, proposed him for the duchy of Courland. Vorontsov showed the letter to the empress, who ordered him to reply with a refusal. The grand duchess, thanks to Poniatowski's prompting, also had no love towards the house of Saxony and saw an injustice in respect to Biron[32] in the gift of Courland to Prince Karl, an injustice harmful to Russia, for this strengthened the king of Poland in respect to Polish freedom. Of course such an opinion was expressed by Catherine in an agitated state of mind, for it was difficult to imagine how the dying August III could be made an autocrat merely because his third son became duke of Courland. It is interesting that in reports to his court in relation to the Courland question Prasse was expressing already the suspicion that Poniatowski, reassured by the patronage of the future rulers of Russia, might have in mind the throne of Courland for himself, if not a higher position.

After the battle of Zorndorf there was a severe shortage of generals, and Prince Volkonsky was ordered immediately to join the army in the field. Gross alone remained to act as an observer at the Sejm, which began on September 21. The day before its opening Gross wrote that Hetman Branicki, through his emissaries, had found a way secretly to insert into the instructions to the deputies that no permission whatsoever be given for Gross to speak to them before the departure of the last Russian soldier from Polish provinces. The deputies of the Brzesc and Vol-hynia provinces, at public audiences, had proposed already to the king that he try to free the Polish provinces from Russian forces and demand compensation for damages suffered. The crown chancellor answered in the name of the king that there were no longer any Russian forces in Poland, and that the empress long ago had sent commissioners to assess compensation for losses. The people received significant sums from the passage of Russian troops, and the actions of these troops served Poland's own security.

On the fourth day of the Sejm Podgorski, a deputy from Volhynia, declared that he could not agree to the Sejm coming to any decisions until the possessions of the Commonwealth were cleared of Russian forces. After this he left Warsaw and so broke up the Sejm. No one doubted that this was a stratagem by Hetman Branicki. Somehow he must be reconciled with the court, and eventually this was achieved. From the Russian point of view there was also an effective remedy. The restless hetman was given the Order of St. Andrew the First-Called. On the breakup of the Sejm the senatus-consilium[33] remained for the solution of important matters. It wanted to accomplish the matter of Courland, but the Czartoryskis declared that the constitution forbade the senatus-consilium from interfering in government matters. They, the Czartoryskis, by their honor and conscience, and in order to preserve their favor in the nation, could in no way permit this, but to resolve the Courland affair the king might call an extraordinary Sejm, the success of which they would each promote. The court, relying on the agreement of two-thirds of the senators present, wanted to facilitate the Courland business in the senatus-consilium. On October 19 this senatus-consilium met as twenty senators. Sixteen of them declared their agreement to the elevation of Prince Karl to the duchy of Courland. Count Poniatowski, castellan of Cracow castle, the Russian governor Prince Czartoryski, High Hetman Prince Mosalski and Governor Wielopolski of Sandomir submitted that an extraordinary Sejm must be called. They were told there would be no point in this. Because of the usual disruption of the Sejms it was all the same whether any matter were postponed until the next meeting or were cancelled altogether.

They adhered to their point of view and the castellan of Cracow declared that even with a majority of the votes in the Senate the Courland question would not receive legal sanction. "Now nobody really knows," wrote Gross, "why these senators, on whom we rely in particular, oppose the king's intention, although generally this behavior is ascribed to their envy. On the reconciliation of Count Brühl with Hetman Branicki, the first minister, by dint of the marriage of his son with the daughter of the military governor of Kiev, has become joined to the Potocki family."

Yet another difficulty arose. Schelling, a delegate from Courland, offered the ducal crown to Prince Karl, but the senior councillors of Courland sent a protest to Warsaw saying the delegate had acted against his instructions, having put forward a Catholic as a candidate[34] when in his instructions it was clearly laid down that he demand a Lutheran as duke. The court did not want to take this into consideration, asserting that there were no rules whatsoever determining the faith of the duke of Courland. At last, at a full meeting of the senatus-consilium, the Courland question was passed in agreement with the king's wishes. Seven members refused to put their names to it.

After this Gross was recalled from Warsaw and appointed a member of the College of Foreign Affairs. In his place Lieutenant General Voeikov, a former deputy-governor of Riga, was appointed envoy extraordinary and minister plenipotentiary to Poland. Immediately before his departure Gross held an interesting conversation with Prince Czartoryski, chancellor of Lithuania. Czartoryski asked Gross whether he had reported to the empress the reasons why he opposed the resolution of the Courland affair in the senatus-consilium. Gross replied that he had, but the empress did not consider these reasons sufficient. "It is a pity," Czartoryski said. "With time the empress will give me credit when she sees that by this example in the future the Polish kings can try to decide all important matters in the Senate without calling a Sejm. In this way the entire Polish constitution will be distorted." On December 28 Prince Karl ceremoniously was invested with the duchy of Courland by his father.

TURKISH AFFAIRS

From Constantinople Obreskov reported at the beginning of the year that all efforts of the English ambassador Porter[35] to force the Porte to declare war on Russia, and particularly on Austria, were unsuccessful. In general Obreskov was very pleased with the state of affairs in Turkey, praising the gentleness of the new sultan,[36] the good management of Grand Vizier Raghib Pasha,[37] even the loyalty of the khan of the Crimea, to whom he advised the governor of Kiev to send presents, following the example of the governor of Astrakhan. Obreskov described the French ambassador Vergennes as carrying out their common sublime interests with the diligence to be expected from a sincere ally. Beginning at mid-year Obreskov reported a new-found warlike spirit in the sultan. Significant military preparations were being made in the Danubian provinces. In spite of this the envoy reassured the empress. "The danger is not very great," he wrote. "Judging by the quality of the local government and forces, without any extraordinary expense and without relaxing any measures taken against the king of Prussia, in one or at the most two campaigns we may bring the Porte to the point of complete repentance and disgrace." After this Obreskov reported that the sultan certainly wanted war with Russia, but the vizier and the mufti, leaders of the peace party, were opposing war as vigorously as possible.

DIRECTIONS RELATING TO MONTENEGRO

If the sultan was seeking a pretext for war, Russia must not give him any. On May 18 a rescript of the Foreign College was signed which declared both to Metropolitan Vasily Petrovich and to all Montenegrins in general that their people's enthusiasm for our empire and their desire to become our citizens merited our customary goodwill and favor. At this moment any formalizing of such a request could publicize the matter and be very disastrous, bearing in mind the great proximity of their surrounding enemies and the great distance of our empire. This matter must be put aside until more propitious times. For the time being they may take satisfaction in the assurance of our certain goodwill. As a sign of assurance, a sheet of paper signed by our deputy chancellor should be sent to all the Montenegrin people, on the pattern of those sent before, signed by Chancellor Count Golovkin.[38] On that single sheet should be expressed the fact, in general terms, that we, through those who have travelled here, such as the metropolitan and others, and also through our Colonel Puchkov and First Major Stepan Petrovich, being informed with pleasure of the enthusiasm of the Montenegrin people for our empire, moreover of their firm adherence to the Orthodox faith, want to bear witness to our goodwill and to assure them that our favor to them will be always inalienable, as a sign of which we also send to all the people a thousand of our golden portraits. As a sign of our particular favor we give instructions that gold medals of our coronation, to the value of fifty chervontsy each, be awarded to the serdar Vukotich and Governor Plamenats, and the same golden medal, to the value of thirty-five chervontsy, to Peter, the son of Governor Yurash-kovich. They should all be given two thousand rubles for distribution on preparing for the return journey. Metropolitan Petrovich should be given one thousand rubles in particular.

The metropolitan maintained that it was necessary to donate up to fifteen thousand rubles every year for the establishment of good order among the Montenegrins and to create unanimity. He further urged that one of the Russian diplomatic agents be sent as resident to Montenegro. The empress agreed to the first request, but to the second replied that present circumstances did not permit it. Even Colonel Puchkov, who was in Trieste to receive and dispatch Montenegrins entering Russian service, was recalled to St. Petersburg in order not to give the Turks any cause for suspicion. The Montenegrins already knew the way, and could travel to Russia by themselves. Metropolitan Petrovich asked for a donation to be set aside for certain sons of Montenegrin boyars assigned to the Cadet Corps so that they could support retainers and for other expenses. There were thirteen Montenegrins in the Corps, and the Senate ordered each to be given fifteen rubles a year.

Of these young Montenegrins, ten appeared before the Senate. Two of them, Rafail and Ivan Petrovich, presented a petition stating that Filipp Petrovich and Peter Radonich were on the register with them, but that they should not be called by these surnames. One of them was Filipp Sharovich, and not Petrovich, the other Peter Stanishich, and not Radonich. Sharovich was from the Turkish town of Podgoritsa, and Stanishich was not of a preeminent family, such as Petrovich, but of a family of moderate status. Filipp Sharovich erroneously had in his keeping a portrait of Peter the Great. There should be an investigation as to how he, a former Turkish slave and artist, came to have it. They requested that Peter Stanishich not be given the seniority and dignity of members of the Petrovich and Vukotich families. The Senate ordered the matter be investigated by the College of Foreign Affairs.

CONDUCT OF MONTENEGRINS IN MOSCOW

There was even more trouble with the adult Montenegrins. They first had been sent for settlement in Orenburg province but did not like it there and had to be removed to southwest Ukraine. On the way to Moscow they began to brawl. On one occasion two corporals and eighty-one other ranks gathered and went to the apartment of Lieutenant Kosetsky. One corporal entered the lieutenant's room, took off his own coat, flung it aside and, going outside, called to the others. At his cry all the Montenegrins were about to rush into Kosetsky's room, but were held back by the guards sent with him to protect the government money he had [for safe keeping].

Then all of them, removing their uniforms and equipment, threw it about and "in great desperation" shouted "We no longer want to serve in Russia. We are going home!" The Senate ordered they be treated according to military regulations because they had been pardoned repeatedly for their audacity, allowance being made for their newness to Russian service but, without appreciating this, they once again were creating considerable trouble.

DOMESTIC ACTIVITIES OF THE GOVERNMENT

From the Montenegrins' behavior it was clear that they were dissatisfied with their uniforms and equipment. The chancellery of Voronezh province accepted cloth from the local manufacturers Gordenin, Pustovalov and Tulinov. The cloth was of poorer quality than the samples upon which the original orders were based, and therefore priced more cheaply than the sum originally appropriated for the cloth ordered. The Main Commissary submitted that the cloth, priced lower than the prices of the originally ordered material by three to ten copecks, be issued to army regiments, but that which was cheaper by ten to twenty-seven copecks be issued to garrison regiments. The money remaining, as a result of the reduction of prices, should be passed on to regimental servants who would wear the cloth, or a reduction should be made in the period of time a uniform had to be worn. The Senate agreed but ordered that the sum equal to that remaining after the adjustment in pricing be recovered from the governor of Voronezh, his colleague and secretary.

In respect to the transport of stores from Russia to the army abroad, at the end of the year the firm Anisim Abrosimov and Company undertook to supply to Königsberg and other frontier locations flour and oats at two rubles fifty-nine copecks and groats at five rubles. The merchant Yamshchikov reduced the price of groats by five copecks. The Conference agreed to pay this price. The merchants supplied provisions at their own risk in foreign and Russian-owned seagoing cargo ships, some of which were leased.

FINANCIAL DIRECTIVES

In addition to these provisions transported to the army from Russia, stores and forage were bought on the spot. Consequently money must be sent for this purpose as well as pay for the troops. In the middle of the year the Conference told the Senate that the commander-in-chief General Fermor, by the letter of credit sent him to negotiate for up to a million silver efimoks, was unable to find any takers either in Danzig or in Warsaw. The Warsaw banker Riokur declared plainly that he was not in a position to lend such a sum. The Danzig banker Wernik offered terms to which it was impossible to agree without significant loss to the Treasury. The Dutch banker Pelsy was so slow in the transfer of a half-million sum that so far not more than forty thousand chervontsy had been transferred to Musin-Pushkin, the resident in Danzig.

General Fermor wished to avoid delay in preparation of the necessary supply depots because of insufficiency of cash. That is why the Conference recommended that the Senate once again make every effort to supply money to the army. The Senate replied that almost all the sum requested for army pay had been sent. Only 149,172 rubles remained to be sent for the rest of the year. At present because of unforeseen circumstances all money supplied to the army for stores and forage before the end of the year might not be realized. The most recent transfer of chervontsy and efimoks to Danzig at the present fallen rate of exchange would be at a loss.

Because of the fall in value of the rate for bills of exchange in St. Petersburg the Senate decided to borrow the gold and silver on hand from the Easter festival, namely thirty puds of gold and two hundred puds of silver. This was to be sent secretly to Holland to prop up the rate of exchange. Ready money for this gold and silver might then be sent to Danzig quickly. The 529,162 rubles taken on credit from the commissariat in 1757 must be paid from a contribution imposed upon conquered Prussian lands. Would it not be possible, in order to leave a significant sum there, to take three hundred and fifty thousand rubles on credit from the Synodal Department and the estates of the archbishop of Novgorod? It appeared that this was possible, and one hundred and twenty-six thousand rubles was taken from the Economic Chancellery,[39] thirty-four thousand from the Moscow synodal office, twenty thousand from the Moscow typographical office and one hundred and seventy thousand from the estates of the archbishop of Novgorod.

COMMERCE

Following the proposal of Count Peter Shuvalov already known to us,[40] copper coins were remade into a lighter coinage and delivered throughout the cities to the tune of ten million rubles. From a proposal by the same Shuvalov, bank offices were established in Moscow and St. Petersburg called "bank offices for the execution of bills of exchange for circulation within the realm of copper coins and maintenance of their balance." Copper coins were issued to merchants, owners of land, factories and mills, for a bill of exchange at six percent per annum. On receiving payment they were to take a quarter in copper coins and three quarters in silver coinage. Owners of capital would place money for increase by interest both in this new bank and in all the others also, while the bank would receive one percent for its expenses and risk, and the remainder would go to the owner of the capital.

The bank accepted from merchants copper coins, which were difficult and dangerous to keep safely at home. When brought in, the sum declared would be entered into a special page in the main ledger. A receipt would be given to the depositor. Should one merchant want to give money to another, both merchants could go to the bank office, or send a steward with a bank receipt made out to the first merchant, and the office would write on his page the sum he had to pay to the other merchant. He would then be given a new receipt for the balance. The other merchant, if he did not want to take copper coinage, could take a similar receipt and debit the page in the ledger. The same thing was done when a merchant did not wish to take copper coinage from the revenue department. He would be given a banknote for the bank office.

In addition to military expenses, other disbursements were necessary for which it was not known whence the money would come. The director of the Gentry Bank[41] reported that a decree of the Senate ordered the office of the bank to pay seven thousand rubles to Locatelli,[42] manager of the Italian opera company, to pay expenses for bringing the company from Italy and its maintenance in Russia. Yet there were only three thousand rubles available at this time at the bank. The Senate ordered the remaining four thousand rubles to be paid by the Merchants' Bank.[43] The Chancellery of Works asked for one hundred and thirty thousand for the construction of the Winter Palace, and the Senate ordered the release of twenty thousand. The chancellery maintained that this twenty thousand was quite inadequate because of the large number of craftsmen and workers. Failure to supply them with money would result in embarrassment for her imperial majesty. A further forty thousand were ordered released. Yet the following month Field Marshal Buturlin announced that the empress was pleased to give orders to the Senate to find funds for building her Winter Palace to the tune of one hundred and twenty thousand rubles a year.

The idea was not discounted of discharging all the disabled from the monasteries and giving them a special lodging, only not in Moscow, as Shakhovskoy had proposed. An imperial decree was sent to the Senate on January 6 stating that instead of dispatching soldiers retired from the army to monasteries for their subsistence, to look for some stone building in Kazan or its vicinity for their better maintenance in respect to their service and their injuries. As her majesty knew there was an ancient stone palace in Kazan, it should be repaired. If it was unsuitable, a stone building should be erected anew to maintain the retired soldiers in the same conditions as they were maintained in European states, in particular conforming to the standards of such institutions to be found in Paris.[44] The funds set aside for the financial and nutritional maintenance of those placed in monasteries should be allocated to build the new establishment for retired soldiers. Where was it possible to find the money to build this establishment for retired soldiers? It would have to be requested from the Synod.

From the revenue of the Synod 10,600 silver rubles were taken to complete the construction of a stone church begun in Mogilev as an additional contribution towards the archbishop's house and for the reestablishment and maintenance of the seminary. In addition a stipend of five hundred rubles a year was released for the bishop of Mogilev. This bishop, Georgy Konisski, expressed his thanks to the empress. "Most pious empress beloved of Christ, great Elizabeth! Most gracious sovereign! Having received the highest favor from your imperial majesty by the donation of a sum of money for the completion of construction of a church, for the maintenance of the seminary and in addition an annual salary to myself and my staff, as I take the liberty with this most humble letter to convey my servile thanks to your imperial majesty, there come to mind the words of the elders of Capernaum, who earnestly entreated Jesus on behalf of a certain centurion, saying, 'He is worthy to have you do this for him, for he loves our nation, and he built us our synagogue.'[45] These words of justification for giving thanks to Christ were not without effect and he went from these elders and gave his blessing to the centurion. Oh! I have incomparably more reason to give thanks to Christ the Lord because your imperial majesty, loving that same Savior and benefactor, rather than the children of men, has most graciously donated such a sum for the completion of a temple to Him and not simply a prayer and thought! Your most humble servant and footstool, Bishop Georgy of Belorussia."

In spite of repeated demands the Senate was unable to obtain full and detailed figures for receipts and expenses. The College of Audits presented the accounts. From 1730 to 1757, 33,335 accounts were settled. It had been notified to recover 263,459 rubles of unauthorized expenditure. To date 63,086 rubles were recovered. The sum of 200,372 rubles remained unrecovered from 1757. Since that date there were an additional 21,911 rubles. There were 17,711 unsettled accounts. In respect to the whole of government, the college had not drawn a general table in detail of receipts and expenditure, the balance and collection of income, because it had not received information from many offices.

Of course trade could not be ignored in the concern for the growth of revenue. Count Peter Shuvalov suggested to the Senate that to increase commerce the customs commission established under the Senate should be abolished and a commerce commission established in its place, to which men should be appointed who knew about business matters. They should be asked to discuss how to extend Russian commerce abroad. For example on what basis should offices be established at our main ports for such trade in particular? How should Russian merchants be divided into companies? They needed to form actual trading organizations by ordering merchandise from other states through such firms in their names. A way needed to be found to overcome the caution of foreign firms and their commissioners, so that they did not damage trade. Foreign merchants must acquire taste for trade with Russia, so that more trade may take place with us. All Russian merchant business needs to be examined to find a way of bringing foreign trading merchants to the port of St. Petersburg, and to decide whether sons of merchants should be sent abroad to gain commercial experience, as well as to make friends and influence people. Our factories need to be examined to see which are necessary for the state and what new factories should be established. We need to discuss whether to send consuls to foreign states; whether to build ships for merchants and how to make use of them; whether to leave state goods in the care of the state, or to release them to private enterprise. When commerce is improved each year it will be possible to give the profit to the commissariat for replacement of the poll tax. People are the great strength of the nation, and therefore it is to be hoped that those paying poll tax will be freed completely from this payment. The Senate agreed to the establishment of this commission.

The Tver city council sent an interesting report to the Senate, pointing to the state of the trading sector in the cities. All merchants in Tver were generally impoverished as a consequence of poor trade in that city, of major fires, of the continual passage of men on foot and by vehicle and their customary burdensome billeting. The chairman of the city council, the two senior deputies and a councillor paid the same tax as all other merchants. They were carrying an extreme burden because they had been in service on the city council for a long time and had not been free to conduct their business, for this reason their commercial interests were coming to great harm. Therefore the city council requested that the chairman and other members be elected for a three-year term, and that those newly selected swear their oath in Tver rather than go away to Moscow to the Chief Magistracy. The Senate agreed. The sad state of the roads, even between the two capitals, could not, of course, assist the success of trade. The procurator general told the Senate that post from Moscow took as much as twelve to thirteen days owing to the poor state of the roads.

The Tver city council complained about fires. The procurator general read out a letter to the Senate from the metropolitan of Rostov, Arseny (Matseevich), about a fire that occurred in Rostov on October 29. The metropolitan's house burned down, as well as churches, sixty-five other houses, the city council offices and shops. No effort was made to put the fire out by the governor's chancellery or the city council. Not only were no citizens compelled to beat a drum, there was not even a single rattle. There was no money in the archbishop's house to repair the building that had burnt down. Only 2,014 rubles had been set aside for the maintenance of the metropolitan's house and the churches. From his house, out of diocesan and patrimonial revenue, 4,395 rubles were paid into the chancellery of the Synodal Economic Administration. Therefore would it not be possible to leave this revenue in his Treasury for five years? The Senate agreed.

UNREST OF MONASTIC PEASANTS

The old economic management of monastic and episcopal revenues, the ownership of populated lands, was evidently falling apart. Conscious of the need to build charitable institutions on a more sound and regular footing on one hand, and the dissatisfaction, the frequent uprisings of the monastery peasants on the other, there were obvious signs of its decline. From 1748 the case of the Viatka peasants dragged on. Calling themselves the "people of the black lands,"[46] 11,582 souls had de-registered themselves from the bishop's estates and the monasteries. An investigator decided the case in favor of the clergy, and the Senate agreed with him.

The Senate was unable to approve the request of the Synod in another matter, the case of the uprising of the peasants of the New Savior monastery already well-known to us.[47] The Senate appointed an investigating commission on which a member of the clergy was to sit. The Synod maintained that no commission was necessary, as a commission was appointed by the Synod following the complaints of these same peasants, yet they did not appear before the investigation and, bypassing the Synod, had the effrontery to trouble the empress with their complaints. They should be punished without any commission.

The Senate replied that an investigating commission was necessary because otherwise it was impossible to know who the culprit was. The peasants could not be blamed for the fact that they had not appeared before the Synodal commission, as the commission was set up in the New Savior monastery and the peasants were complaining about the steward at that monastery. The bishop of Krutitsa complained that the peasants of the Transfiguration monastery in Belev were rebellious. They would not pay their quitrent. The monk who acted as steward was ducked under water. The chancellery at Belev strove to please them, yet the military governor of Belev,[48] because he had been bribed, released fourteen without punishment.

ADMINISTRATION OF CHURCH ESTATES

Naturally the idea had to be addressed of freeing the state from the sad necessity of curbing peasant uprisings and of freeing the monasteries from the obligation, unbecoming to them, of managing the peasants. Financial necessity also supported such an idea. Again on September 30, 1757 the empress ordered the Senate and the Synod to give some thought to the possibility of handing over the monastery landed estates to officials, and to introduce greater regularity into the assignment of revenue. An extract from the protocol of the Conference was sent to the Synod on this matter. A copy clerk of the Synod, Ivanov, gave a copy of this extract of the Conference to a synodal peasant Sumotchikov. He gave a copy to Davyd and Sidor Kononov, Ivan Dorofeev, Nikita Ivanov and Konon Petrov, peasants of the Trinity-St. Sergius monastery. The peasants let it be known that all monastery estates were about to be given to the sovereign. They were arrested as propagators of false information, and the College of Justice passed a stiff sentence, which the Senate commuted. The copy clerk was to be lashed and sent into the army, but he was not sent to the galleys as the College of Justice decreed. This was because Ivanov wrote a copy from the extract not because he was bribed, but because of his acquaintance, out of credulity. He simply did not know of Sumotchikov's intention to give it to the Trinity peasants. The peasants, Kononov and his colleagues, were not to be executed, because they were found not to have taken part in any fictitious affair or escapade, but acted on the copy given to them from an extract of the Conference, and because of Sumotchikov's verbal declaration which they, as simple and illiterate men, misunderstood. Because they did not inform their authorities about the copy, and led their fellows into disobedience, they and Sumotchikov were to be punished with lashes.

Serdiukov, overseer of the Vyshny Volochek canals, complained about coachmen who beat the tocsin and came to his house three times. A commission found that Serdiukov himself was guilty. He embittered the coachmen because he beat them with whips without authority. He should have sent them to the authorities. Therefore he was to pay a fine of one hundred rubles to the hospital. In Tambov, Shatsk, Kozlov and other districts uprisings continued among the peasants. Whole villages and families fled. Moreover they stole from the landowners. The matter did not end without bloody encounters. Those caught testified that they were going to the Akhtuba river and to Astrakhan to settle on crown vineyards and in silk mills, where Lieutenants Parobich and Tsypletev would accept them and take two or three rubles from each of them for this service. Up to three thousand had settled on the Akhtuba with their wives and children, and up to two thousand in Astrakhan. The governor of the Kalmyk khanate, Duduk-Dashi, sent a complaint against those who settled at the silk mills in Tsaritsyn. They were building a town and seriously hurting the feelings of the Kalmyks who had lived there for many years. They were stealing from them. The Lower Salt Bureau reported that the reception and harboring of escapees was being practiced by Shcherbakov, a clerk of the governor of Saratov's chancellery.

Peter Ivanovich Shuvalov thought that peasant uprisings could be prevented by observance of a few precautions. "The lack of faith of the peasant," he told the Senate, "entails such sad consequences in respect of the decrees sent to them! I will mention only two examples. We are compelled to seek means to preserve people from severe punishment and the spilling of blood, the more so as the peasants undergo such punishments not because of their ill-intentions so much as out of credulity. The first incident is related to the peasants of Demidov. This shameful event, in which blood was spilled, was as a consequence of the distrust of the peasants of a decree in the hands of the commander of a military detachment.

In the second incident the bureau of the potash management in Pochinki made a submission to the Senate that some of the local peasants, who regarded the written decrees of the Senate as false, directed the workers assigned to the mechanized ships being built to transport salt to request a printed decree. As this was not produced, three hundred and thirty-three of them, after beating the non-commissioned officer of the convoy, ran off to kill the judge and the land elder, the first for issuing the warrant to make them do such work, and the other for obeying this warrant. Rushing into Pochinki they beat the elder to death. In order to put down further unrest, they suffered severe punishment. Yet punishment cannot stave off similar harmful incidents indefinitely, especially when the solution is simple, that is to proclaim a printed instead of a handwritten decree, and the observance of a few other precautions. The Senate agreed.

DRAFTING A LAW CODE

Drafting the Code of Laws continued, although in the Senate's opinion it was proceeding slowly. The Senate asked the Commission for the Composition of the Code of Laws[49] to ensure that the remaining parts were completed as quickly as possible and that the members of the commission work full-time through the stipulated hours. The commission replied that it had decided to draw up the incomplete chapters of the third part immediately, and entrusted the supervision of the clerks and responsibility for the completion of the task to State Councillor Yushkov. Drafting of the fourth part was entrusted to Professor Schtrube, together with Senior Councillor Vikhliaev. Until these chapters were completed, the members of the commission were to meet every day to some purpose. On receiving this reply the Senate ordered the commission to make every effort until the remaining parts and chapters of the Code of Laws were completed, and to press its members unremittingly to this end.

COMMISSION ON FREE HOMESTEADERS

Yet another commission, on free homesteaders,[50] continued its work. Among the free homesteaders there were former house serfs and peasants. According to [land] boundary instructions they were placed in the same tax bracket as the free homesteaders, and were called free homesteader sharecroppers. The commission stated that, in its opinion these sharecroppers should be released from the jurisdiction of the provincial and military governors' chancelleries and placed under the free homesteaders' managers, except for criminal matters. The Senate agreed.

AFFAIRS IN UKRAINE

In southwest Ukraine, in Little Russia, the hetman, who did not know how to get away from Glukhov to St. Petersburg, stubbornly defended himself against every statute that applied generally throughout the empire as though it did not apply to him. At the start of the year he sent a complaint to the Senate that the Chief Magistracy had appointed two representatives of Little Russian merchants to Little Russian towns for verbal disputes between merchants. In Kiev, Nezhin, Romny and Borzna a public notary was appointed for the protest of promissory notes, even though he, the hetman, asked for this not to happen. An inquiry was carried out and it turned out that in 1754 items drafted in the Kiev government chancellery for the benefit of all the people were sent from there to the Senate for consideration. (1) There should be a court for Little and Great Russian merchants concerning promissory notes following the exchange rate regulations, and not as was done currently between them. For example, a Little Russian merchant borrows money and returns it according to its face value. If he does not return it within the allotted time, written proceedings take place in the Little Russian chancelleries which drag on, and the merchant who has loaned the money is forced to lose business or abandon the claim. (2) Merchants should be selected for a verbal court.

These items were sent by the Senate to the College of Foreign Affairs, the department in which matters relating to Little Russia were dealt with at the time, but the college sent them to the hetman with a request for his opinion. The hetman sent back his opinion that in Little Russia the administration of justice and the meting of punishment in all cases must be according to Little Russian law in Little Russian courts of justice. Therefore he requested exemption of all Little Russian citizens from the new institution. The Senate ordered that the new institution be abolished. The merchants and notary were to be removed from Little Russia.

Later the Senate was presented with the necessity of conducting verbal courts in Little Russia and it sent a document relating to this to the hetman. The irate hetman replied that a great deal of ignorance was being created hour by hour, as well as difficulty in the administration of Little Russian affairs. The cause was the imprecise interpretation of the decrees concerning the Little Russian people to which Hetman Bohdan Khmelnitsky acceded under All Russian rule. There were points of confusion between Khmelnitsky's clauses affirmed by the tsar, and points mentioned only in conversation between the boyars and envoys of the hetman, from which inconsistencies developed. The Senate was angry in turn and replied "the Senate cannot make out from the report sent by the hetman which ignorance and difficulties are being created for him in the administration of the affairs of Little Russia, and what imprecision there may be in the interpretation of the decrees concerning the Little Russian people. Moreover the hetman did not spell out in his report any explanation, neither did he refer to any specific case, with the exception of one matter, concerning verbal courts between merchants. It is pointless to relate one of these cases in isolation from all other Little Russian cases, or to consider it related to the difficulty of administration of Little Russian affairs and the imprecise interpretation of the decrees concerning the Little Russian people. All the decrees confirmed by her imperial majesty concerning the Little Russian people must be maintained in all matters without the slightest alteration in their application.

"The matter mentioned above relating to rescinding of decrees concerning the Little Russian people has not the slightest bearing upon the case. In particular it did not have anything to do with the difficulty in administration of Little Russian affairs. It related only to the verbal courts between merchants alone, who must comply with government commercial regulations through establishment along the borders of customs posts and the public commerce carried out through them, not only by Little Russian merchants but also by Great Russian and foreign merchants.

"When all the aforementioned points, both verbal and written, covered in the first place by the document sent to Hetman Bohdan Khmelnitsky, and in the second place by the verbal points written down and affirmed already by the signature of Peter the Great in 1722, as well as those of 1754 inserted into the report to her imperial majesty concerning induction, and confirmed by her signature, for that reason even the State Senate cannot consider these verbal points invalid, especially for the hetman. It is unnecessary to ask whether they are invalid and lack admissibility as the basis of law. Lastly there is no contradiction between the verbal and written points."

The hetman received yet another unpleasant document from the Senate, because it was difficult to fulfill the injunction it contained. The Senate ordered all those who fled Great Russia to Zaporozhia be returned to their places of origin as quickly as possible. In future they must not be accepted, under pain of a fine. The War College reported that three dragoons caught among the runaways gave evidence that they were living in Zaporozhia, and knew of other runaway regimental servicemen there.

Russian manufacturers in eastern Ukraine, not intimidated by the Bashkir revolt,[51] continued to develop natural resources. It was reported to the empress that Ivan Tverdyshev, the manager of copper and iron mills, with his colleague Ivan Miasnikov, was the first to look for minerals and build mills in empty, wild and distant places inside Bashkiria. In spite of intimidation from Bashkir agitation he earned a considerable profit for the government, surpassing all previous mill-managers, in particular in smelting copper. He had paid into the exchequer the money lost because the government mill at Tabyn was destroyed by the Bashkirs, and had constructed fortresses under the auspices of his mills for protection from the enemy. He furnished these with arms and powder and all this with his own funds. He did not ask for any additional registration of peasants, without whom none of the previous mill-managers could cope. For this the Senate recommended his promotion from the status of assessor to collegiate assessor.

III

RUSSIA DRIVES PRUSSIA TOWARDS PEACE, 1759

FERMOR RECALLED TO ST. PETERSBURG

The year began with military preparations. On January 12 the Conference sent a rescript to Fermor asking him to come to St. Petersburg as soon as possible "in order to hear our wishes more closely" the rescript stated, "and the better to present your plans." Major General Panin (Peter Ivanovich) asked for leave from the army to go to Moscow to arrange his domestic affairs. The empress wrote to Fermor that she was astonished by such a request "when his service is absolutely necessary and when he must demonstrate that he prefers his duty to us and the love of his fatherland." Fermor had to tell Panin in the name of the empress that permission was refused, and if anyone later wanted to make a similar request, he was to refuse it with a reprimand.

Manpower shortage forced Fermor to be instructed to invite Prussian citizens to enlist in the Russian army. Fermor wrote that Prussians scarcely would agree to serve on equal terms with the Russians. He received the following reply. "Even the slightest difference in pay to those accepted in this way, in contrast to what is paid to our citizens, is of course incompatible with our imperial maternal favor to our loyal citizens. We cannot therefore act on this matter in any other way." Fermor's request demonstrates that service in the Russian army could not in fact have been attractive to foreigners. "The generals, the staff and senior officers, who have been in the army abroad from the beginning of the present war, now have come to such a state of poverty that they are not only unable to conduct themselves according to their rank but they cannot even provide sufficiently for themselves. This is due to the distant campaigns, to their considerable expenses and to the fact that many were deprived of everything and others lost some their equipment in the battle of August 14 last. They suffer extreme want in everything, the subalterns in particular." Fermor requested that at least a third of the indemnity money available in Königsberg be given to the generals and officers over and above their salary. This request was granted.

St. Petersburg continued to be angry with Fermor because of his failure to send information. Lieutenant General Kostiurin[1] was sent to the army with a request that Fermor furnish the following information as soon as possible. (1) The current condition of the forces in all regiments and corps, "about whom to our particular astonishment," the rescript stated, "we never have reports." (2) The number of horses presently fit for service, as well as the number of draught horses. (3) The number of weapons lost in the last encounter, the number available in the regiments, the number in addition that need to be sent from Russia. (4) About uniforms. (5) The briefest account of money in hand. (6) The briefest account of stores. (7) A schedule of promotions to positions vacated by the fallen, which has been requested many times. (8) Information as to who and how many are absent. (9) Information about all supply depots and troops with them, about whom the most astonishing rumors are circulating, namely that they are suffering considerable want, not receiving any pay. (10) The number of Prussian prisoners, and where they are held. "This information we await with impatience," stated the rescript.

On his return to the army from St. Petersburg Fermor was instructed in March to make a great effort to bring the army up to strength and furnish it with supplies. An interesting observation was made. "It has come to our attention that your troops, in quarters in Prussia, have none of those benefits which Prussian forces usually enjoy in quarters. We have indeed recommended that you maintain the strictest discipline and do not tolerate the local inhabitants being subject to offense or ruin. At the same time we have no doubt that our forces in a conquered land naturally should have the same benefits as Prussians enjoy. For once it becomes the norm the inhabitants cannot consider it a burden. To this end we command you always, whenever our forces are quartered on enemy soil or are stationed in a garrison, to act exactly in the same way as the Prussian forces do."

Once more there were reprimands because no precise information was sent. For example a rescript of March 11 stated, "From the information you have submitted in respect to the number of weapons we observe with much regret that a great many are lacking, especially through losses in battle. You do not explain, however, this deficiency in terms of men available. As we are afraid that the weapons will not be sufficient for the number of men available, we order you at once to send a precise and clear report of just how short you are of weapons and other items of munitions, that we may, on the basis of that information, take appropriate measures."

Korff,[2] governor of Königsberg, was obliged to find everything necessary, especially stores, forage and carts for separate detachments of the army. Korff wrote to St. Petersburg that despite his own reminders not one of the commanding generals with the divisions or brigades gave him any information, either about the movements of regiments, or of the place where they were to be billeted, so that in the end he did not know where to send what.

PLAN OF CAMPAIGN

The plan of campaign, drawn up in Fermor's presence in St. Petersburg, was that the Russian army, that is the regiments with two battalions, be ready to march well before the end of April (Old Style). Although it was difficult to expect good feed in the country at the beginning of May, the army nevertheless must leave its winter quarters and move towards Poznan, where in mid-May or towards the twentieth there must be a significant force, certainly not less than sixty thousand, and including officers, the artillery, engineers and cossacks, not less than ninety thousand. This army must not take with it a single sick or weak soldier, all of whom must remain in the vicinity of the Vistula to protect the supply depots and for their own convalescence, so that by the middle of the year an army of up to forty thousand gradually could be assembled there. From Poznan the army was to go directly towards the frontiers of Saxony as far as the Oder. No matter where the army of the empress-queen might be, the advance of a Russian army into Silesia must strike the king of Prussia where it hurt most.

Fermor left winter quarters and crossed the Vistula on April 20 but reached Poznan only on June 10. News was received on June 16 of the advance of Prussian forces into Polish territory, and on June 19 Fermor handed over his command of the army.

REMARKS TO FERMOR FROM THE CONFERENCE

Even on his return from St. Petersburg the unpleasant discussions between himself and the Conference, opinions and requests sent in the form of rescripts from the empress continued unabated. The Conference could not understand from the reports of the commander-in-chief why he was gathering such large reserves of stores, and on what such vast sums of money were spent. "You gave orders," stated one rescript to Fermor, "to lay in seventy thousand quarters of grain in Poznan. This quantity exceeds what was considered here in St. Petersburg, with your agreement, enough for the whole campaign. Why are yet more vast reserves being gathered on the Vistula, when grain is coming by sea from Russia? We cannot see from the information you have sent by what contract, and for what supplies, you needed to pay the Jew Baruch fifty-six thousand rubles. From what we have seen so far, the entire purchase is being made on single contracts, but we cannot understand why yet more contract grain had to be transported. When we looked further at the information you sent we became even more perplexed. Once again you are counting on at least six hundred thousand rubles for advances through contracts for grain purchased and prepared in advance, and for its transportation from Königsberg and Pillau by water. We cannot see for what grain and for what quantity such a vast sum is to be appropriated. It turns out that just for a single transport of our grain across enemy territory we must pay twelve hundred. It turns out that we have received East Prussia at the expense of the exhaustion of our Treasury and for the enrichment of the Prussians!

"We give the following instructions. You are not to make any new preparations on the Vistula or purchases of supplies. You are to rely firmly upon supplies being brought from Russia, and then make such dispositions that import of grain received from Russia is not ruinous to the Prussian inhabitants and not very burdensome to us. It is evident from our information that on January 27 you had 1,312,863 rubles on hand, and now only 276,281 rubles remain, even including what was brought from Königsberg. After supplies have been acquired, surely such funds should be spent on purchase of horses and regimental replacements. Yet it turns out that most of the money has been used in payments to Königsberg merchants and to goodness knows whom else for contracted supplies to the tune of 453,305 rubles. If during your stay on enemy soil, in spite of the grain transported from Russia, provisions are becoming so expensive and if, on the contrary, by our calculations the whole present campaign and passage through neutral territory should be so inexpensive, we cannot but demand an explanation. We would also like to know how almost four million was used last year in the administration of supplies alone. In 1757 only a little over two million was used despite the fact that the army was almost twice the size, was situated almost always on neutral territory, and significant expenses were involved in bringing cavalry and light horse from Ukraine across the whole of Poland and for preparation of supply depots, from which even now we see a significant surplus."

The commander-in-chief justified himself by saying that he did not reckon on the grain transported from Russia because it would arrive in Pillau in June and July, and then must be loaded on ships going by way of the Frisches Haff. At Elbing it must be reloaded into flat-bottomed vessels, which had to go against the current. Therefore despite all efforts to create supply depots on the Vistula, especially at Thorn, it would be impossible to fill them quickly, as grain would not arrive at Thorn in less than six weeks. Besides, the price of grain on the Vistula in April was so low that, even with transport to the supply depots, it worked out cheaper than a St. Petersburg contract, if purchase in April and May was not let slip for lack of ready money. Out of the four million rubles the greatest sums were used in St. Petersburg and Riga by the chief of the Commissary on organization of the third battalions and sending various supplies for the army.

SALTYKOV'S APPOINTMENT AS COMMANDER-IN-CHIEF

Even before these explanations were received on May 8 a rescript was sent to Fermor. "In seeing fit to send our General Count Saltykov (Peter Semeonovich)[3] to our army abroad, at present under your command, we wanted to make it clear by this [rescript] that, as the count has seniority over you, he is required naturally to take senior command over all the army. Therefore you are to hand over [the command] to him. In these circumstances we are firmly convinced that you will endeavor to continue your service no less assiduously and, in particular, that you will give all necessary information to General Count Saltykov, and that you will endeavor to assist him with every service and advice in all things." "Seeing the gracious continuation of maternal favors and the trust of your imperial majesty in your humble servant," Fermor replied, "I do not only not take this as an insult but, prostrating myself at your feet, offer you my humble thanks."

The members of the Campaign Supply Chancellery set up by Fermor were Major General Dits, Brigadier Khomutov and Colonel Maslov. Dits and Khomutov now were dismissed and the management of the chancellery given to Lieutenant General Prince Alexander Menshikov under whom, of the previous members, Colonel Maslov remained. Menshikov was told that the army always had on hand provisions for one month. Being on enemy territory, it must receive supplies from local sources through use of written orders to cover rations for individuals or for periods of time, and war indemnities. Should this prove insufficient, supplies could be purchased in neighboring Poland at above the customary price by a ruble or up to two rubles on condition that the sellers deliver the grain. The soldiers must not find it difficult to bake bread and dry rusks on the march. For this reason when routes have been selected and knowledge about the places and villages that lie upon the road assembled, courier officers should be sent ahead to those places with written orders stating by what date so much bread must be baked by the residents, so that the soldiers not only receive prepared bread but also take baked bread with them to the next place.

The replacement of Fermor was unexpected. Also unexpected was the appointment of his successor. For some reason Fermor had a reputation in the art of war. Peter Semeonovich Saltykov had no such reputation. He could not have been welcome to the new government because of his kinship ties with Empress Anna and the regent Anna Leopoldovna,[4] and for that reason was posted far from St. Petersburg in command of the regiments of the Ukrainian provincial militia. Both foreigners and Russians spoke of him in the same terms, that he was an extremely kind, well-mannered, affectionate man, but a simple soldier who never had commanded an army in the field. This is the impression made by Saltykov in Königsberg and noted by an eye-witness. "This gray-haired old man, not very tall, rather simple, in the white caftan of the local militia, without decorations and without anything to make him splendid, walked about the streets and never had in his retinue more than two or three men. Used to splendor and magnificence in their commanders, he seemed strange and surprising to us, and we did not understand how this simple little old man, not significant in any way as far as we could see, could be the commander-in-chief of such a great army, and could be its leader against a king who astonished all Europe by his courage, swiftness and knowledge of the art of war. He seemed an absolute lamb to us and no one thought for one moment that he would be capable of doing anything of significance."

BATTLES OF PALZIG AND KUNERSDORF

On his arrival at the army in Poznan the new commander-in-chief called a council of war at which it was agreed to seek out the enemy, to expel him from Poland and to make for the Oder. This decision was carried out and Russian light horse skirmished with the Prussians. Letters were sent to Saltykov from St. Petersburg expressing pleasure at his courageous and commendable plans. The Prussian army was under the command of General Wedell,[5] who had the task of preventing the Russian army from joining up with the Austrian corps of General Loudon.[6]

On July 12 the Russian army met the Prussian near the villages of Palzig and Kay, not far from the Oder, on the Brandenburg frontier. "The enemy," as Saltykov's report relates, "suddenly turning its left flank, rushed upon our right, and a cannon bombardment began in a most brutal manner, continuing without pause for more than an hour. In the meantime the enemy, closing to its usual range, fired his small arms and attacked the right flank most courageously, but met such bravery and fortitude that he was beaten back in very strong fire from both sides. Having, from his point of view, convenient copses in a number of places, and replacing his forces with new men, the enemy once again made extremely vigorous assaults. In this way he made thrice-repeated attacks of the right flank. They tried, always with equal bravery and courage, by a series of defensive cavalry attacks to burst through between the Siberian and Perm regiments, which already had suffered very greatly. These regiments did not yield an inch from their positions, and the enemy, having made their way to the second line in the gaps made by the dead and the wounded, immediately was driven back by Lieutenant General Thémicoud[7] with the cuirassier regiments Heir Apparent and Kiev, which stood between the lines in reserve, and that gap was filled by the Nizovsky Infantry Regiment.

"A few squadrons, separating off from the enemy cavalry, rushed upon the First Grenadier Regiment but were repulsed and driven off by artillery. The enemy, without achieving any success by their thrice-repeated malicious attacks on the right flank, rushed towards the left flank, where twice they attacked in an equally most desperate manner, and part of the enemy cavalry marched towards the village of Nickern, hoping to pass through it to burst upon the left flank.

"Major General Todtleben,[8] hearing a heavy cannon bombardment, came from the transports in the rear to the army in the field and remained upon the left flank. Seeing the enemy's intention, he set fire to the village and so foiled their plan. Forestalling the enemy this way, making the most devastating use of newly invented armaments of various types and of Shuvalov's howitzers, by the dexterity and bravery of all the artillery their troops were put completely to flight. Our light horse pursued him but, with night quickly falling, they were prevented from achieving their expected success.

"So, after a most intense five-hour battle, the proud enemy was completely defeated, driven off and vanquished. I cannot describe sufficiently the fervor, bravery and courage of the entire general staff and the intrepid army, in particular its discipline. In a word this praiseworthy and unparalleled action of all our forces astonished all the foreign volunteers. On our side Lieutenant General Thémicoud, two staff officers, two captains, eleven subaltern officers and 878 lower ranks were killed. One lieutenant general, one brigadier, four colonels, four lieutenant colonels, six majors, thirty-six cavalry captains and other captains, 101 subaltern officers and 3,744 lower ranks were wounded. Of the enemy, 4,228 bodies were buried, 605 were taken into captivity, amongst their number being one colonel and fifteen senior officers, but the greater part of these were wounded. There were 1,406 deserters. Fourteen cannon were taken, four flags and three standards. The weapons collected on the field of battle numbered 2,222." "This victory," said a contemporary, "brought about, of itself, a great number and variety of consequences, of which several were particularly advantageous to us. By far the most significant was that all our forces took heart from the enemy's defeat and began to have more confidence in the little old man who was their leader, who had the good fortune from the very beginning of his arrival to capture the affections of the soldiers. Now they loved him even more, and he was held in the greatest respect by all of us."[9]

On July 16 Saltykov and the army moved towards Crossen and on the eighteenth he wrote to the empress, "Everything is going well in the army. Only the transport wagons are in need of repair and the draught and artillery horses are scarcely able to move. Prince Menshikov, being resident in Poznan, is very slow in the delivery of supplies and simply wastes time in unnecessary correspondence, not wishing to subordinate himself to my command. When he comes to join the army with his commissary administration he will be able to carry out the commission entrusted to him more successfully than by staying in Poznan, because then he will understand all the circumstances. He will simply direct his subordinates to carry out their orders, the more so as supplies already will have been put in hand in Poznan before his arrival here."

On the arrival of the Russian army in the vicinity of Crossen the following day, the eighteenth, Saltykov received a letter from the Austrian general Loudon from Rothenburg sent on the seventeenth (Old Style). Loudon wrote that he had been sent with twenty thousand men to the Oder by his commander-in-chief Count Daun, and would march together with the Russian army. He would leave Rothenburg on the nineteenth and in four days' march arrive at the Oder. On the twenty-first Saltykov set out with the army, and in the village of Karchen received a letter from the Austrian general Hadik that the king of Prussia had left Sagan and was proceeding fast. He would arrive that night at Bobergsberg, only one mile distant from Crossen. Therefore Hadik begged Saltykov to lay pontoons across the Oder opposite Fürstenberg so that the Austrians could send their infantry across while the cavalry, thanks to the drought, could ford the river. Saltykov replied that the bridges would be put in place during the night, and that the Austrians could cross on the night of the twenty-second. When the Russian army arrived at the village of Auer, however, Loudon came to meet Saltykov with a large retinue and declared that Frederick II with all his troops had gone back against Count Daun, and that General Hadik had turned to join him. Loudon, with twenty thousand troops, would stay where he was, because it would be very difficult to join Count Daun's army.

After giving this information Loudon, on behalf of Daun, demanded that Saltykov send thirty thousand infantry to assist Count Daun. "Without specific orders," Saltykov replied, "I cannot fulfill your request, because nothing was said about this in the operational plan already agreed. Both imperial armies have been directed to join on the Oder and attack the enemy with their combined forces. Besides, the horses are in such poor condition that without rest we cannot set out upon the march." Then Loudon asked whether he might receive provisions and forage. He then went on to say that Count Daun had instructed him to take a million thalers of indemnity from Frankfurt and divide this money equally with the Russian army. "We have insufficient provisions and forage," replied Saltykov to this request, "and the city of Frankfurt was taken by the Russian army alone. Consequently I can share with you neither the one nor the other." With this the conversation came to an end.

On July 23 Saltykov arrived in Frankfurt. He was met with the keys by General Villebois who had occupied that city, and who declared that an Austrian corps was situated in camp half a mile away. After this an Austrian officer appeared with a request that his colleagues be given permission to enter the city to purchase necessary materials, and also requested ninety thousand rations for three days. Saltykov replied that he should come again the following day and report to him the number and condition of the Austrian force. About the other matter, he must present his request in written form. "I intend," wrote Saltykov to the empress, "to send Lieutenant General Rumiantsev to Berlin to take a monetary indemnity, horses, oxen and provisions, as our horse and oxen have arrived in a state of extreme exhaustion owing to the heat and sandy roads. A large proportion of the transports need repair, and we cannot neglect the repair of the artillery after the battle. Provisions in the army have become severely depleted, and Prince Menshikov has not sent any. Therefore I am obliged, becoming firmly established in this favorable camp, to make good our necessities and wait to hear what success Count Daun has over the enemy so that later, having put our deficiencies to rights and having rested the army, I can take appropriate measures to prosecute further military operations. At this moment I do not dare to set out on a long campaign lest I expose your majesty's armies to any unpleasant consequences, or cloud the reputation achieved by the victorious arms of your imperial majesty."

In St. Petersburg the College of Foreign Affairs was instructed to send the following communiqué to Count Esterhazy. "The principal content of the operational plan consists in the fact that there should be decisive operations in Silesia, and to that end that both armies must approach the Oder. Therefore we have given instructions to our general to cross the Oder should our army arrive there sooner. By crossing the Oder it may facilitate the junction of the two armies. Moreover we have given instructions that if Count Daun is not in a position to approach either Carolath or Crossen, and the king of Prussia has cut any communication, he should make a strong diversion against the enemy and hold more firmly to those positions where in favorable circumstances perhaps he can join up with Count Daun.

"As proof of the sincerity of our intentions, these resolutions were communicated to Count Esterhazy in a note of June 19, and we did not doubt that knowledge of them would serve as an inducement to Count Daun to fulfill the agreed plan with the same zeal as that with which we have carried it out. Extremely unfortunately for the common cause it has turned out quite the opposite. Hardly did Count Daun learn that the Prussian army had entered Poland and was approaching Poznan than he immediately doubted that the plan would be adhered to on the Russian side. He let it be known that although he was ready to march against the king of Prussia this news stopped him, when it should have impelled him to occupy the king of Prussia's attention so that our army in Poland might have less delays and the more swiftly reach the Oder. When our army overcame all obstacles in Poland it drove out the enemy's army, finally defeated it, and arrived at the appointed time at the Oder. In this way we did enough to keep the king of Prussia occupied, leaving Count Daun's hands free to turn towards our army with almost all his forces. Then Count Daun, instead of immediately supporting our operations, evidently considered the opportunity arrived for our army to implement the order given it to join up with him. He sent Count Loudon with the suggestion that our army, abandoning its transports, send him thirty thousand infantrymen for support at the very time when, according to the information of Generals Hadik and Loudon, the king of Prussia was marching with the utmost speed to attack our army."

A rescript was sent to Saltykov together with a copy of this note. "You have made such a fine and sensible decision to remain in the advantageous position at Frankfurt, to give our forces a respite, to coordinate the transport teams, to gather everything necessary for our army from enemy territory and at the same time to be in readiness to take on the enemy courageously, that in justice it would have been impossible to think of anything better. The agreed plan has been more than fulfilled because you left Poznan at the appointed time in spite of the fact that an army, of such strength as it was impossible to foresee when drawing up the plan, arrived in the area to drive you from that position. You arrived at the Oder within the prescribed time, first defeating an enemy army. By doing so you forced the king of Prussia to turn almost all his forces against you while leaving Count Daun's hands free.

"You could do one more thing. Perhaps you could join up with the Austrian army, and together completely rout the king of Prussia, as the note given to Esterhazy in June has been interpreted in this way in the Austrian camp. In this note it did not say that in the meantime there was nothing for the Austrian army to do. Nevertheless let us explain our ideas to you. If Count Daun advances closer to you or does something substantial and useful, perhaps by your good offices you can speed up a resolution of the matter and increase the advantages already gained. Our army in the meantime will not be exposed to any unnecessary and apparent danger. Naturally you will not let the occasion go by to make even more significant our service to a Europe suffering from war, our goodwill more important and our friendship more binding on our allies. Although their present conduct exposes their great selfishness and insincerity towards us, we nevertheless would lay ourselves open to reproach if, by repaying this prematurely, we lose a favorable opportunity to end the war.

"If the matter between Count Daun and the king of Prussia remains undecided, or if the king of Prussia gains certain advantages over him, you must see to it that our army is not exposed to any danger. If indeed the king of Prussia turns upon Count Daun, you must act with extreme caution, remembering that Count Daun is a past master at choosing impregnable positions, and the king of Prussia is extraordinarily adroit at making swift marches. You must act very cautiously, even if the king of Prussia has not put a large force against us. In the event of a crossing of the Oder, you must not be more than three days' march from it. If the king of Prussia put a small corps against you, it would be correct for you to attack and defeat it, but having defeated it you must once more return to this side of the river.

"In the event that the king of Prussia, while turning on Count Daun, leaves a significant force against you, try above all to preserve the advantages already gained. However much Count Daun solicits you to render him assistance or the strongest action from our side, you may reply to him directly that since you have to fulfill the plan to the letter, you must let no difficulties stand in the way. Now, having against you a distinguished army, you cannot bring yourself to give battle, for if you win it is too late to exploit it, but if you lose, you have lost everything. You cannot imagine how pleased we are with everything that you have done to date, in particular your firmness in reply to the absurd requests of the Austrians."

"The king of Prussia is extraordinarily adroit in making swift marches," the rescript said, and Frederick II hastened to justify this opinion of the

St. Petersburg Conference. The "immanent" king decided not to let the enemy armies come together, and to that end he had to attack the Russian forces and defeat them. The battle of Zorndorf gave him the hope of carrying this off with complete success. He hoped *to destroy* the Russian forces. On August 1 he attacked Saltykov, having positioned his forces on the hills near the village of Kunersdorf. In his reports the Russian commander-in-chief described the battle the following way.

"The Russian army took up a position on high ground, its right flank reaching almost to the Oder and the left beyond the village of Kunersdorf to the point where the high ground and the forest come to an end and where, across a small stream, the ploughed fields and meadows begin. The right flank was made up of the first division under the command of General Fermor and the regiments of the advance guard corps under the command of Lieutenant General Villebois. The second division, under the command of Lieutenant General Count Rumiantsev, made up the center of the army, while on the left flank was placed a newly formed corps under the command of Lieutenant General Prince Golitsyn. The Austrian corps under the command of Lieutenant General Count Loudon was placed behind the right flank. At three in the morning the enemy began to march and, going around to the left, moved solidly towards the right flank and gave the appearance, through ceaseless maneuvers, of being ready to attack the army of your imperial majesty from all sides. At nine in the morning it was evident that he was placing two large batteries on a hill opposite the left flank, under cover of which some cavalry and infantry were brought into a depression near the left flank. At ten the enemy approached the forest and began to draw up into battle order, its left flank before the right flank of our army.

"Perceiving that he was preparing to attack our right flank which because of its situation did not have as strong a defensive position as our left, and in order to hinder him in his intentions, I ordered Count Todtleben to set fire to a large bridge across the marsh. Seeing his way cut off in this manner and the crossing made difficult the enemy, except for a small part of the cavalry, which at a leisurely pace followed after it, suddenly and completely turned on our left flank. So at half past eleven, under heavy cannon fire on the left flank, he rushed upon the flank and took the offensive. The Prussian regiments, which in the meantime were stationed in the depression, advanced just after midday and approached under the guns of our batteries. Suddenly from the flank they directed an attack in columns on the grenadier regiment of the recently formed corps. Although they were met from our side in a forceful manner, nevertheless because the opposition was short-lived, the enemy, increasing in numbers, with renewed energy dislodged the grenadier regiment from its position.

"At this time the commander of this corps, Lieutenant General Golitsyn, immediately ordered the Third and Fifth Musketeer regiments of the same corps to form a new line, and later also committed the Fourth and the First. The enemy, reinvigorated with fresh regiments, brought them down and took possession of two batteries. Moreover, having created a column from his entire army, he poured with all its strength through your majesty's army, fighting his way to the river itself. He left the first line on his left and, advancing in this way, delivered very heavy fire from all his batteries with bombs and shot from two hundred cannon, so that there was scarcely anywhere that the cannon could not cause harm. Because of this, a great many of our boxes of cartridges were blown up and the gun carriages of our cannon were damaged.

"No sooner did I catch sight of the enemy success and such an energetic rush towards the river than I immediately ordered Lieutenant General Panin to support the waverers with new regiments. He brought up for reinforcements the Second Grenadier Regiment from the second line under Count Bruce, and the Austrian lieutenant general Count Campitelli brought up the companies of the German Grenadier regiments. Later he added to them the Belozersk and Nizhny Novgorod regiments under General Panin. It was impossible to place more than two regiments between the defence works in the direction in which the main enemy thrust was proceeding. Behind them the St. Petersburg and Novgorod regiments were brought up as well, having endured the most severe fire, and stopped the enemy's progress a little. The Austrian grenadier companies of the same corps were reinforced by the Loudon and Baden-Baden regiments which were in the vicinity.

"At that very moment the enemy cavalry entered the defence works but were turned back and driven off by our forces under the leadership of Lieutenant General Count Rumiantsev and the Austrians under the command of Lieutenant General Baron Loudon. After that Lieutenant General Prince Lubomirski with the Pskov, Apsheron and Vologda regiments and Major General Prince Volkonsky with the First Grenadier and the Azov regiments threw even the enemy infantry into confusion. In order to set this to rights the enemy made an attempt to pass its column behind our second line to cut off the regiments reinforcing their colleagues. Major General Berg with Brigadier Derfeld, who were at that moment going to reinforce their colleagues with the Siberian regiment of the first division of the second line and a battalion of the Nizovsky regiment under their command, were placed against the enemy column. The enemy, who met with a cannonade from 'unicorns,' from Shuvalov howitzers and from a battery of the Austrian regiments placed upon a hillock, were destroyed and scattered.

"Victory was still very much in doubt until five in the afternoon. Then the Voronezh and Narva regiments of the advance guard were brought up by Lieutenant General Villebois and Major General Prince Dolgoruky. At once behind them appeared the Second Moscow Regiment, one company of the Nizovsky and the Kazan regiment with Major General Berg, who struck the enemy flank with the Second Moscow and, joining up with Lieutenant General Villebois, dislodged the enemy already beginning to withdraw from the defence works. They liberated our batteries, on which several cannon already were spiked by the enemy. They even saw them off as far as the depression. There, following the king's command, Lieutenant Colonel of the Life Cuirassiers von Biderbe attacked the Moscow and Narva regiments with two squadrons, only to be defeated by the Chuguev Cossacks. The lieutenant colonel was wounded and taken prisoner.

"Then the enemy army totally took to flight. Lieutenant General Loudon with his own and with our cavalry, and Brigadier Stoianov with his regiment from the left and Major General Todtleben with the other light horse from the right began to pursue the enemy. Thus this terrible and bloody battle, which began at half past eleven and continued without pause until seven, ended with the defeat and expulsion of the enemy." The Russians lost 2,614 dead and 10,863 wounded. Of the enemy, 7,627 bodies were buried on the spot, 4,542 were taken prisoner and there were 2,055 deserters. Loudon's Austrian corps lost 893 dead, with 1,398 wounded. The victors took twenty-eight standards and 172 cannon.

FREDERICK II'S DESPERATE POSITION

Frederick II intended to destroy the Russian forces, and at the moment of success on the left flank sent a messenger to Berlin with news of victory. Yet Frederick II barely was saved from death or capture, and was beholden for his salvation to Captain Prittwitz, who with forty hussars managed to lead him away unharmed from the battlefield. Frederick informed Count Finckenstein[10] about the state of his affairs in these words. "Our losses are very significant. From an army of 48,000 men I do not have even three thousand at this moment. They are simply running away and

I no longer have control of the military forces. They would do well in Berlin if they looked to their own security. It is a terrible misfortune. I shall not survive it. The consequences of the battle will be worse than the battle itself. I no longer have any resources and, to tell you the truth, I believe that everything is lost. I shall not survive the ruin of my fatherland. Farewell."

During the period of time of his severe illness Frederick gave command of the forces to General Finck with the instruction that, as the unfortunate army was in no condition to do battle with the Russians, it should at least attack Loudon if he moved on Berlin.

When Elizabeth received news at Peterhof of this "most glorious" victory gained over the king of Prussia himself she hurried to St. Petersburg, where a service was conducted in the chapel of the Winter Palace to a salute from all the cannon around the fortress and the Admiralty. Saltykov was promoted to the rank of field marshal. Fermor and Browne were given property in Lifland. Prince Golitsyn was promoted to full general, Volkonsky to lieutenant general. The other lieutenant generals, including Rumiantsev, received the Order of Alexander Nevsky. Panin and Loudon were given swords decorated with diamonds. Maria Theresa sent Saltykov a diamond ring, a snuff-box studded with diamonds, and five thousand chervontsy. Count Rumiantsev was given two thousand, Villebois the same amount, Panin fifteen hundred and Quartermaster General Stoffel one thousand. On August 5 the Russian army crossed the Oder by two bridges constructed near Frankfurt.

ALLIED INACTIVITY

On August 11 Saltykov rode into the town of Guben for a meeting with Count Daun. The Austrian field marshal began the conversation by saying that the Russian army should now take a rest, and the Austrian should set to work. Therefore the Russian army should remain for some time in the vicinity of Frankfurt and later march into Silesia with the Austrian army. Saltykov agreed to remain near Frankfurt for about two weeks or ten days, depending upon how long the forage held out. Soon there was a shortage of forage, and Saltykov sent to Daun to tell him that he must move to Müllrose and from there on towards Guben to obtain supplies and forage from the Austrian supply depot situated there. In the meantime would it not please Count Daun to attack the defeated king of Prussia with their united forces?

On arrival at Rogenwald, about three versts from Müllrose, Saltykov sent once more to Daun with the same suggestion, adding that should the Russo-Austrian army defeat the king of Prussia it could go anywhere it wanted, to Berlin, into Saxony or into Silesia to attack Prince Henry, and so hasten the end of the war. Saltykov went on to point out that, abandoning Frankfurt and not finding forage near Müllrose, he would have to move on to Lieberose, and at such a distance from the Oder he would lose communication with East Prussia, Poznan and the Vistula. Saltykov indeed moved towards Lieberose and set up camp in the vicinity when he received news that Frederick II, having recovered his spirits and gathered his forces, had left Fürstenwalde and positioned himself on the other side of the Spree river, compelling the Austrian advance posts to cross to this side of the river. On the other hand news was received from the Austrian general from Guben that the enemy was in Sorau. From this Saltykov understood that the enemy wanted to attack the Russians from two directions, the king himself from one side and Prince Henry from the other. Therefore he sent to ask Daun what measures he was taking.

Saltykov was in considerable anxiety over the fact that Daun, as was clearly evident, did not want to give battle to Prince Henry. On August 20 the Austrian general Hadik, finding himself near the Russian forces with his detachment, gave Saltykov to understand that the enemy marching near his camp was exchanging fire with his men. Saltykov immediately rode there with his general staff and found the enemy marching under the escort of its cavalry. The Russian and Austrian hussars, with the Chuguev Cossacks, harried the enemy until sunset, but things did not reach a significant stage. The next day, after two in the morning, Daun sent word to Saltykov that if the king of Prussia turned into Saxony, the Russian army should move towards Lieben[11] in order to prevent him from entering Saxony for six or seven days. During this period Daun would go to meet Prince Henry and give him battle, preventing him from joining up with the king. Saltykov replied that he would not go after the king towards Lieben, as, being too far distant from the Oder, he did not want to expose his army to the danger of being cut off from communication with Poznan, whence not only supplies were expected but also a significant sum of money, several regiments, horses and artillery. Should the king of Prussia march to Cottbus the Russian forces would try to prevent him from joining Prince Henry.

On the twenty-fifth General Bukkow came to Saltykov from Daun once more with a request for the Russian army to move towards Peitz to prevent the king sending his troops into Saxony. Saltykov replied, as previously, that he would not march towards Peitz, lest he lose communications with Poland and East Prussia. "The enemy," Saltykov continued, "already has taken up positions near Peitz. Do you really expect me to attack him and drive him out of there? I do not want to venture the hazard, as the army entrusted to me has held the enemy sufficiently in check, suffering a good deal in the process. We should now be given some respite, and it is for you to do the work. You have let almost all the summer pass to no purpose." "Yes," Bukkow replied, "thanks to you our hands have been tied for three months," giving Saltykov to understand that the Russian army had acted very slowly. "It is true," retorted Saltykov. "We can be reproached for the fact that we drove the enemy out of Poland, defeated him and arrived at the Oder according to plan. Passing over the second defeat of the enemy, we have done so much by ourselves that all the impartial world is duty bound to sing our praises. I will not expatiate upon this further but, returning to the main subject, will tell you that I cannot stay here for long. There is no food for the horses. I will remain as long as I can, then I will march towards Guben and take up a position between the Neisse and Bober rivers, where there is still some forage."

In the meantime on August 18 a decree was written in the Conference to Saltykov. He should suggest to Count Daun that he remove Prince Henry from the center of present operations and reduce him to inactivity. He had a number of ways of doing so. Having drawn Prince Henry off into Upper Silesia and keeping him there with the corps of General Harsch, Count Daun himself could cut Silesia off from Lusatia, could take possession first of all of Liegnitz and Glogau, and then could try to take Schweidnitz as well. In this way he would cut Prince Henry off from the king for good and all, and confine him to Upper Silesia. He should suggest to Daun that in that case he, Count Saltykov, together with the corps of Generals Hadik and Loudon, would attack the king in Brandenburg in order to cut him off in that province exactly as Prince Henry would be cut off in Silesia. Should Count Daun manage to complete all this, Count Saltykov would of course take up winter quarters there. With Glogau as a center and with Crossen in front or on the right flank, he should take up a position between the Oder and Bober rivers. Should Count Daun not fulfill these tasks, all the advantages received from the victory would slip through their fingers.

"Although," the decree continued, "we may be able to assemble an army twice the size for a future campaign and be victors twice over, all these victories would merely serve the destruction of the human race and prolong the war. Our army, after these victories at such a distance from their borders and supply depots, cannot gain a firm foothold in enemy territory unaided. General Daun, in all justice, must at least prepare comfortable and safe quarters. However disappointing it may be to Count Saltykov not to be able to take advantage of these gains and not to extend his victories, or to stop operations at such a time when it remains simply a matter of bringing the war to an end or at least of laying a firm foundation for doing so, he will have to retreat to locations where the army can find the necessary repose after such labors."

On September 3 Saltykov sent Lieutenant General Count Rumiantsev to Count Daun to tell him that the Russian army was suffering an extreme lack of fodder for the horses. Therefore it was leaving Lieberose for Sommerfeld, Christianstadt and Freistadt by way of Guben, keeping close to the Oder river and Glogau. The hope was that in these districts, where there were not yet considerable numbers of troops, they would find some fodder. As, in accordance with the empress's will, they were to take up winter quarters in Silesia and the army could not be stationed on enemy territory because they had not taken possession of a single fortress, he begged the Austrian field marshal for an auxiliary corps of ten to twelve thousand men and siege artillery, together with reassurances that there would be no shortage of supplies and fodder. Rumiantsev returned with the promise that all these requests would be met, and this found Saltykov already near Guben. An auxiliary corps did indeed arrive. When the Russian army approached Christianstadt, instead of a promised twenty thousand centners of flour only six hundred centners were discovered in the town magazine. At this time news was received that Frederick II was moving to join Prince Henry. Count Daun, instead preventing this union from taking place or, once it had taken place, of pursuing the Prussian army in order to place it between two fires, decided to move towards the Elbe in Saxony. Seeing that with this removal of the Austrian army there was no possibility of gaining tranquil winter quarters in Silesia, Saltykov decided to cross the Oder.

It turned out that king Frederick II did not join up with Prince Henry. Daun did not march into Saxony, but pursued Prince Henry. In spite of this Saltykov reported that the season was well advanced and it would be difficult to take the fortress of Glogau, as there were calculated to be up to thirty thousand men in the enemy army; therefore Saltykov should cross the Oder. If Loudon also crossed with him he would remain in Silesia until October 4, but should Loudon move away from the Russian army Saltykov would move towards the Vistula a little sooner.

CONFERENCE'S REMARKS TO SALTYKOV

Later, on September 28, the following rescript to Saltykov was composed in the Conference. "As your army is greatly superior in number to the king's, even without the auxiliary Austrian corps, we shall not hide from you the fact that we did not expect the decision you have taken. It is true that you have an important reason, a lack of grain, but we cannot but notice that even this justification is becoming very weak. This pretext was put forward immediately after the engagement at Frankfurt, to keep our army from action. Yet it then remained in that district for more than a month. It is true that Loudon took it upon himself to supply our army with sustenance, but did not do so. You should at least have considered whether there was the time and means to effect that responsibility. You should not have demanded that what was agreed today should be carried out without fail tomorrow. In that way it is easy to arouse the suspicion that you simply are looking for any pretext. We have told you repeatedly that we want to surpass our allies in sincerity and to convince them of our good intentions, even though they have been somewhat at fault in that respect to us. The grounds for suspicion may increase, for when Loudon received six hundred thousand imperial gulden and wanted to send them to Poland for the purchase of supplies, merely requesting from you permission to give orders for several regiments to go there, you very tersely refused him this request. Equally tersely you notified Count Daun that he would, of course, be in a difficult position should he leave General Loudon with a corps in your command, or attach him to himself, as you had not written anything to him about this.

"Also we shall not hide from you the fact that, to our dismay, we have noticed a certain intrinsic coldness between you and Count Daun which, of course, ought to have been dispelled at the very beginning rather than intensified. We instructed you not to expose our army to any apparent danger to no purpose, but this injunction cannot be applied on all occasions. You were given other instructions as well of a general nature, but more applicable to actual circumstances. For example you were told that, although you must certainly concern yourself with the care and protection of our army, care and protection are inappropriate when you have to wage war for several years instead of bringing it to an end in a single campaign with a single blow. Later you were given a precise instruction to try to reduce the forces of the king of Prussia and not to let any opportunity slip through your fingers where it might be possible to render an outstanding and consummate service to the whole of Europe.

"In this respect, even now if you do in fact stay in Silesia until October 4, the king of Prussia is at a distance from his brother and happens to be near you, with General Loudon not far away. Consequently you have a superior number of men and artillery. We therefore trust that you will of course make every effort to attack the king and destroy him." The rescript finished with an instruction to take up winter quarters near Poznan and to withdraw towards the Vistula only in the extreme event that Daun's affairs went very badly and Loudon abandoned the Russian forces.

In the mean time, on September 29, Saltykov sent to St. Petersburg a copy of a letter from Loudon. From this it was clear that, owing to Saltykov's maneuvers, the king was so contained in Silesia that, being afraid for Breslau and Upper Silesia, he could not part with a single detachment from his army to assist Prince Henry. This was very beneficial for the common cause, for it enabled Count Daun to take the field. In his letter Loudon also expressed the opinion that the Russian army should stay in Silesia until the end of October (New Style).

"On this matter," wrote Saltykov to St. Petersburg, "I can in no way agree. The Russian army has done too much for the allies. No one can deny this. No one can demand more at such an advanced season of the year. Of course the presence of the Russian army in Silesia until the end of October would serve one purpose, namely that the king would not be able to force his way through into Bohemia this year. Therefore Count Daun would gain a foothold in Silesia. Yet can this purpose be of greater significance than the harm which will ensue for the Russian army by its protracted, exhausting residence in Silesia, where daily it must practically tear feed for the horses from the hands of the enemy?

"After the meeting in Guben I suggested to Count Daun an attack by our joint forces upon the king that would lead to his destruction. Then we would force Prince Henry out of Silesia and take the fortresses to secure our winter quarters. For this sufficient time remained. Had we spent the winter in the vicinity of the enemy we could have opened the campaign early, taken Saxony and pursued him into Brandenburg. Thus we might have achieved a swift peace. Now nothing more remains for me other than to be concerned for the preservation of the army, and to conclude the present campaign with everlasting glory. We cannot prolong the army's presence in Silesia until the end of October because of an insufficiency of grain, feed for the horses, cloaks and footwear. I am prepared to hold on for the period promised, that is to remain until October 15 (New Style) and perhaps several days more. Then I shall make my way towards the Vistula to winter quarters.

"Therefore, most gracious sovereign, I trust that the sublime allies can be satisfied with your majesty's army and with my own actions. The king of Prussia's position on this side of the Oder near Herrenstadt, at a distance of about two miles, gives occasion for daily engagements between the light horse. Should I find occasion to attack the king, even victory, because of our present circumstances, would be more of a burden than an advantage, not to speak of the fact that we would have to sacrifice a considerable number of brave warriors who will be much more useful in the next campaign. Above all the enemy always establishes camp in such strong and inaccessible places that it is impossible to approach him in any way."

Justifying himself in respect of Daun, Saltykov wrote, "Count Daun stated that he intends to march towards Saxony and that he set off in that direction on September 9 (20) when he received news from me that I had decided to cross the Oder. Yet could Count Daun have received my letters on September 9 (20) concerning the crossing of the Oder, when it was sent on September 15 (26) and another on September 18 (29)? Is it not clear that rather earlier, not only than the receipt my letter, but even than *dispatch* of my letters, he made up his mind to march into Saxony and to move away from the Russian army, which prompted me to cross the Oder and make my way towards the Vistula."

In respect to instructions from St. Petersburg to make his way to Poznan as the place selected for winter quarters, Saltykov wrote that Poznan was insecure and inappropriate. The surroundings were trampled down. There was no hay or stubble. Saltykov was informed from St. Petersburg that Esterhazy, on the instruction of the empress-queen, had brought bitter complaints, not only in respect of the inactivity of the Russian forces, but even more at the fact that he could never receive either a decisive or a satisfactory reply from Saltykov about anything. A letter of September 9 (New Style) from Count Kaunitz to Saltykov remained almost a whole month without reply. Therefore Esterhazy demanded that Saltykov and Loudon not only carry out aggressive operations in Silesia, but even try to remain there in winter quarters, so that at least the Russian army remain active as long as the Austrian army stayed in the field. Alternatively, Saltykov should send a combined corps, made up of twenty to thirty thousand Russians, with Loudon's forces into Maria Theresa's hereditary lands.

A rescript of October 7 informed Saltykov of this. "We have attempted to deflect these complaints, cutting them short in a seemly manner for a number of very important reasons, in particular, in accordance with the proverb that one does not quarrel when sharing. Such a great and glorious alliance should not result in disappointment, reproofs and coldness, as scarcely has been seen before. That would be harmful for the future and indeed ought to be avoided. Rather it should result in the expected glory and satisfaction. The king of Prussia is trying to enter into an alliance with the Porte, but even from the Porte a great deal of pliancy is to be found. By your two victories the Porte has been forced to give the matter some thought and, thinking the downfall of the king of Prussia unavoidable, has refrained from entering into any undertaking with him.

"Our apprehension has not gone away. The inactivity of the victor when the king of Prussia has been reinforced with new and fresh troops lessens his victory. The king of Prussia's salvation, which must be ascribed not to his knowledge of the arts of war but to blind fortune, may add to his fame and may perhaps enhance his reputation in the eyes of the Turks especially if, in the light of this, there is suspicion that the close friendship between us and the court of Vienna has turned into coldness. Therefore we recommend most diligently that you commit to eternal oblivion everything that has made you displeased with the Austrian general staff. Equally we have declined for important and well-grounded reasons, *and not for the sake of dry and vexing repudiation*, all other Austrian demands, and have explained the necessity and value of Loudon remaining to winter over in the vicinity of Poznan."

The rescript of October 13 contained further very harsh statements. Saltykov discovered in it an unambiguous reprimand for his foolish handling of Loudon, as a consequence of which our allies very likely never again would send their forces to our assistance. It was suggested that he take as a model Admiral Mishukov, who so successfully handled the Swedish fleet put under his command that the following year the Swedes even sent their ships to be placed under the command of Admiral Poliansky. It should have been borne in mind that this foolish handling of Loudon's corps may have caused anger even amongst our fellow-believers (the Slavs) in that corps. "You write," it continued, "that our movements along the Oder gave rise to misgivings in the king with regard to Breslau and gave the advantage to Count Daun. Your movements along the Oder are deserving of considerable praise and have been very useful to the general cause. If during your prolonged stay in the vicinity of Müllrose and Lieber- ose, even by insignificant movements, you caused the king of Prussia to fear taking some step, then even by holding your position you have enhanced your victory. You think we must place Loudon's corps near Poznan and along the Warthe as far as Kalisz. This is very good, and conforms with our intentions.

"We cannot, however, hide our astonishment at the way in which ear- lier you put forward the fact that there was no forage or dry feed in the area. Yet when the need arose to place Loudon's corps there, has forage indeed been found? Then in your report, of course through a clerical er- ror, the incautious remark already referred to crept in, namely that with Loudon's presence in these positions our army would be covered from the direction of Silesia and Brandenburg. Such a self-interested statement, so offensive to our allies, is very far from *the tenderness of our sentiments*, not to mention the fact that it is dishonorable to our army that, triumphant in the field, it is protected in quarters beyond the Vistula very far from the enemy by an Austrian corps that is weak in comparison to itself. You write that, had you attacked the king of Prussia and defeated him the vic- tory now would be more burden than advantage. We regret this for im- portant reasons. Firstly, as the king of Prussia already has attacked the Russian army four times, the honor of our arms demand that we attack him at least once, the more so now that our army exceeds the Prussian both in numbers and courage. We have explained to you at length that it is always more advantageous to attack than be exposed to attack. Sec- ondly, the king of Prussia, although he has been beaten, has not only not moved away from our army, but within sight of it crossed the Oder with a small corps. This happened in the confidence that naturally he would not be attacked. From here it is extremely galling that, even defeated, he does not run away but harries the victor. Were he to be exposed to attack even once and defeated, he would retreat further with his small forces and our army would have greater peace of mind and most proper rest and sustenance. The only reason the king of Prussia comes close to you is that he does not expect you to attack him. Without a doubt that is the reason it must be supposed that if he expected an attack he would have retreated immediately beyond the Oder. Had you launched an attacking movement it would not have come to a battle. In the meantime you would have been able to declare, as Count Daun now does, that you would be glad to take to the field vigorously, but the enemy is running from you and you cannot keep pace with him in alien territory."

SHARP EXCHANGES BETWEEN IMPERIAL COURTS

In St. Petersburg the Austrian court made three demands. (1) That the Russian army, together with Loudon's corps, continue military activities in Silesia and occupy winter quarters there. (2) That the Russian army remain active at least while the Austrian army was in the field. (3) That a corps of Russian infantry of twenty to thirty thousand men, together with Loudon's corps, be sent into Maria Theresa's hereditary lands.

In light of these demands Esterhazy allowed himself to add in conference with Vorontsov, "The public and various courts have blamed Daun for not having pursued the king of Prussia alone, as the Russian army was not prepared follow up its victories. Our court, however much it concerns itself with the glory of its arms, prefers to leave its general with a reprimand rather than reveal the direct cause of its inactivity, which lies in the behavior of the Russian general staff. Many of the foreign officers present in the armies are beginning to denigrate the conduct of the Russian commanders, accrediting victory in the last battle more to the desperate attack of the enemy than to the commanders' skill in warfare. It is also said that the reason for all the inactivity is that Count Saltykov has received secret instructions from his court, and that there is a hidden agreement between Russia and England."

On October 8 Esterhazy was handed a reply. In respect to the first two demands it was pointed out that it was too late to satisfy them now that Russian army was across the Oder. The following extensive reply was given to the third demand. "Is it possible that at the court of the empress-queen it is thought that a corps of Russian infantry between twenty and thirty thousand men can render the common cause greater service than the whole of the Russian army? It is simply with regret that we must add that we could not make use, or use was not made, of the fortunate circumstance when the greatest part of the Prussian forces was turned against our army. When subsequently the enemy was defeated by our army it would have been very desirable if we could have sent the corps requested into

Austrian territory and then, with not inconsiderable force, have taken the field against the king of Prussia. This simply was not possible.

"According to the latest reports from our army, it is made up of sixty thousand men of all ranks and types of forces, apart from those stationed in East Prussia and along the Vistula, except for fifteen thousand sick and a greater number wounded. In this sixty thousand, of course, there are only a little more than thirty thousand infantry capable of bearing arms and taking the field, and whom we would want to send to the assistance of the Austrian army. Therefore we would have to send all of our infantry regiments. In this way we would destroy our army for good, for the infantry regiments we would send, without being able to recruit on Austrian territory, would disappear imperceptibly. Whatever levies we might raise here could not be put together into new regiments quickly and be brought up to a suitable condition. This is not to mention that the forces remaining would be exposed to inevitable ruin, or that new arrivals need to be given heart by the older soldiers, that rapidly they might take on the appearance of veterans worthy of victory, whereas completely new recruits need to be trained to victory through defeats.

"So, in sending thirty thousand infantry into Austrian territory and without the possibility of putting against the enemy a new and, to him, terrible army, we would be obliged to transfer our supply depots, the sick and our artillery to Russia. Then indeed everyone would have every right to think that we were tired of the war, and that by sending the thirty thousand troops we simply wanted to fulfill the obligations of an ally but in every other respect to be neutral. Then indeed you would have the right to ascribe to us covert plans and agreements with England, whereas now there is no cause whatsoever to entertain such a suspicion, so insulting to us and unworthy of the empress-queen.

"We have never given occasion to be accused of duplicity. We have never promised what we have not endeavored to fulfill in actuality. If at any time, through the self-interested behavior of our allies, we felt obliged to lose touch with the present system, we would have warned our allies directly of this in advance, and our forces would have returned. Then we would not have been distressed by the perfidy of glory, achieved by the precious blood of our subjects. We shall withhold from any further explanation at this time, while regretting that we have had to say even as much as has been said."

The complaints by the court of Vienna against Saltykov also were not left unanswered. The complaints consisted in the fact that the field marshal let slip through his fingers every opportunity to exploit the advantages he received, that he rejected all proposals put to him, that he expressed himself in an inadequate and ambiguous manner, that he did not carry out promises given, and even acted contrary to them. "We will not repeat here," the reply stated, "what has been achieved by our army for the glory and benefit of the common cause, as a consequence of which its subsequent inactivity could be tolerated lightly. We agree that the caution of our general staff was excessive after the engagement at Frankfurt (Kunersdorf), that the defeated Prussian army could have been destroyed as a consequence of a few maneuvers by our army, and that in these circumstances there should have been no need to fear a third battle. When with complete impartiality and with no less attention everything that took place before and after the battle of Frankfurt is considered, naturally one must on one hand be astonished that our army for so long could hold the Prussian army back, and on the other must regret deeply at the same time that perhaps the main reason for our mistaken idleness was that we did not expect such overwhelming success as that achieved by our army.

"So when Count Daun received news of the approach of the Prussian army in the direction of Poznan and, fearing that perhaps our army would not arrive at the Oder on time, ceased his operations so successfully begun, he did not take those measures which, of course, he would have taken had he not doubted so much the definite fulfillment on our part of everything promised. It can be seen from this that even at that time there was an attempt to lay the failure to fulfill the plan on our general staff, rather than in carrying it through, to make its fulfillment, from their point of view, also most convenient for us. Our field marshal Count Saltykov hardly arrived in Poznan to take over the command of our army than he took measures such that the enemy not only was obliged to turn back, but did not even succeed in retreating. Proof of this lies in the fact that the route to Crossen was denied him as well through his defeat at Palzig. During his campaign Field Marshal Saltykov received from Count Daun only the vexing intimation of doubt that our army could set out from Poznan. No enterprise by Count Daun would have given rise in Count Saltykov either to jealousy or the prospect of fulfilling his intentions. When Count Saltykov arrived at Crossen he did not even know where

Count Daun's army was. To find out he had to dispatch special detachments.

"In fact General Loudon came to meet him. Yet the proposals he brought would have exhausted the patience of the most phlegmatic. He arrived to tell him that the king of Prussia, with a large part of his forces, had turned against our army and had joined up with Wedell's defeated army. Instead of immediately asking the approval of our army for the measures Count Daun was taking, as he wanted to take advantage of the weakness of the Prussian forces still against him, he demanded that thirty thousand of our infantry be sent with him to Count Daun, and that he be given permission to take from Frankfurt, already captured by our forces, a million in war indemnities and to divide this equally with our army.

"Count Saltykov gave such battle that, even if it was not completely successful in undermining the forces of the king of Prussia, it would have been useful to our allies, and with the blessing God could have been decisive for the whole war. So the criticism by foreign officers of such a glorious battle, which naturally will be the greatest event of their lives, is quite absurd. Still less could it have been expected that our very best allies would use this to accuse our general staff. It must be admitted that to stop the successes gained at first by the enemy, to re-form the army in its entirety during a bloody and fierce battle, and ultimately to be totally victorious, when for many other armies defeat would have seemed unavoidable, serves as proof of undaunted courage and presence of mind. Almost a new model in warfare has been demonstrated, which of course will force the king of Prussia to follow other rules and to rely less on his good fortune and the fury of his attack.

"You easily may imagine with what regret we now see that our greatest campaign coming to an almost fruitless end. Everyone has been deceived in its certain expectations. We are in the unfortunate position of listening to censure and of entering into most unpleasant explanations of our position at a time when we should be agreeing on the future welfare of Europe! After the battle of Frankfurt, Count Daun did indeed send us the suggestion that it was high time to be thinking about winter quarters. This was very true and commendable. He chose, however, Upper Silesia for this purpose, and proposed the preliminary siege of Neisse and Brieg. These are so distant from the center of activities and from our frontiers that naturally Count Saltykov was convinced firmly that they were trying to make our army an auxiliary corps for the Austrian army, instead of conducting a strong campaign against Prince Henry and, with the siege of Glogau, clearing the way for the best winter quarters and the liberation of Saxony. Instead, while waiting upon hypothetical events and without taking sufficient measures for supplies, it was found necessary finally for the Austrian army to cover its supply depots, while our army sought to feed itself and also to convey sustenance to Loudon's corps, when General Loudon ought to have been concerned with the supply of our army. As insufficiency of provisions forced Baron Loudon also to cross to this side of the Oder to join our army, we fail to understand in what way the whole of our army could have conducted a campaign there with the earnestness desired.

"We have no intention whatsoever of complaining about Count Daun or of justifying the excessive displeasure and intractable behavior of our general (although perhaps occasion was given him at first by the doubt cast upon his success. Maybe rumors also reached him that he was being held up to criticism). While trying as far as possible to set right what has been marred in our relations, we have instructed our field marshal Count Saltykov scrupulously to commit all that is past to eternal oblivion, and to try by every possible means to create that trust and concord between the commanders-in-chief corresponding in full to the friendship and trust between the two imperial courts. For this to be possible, the empress-queen must also give similar instructions to her own general staff. The trust merited by our forces should not be diminished by such doubts and conjectures which possibly are based upon outrageous presumptions."

The displeasure between the two imperial courts was the more damaging, as hope was waning for the continued and energetic assistance of France, the other ally. At the start of the year the disquiet of the imperial courts lest France conclude a separate peace was dispelled by the resolute announcement of Louis XV that, despite the fact that he was not receiving any support from his allies in conducting a two-fold war, on land and at sea, and despite the fact that expenses in the war with England were enormous, nevertheless he was prepared at all times to do everything possible in the interests of the common cause. He renewed the reassurances given in a letter to the empress of Russia relating to his firm desire to remove any suspicion harmful to the successful alliance between France and Russia. He repeated his promise and reassurance that he would not enter into any talks whatsoever with the common enemy without the agreement of the empress of Russia and the empress-queen. The king was prepared to confirm this through new agreements if both empresses desired them. He was prepared to increase his undertakings for the preservation of an alliance with Russia that was so precious to him.

Although the king very much wanted the Russian sovereign, both in respect of the common cause and of his particular interests, to enter into specific undertakings with him against England, the chief architect of the current misfortunes in Europe, nevertheless if the Russian sovereign thought that she could not enter into an agreement on this subject with the king, then despite all the burden of the war with England he was prepared to use all of his resources against the king of Prussia on behalf of his allies, to demonstrate that he was as zealous in the cause of both empresses and the king of Poland as he was on his own behalf.

The exhausted revenues of France compelled it to wish for a swift peace settlement. The duc de Choiseul turned to the Russian ambassador with a reproach as to why Russia, in such an unheard-of manner, was giving benefits to the Prussian possessions occupied by its forces. Why did they take such insignificant ordinary taxes and extraordinary indemnities from them when the king of Prussia, as soon as he took possession of any country at all, not only Saxony and Mecklenburg, or even simply passed through it, completely ravaged it. "Therefore you should in no way spare the kingdom of Prussia. Likewise you must extract great sums of money from the Prussians, which would relieve costs for the upkeep of the Russian forces. Otherwise not only would the kingdom of Prussia be spared but would become even more wealthy from the money the Russian forces were leaving there. Such a model of behavior is in no way in accord with either Russian or the common interests because the king of Prussia, seeing his lands in such fine condition, has no incentive to yield to a swift peace."

Vorontsov made a note on this despatch of Bestuzhev's. "Out of ignorance of the actual state of revenues in Prussia anyone may make a comparison of the collection of indemnities with those from Saxony and Mecklenburg. From our own sources we are now assured that the people of Prussia are not in a position to pay the indemnities imposed, both on account of their lack of goods and chattels as well as their lack of ready cash, which has been removed from the country by the king of Prussia. The great sums of money used from here for the maintenance of our army have been spent almost entirely in Poland, to the considerable enrichment of the Poles. Nevertheless we do not have to follow the bad example of the king of Prussia."

In August Bestuzhev reported that everyone in France generally was astonished as to why General Daun thus far had not undertaken a campaign. They vehemently complained about him for still conserving his forces too carefully, and that he was content to let others sacrifice themselves for Austria. The duc de Choiseul gave the Austrian ambassador Count Starhemberg to understand this in the presence of Bestuzhev, showering praise upon the Russian forces over the battle of Kunersdorf.

PEACE PROPOSALS FROM ENGLAND AND PRUSSIA

The displeasure between the two imperial courts strengthened the hope for peace in Prussia and England. Even in the month of June Frederick II wrote to George II of England that every effort on their part to break the enemy alliance had been futile. Such a relentless and bloody war must be brought to an end and, using the first opportunity, their enemies should be informed that in London and Berlin there was an inclination towards opening a peace congress. In England this suggestion was accepted very willingly. In London a declaration was drawn up, and favorable circumstances merely were awaited to put it forward. Instead of favorable circumstances, news came of the battle of Kunersdorf. The Prussian minister Finckenstein wrote to Knyphausen, the Prussian ambassador in London, "Only a miracle can save us. Have a word with Pitt[12] as a friend, not as a minister. Point out to this great man the terrible danger to which this most loyal ally of England is exposed. Perhaps he is in a position to make peace." "Make every effort, as a dear fellow citizen," wrote Frederick himself to Knyphausen, "to see whether peace negotiations cannot be started between the English and the French. When the English receive good news from America, that will be an opportune moment. A great many enemies are causing me distress." In fact soon after this news arrived of the brilliant success of the English at sea and in America,[13] so the subject of a congress came up once more.

At a meeting with Vorontsov on October 23 Keith suggested that the kings of England and Prussia were prepared to renew their previous agreement with Russia, and that the Russian court might wish to discuss this even without its allies. "From the point of view of the empress," Keith said, "she has exceeded her obligations. For Russia there is no virtue in being in an alliance with France, which always has been envious of Russia and now has its own designs, about which I have clear proof, relating to the succession to the throne of Poland." "The chancellor," states the note of this meeting, "avoided entering into any further discussion on this matter. While clearly understanding the proposal, even though in general terms, to which these references were being made, he showed astonishment that the court of France should contemplate placing anybody on the Polish throne."

A month later, on November 24, Keith handed Vorontsov a copy of the declaration drawn up at The Hague from the kings of England and Prussia to the Russian, Austrian and French ambassadors. The declaration stated that the kings of England and Prussia were prepared to send their representatives for talks related to a durable and general peace settlement with the representatives of the warring parties, in a place considered most suitable for the purpose.

To both suggestions the following reply was made on December 1. "The empress has received with thanks the note of his britannic majesty expressed in a prior communication concerning the declaration drawn up at The Hague. As this declaration must have been made not to her alone, she cannot really reply to it in detail until she has come to an agreement with her allies. In the meantime the verbal communications of your ambassador, made to the chancellor on October 23, have been reported to her imperial majesty, to which the empress has given instructions for the following reply to be made. Naturally her chief endeavors were always and will ever be to live in concord with all powers. Everybody knows that, though she pursues this war most unremittingly, she was most unwilling to start it, and started it only when all her declarations failed to achieve any reactions at the court of Berlin, and her allies already were attacked. The empress is very upset by the shedding of so much innocent blood. Yet the peace we all desire is still very far off, if there is no other hope for it than the peaceful intentions of her majesty. The empress is unshakably determined, as a sacred duty, to fulfill punctiliously her solemn declarations, to give the aggrieved parties worthy and just satisfaction, to conclude peace on none other than honorable, lasting and advantageous conditions and in agreement with her faithful allies, and in no way to permit, through a spurious compassion of the moment for innocent blood, the peace of Europe to be left to its former peril. If the proposed conditions are satisfactory to the aggrieved parties and are acceptable, the empress will agree immediately to everything deemed to the good of her allies."

PROPOSALS DISCUSSED BY ALLIED COURTS

At the same time a note was given to the Austrian and French ambassadors. "We are reliably informed that the king of Prussia, with the knowledge and consent of England, has informed several courts that France has not so much become weary of war as, envying the success of our arms, it is disposed towards a reconciliation with Prussia, and has made proposals relating to this matter. The court in London evidently endeavored to bring this information to our attention, from which we have concluded that by such perfidious means they wanted to reassure only their allies within the German empire, and to cause awkward relations between us and our allies. We wanted to leave this matter in scornful silence, the more so as we were assured of the resolution and sincerity of our allies. We know with what dignity his Christian majesty has rejected the peace proposals made by the general staff of Hanover. Ambassador Keith consequently suggested that Russia might conclude a separate peace with the king of Prussia. At the same time the Prussian commissioner Major General Willich, appointed to arrange an exchange of prisoners, relayed to our Major General Yakovlev the information that Count Finckenstein had informed him that peace talks already had begun with France; on the other hand, a declaration for a general peace settlement was drawn up in The Hague.

"It seems that Prussia and England, by proposing a separate peace to us and to France, are trying to sow suspicions between the allies and to weaken our great alliance. As soon as one power concludes a separate peace the others will endeavor also to do the same. By the declaration drawn up in The Hague they are trying to show the world merely that they are ready for peace. Later they will drag out general negotiations for some time and render them futile. We do not want to say and to communicate by this note that we should not listen to peace proposals, even if the courts in London and Berlin suggest the most advantageous conditions. We find, however, that such a glorious alliance of the greatest powers in the world will not bring about the desired result, and peace cannot be lasting, if these powers do not achieve their objectives and if their mutual interests in the future peace settlement are not observed equally. This will be impossible to accomplish unless the allies unanimously recognize they should conclude an honorable, lasting and advantageous peace. Such peace settlement will not be concluded soon unless the courts in London and Berlin abandon any hope of sowing doubt between the allies and of inclining any one of them to a separate peace.

"In our opinion we must respond to the declaration drawn up at The Hague that the allies, no less than Prussia and England, desire a swift but honorable and durable peace. There will not be any difficulties over the choice of a site for these talks and the dispatch of representatives when it is explained a little more precisely how it is contemplated to reach a durable peace. The way matters stood before the present war were not conducive to the preservation of peace, and with the declaration of war all previous agreements were broken. At the same time it seems to us essential to draw up a specific declaration in the imperial diet, through the court of Denmark, and in Holland, that the allies have heard with great displeasure the disclosure of the enemy that apparently each has been endeavoring to conclude a separate peace. On the contrary now, more than ever, they are endeavoring to make their alliance indissoluble and steadfast. If they have been in agreement up to now to wage war, then if they stand united in any future reconciliation they will accept no other peace but one that is honorable, durable and workable, and which will deliver to all aggrieved parties worthy and just satisfaction.

"A firm and diligent preparation for the next campaign in these circumstances is of paramount importance. So it is vitally necessary that the allies now, as soon as possible, agree with us precisely and resolutely on all conditions for the future peace settlement. In the first place peace negotiations themselves will be much easier if this is done and, in the event of a success of arms, may be concluded right away. If the courts in London and Berlin observe substantial disagreements between the allies during negotiations they will see in this the possibility of prolonging the talks and later even of dividing the allies, and of achieving what has been impossible by force of arms through the conclusion of peace by negotiations.

"In the second place the undertaking accepted by the allies not to conclude either a separate peace or an armistice with the common enemy is imperative to a preliminary and precise resolution of conditions. A precise and strict adherence to this undertaking will almost always make peace difficult, but when the allies are agreed about future conditions for peace beforehand each may listen to proposals and communicate them to the others if they are easily acceptable, or reject them straightaway if they are not in accordance with the common view.

"In the third place if in this way there is complete agreement between the allies there will be no need to conclude a disadvantageous armistice. In respect to the site of the talks, as the duke of Mecklenburg has suffered innocently a great deal in the present war, it would be some compensation to him if the congress were to convene in one of his cities. Should this not prove possible, the best solution would be to convoke the congress in Hamburg or Lübeck. We will agree, however, to any decision of our allies."

The court in Vienna was greatly alarmed by the Anglo-Prussian declaration drawn up at The Hague. It feared that France, exhausted by the war, would be pleased at the opportunity to conclude peace as soon as possible, as a consequence of which the other members of the alliance would be obliged to do the same without gaining from the war any of the expected benefits. Maria Theresa wrote to Esterhazy that she placed all her hope on the allied friendship and the steadfastness of the Russian empress. She begged the Russian court to put aside any distrust and particular interest and not to conceal anything from the court in Vienna for the anticipated achievement of a great objective. She expressed the hope that Russia would renew undertakings already made in regard to herself and her house. For her part she promised ardently to fulfill her obligations, and besides to give her royal word that, both through strength of arms and also in any peace negotiations, she would use all her power to afford Russia all benefits and rewards it desired and found possible to achieve. She asked that no armistice be concluded, but suggested they agree to a peace congress at which they should try to win as much time as possible in order to identify the real intentions of the other courts and, making use of this information, undermine the friendship between England and Prussia. They should endeavor to ensure that peace be concluded between England and France in such a way that Austria and Russia remain free to continue the war against the king of Prussia.

The empress commanded the following reply to be made. "There is no doubt whatsoever that because of the solicitations of the king of Prussia, England was disposed to draw up a declaration with him concerning a peace congress. It is no less true that England would not have understood its own vital interests if it did not make use of present circumstances to conclude an advantageous peace and to save its ally the king of Prussia. It is impossible for England not to see that, however unremitting the success of its arms, it cannot achieve greater advantages when in North America it no longer has anything to fear from France and, what is even more important, the fleet and trade of France cannot recover for some considerable time. French revenues are quite exhausted, and in prolonging the war England can only risk the possibility that France by some courageous and successful enterprise might change the situation to its advantage. England naturally feels that if the king of Prussia is disabled completely it will lose all its allies in Germany. Consequently the considerable successes of its arms would not make up for its loss of standing in European affairs. England, through the concessions of a most advantageous peace with France, would in fact leave it in a considerably impoverished state, and by such a peace, in rescuing the king of Prussia, would incomparably increase its own standing and influence.

"So in our opinion it is more to be hoped than expected that we shall be able to succeed in persuading England to conclude a peace settlement with France with the complete exclusion of the king of Prussia. We must take the utmost care in any conspicuous distinction between the Anglo-French war and ours with Prussia, that we not alarm France and thereby do harm to the matter in hand. We consider it necessary that our ambassador Count Bestuzhev-Riumin and Count Starhemberg, with their full agreement and intelligence, make clear to the French court that it is not our wish and intention to exclude his most Christian majesty from the war against the king of Prussia. On the contrary, with grateful acknowledgment of his strong assistance, we earnestly desire that in any peace settlement with this sovereign the interests of France and of all the allies, in particular Saxony and Sweden, are observed on a par with our own.

"We are even further from any thought that, having concluded a particular peace settlement with the king of Prussia, we should leave him free to render assistance in any way to England. We very well understand why at this particular time England and Prussia are in such haste with their proposals. England observed long ago that its apparent superiority in forces at sea will become effective only when it has strong reinforcements on land. For that reason it appears that in the present war it has concerned itself more with the interests of the king of Prussia than with its own. Therefore we may be led to believe that in any conclusion of a peace settlement it will take greater pains over the interests of Prussia. Perhaps indeed all of its hopes for a peace settlement are based upon this, sacrificing some of its own advantages in order to preserve the power of the king of Prussia, which is so useful.

"Russia and Austria will never demand that France sacrifice anything at all for them. His most Christian majesty will observe of course that, whatever advantageous peace settlement might now be reached with England, it will always be of incomparably more assistance to that power, and more injurious to France, if at the same time the forces of the king of Prussia are not reduced. England will retain an ally who is obligated in all things, and with whose assistance it will easily be able to exercise dominion over all Germany and the North. Of course the onerous war itself will cease for a space of time, but we must always be prepared for a new war, more onerous because the coalition of the king of Prussia will become incomparably stronger. England and the king of Prussia together are putting forward a proposal for a general peace settlement at this time, thinking by the successes of England at sea to make up for what has been lost on land. In our opinion, with the intensification of the war on land we must compensate with interest what has been lost at sea. The means to retrieve all that has been lost, we believe, are there. To fulfill our obligations and not concede anything anywhere, we simply must follow this advice. In a French reply it must be pointed out that the king is ready to make peace with England, but only if the peace is honorable. As to the war begun by the king of Prussia against Austria, Saxony and Russia, insofar as the king entered it merely in his capacity as a supporter and guarantor of the Treaty of Westphalia[14] he must carry out his obligations religiously, assisting his allies and trying in the forthcoming peace settlement to ensure that they receive just compensation for all losses."

RUSSIA'S RELATIONS WITH SWEDEN, POLAND AND TURKEY

Sweden was the one other power which had entered the war against Prussia to preserve the Treaty of Westphalia. Panin sent sad news concerning the lack of success of the Swedish forces. "The present campaign has cost Sweden twenty million thalers," he wrote. "Her majesty knows how much foreign subsidies have been received to this end. Were you to take into account the number in the Swedish army and what it was doing all the time, having spent the month of June in Stralsund and then going backwards and forwards no more than fifty miles, practically without coming in sight of the enemy, it is not difficult to prove how at least a third of these millions has passed through their hands. As far as preparation for the forthcoming campaign is concerned, this question poses a number of difficulties. The Senate commission on equipment has not met for several months for want of money, not knowing how to satisfy its contractors, even for those many items which even last year were supplied to the army. One senator told me in strictest confidence that they have no expectation the court in Versailles will pay them a subsidy for this year. The well-known local lottery here has no hope of the desired success. Few punters take tickets, for when they ask the bank to take these tickets as security, the bank refuses."

On June 1 Panin wrote that there was no prospect of anything new from the military arrangements and preparations, except for a muster of up to six hundred recruits from various provinces. It was said they would soon be sent to places on the coast ready for embarkation. There were no other departures for the army. All the forces would remain with their provinces and garrisons. The reason was clear to everyone. The state Treasury was at present totally exhausted, and arrears in foreign subsidies remained unpaid. What was being paid went towards the maintenance of the army at that time in Pomerania. In August, referring to the situation upon the death Count Gyllenborg, leader of the governing party, Panin wrote, "Up to now there has been little time for the Senate to think about its army because it has had to deal with various factions. With the death of Gyllenborg domestic affairs will become even more confused."

At the beginning of September Panin informed them that the State Bank finally gave the crown a loan of thirty casks of gold with notice that this was a final effort to assist the state's deficit. Out of these thirty casks, twenty were held back by the College of State Accounts for the payment of salaries to state and military officials for this year, for the government had taken this salary in advance from its usual state revenues and used it for military expenditure. Four casks were taken by the Military College to pay off contractors for the supply of goods this year, and so there remained only six casks for the government to use for new military expenses. Panin considered it his duty to confirm that in 1759 no soldiers and recruits would be sent to Pomerania. Only empty reassurances would be made to keep the allies quiet and to maintain morale among the people. In the provinces nobody wanted to obey government orders. Next year the Riksdag must meet and, over and above everything else, it would be occupied with the election of a land marshal. The Court party, together with the old *Caps*,[15] was acting calmly and was not interfering in this matter. The French party wanted Baron Scheffer, at present minister at the court of Versailles, as land marshal. Senator Höpken and his followers did not want to listen to this, and Höpken was putting forward his friend, the retired senator Vrede.

The new Russian minister in Warsaw, Lieutenant General Fedor Voeikov, had to concern himself with old matters. He began his reports with news that the first minister, Count Brühl, his son-in-law Crown Marshal Count Mniszech, together with Archbishop Soltyk of Cracow, had almost a free hand. The party in opposition to them was led by the Princes Czartoryski and Castellan Count Poniatowski of Cracow. The greatest disorder and detestation between distinguished Poles proceeds from the dissensions between these two parties. Crown Chancellor Malachowski came to see Voeikov and, while reassuring him of his devotion to Russian interests, at the same time expressed his strong displeasure at the actions of Brühl and Mniszech. In defiance of the constitution and the customs of the Poles they were intervening in all matters relating to the jurisdiction of other dignitaries to the extent that Malachowski, in order to avoid any further insults, decided to retire to his village for a while, which is what in fact he did.

"I have also heard," wrote Voeikov, "about similar dissatisfactions from other distinguished Poles. It seems to me that these dissatisfactions are excited by the Czartoryskis and Poniatowski, who have considerable importance. I also have been able to observe that most of those clearly belonging to the court party are scarcely genial, others are only outwardly friendly in order to receive office and other advantages. My actions and behavior are very carefully observed, and everyone tries to draw me to their party. For this reason I have decided to observe caution, modesty and courteous behavior, to hear out any complaints and sometimes even those without foundation. I can see that in this way I am held in sufficient respect by both parties, and I hope that should I solicit some information in such circumstances, I will not meet any major obstacles."

"I have observed," wrote Voeikov later, "that the Russian commandant, Prince Czartoryski, is on very friendly terms with the English envoy Lord Stormont[16] and with the other English here. They are at his house almost every day. Count Poniatowski shows the same goodwill towards them. Such conduct gives just cause for the greatest dissatisfaction and suspicion, both from the point of view of the king, and equally of his first minister. Perhaps they do this only in vexation at the court party opposed to them, without having any ill intentions. In my opinion, however, this idea is not at all praiseworthy."

Voeikov received a rescript from the empress in response to this report. "The young Prince Czartoryski arrived here recently asking our support with the king to obtain a papal bull for Bishop Szepticki of Kamieniec and to make Abbot Mosalski coadjutor of Wilno, by which the Russian party may receive significant encouragement. Although in truth the Czartoryski princes and their party seem devoted to us, for which reason indeed they have received many favors from us, nevertheless time and experience have shown how little they respond. Through their particular malice towards Count Brühl and his son-in-law they appear hostile not only to our own, but even to the king's interests. They displayed explicit evidence of their malevolence when they showed no embarrass-- ment in opposing directly the king's proposal to ask the king of Prussia, through a deputation from the Commonwealth, for an explanation regarding his hostile behavior in respect to Poland. Because of their stubborn insistence, this proposal was not adopted. This shows what we and the king may expect from the Czartoryski princes and their party. In the hope that they will change their behavior we grant our pardon to young Prince Czartoryski, and command you in our name to intercede on behalf of Szepticki and Mosalski. Before you do so, carefully ascertain whether by these recommendations we will not cause any ill-feeling towards the king, and in this way compromise our dignity."

Voeikov, following the example of all his predecessors, complained about the persecution of the Orthodox on Polish territory. A rescript to him from the empress dated August 10 stated, "Because of all the impediments placed upon those of the Greco-Rus faith living in Lithuania and Poland by the Poles in the renovation and repair of their dilapidated churches and in the construction of new ones, your predecessors clearly were recommended to obtain from the king the common right for them to have complete freedom. Nevertheless such a right has not been granted so far. Those of our faith have great need of it because the Poles, and in particular the bishop of Wilno, do not allow them to repair or build their churches."

Voeikov referred the matter to Count Brühl, and received the usual reply that the king would do all he could to help. Voeikov wrote to the bishop of Wilno, who replied that the matter must be deferred until the meeting of the Sejm, because without a decision of the whole Commonwealth he could not give permission to build or to repair the churches of another confession. "These empty excuses demonstrate his ill disposition," wrote Voeikov, "for it is well known that almost all Polish Sejms break up in disarray."

At the same time the Poles demanded immediate compensation for damages resulting from passage of Russian troops through Polish territory. Two deputies were chosen, of whom one was to be sent to St. Petersburg and the other to Field Marshal Count Saltykov, to seek compensation for these damages. Voeikov tried in vain to hinder the dispatch of these deputies. He asked to no effect why complaints were made about Russian troops and no others. The Prussians burst into Polish territory and laid them waste, but there was not the slightest complaint. Count Brühl replied that such a motion from the Polish magnates to the king was very disagreeable, but he could not to stop it. Brühl added on his own behalf that nothing could be done about it. The obstinate and reckless Polish gentry had to be satisfied in order to restrain them from any reprehensible behavior, because of their proximity to the borders of Brandenburg and Silesia.

In October Voeikov received a rescript with new demands to obtain common rights for the Orthodox. The bishop of Wilno was sending missionaries who were behaving in an unheard-of manner among the ordinary people. Because of their incitement, such dishonor and abusive language was inflicted on Bishop Georgy Konisski of Belorussia, in the town of Orsha, that he was afraid he might not be able even to live undisturbed in his own house, and begged her majesty to defend all those of the same faith in Poland and Lithuania. Voeikov received the previous replies to all his representations and wrote, "The clergy here in Poland have great power, which is why they are puffed up with such pride that they not only make light of ministers, but scarcely even obey royal commands."

In Poland Frederick II could not entertain any hope of stirring up any movement capable of distracting Russian forces. He did not, however, despair of Turkey. At the beginning of the year Obreskov reported from Constantinople that everything was quiet, but on April 3 he reported the arrival of a new Prussian emissary. On March 22 the grand vizier had a secret meeting in one of the sultan's palaces outside the city with a secretary of the English embassy and a senior interpreter. The English ambassador received an instruction from his court to try by every means to forge an alliance between the Porte and the king of Prussia and gave him permission, if necessary, to spend as much as £100,000. The vizier agreed to a simple alliance or treaty of friendship, but the king asked for an offensive, or at least a defensive, alliance. The vizier would not agree to this at all. "In the mean time the allied ministers and I," wrote Obreskov, "have used all our resources to frustrate the conclusion of this policy. Although we can see that in general the Turks are far from the Prussian alliance, nevertheless if the vizier is disposed towards it and their allies do not receive a distinct advantage over the king of Prussia, I cannot predict what might happen."

Indeed, immediately after receipt of false information that the Prussians had been victorious over the Russian forces at Palzig the vizier entered into negotiations with the Prussian emissary, cutting them off when verified information concerning the Russian victory at both Palzig and Kunersdorf was received. "The Prussian emissaries," wrote Obreskov on October 1, "are still here, but their situation has not improved, as the Porte repeatedly tells them to be patient and await a suitable opportunity. This behavior of the Porte concerns me and the allied ministers not a little. We can see from this, on one hand, the cunning of the Porte, which wants to preserve full freedom to accept or to reject the Prussian proposals, depending upon circumstances. On the other hand the Prussian emissaries, living here incognito, can hold on a little longer, and it is obvious that they can bide their time. Therefore, with the allied ministers, I have made every effort to get these emissaries expelled, but without success. Owing to the predisposition and firmness of the vizier, we have little hope of future success unless our forces or those of our allies have further victories. The Porte constantly is concerned with the provisioning of border towns with military supplies. The sultan wants war, but little desire for war can be found amongst the nobility."

According to the reports of von Reksin, the Prussian emissary in Constantinople, the grand vizier told him that the Porte was ready for an alliance with Prussia, but on condition that England also enter this alliance and guarantee it. The three allied powers must conclude peace only by mutual agreement. The English minister told the Prussian envoy that England simply had concluded trade talks with the Porte, without concluding any alliances. An alliance with the Turks would excite indignation in the Catholic courts in Spain and Naples, and amongst the English people. It was impossible to accept an article relating to the conclusion of peace only by mutual agreement. It would be unacceptable to the English. Only one thing remained, to send an instruction to the English envoy to incline the vizier in favor of Prussia, without tying his hands.

DOMESTIC POLICIES

There was need to be concerned about the preservation of peace in the South because the war in the West was becoming very expensive. All discrimination in conscription of reinforcements for the armed forces came to an end. The War College reported that it could not assign the estate manger Krivtsov, formerly in the College of Mines and sent to the War College, to the regiments and garrisons. A decision of the War College in 1756 determined to promote men to officer rank in the army only after receipt of reliable testimonials that they were hard working, expeditious, quickly resourceful, solicitous in everything, with a retentive memory, knew the military regulations completely, had good eyesight and were efficient. Krivtsov was never in military service, but in the mines.

Furthermore he was dismissed for unworthy conduct and, moreover, was no longer a young man. Even so the Senate ordered Krivtsov assigned to a post wherever he seemed capable of service. If he was passed over for promotion as officer of mines for incompetence, that was because officers of mines were promoted according to their knowledge of those sciences necessary to expertise in mining. Krivtsov was only forty-nine and therefore still was capable of continuing in service. The War College did not mention areas of incompetence, apart from his age, which might prevent him from serving in the regiments.

The Medical Chancellery sent the Senate the opinion of Doctor Poletiki that the sick in the military hospital were suffering for the most part from fever and diarrhea. This was caused by the stuffy atmosphere, the distant and difficult journey for conscripts, poor food, close confinement in quarters and lack of hygiene, the changeable and wet winter, as well as fatigue from military exercises. Moreover the sick were sent too late to the military hospital, where they were already dying from the close confinement and stench. The military hospital must be expanded and the number of the sick living in tents reduced at least by half. The Senate ordered new buildings to be found to enlarge the hospital.

Instructions were sent to the senior police responsible for finding runaways, that out of those at present under their command they should return only the most essential, without supernumeraries. Because of the pressing need in the army all others were to be sent to the regiments.

LACK OF MANPOWER AND ITS CONSEQUENCES

The forces available to the police were reduced and the consequences were common knowledge. There was a noticeable increase in brigandage. Brigands appeared near Moscow along the Vladimir road near the menagerie. They found asylum in the Lefortovo district amongst men of indeterminate rank[17] living in the district. Formerly the gendarme general had two companies of dragoons, but now this number was reduced. The gendarme general reported that daylight robberies occurred along the Moscow road and in the vicinity of St. Petersburg, the robbers being armed with broadswords and pistols. This report was followed by an edict signed by the empress once again to establish two companies of dragoons. It was difficult to carry out the edict swiftly. Confirmation of the speedy dispatch of two companies of dragoons for police work arrived from the Cabinet because not only were domestic robberies taking place in St.

Petersburg, but also in the port. Behind stalls for flour and candles some bast matting was found in which a pot with wineskin and gunpowder was wrapped, from which the bast matting was scorched. The empress also ordered gypsies be driven out of St. Petersburg and surrounding districts. News arrived that in the Novgorod and Staraia Rusa districts brigands had destroyed many houses. The number of brigands there so increased that at the end of the year all military personnel serving in the land-survey of the district had to be seconded to hunt them down. They were ordered to take retired officers to assist them and, where necessary, even local residents. An interesting imperial edict was reported to the Senate on December 13. "It has become known to her majesty that many are causing offense to residents on their way to the newly discovered miracle-worker Dmitry in Rostov,[18] and to the miracle-working image in Akhtyrka. They are taking carts without paying for them, and for this reason drivers and peasants are being ruined."

LACK OF MONEY

At the beginning of the year the Senate was obliged to reply with a resolute rejection to the financial demands of the Conference, as the Conference requested that eight thousand four hundred rubles be given to Captain Prince Nikolay Repnin, who was sent to France, and to Cavalry Captain Count Peter Apraksin, who was leaving to join the Swedish army. The Senate instructed that the Conference be informed that these sums could not be released at present. There was an extreme shortage of money in all branches of government because many money requisitions were not met. The very day after receiving this response the Senate decided to send available couriers, staff and senior officers, with instructions to the government, provincial[19] and municipal magistrates to send all money available from collection of revenues found in council offices and town halls, as much as there was available wherever it might be, everything, leaving no stone unturned. A report of the Chief Commissariat was presented at this point. More than six hundred thousand rubles must be sent to the army abroad for annual expenses, and that day the Senate ordered four hundred thousand in copper coins sent to Königsberg. Yet in various accounts, including that of the military hospitals, the Treasury had only 289,276 rubles on hand.

The collection of customs was farmed out to Chief Inspector of Customs Shemiakin and his company. At the end of the year Shemiakin reported that dispensations were being made by detachments because of the scanty amount of customs revenue in many places. Several commanders were creating obstacles to the collection of revenues. Customs officers were beaten mercilessly and held for long periods under arrest. Those with merchandise passed the frontier in secret through bribery. Those who made false reports were not sent for investigation. Those sent on mounted patrols were beaten mercilessly and at the Kolybelsk frontier post there was a murder. No assistance whatsoever was rendered by those living in the vicinity of the frontier. On the contrary, in collusion with Polish and Russian merchants, each in companies of a hundred and more with guns and spears, they constantly carted merchandise across the frontier. It was impossible to suppress them because of the small number of military companies at the frontier posts. In many places there was only one soldier, and every military company offered the excuse that there was nobody to reinforce the men at frontier posts. Major General Albedil wrote that it was necessary to halt these parties of smugglers, and in addition to detain the many families of runaways from Russia to Poland. Besides the present route, the escapees had established several other routes across the frontier.

INDUSTRY

In this state of financial insolvency the news from Siberia brought some joy. The Nerchinsk expedition suggested publicizing in the newspapers, for the glory of the Russian empire, a previously undiscovered rich silver mine called Kadainsk. The Senate, nonetheless, ordered publication withheld for a little while.

Interesting developments were taking place among other industrial enterprises. The Conference sent a report to the Senate from the chief inspector of customs and tax farmer Shemiakin, who asked permission to import silk, gold and silver into Russia duty free in order to supply Russian mills. The Conference told him that consideration and resolution of this matter belonged strictly to the Senate. Still it was decided to mention, in forwarding this report, that Shemiakin's suggestions were well founded and that his diligence deserved praise. In addition it recommended that, because of the importance of this matter, its resolution be accelerated. If Russian manufacturing were to be improved it was necessary somewhat more swiftly to take advantage of the present confusion throughout almost all Europe. In his report Shemiakin wrote that, although the number of silk manufactories had expanded greatly, this business was far from perfect, and could serve as a reliable road to ruin. A French manufacturer was concerned solely with designs, and gave not a thought about where to obtain silk and how to dye it. There were merchants and dyers to do this. With us, on the other hand, the manufacturer must be both a merchant and a dyer, which brought us to ruin, for it demanded the immediate outlay of much capital. Every manufacturer must have at least fifty thousand puds of silk in reserve, if he wanted to guarantee that his mill would not come to a halt. The manufacturer might hold forty puds of yellow silk yet not fabricate a single pud of this in a whole year. To fill his order book he might have to produce thirty puds of violet in one month, of which he had not even a hundredth. What was he to do? To re-dye would waste dye stuffs and the color would come out badly. The material would lack the same purity and durability.

Shemiakin undertook to maintain as much silk in as many varieties and colors as might be needed in St. Petersburg and Moscow, to avoid a break in production. In exchange he asked for this concession for thirty years. In addition he requested exclusive rights to export squirrel, lambskin and beaver. The managing director of a braid factory, Rogo-vikov, reported that Shemiakin's request was to no purpose. He was slandering Russian manufacturers simply out of envy, as many silk mills had reached a prosperous stage of development. He, Rogovikov, had spent more than one hundred thousand rubles on his factory, and his goods gave great satisfaction. Shemiakin had no factory of his own, but wanted to undermine all those who had. If desired, Rogovikov would accept the concession on the very same conditions, and would take other manufacturers into his company as well. Moreover he would undertake to pay thirty thousand rubles every year into the Treasury.

The Senate ordered that Shemiakin be permitted the duty-free import of silk only, but not of gold and silver. Other manufacturers might import silk free of duty for their own mills, not for resale. Shemiakin might let beaver cross the Chinese border in exchange for silk, but duty should be charged. He could take lambskins and squirrel across other borders with duty being charged but the export of these should be prohibited to others. Rogovikov's unfounded statement was to be ignored, and he be told not to make any further such statements.

Lieutenant General and Marshal of the Court Baron von Sievers submitted an application for the destruction, no more and no less, of the paper and cardboard mill of the St. Petersburg merchant Olkhin. In Sievers's mill at Krasnoe Selo paper of every sort was made by the very best craftsmanship and in such quantity that not only the whole of the St. Petersburg province but all surrounding provinces could be supplied. It was necessary to put a stop to what he saw as the clear detriment to his trade from Olkhin's mill. In 1754, following a decision of the Senate, Olkhin was forbidden to expand his unnecessary mill. In his submission Olkhin stated that Sievers was undermining his mill. For this reason Sievers was seeking satisfaction. The Senate ordered the College of Manufactures to inspect Olkhin's mill and thereupon to report whether this mill had expanded previous production, and what that increase was. In regard to satisfaction, let Sievers make any petition he cared permitted by law, but in a lower jurisdiction, not the Senate.

LANDOWNERS AND CITIES

The war was dragging on. Landowners with the forces abroad had no opportunity to take leave for supervision of their estates and repay the bank money borrowed. Peter Ivanovich Shuvalov proposed deferment of such payments as the nobility, "this foremost member of the state," should not be deprived of its property, especially at this time, being abroad and fighting a war. A landowner might be with the forces and his neighbor take advantage of his absence, attack his estate and beat his peasants. Shamardin, a landowner from Orel, with his servants and peasants, attacked the servants and peasants of Major Shenshin, killed four of them and even thrashed an investigating detachment sent against him.

The towns must be protected from fire, from the arbitrary rule of the Chief Magistracy and from military governors, who in turn complained about the merchants. The chancellery of the provincial governor of Yuriev-Povolsky reported that local merchants were not fulfilling their police duties and had nothing with which to fight fires. Many people gathered together at night. There was mischief and threatening behavior, with violence against the military governor and chancellery officials. Spiridon, the military governor of Rostov, was replaced because he made no effort to acquire fire fighting equipment. The Chief Magistracy reported to the Senate that it elected into the ranks of town councillors the Moscow merchants Strugovshchik and Serebrenikov, acknowledged as worthy of this distinction. The Senate gave orders, in line with the regulations, that the merchants of Moscow be instructed to select candidates and present them to the Chief Magistracy, which must nominate them to the Senate, emphasizing in their report who in their opinion was most worthy. The

Chief Magistracy must act according to these rules and not confer this honor themselves. They shall bear in mind the regulations and the edict of the empress of 1757 with a rebuke for a similar imprudent act, but all of this was disregarded.

A petition of the College of Justice is notable regarding military governors. Was it not possible to appoint a special commission of outsiders for an action against Zhukov, military governor of Penza, as there was no possibility of conducting the business by it [the College] owing to a shortage of secretaries and officials? A special commission was appointed to investigate a councillor of police Nepliuev, although there were only twenty charges against him and 223 charges against Zhukov! The Senate disagreed, and ordered two days set aside for consideration of the Zhukov case, in a week when it was not occupied with other business.

RURAL POPULATION

In the village uprisings of the monastic peasantry was by no means a new phenomenon. The Synod sent notice that Archimandrite Irinarkh of the city monastery in Archangel was complaining about the disobedience of peasants attached to the monastery. The peasants complained at the burden of excess work and extortions. Before conclusion of the case a written pledge was presented to the peasants to obey the monastery. The peasants would not do as they were told. The cellarer was knocked from the front steps. Later even the archimandrite was driven off, pushed with fists to his ribs, and the provincial chancellery did nothing about these assailants. The Synod complained at the indulgence of the government official Cherevin towards the peasants and in appointment of the secretary Ivanov. In the Shatsk district the newly baptized Mordvinians in the village of Tumagi seceded from the St. Sabbas the Guardian monastery and had not paid their quit-rent since 1753. The peasants of the Kaliazin monastery in Tver sent a petition stating that the archimandrite and monastery officials were bringing them to ruin.

The infamous case between Safonov and the Lvovs has been mentioned. The Lvovs attacked Safonov's peasants, killing eleven and mortally wounding forty-five. This matter had dragged on since 1754. In the period under discussion the Lvovs made their peace with Safonov when they offered, in the suit, to give him about four thousand rubles and an estate, all their fixed assets in the Kaluga district and to add to that estate a deed of purchase worth five thousand rubles. The Senate agreed to this transaction.

UKRAINE

In the South, on the Ukrainian steppe, raids of the Zaporozhians continued on the Don Cossacks. The ataman of the Don Cossacks, a certain Yefremov, as a mark of the particular favor of her imperial majesty, was made a privy councillor for his campaign abroad. With some difficulty the hetman of Ukraine obtained compensation for Zaporozhia, an increase in monetary payment because of the increase of this military unit, and because it was restricted in catching fish and game by the establishment of New Serbia and the new regimental settlement. Besides, the cossacks had abandoned manufacture of salt and other trade as a consequence of the increase in customs duty at the border posts. The hetman further asked that Zaporozhia be given artillery. The Senate agreed to grant an additional two thousand rubles to the monetary payment, to make 6,660 rubles with what had been granted before, and to let them have three new cannon to replace three which were now unserviceable.

The settlers in New Serbia began to get involved in illegal activities. In exchange for bribes two of them let into Russia Ukrainian cossacks from abroad. A third accepted stolen property from Ukrainian cossacks and gave them in exchange arms, powder and bullets in order to carry on their brigandage. A military court sentenced them to death, but Khorvat obtained a pardon in order "not to send an echo" to potential immigrants to New Serbia and not to discourage migration.

Mention has been made of the Montenegrins' unruly conduct.[20] At the beginning of the year under discussion the Senate received a communication from the Cabinet. The considerable amount of mischief, fights and daylight robbery of the Montenegrins in Moscow came to her majesty's attention. It came about, it seems, from their extreme poverty and lack of pay. The Senate authorized the following response. The Montenegrins had permission to emigrate to Russia with permanent citizenship to settle places assigned to them in the province of Orenburg. They had inspected these places themselves. At first they were satisfied with their benefits, which is why they went there from Kiev. Soon they not only began to abandon settlement in these places but even, when they were in Samara, made a great deal of mischief and gave offense to the citizens. For that reason the Senate determined to keep them there until preparation of an edict envisaging the formation of a hussar regiment from the Montenegrins when their number was sufficiently increased. Later some of them expressed a desire to serve as a special squadron in the army and in the established hussar regiments. For that reason they were ordered to Moscow for arms and uniforms. In Moscow not only were they involved in fights and offended the citizens, they even disobeyed their commanders. They refused to take the oath without the permission of the metropolitan of Montenegro.

In September 1758 Metropolitan Petrovich was sent to Moscow to bring them under control. He was ordered to punish those guilty according to the custom of their country. Later these Montenegrins once more became involved in frequent acts of mischief, in fights, assaulting and robbing citizens. Therefore it was resolved to treat them under military law, banish them out of Moscow and into the army as soon as possible. There was no petition to the Senate in respect to their poverty. They were given the same salary, every third of the year, as others in the hussar regiments. Incidentally Baroness Maria Stroganova complained that on January 7, 1759 a crowd of Montenegrins came to her house with naked sabers, broke through her gates, hacked to pieces a railing, severely beat those whom they caught, even ran into her private rooms and felled the columns on her porch. Later a tocsin was sounded in the belfries of the churches close by. People came running, and the Montenegrins had to retreat.

IV

RUSSIANS OCCUPY BERLIN, 1760

NEW YEAR CELEBRATIONS

The new year began with recollection of the victories of the previous year, victories the like of which were unseen since the glorious days of Peter the Great. Therefore there was some justice in comparing the days of the father with those of his daughter. In St. Petersburg there was a magnificent firework display. The brutal conflict near Frankfurt, the most glorious victory won by the Russians, was portrayed. A burning sun with the name of Elizabeth the Great could be seen over the site of this terrible conflict, and on either side were two magnificent buildings signifying the two great victories. Then Glory was represented in the sky handing down two laurel wreaths, signifying the two victories of Palzig and Frankfurt, to Eternity sitting on an ancient rock and listing her majesty's achievements. Then there was a magnificent temple in which the glory of Peter the Great as the founder of the present prosperity of Russia was represented. Through doors in the heart of the temple could be seen a half-length image of that greatest of monarchs, Peter the Great.

PREPARATIONS FOR THE CAMPAIGN

The most glorious victories of Peter the Great led to a most glorious peace settlement. The chief concern of his daughter was to be compared, if only a little, with her father in this respect. An honorable peace settlement for Russia and its allies could be concluded only with the overwhelming defeat of the forces of the king of Prussia. "I do not make up my mind to anything quickly," Elizabeth told Esterhazy, "but once I have made up my mind, I never change my decision. I shall continue the war, together with our allies, even if I am forced to sell half my dresses and diamonds."

On January 3 an order was sent to the commander-in-chief Count Saltykov to come to St. Petersburg as soon as possible and hand over command of the forces to Count Fermor. This summons followed as a consequence of a report by Saltykov that he did not know in which direction the army would move in the upcoming campaign and therefore he would refrain from sending detachments to inflict harm upon the enemy. Should the army advance to the right, that is into Pomerania, detachments could be sent to lay waste this still untouched country. If on the other hand detachments were sent to the left, this district had been laid waste completely already.

INSPECTION OF ARTILLERY

Artillery Lieutenant General Glebov[1] arrived at army headquarters before Saltykov's departure for St. Petersburg in order to make a detailed comparison of the new artillery with the old in the presence of the field marshal, the general staff, the officers and even the soldiers, at least a small number from each company, and in that way resolve all doubts. When giving notice of his instructions for conducting this comparison Saltykov wrote, "I have taken into consideration those harmful consequences which may easily arise from the tales of military personnel present on such an occasion. They should be kept in mute obedience to their commanders, and by no means given cause and occasion for discussion of such matters. Therefore, in the most humble hope of the highest approbation, I took the liberty to rescind the command for ordinary soldiers to give testimony regarding the artillery."

The "highest approbation" did not follow. "We consider it is necessary," Saltykov read in the answering rescript, "the more swiftly and accurately to ascertain any strong preference of the ordinary soldier for the new artillery over the old. With this intention, while greatly respecting the fact that however accurate the inspection, and however much the advantages of the new artillery has been proven, perhaps it will not be attain the benefit desired. The only way to overcome the doubt that has taken root in the army in respect to the new artillery, in particular among the soldiers of the line, is if its advantages are clearly proved and explained definitively by their commanders. Therefore by this rescript we instruct you, under penalty of severe punishment for failure to observe these instructions, to give directions that the entire army general staff attempt to explain and to give confidence to staff and senior officers, and officers to the rank and file, at every opportunity, inculcating in them a greater trust in the new artillery. It is in reality to their own advantage, and its operation is, of course, superior and more powerful than that of the enemy."

The artillery inspection began in Marienwerder on January 28 and continued January 29-31, after which a detailed register was sent to St. Petersburg, signed by all generals present. The following broad conclusion was attached. "The newly devised artillery naturally has advantages over the old, when a three-pound cannon is compared with a twelve-pound 'unicorn' and even other arms. Yet as the skillful art (experience) of past campaigns has demonstrated, both the one and the other in its own way is necessary and useful. Consequently both types of artillery may still be used successfully. Therefore in our judgment, both because of long familiarity with the previous artillery, not only of the lower ranks within the artillery but, in case of need, even of the soldiers, the undersigned find it desirable to maintain both the old cannons and mortars in the army as well as the newly devised armaments."

THE PLAN OF CAMPAIGN

Soon after the inspection of the artillery Saltykov set off for St. Petersburg. There on March 7 he offered his opinion on the plan for the future campaign. In his judgement the reputation of the Russian army had been established and confirmed by victories over an enemy which had defeated all other armies apart from the Russian. "This reputation must be maintained. Therefore they must not engage in general battle with this desperate enemy except with overwhelming superiority on their side. The Russian army may set out on the campaign with a force of no more than sixty thousand infantry and regular cavalry. Yet this army would scarcely surpass the forces the enemy could put in the field against the Russians, should he be permitted to do so by the allies. As the enemy on his own territory has a better chance of hiding his movements, and the speed of movement of the king of Prussia is sufficiently well known to everyone, a great deal of care must be taken lest he attack us in the rear with superior forces, as without warning we could not avoid a general engagement. Therefore it is considered most appropriate in bringing the Prussian army into a state of general exhaustion by the allies, not only not to cross the Oder, not only not to undertake the siege of those fortresses lying on the river, but not even to approach this river without great caution and, following the Austrian example, try to lead the enemy into a state of exhaustion more by constraints rather than by victories, from which our own forces may be diminished significantly."

On this basis the future campaign might, in Saltykov's opinion, take the following form. "(1) Occupy the whole of Pomerania up to the fortresses along the Oder and take measures to become firmly established there, so that we may remain there for the winter. (2) Occupy Danzig at the very beginning of the campaign, both for our own security and to deny its advantages to the enemy, as he receives grain from Danzig, recruits soldiers there, buys horses and obtains good coinage for minting into his own. (3) On taking Danzig, go into the interior of Pomerania as far as the Praga river, build a fortified camp there and dispatch a corps for the siege of Kolberg, covering the siege with the main army. (4) We can hope that during the siege of Kolberg the allies may achieve some advantage over the enemy which will make apparent the best way of continuing military operations. Even if they did not manage to achieve anything substantial, then even by taking Kolberg, providing it with a small garrison, making depots and leaving behind all major liabilities, we may move towards the Oder, making the enemy believe that the intention is to cross that river and occupy Berlin. (5) With this movement the enemy must detach a significant number of his forces to repel the danger threatening him, of which the allies must take advantage to attack him with superior forces. (6) If the allies destroy the enemy, the Russian forces would move to the siege of one of the fortresses on the Oder. (7) Should the Russian forces not manage to occupy a fortress on the Oder, the reputation of the forces would be maintained by the occupation of Pomerania, the army would be preserved and more hopes for a peace settlement would be realized, as the enemy would lose a significant part of his territories."

This plan was not accepted. On April 30 the empress signed another plan of campaign, in the foreword to which was stated, "If we were prosecuting the present war with the king of Prussia alone, or if matters consisted merely in us keeping East Prussia within those boundaries which we now control, or if we had to conduct a defensive war, there would scarcely be the need to concern ourselves with any plans for military operations. It would be enough merely to maintain the army in sound condition, to be ready for any eventuality and to undertake only what circumstances themselves dictate. We are conducting a war together with the empress-queen, however, and the matter consists not simply in keeping East Prussia in our possession but in fulfilling our obligations to restore the king of Poland to his hereditary possessions. Therefore we must defeat the forces of the king of Prussia, fulfill what we have promised frequently by solemn declarations and not show any less commitment when the war is coming to an end. At such a time we must anticipate the fruits of war to the extent of our assistance. We must anticipate the gratitude of our allies and of all Europe for that peace and security to which it is restored by the defeat of the forces of the king of Prussia. Therefore we cannot put together a plan of military operations for the current year in any other way than with the agreement of the empress-queen.

"More especially, however numerous the forces gathered by the court in Vienna against the king of Prussia, they will not be sufficient to end the war as we would wish. We must also confess that, however glorious the successes of our arms, we cannot follow up these successes without the assistance of Austrian forces. The last most glorious campaign for our arms and for your name affirms this truth more than anything else. The most decisive conflict at Frankfurt, where the king of Prussia considered everything lost, did not end the war because our army could not follow up its victory given the remoteness of the war zone. Count Daun refused, or was unable, to reinforce or to supply our army as necessary. About this we do not wish to go into detail, lest we recall to mind everything that was unfortunate in this matter.

"Therefore a plan of general operations for the current year has been drawn up between us and the empress-queen, and consists of the following points. (1) The empress-queen will gather together yet another army, this time in Lusatia, in addition to that already gathered in Saxony, and will try to drive the enemy forces out of there. (2) Our army must move towards the Oder between Frankfurt and Glogau.

"Of course this plan is not in agreement with yours. Besides the fact that you were unaware of the actual intentions of the Viennese court, your opinion very easily may be made to conform to the new plan if the principal arguments are explained further. You have reasoned as a skillful general taking care to preserve the army and the reputation it has gained, and in addition have in mind only past precedent. We, on the contrary, are forced to take into account the extent to which our state has become impoverished since the beginning of the aggravation of the king of Prussia, by conscription levies, by the increase of the army and by the customary maintenance of considerable forces on the Livonian frontier in readiness to restrain the king of Prussia from his harmful enterprises. Our empire would have been in extreme danger many times over had the Ottoman Porte conceived the desire to declare war upon us, had we been obliged to defend ourselves against it and at the same time fear trouble from the direction of Prussia.

"Necessity would have forced us sooner or later to embark upon this war ourselves, even had the king of Prussia not started it. That sovereign, formerly dependent upon all of his neighbors, wanted in the end to put all the courts into a state of dependency upon him. He has demanded everything from everybody, while not wanting to give satisfaction to anyone himself in anything. He has shown, in embarking upon the present war, that he would not permit the court of Vienna to make the slightest movement in any of its own lands. If the king of Prussia is not incapacitated by the present war, his significance will have increased incomparably, as the world will consider him invincible. Our influence and that of our allies will have suffered immeasurably, as we could do nothing even when Providence itself created all the circumstances to give us victory.

"In this case our empire, even if not exposed to greater danger than the court of Vienna, nevertheless would be much more excluded from participation in European affairs as the king of Prussia, standing in the way, would cut us off for all time from any communication with the court of Vienna, and we would be left surrounded either by enemies or unreliable neighbors. The long-term maintenance in readiness of significant forces on the Livonian frontier would, of course, cost our government more than even the present war. That is why further prolongation of this war will become incomparably more expensive than its conclusion in a single campaign, however expensive such a campaign might be.

"We always have been of the opinion that we ought not to venture upon a hopeless and premature conflict. Yet the examples of last year have taught us that these days it is not so necessary to fear a general engagement because they are more bloody and desperate than formerly. At that time the king of Prussia had a quite different comprehension of our forces. It seemed impossible to him that they could stand up to the Prussians because either they had not been in the present war for long, or they were used to fighting less sophisticated peoples; the more so as the Austrian forces, although constantly at war and often victorious, very rarely stood their ground against the Prussians. Therefore at the beginning of the war he had no doubt that Lehwaldt's army alone was sufficient to destroy all our forces. As soon as he was unsuccessful in the battle of Gross-Jägersdorf he took other measures. He quit East Prussia. When in 1758 our army crossed into Pomerania, subjugated the greater part of it and reduced Küstrin to ashes, the part of Lehwaldt's army under the command of Count Dohna no longer dared to show itself in our vicinity.

"The battle of Zorndorf, always remembered with distress, gave him a rather different impression of our army.[2] He basically concluded that our army would allow itself to be attacked whenever the enemy liked, that there were many ways of causing it extreme harm, but it was difficult or impossible to enjoy complete victory, so great is the courage of even beaten soldiers. At that point he could satisfy himself that it was worth simply placing a small corps against our army, and it would not shift until the season of the year obliged it to retreat. Therefore last year the king of Prussia made up his mind to send the army of Dohna or Wedell to Poznan, in no way regarding it as having sufficient strength to gain a victory over us or to stay there. He was assured that our army would not set out because his forces were there, even less attack them. The whole campaign therefore would end in frustration and ignominy, with the army standing idle in the vicinity of Poznan. So it would have happened had you not accelerated the pace by your arrival there, and had you not taken the prudent and courageous decision to march straight into enemy territory.

"Now the king of Prussia needs to be given a totally new impression of what our army is like. He has been able to reassure himself that there was no general engagement at Palzig. The battle of Frankfurt alone was enough assurance for him and everybody that our army is not yet defeated, even when all advantages have been achieved against it. In fact what army would not have been brought to disarray and put to flight, being outflanked and a significant part of it brought down, much of the artillery lost and by far the greater part reduced to inactivity?

"At Frankfurt we proved that the fortitude and sound common sense of a commander and the discipline of the troops gain the most complete of victories even when it seems impossible to expect anything but devastation. After Zorndorf and Frankfurt the king of Prussia was assured that it was useless to attack our army, the more so as it would never take the initiative. Consequently there was no need to anticipate an attack. With the onset of autumn the Russian army would return to the Vistula, whatever victory it may have gained, so why venture into battle? Believe us, the enemy's courage comes principally from the fact that he in no way expects an attack and that he would never have approached our army so importunately and brazenly, if even once one of his corps were to be exposed to attack. In our opinion it is now less necessary than at any other time to expect engagements which it would be impossible to avoid.

"The vast difference even now compared with previous campaigns consists in the fact that at that time our army was always marching through completely unfamiliar terrain. It is impossible now to find any place to march, about which we do not have complete knowledge. Some danger remained last year as to whether the battle of Zorndorf had a negative impression on our men. Though our single edict and your arrival took effect, and the men understood how harmful their lack of discipline and drunkenness had been to them, how much more now they understand the necessity for blind obedience, when they have witnessed two great victories gained by discipline and steadfastness? The cavalry is now much greater in number than it was before, and by your own admission has never been in such good condition. In a word we are sure that the entire army is now awaiting with extreme impatience your arrival and the start of the campaign, so that it may offer service anew to its native land under your leadership, and may crown the reputation it has already gained by the restoration of a peace so much desired. Almost everyone with us would almost begrudge it if Count Daun, even in conformity with our wishes, should bring off something substantial and decisive before your arrival or without your assistance.

"The opinion you have offered is very well-founded, and the plan set out according to the military rules. We regret that we did not give instructions for the campaign of 1758 to begin in that way, and Count Fermor did not so conclude it. Not only did he not attempt in any way to avoid a purposeless battle forced upon him, but was almost marching himself to meet it. Then the war had scarcely begun. That is why we had to prepare for the eventuality of retreat. Now circumstances are completely different. Should it happen against our wishes and expectations that yet one more campaign is necessary, it shall be done. We will just have to take some steps to that end. Nothing on this earth can harm our interests and the general cause more than the belief that the war will still not be concluded by the present campaign, and that therefore we must make preparations for another.

"The war is in fact coming to an end. England and Prussia have made a formal proposal for a congress, and we and our allies cannot ignore that. Whether there will be the same agreement among the allies for a congress as there has been so far, it is impossible to foresee. It is clear that in the event of a swift reduction of the forces of the king of Prussia by the energetic operations of our own and the Austrian forces, we may keep the other allies on our side, whereas if we operate in the present campaign without fervor, slowly, there is no doubt that our already exhausted allies one after another will give us up. Each will seek a separate peace settlement, will enter into undertakings with the king of Prussia and, worst of all, instead of gratitude for our staunch assistance perhaps even will reproach us for the fact that we, in acting indecisively and slowly, were seeking a separate peace settlement ourselves and were anxious to abandon them.

"The Swedes are simply holding out in this way, and the king of Prussia does not even have to consider them. The French court frankly confessed its complete impoverishment, and if the empress-queen and we do nothing substantial before the opening of peace talks we must fear that France will agree immediately to the most disadvantageous conditions. The empress-queen, of course, is happy to continue the war to the point of complete attrition in order to regain Silesia. Yet her own total depletion is already so great that it is only through any substantial successes of the present campaign, and therefore in certain expectation that the next campaign will be the last, that she will be able to find new resources. If we act indecisively and the others also give up completely, it will be impossible to reproach her should she put off the recovery of Silesia to another time, or even abandon any further thought of it.

"In a word at present there is a choice between two things: either to act in the present campaign with all our strength and anticipate an honorable peace settlement or, much better and shorter, without incurring any further losses, to accept any peace settlement the enemy may permit. You know how far we are from such faintheartedness. We deplore what has been said in this respect. Moreover there is no need to imagine that the war will be long drawn out. There is no obstacle, no doubt or fear to stop our forces marching to the Oder between Frankfurt and Glogau. When our army arrives successfully at the Oder and the two Austrian armies are close by and in communication with us, nothing more is needed to bring the war to an end than the agreement of the commanders, the taking of swift and purposeful decisions and the earnest endeavor to carry them out."

SALTYKOV'S ADVANCE

With this decision Saltykov then returned to the army in Marienburg, where he arrived only on May 31. From June there began to appear in the newspapers items relating minor successes of the light cavalry under the command of Major General Todtleben. Then news appeared of a victory of the Austrian general Loudon in Silesia over the Prussian general Fouqué,[3] the entire enemy corps being either destroyed or taken prisoner. At last appeared in the newspapers that on June 13 Field Marshal Saltykov had left Marienburg and had arrived at Poznan on June 24. A detachment of fifteen thousand troops was dispatched for the second siege of Kolberg.

SALTYKOV'S CORRESPONDENCE WITH THE CONFERENCE

At first Saltykov received rescripts of approval. Then the following rescript was sent to him on July 15. "We would have wanted to reply at length to your communiqués (of June 27 from Poznan) but the contents of these communiqués were extremely confused, the one completely refuting the other, with no way of making out which was the more reliable. Apart from the fact that these different versions were written on the same date, in the very latest you merely confirm events that have for the most part or even completely passed. Therefore, in order not to enter into controversy with you, and in order not to lead you into confusion with any precise instructions regarding such unreliable and unclear events, we consider it better to refer to our last rescript in which you were instructed precisely to undertake and to set in motion everything pertinent to the general cause and conducive to the decisive conclusion of the present war. On the other hand you must not expose our army to any purposeless and apparent danger. In this respect we note that there is no necessity for the large number and the extensive character of your communiqués.

"For our pleasure and peace of mind you should endeavor to send us reasonable communiqués as frequently as possible, observing the following order in drawing them up. (1) Outline in brief the state of affairs and of the army. (2) State what changes have taken place of late. (3) State how matters and the army are at present. (4) What therefore do you intend to do, or where do you wish to direct the campaign?

"It is regrettable and incomprehensible to us to see such scarcity of ready cash, that officers are eating the same food as the soldiers because they have not received any pay. From the enclosed report of the Chief Commissioner of War you will see that 758,000 rubles were spent on salaries up to May 30, and are still being forwarded. We believe that even the three hundred and fifty thousand rubles sent to you from the College of Foreign Affairs have been delivered and soon an even more significant sum will be dispatched. We await with impatience from you some positive information, having no doubt that you will look not to trifles but to the most important matter in hand, and that you will be eager to augment your own reputation and that of our arms gained during the last campaign."

There was great alarm in St. Petersburg in July caused by a letter from General Springer with the Austrian army from the Russian side, and on July 18 a rescript was sent to Saltykov. "To our astonishment we have no news whatsoever from you, but Major General Springer reports on July 6 that the king of Prussia and Count Daun are now in full advance in Lower Lusatia, that the king of Prussia is attempting to join up with the army of his brother Prince Henry, and that Count Daun is making every effort to hamper this intention and to maintain communication with all his corps. We hasten to send you a courier, not out of fear for our army, but lest the present campaign be rendered not only as indecisive as the last, but even less glorious for our arms. From the present critical circumstance now depends both the fatal prolongation of the war and its successful conclusion. If the king of Prussia manages to join up with Prince Henry, we must be sure that he does not defeat Count Daun with these united forces or, if you take Daun's great caution into consideration, that Frederick does not lead him into a disaster such as he has not experienced thus far. This is almost as harmful as losing a battle, for if this summer nothing of material significance is accomplished, in the last months of the year it will be impossible to make it up in any way.

"The direct and most reliable means of averting misfortune is for General Loudon to undertake something substantial in Silesia, and for you to hasten to Breslau. We see no danger whatsoever in this. Not only is Loudon in front of you and cutting off the way to Prince Henry, but all the Austrian forces have now come close to Silesia as well. The use to which this might be put cannot be overestimated. The king of Prussia will be obliged to divide his forces and you, being the prime cause, will have the right to direct all the operations of the present campaign. Even should the king indeed join Prince Henry, even should Count Daun be beaten, you would be far to the rear of him and close to Poland. In that unlikely event, at least retreat would not expose you to any danger or difficulty."

As this rescript was sent off a dispatch was received from Saltykov dated June 6. "I am," wrote the field marshal, "by no means of the opinion now, nor shall I ever be, that as the Austrians did very little in the last campaign, there is nothing for the army of your imperial majesty to do now, the more so as I have always fulfilled my humble duty, in spite of any differences, to carry out your majesty's pleasure and command as precisely and as far as possible. In particular at present through so splendid a success granted by the Almighty to Austrian arms at the beginning of this campaign (the destruction of Fouqué's corps) I am doing my very best to hasten my departure. Furthermore I am obliged most humbly to report that the troops that have arrived here, the cavalry in particular, both men and mounts, are in the very best condition and, if I may be so bold as to say so, better than ever.

"I have just received from the Austrian general Baron Loudon a letter with an inventory of Prince Henry's corps. You will be so good as to observe that he is at present situated near the town of Liegnitz, from which Breslau may be reached in one or two days' forced march. Finally he asks that a corps of your imperial majesty's troops go ahead to Breslau to take it and seize the supplies there. I shall reply to him immediately that in a few days, on the arrival here of the remaining third division, I shall advance directly towards Breslau with all the army entrusted to me. As soon as I can rectify certain dispositions and dry a quantity of biscuits, I shall make all haste."

On July 10 Saltykov wrote, "Although I shall not fail immediately to advance directly upon the campaign with which I have been entrusted, and to do so as quickly as possible (in order to make recompense for that time which, to my extreme regret, has been lost), nevertheless I am obliged to point out that because of the expenditure for laying in supplies and for distribution to the regiments a small part of their salaries for the satisfaction of the men, with the small amount of money in all departments available in the army there is almost no money whatsoever now available anywhere. Nothing yet has arrived of the sums assigned for provisions, the commissariat and other purposes, and I have no report as to where they are at this moment.

"On the other hand men are even beginning to desert because, in addition to their increasing indignation, their pay is in arrears. In the past week about fifty have deserted from the entire army, and six only yesterday. I have received a Prussian manifesto from Prince Henry distributed in Poland about their intention to advance into that kingdom. On the other hand news has reached me that the enemy intends by a march straight to the Vistula to create a diversion for the army of your imperial majesty and to cut off communication with that river. Although it is in no way possible to believe that the enemy, without any source of supplies, has undertaken to make for the Vistula, the likelihood must really be considered that he sometimes takes pleasure simply by making his way through the local districts to the rear of your majesty's army and thus cutting off any supplies from the Vistula. In that way he can not only prevent any supplies reaching Silesia, but can even turn them back. All this, however, is best accounted for inevitably by my imminent departure from here with the army. In the meantime in the event of an enemy movement to the rear of us just mentioned, your majesty's army must turn back. As we do not have any longer any prepared stockpiles in Kalisz and as there is less money available, there will inevitably be extreme discomfort for your majesty's army, the more so as there is no longer any hope of obtaining anything here in this territory on credit. On the other hand, should the enemy march into Silesia parallel with us, following last year's example, I would not in any way let this very desirable opportunity slip to attack and destroy him, the more so as the present change of direction of the king of Prussia in Saxony may be greatly conducive towards this end, as news has reached me here from various quarters that he has turned once more towards Dresden. Consequently, if this is true, instead of joining Prince Henry, he will find himself between two fires."

There was great delight in Tsarskoe Selo on the receipt of this report. On July 22 a rescript was sent to Saltykov. "We have observed with extreme pleasure and favor that your opinions in respect of the king and Prince Henry are now in conformity with our own. Your prospects and hopes of defeating the enemy, of augmenting your laurels and crowning our arms with new glory are reviving and increasing as you approach enemy territory and the enemy himself. It is no less pleasing for us to see that our army, both the men and their mounts, are in such good condition, better than they have been at almost any other time. We properly acknowledge in the first instance the blessing of the Lord, and we shall give our thanks for this, and then for your own efforts and care.

"On the other hand it is very regrettable to us to observe that you cannot see an end to the shortage of money by the transfer we expected of various sums sent from here, and that it is beginning to have very unpleasant consequences. Our anxiety about these unpleasant consequences is not particularly great, because the enthusiasm of our loyal subjects is well known to us, and we may be confident of your good sense and that of the other members of the general staff.

"We have certainly considerable sympathy for the fact that for a short period of time officers and men are experiencing considerable hardship. In this respect we are writing by this courier to the governor of Königsberg, Lieutenant General Korff, that he make every effort to deliver to you as soon as possible sums of money still in transit. We are presently hastening to send you new sums of money from here, and we authorize you to negotiate for money from the bankers Riokur and Tsiman or however you can. We give you permission also to act, in case of need, on conditions which may be not be too advantageous to our Treasury, to raise a sum not exceeding three hundred thousand rubles, and in extreme circumstances up to half a million. We consider the welfare of our army and the supply of provisions without shortages more important than anything else."

A rescript of July 26 was sent in the same tone. "We have observed from your communiqués with great pleasure that our army has begun to advance from Poznan on a further campaign. The campaign is very well founded. It is prudent and consistent with the art of war. Though perhaps it has been accelerated, there appears to be no fear even of a shortage of forage. Coming together with other forces, in the event of the enemy's approach, can take place swiftly. Your intention to attack Prince Henry, should he want to hinder your movements, also gives us great pleasure." On July 15 the army indeed advanced from Poznan to Breslau to join up with Loudon's Austrian corps.

SALTYKOV'S RETREAT AND ILLNESS

In August matters changed. Saltykov made known his retreat because Frederick II quickly returned to Silesia and managed to join, or at least to restore unrestricted communication, with Prince Henry. By this means he hampered Loudon's conjunction with the Russian forces. The field marshal put all the blame on the Austrian commander-in-chief Count Daun, who allowed Frederick II to move over to our side of the Oder. As a consequence Saltykov, without hope of receiving any assistance from the Austrians, refused to expose his army to obvious danger.

Finally Saltykov told them of his own illness. A rescript in reply to these reports, sent on August 22, betrayed considerable irritation. "All of this will simply lead to unpleasant and useless explanations with the court in Vienna. The matter will be little improved thereby, and we will only lose valuable time. That you have retreated so precipitately and cancelled all your plans cannot be welcome for us to hear, and even less so that you, begging new orders for further action, not only fail to suggest any ideas for your part, but merely try to discover and to demonstrate difficulties and obstacles everywhere. We well understand that your situation is difficult. You must agree, however, that you already have sufficient directions for almost every eventuality that might arise. In a word, during the whole of the present war we have not yet been in such embarrassing circumstances. It is quite intolerable that the campaign, having begun so splendidly, and having promised without any doubt the desired end to the war, should become so fruitless. At this point yet other arguments become associated with these circumstances. We have agreed crucially with the court of Vienna matters relating to expected advantages from this war and it has acknowledged us directly as a belligerent against the king of Prussia. Having ceased to be assistants and getting out of liabilities that were burdensome and useless to us, naturally we had to intensify the operations of our arms for our reputation and to attain our goals. We must still win over France and the other powers. In face of the poor successes of French arms, if we cannot show the court of Versailles and the whole world that at least on our side everything possible has been done sincerely, any proposal regarding our rewards will not only be untimely but may produce unpleasant consequences at the French court and, increasing disgust at an unsuccessful war, may force all the alliance towards an injurious peace settlement.

"For that reason we have been holding out all this time, waiting to see whether by some fortunate circumstance you would present some useful reinforcement to our negotiations. The Danish court is already threatening to join with England and the king of Prussia, and the poor success of the present campaign may spur it on all the more to unite with our foes. It may appear to a public not knowing all the details that our army has undertaken the campaign in Silesia merely with the intention of making use of any advantages the Austrians prepare for us, and not to do anything ourselves. As soon as the king of Prussia made contact with Prince Henry, even though they had not even joined forces, the decision immediately was taken by our army to retreat to Poland.

"We have no intention of minimizing the faults of the Austrian general staff. As for Count Daun, we have given instructions for what amounts to a formal complaint to be brought against him. We are in no way satisfied, however, that reprimands proceeding from the poor direction of our affairs can be blamed on Count Daun alone. The matter cannot be corrected in this way. Rather we must try to correct it in actuality. We are sure that had matters in Silesia taken on a positive appearance before sending these instructions you would not have given up, naturally, making use of our previous instructions, especially where they enjoined an extreme effort to make the campaign decisive. Perhaps matters will correct themselves on receipt of these instructions, and you will see that you can improve them still more without further danger and make them most decisive. In that case, of course, you must make every effort to this end.

"Should matters between the Austrians and the king of Prussia nevertheless remain undecided, and if in the meantime Kolberg falls into our hands, you must consider taking up winter quarters in Pomerania. As regards the march there from Silesia, we leave this up to you. If neither the king nor Prince Henry follow you, both being detained by the Austrian forces, you will have to send a small corps to reinforce the siege of Kolberg and gradually proceed there yourself. It would be best of all to send Count Todtleben with light cavalry by another road to Berlin and to give him instructions to return to you in Pomerania by way of Schwedt. If matters are not corrected, and should the army be in danger, nothing else remains but to concern yourself for its preservation."

Saltykov continued to report that he was ill. On August 30 he was sent the following rescript. "The contents of your communiqués we find very regrettable. Obviously the army is being brought to a degree of idleness by your illness. At least decisions cannot be carried out as swiftly as necessary, this at a time when we must expect the resolution of the campaign, when there is no enemy against our army, when there is nothing to stop us taking measures along the lines we have advocated, when the slightest activity of our forces could mean so much, giving the enemy great anxiety and rendering considerable assistance to the Austrian army. From a letter which has been seized, written in the king of Prussia's hand, and also according to the number of deserters coming openly to you, the enemy is in extremely difficult circumstances, but out of despair is considering a move of considerable significance, namely an attack with all his forces on Count Daun. Despite knowing all this at first hand, you are not only doing nothing to avert or even to lessen the danger, but have not even told Count Daun about it, whereas we understand that this important letter of the king of Prussia is known to many in our army who have no need to know.

"Now what we told you over and over again indeed has happened. The king of Prussia will not seek an opportunity to attack you as brazenly as in the past but will avoid any chance of doing so. It is rather more important for him to rush upon the Austrian troops with all his forces. Yet we do not see that your previous convictions have evaporated completely. We hear, by the way, that discipline in our army has become extremely lax. Many who are quite healthy are malingering. You have under your command such fine generals that, thanks to their zeal and in the event of your own absence, the fulfillment of our aims need not stop or be delayed. Therefore we give instructions to make it clear to all generals in our name that if anything be let slip, your illness will not serve them as an excuse but, on the contrary, will be a charge against them. Neither they nor the whole army has any need to relax because of your illness. Get over your condition, have the courage to carry out our will and strictly force others to carry it out.

"We long ago instructed you that we would rather see good planning than good luck, and that the services of the general staff under your command will increase your merit before us. We give you leave, should you happen to undertake anything substantial and helpful, to make use of anyone who is more competent and diligent, regardless of seniority. You must combine twenty-five, or at least twenty thousand, of our forces with General Loudon to cover the siege of Glogau, to which fortress you must lay siege with the remainder of our army. At present not one of your fears has come to pass. The king of Prussia has not come after you. So assure yourself even now that there is not a single one of those dangers to our army you imagine."

Indication that there was a slackening of discipline in the army mentioned in this rescript is explained by a paper of the Conference to the empress. "Your imperial majesty has been pleased to observe in the latest communiqué from General Field Marshal Saltykov that, while gaining some alleviation from one of his ailments, he is not only in a state of extreme weakness and feeling worse hour by hour, but feels the onset of yet another inner sickness. To this unfortunate circumstance is added another even more unfortunate, namely that Lieutenant General Chernyshev writes to the chancellor that the rule of anarchy continues in the army. The field marshal is such a hypochondriac that he often weeps, neglects business and says, without concealing it in any way, that he intends to ask to be relieved of his command, that indiscipline in the army is increasing and there is almost no hope of correcting it." The Conference then suggested appointing Field Marshal Count Alexander Borisovich Buturlin commander-in-chief of the army.

SALTYKOV HANDS COMMAND TO BUTURLIN

On August 31 Saltykov informed the Conference that his illness was continuing, and that he would have to hand over the command to Count Fermor. He asked permission to leave for Poznan. He was given this permission in a rescript on September 18, in which he was informed that Field Marshal Count Buturlin[4] was appointed commander-in-chief of the army. A rescript then also was sent to Fermor. "Even should you have been commander-in-chief for only one day, you must think in such a way as though you always had command and therefore should never postpone anything. From his undoubtedly insubstantial corps the Prussian general Goltz has sent Major General Werner to Frankfurt. Knowing about the expedition to Kolberg, it would not have been difficult for you to guess we are vexed that this exercise was carried out to save this small fortress. To our extreme regret not only has nothing been done to stop this, but it never even dawned on anybody that by this move Goltz's insubstantial corps was made even weaker. Yet not even a party of light cavalry has been sent to warn our corps near Kolberg, so that now our best measures have been frustrated and the ill-fame of our army has been revived that proceeded from the unsuccessful siege of this nest in 1758. As there is still time to set this muddle to rights, we trust that General Goltz will suffer a perceptible defeat, or at least that General Werner does not return from Pomerania to boast of his good fortune, but is punished for his endeavors."

The instructions to the new commander stated, "Order and strict discipline are the heart and main strength of the army. You know that in part because of the prolonged illness of Count Saltykov and in part from other circumstances, a considerable degree of negligence and indiscipline has occurred in this respect. Our army is not obtaining any sustenance from this fruitful land, which is completely destroyed and its inhabitants driven away. Apart from this we hear with extreme annoyance that army transports have been increased with an unbelievable number of horses. The horses, it is true, have been taken on enemy territory. For all that, apart from the fact that horses should not be taken from innocent inhabitants, these horses have not been taken for the army, not for our service, not in order to relieve our forces and carry all essential equipment after them. They carry only personal belongings, and are a burden to the army. They hinder its movements, use unnecessary manpower, causing physical exhaustion and, finally, in their large numbers deprive it of forage. We give instructions that, as soon as you have reduced your own transport as much as you can, you immediately make an inventory of all the horses in the army, with the number that everybody has and, leaving everyone no more than they really need, take the remainder for us. Supply government transports and the artillery with good horses out of these, and put the poor ones out to pasture in East Prussia, so that at least they might be of some use later, that in a future campaign there should be no need to drive horses from here or to waste vast sums of money buying them in Poland. We cannot give any instructions at present in respect to military operations, because time is very short and you can better see and set up everything on the spot yourself. Should the king of Prussia be beaten decisively by the Austrians, we would very much hope that our winter quarters be established near the Oder. We should be almost equally pleased were this done in Pomerania or else, owing to a scarcity of resources, we would have to return to the Vistula, for it will not be at all worthwhile to winter in Poland, and supply depots already have been established on the Vistula."

OCCUPATION AND ABANDONMENT OF BERLIN

In the meantime at the military council held by Fermor it was decided to move into Brandenburg and carry out the empress's edict regarding the taking of Berlin with light cavalry.[5] On September 12 the army was near Carolath on the near side of the Oder, but the corps of Count Chernyshev and Major General Todtleben with a section of light cavalry was on the other side near Beuthen. On the September 15 the army crossed the Oder. Todtleben with the light cavalry moved ahead, and after him at a short distance was Chernyshev. On September 22 the army was in Guben. On the same date at ten in the morning Todtleben appeared near Berlin with hussars and cossacks and occupied all three roads from the Cottbus, Köpenik and Brandenburg gates. Prussian hussars rode out of the Brandenburg gate but almost all were killed or taken prisoner. After setting up a battery between the Cottbus and Brandenburg gates Todtleben sent to demand the surrender of the city and, on receiving a refusal, ordered this battery to fire on the royal castle and the foundry. Although this bombardment caused fires within the city, they were put out quickly by the citizens, and by nightfall the Russians moved their battery and established it by the Brandenburg gate. Deserters said that there were only three battalions of infantry in the city, together with a few mounted troops. Moreover these all were recruited from Russian, Saxon and French prisoners of war who were immediately ready to lay down their arms. On the basis of this information Todtleben decided to take the Brandenburg and Cottbus gates by storm at night. At ten that evening the bombardment began again. At midnight the grenadiers tried to take the gates by storm, but were beaten back. At three in the morning the bombardment was called off because of a shortage of cartridges.

After this Prince Friedrich of Würtemberg and General Hülsen made their way towards Berlin to render some assistance, while the Russian generals Chernyshev and Panin and the Austrian Count Lacy[6] joined Todtleben. Hourly engagements began, and on September 29 Chernyshev ordered a sudden attack at dawn on the entire enemy corps, while Todtleben was to make an assault towards the city. Hülsen did not wait for the attack and in the night of September 28-29, under cover of darkness, made his way into the nearby forest and lay concealed. When he got to know about this at dawn, Chernyshev immediately sent to demand the surrender of the city, but his emissary was met on the road by an officer sent from Todtleben to tell him that the city would surrender. Todtleben was negotiating conditions of surrender. These conditions stated that all military personnel in Berlin would receive free passage out of the city with all their belongings. The royal castle and other public buildings would remain unharmed. Berlin was to pay half a million thalers in war indemnity and two hundred thousand thalers to the forces. For two days (September 29-30) the victors were occupied with the collection of war indemnity, the appropriation of the royal Treasury and the mopping up of the arsenals and supply depots. What could not be appropriated was destroyed. All the powder mills near Berlin, the cannon foundry, the armament and sword factories in Potsdam and near Spandau were razed to their foundations.

When news of the occupation of Berlin was received in St. Petersburg all foreign ambassadors, with the exception of the English, came to the Chancellery on October 11 with their congratulations. They enlarged upon the gloriousness of this event for the reign of Elizabeth, for her ministry and army. In particular the ambassadors of Austria, France and Councillor Prasse of the Saxon embassy suggested that, for the honor of Russian arms and the common cause, Berlin must be held. They said that in addition to reinforcements already in the city, perhaps it could be strengthened even more very soon, and brought into such a condition that it would be quite safe to remain there. Sufficient supplies and forage probably could be found there. Moreover the districts surrounding Berlin were so far not in the war zone, and it could be hoped therefore that there would be no shortage of forage and grain. The Russian army occupying Berlin could take winter quarters in Brandenburg and Neumark, having the whole of Saxony, from which the enemy had been driven completely, to give it some support in this respect. If contrary to expectations the whole army could not remain there, at least a Russian corps of from twenty to twenty-five thousand could be sent to join up with the Austrian army supplied with sustenance by the empress-queen.

As far as could be seen the king of Prussia cared more about retaining Silesia than anything else. If he attempted any move against the Russian forces in Berlin and Brandenburg he might discover only his destruction in such an undertaking. In addition to the fact that all Russian corps were close to one another and could render each other assistance, the corps of Count Lacy, which had joined the Russian forces, could render not insignificant support. Besides, Count Daun would not give up following the heels of the king. So if the empress were pleased to accept these ideas regarding the retention of Berlin and wintering in Brandenburg and Neumark, or concerning sending from twenty to twenty-five thousand troops into Saxony, the king of Prussia would be so constrained from all sides that a final conclusion of the war must be expected. These suggestions were somewhat belated. Berlin was occupied with a financial target in mind, with a war indemnity to ease the burden of military expenses. Therefore as soon as this booty was taken, Chernyshev and Todtleben evacuated Berlin on September 30-October 1.

Frederick the Great

J.G. Ziesenis, Staatliche Schlösser und Gärten, Potsdam-Sans Souci

Information about a second failure of Russian forces at Kolberg was published at the same time as news of the seizure of Berlin. It was no secret that with news of the approach of General Werner to help the city the Russian officers and men hastened to flee by boat, as a consequence of which a portion of the artillery was left as booty to the enemy.

BUTURLIN'S ARRIVAL

The new commander-in-chief Buturlin arrived at the army only after the occupation and abandonment of Berlin and after the second failure at Kolberg. At the end of October Buturlin reported from Arnswalde that he was leaving for the Vistula with the main army. He was leaving the corps of Count Chernyshev in Pomerania (nine regiments of infantry and four of dragoons), which would occupy a position from Regenwalde to Rummelsburg with the light cavalry covering from Köslin to Ratzeburg. He put forward as the reason for his withdrawal that when ordered to make a list of all the grain and forage in Pomerania, he found that without the complete devastation of this province there would be insufficient supplies for the whole army even for two weeks. In Poland the price of grain was not excessively high, but the horses which up to this point were with the transports for the army were so exhausted, and there were so few of them left, that if they were not allowed to rest now they could not be expected the following summer to transport the material necessary, or even to plough a field. Our supply depots on the Vistula were sufficiently well stocked but we could not transport anything from there except with regimental and artillery horses. Apart from the fact that this transport would not be sufficient to maintain the entire army, it could not possibly leave for the field the following spring.

In a rescript to the College of Foreign Affairs, directed for communication to foreign ambassadors, the empress said, "Owing to the present state of affairs and the great distance from here to the army, any command contrary to this order would be too late and awkward to carry out. Therefore we have confirmed this order and directed (1) There should be every possible attempt to move Count Chernyshev's corps forward, even a little, occupying his present position with other regiments. (2) As many troops as can be accommodated should be brought into the vicinity of Danzig. (3) The light cavalry should be so stationed that the enemy not only cannot obtain anything from Pomerania, but will not be free of anxiety even in Brandenburg itself. (4) Every effort should be made to prepare for the earliest possible start to the next campaign and, even while in winter quarters, everyone should be in constant readiness to take the field.

"We are sure," the rescript went on, "that our allies, when they have taken all this into mature consideration, will acknowledge that on this occasion we can do nothing more or in any other way. It will soon be impossible to provision our army in Pomerania, despite the fact that there may be an inexhaustible abundance of every food. Still less is it possible to take up winter quarters in either Brandenburg or Neumark. Even if the garrisons situated in the vicinity of their splendid fortresses cannot cause the army any anxiety, at least they can make delivery to it of uniforms and ammunition, and particularly horses, extremely difficult. Even if the king of Prussia is preoccupied at present in Saxony, nevertheless there is a sufficient precedent that once more he may hold Saxony and the Elbe behind him with a small army corps at Torgau, and in the meantime make his way at the double to the Oder. Even were we not in any danger from his approach, and even earnestly wished that matters could reach the point of a decisive engagement with him, yet in a manner totally incomprehensible to us not only are roads everywhere open to him, and food supplies available to him far and near. Therefore he may not only swiftly enter a completely impoverished Saxony, but may even pass between the army of Count Daun and the other Austrian forces, having no fear that he will be cut off from all his provinces and confined between the mountains and two enemy armies in a territory where no supplies could possibly be obtained. Thus we cannot but be convinced that the king of Prussia, situated in his own territory, would find every means, without giving any opportunity for an engagement, so to harry our army that it would always be obliged to remain in the field and under arms.

"The situation itself is now neither so favorable that it may be put to good use immediately, nor so bad as to cause despair. Every advantage for the king of Prussia rests on the fact that he acts aggressively and for that reason he almost always has his forces together, whereas Count Daun in acting defensively is obliged to divide his forces. It seems that everything now points to the fact that we should go over to the offensive and force the king of Prussia to act defensively. This may be achieved most expeditiously by the following means. The campaign should commence with taking Kolberg by our army, if it is impossible to do so any earlier. Then we must make every effort to cross the Oder, to clear the way for the Swedish army and to move on Berlin. At the same time we must see

whether we can take Küstrin. Even if we do not achieve this, at least we
can be assured that the king of Prussia, abandoning everything, will hasten there and resolve on a major battle. Noticeably he has been avoiding
this since Frankfurt, and otherwise it has been almost impossible to force
him to battle. Whatever the outcome of this engagement, it will in any
case weaken the forces of the king of Prussia and give the Austrian army
as much time as will be sufficient both to clear Saxony, and for significant gains to be made in Silesia. The College of Foreign Affairs must let
Count Esterhazy know all this to present it to his court.

"As regards the king of Poland, it is enough at this moment simply to
tell him how our army will be positioned, and to reassure him that our
army will do all it can to help in the deliverance of Saxony and the restoration of that honorable and stable peace we all long for. Nevertheless,
so as not to leave him with this promise alone and to avert, as much as
it depends upon us, the execution of Prussian threats, we instruct the English
minister here to read a note (and if he wants then to hand it to him), stating that we are naturally far from following bad examples, and would
have already consigned to oblivion all the stern measures enacted by the
king of Prussia in Saxony, Mecklenburg and elsewhere. As the king of
Prussia once more has entered Saxony and immediately uttered the threat
that Saxony must pay for the losses incurred by him in Berlin, and that
the country will be forced to do so by fire and sword, we are obliged to
declare that from now on we will not look indifferently upon any new
violation of the rules of war and the destruction of innocent lands. Although we are far from following bad examples of vengeance and inhumanity, yet if they do not stop, and as our moderation and our compassion for those regions suffering from the war bear only disagreeable fruit,
we shall give instructions in all those enemy territories, wherever our
military arm may reach, to follow the examples of the king of Prussia and
if possible to surpass them.

"It is not in accord with our dignity to justify our behavior, which has
been humane in the fiercest of wars. Still it is impossible not to mention
briefly that before the declaration of any war Saxony was seized in a most
perfidious manner and was ravaged, not as a prize gained by force of
arms, but as the victim of cruel vengeance. East Prussia, in spite of the
fact that it was occupied by us by right of war, has received confirmation
of all its rights and statutes, and is exercising them at this moment without violation, becoming richer from the presence of our forces and with

all the cash available. A great number of conscripts have been taken forcibly from Saxony and other inhabitants have been deported to the territory of Brandenburg. On the other hand not one man has been taken from East Prussia, and money has been distributed to the inhabitants of that kingdom from our Treasury in compensation for losses suffered from the cattle plague, so that they might continue to sow grain. The king of Prussia, with inhuman beatings and hunger, forces all prisoners to enter his service. We, on the contrary, free these involuntary recruits and return them to their rightful sovereign. With more to be embittered about than the king of Prussia, the seizure of the city of Berlin may simply serve to demonstrate our mercy and generosity. Because of the fortifications and defensive positions made there, where no resistance could be offered, the city deserved punishment, but it was shown mercy. Our soldiers were not quartered in a single house. Leipzig made no resistance, yet it did not receive such merciful treatment. In Berlin the arsenals, the armaments and artillery factories were destroyed, but the expedition was undertaken for that aim. A war indemnity was taken, but according to the generally accepted convention, and there would be no need to mention this war indemnity but for the fleecing of Saxony and Leipzig."

RETREAT TO THE VISTULA FOR WINTER

It was just announced to the allies that Chernyshev's corps was to remain in Pomerania when Buturlin sent a report that it was simply impossible to do so, as news was coming in from all sides that there was nothing to be obtained anywhere. He was sent a reply from St. Petersburg on December 4 that in that case there was nothing to be done but that Todtleben's corps, consisting of light cavalry and two infantry regiments, remain in Pomerania and be spread as far as possible in that province. Besides, Buturlin was not to conceal the fact that the campaign would begin with the siege and seizure of Kolberg. The seaports of Leba, Rügenwalde and Stolpemünde must be taken also. Their harbors must be rehabilitated using soldiers for the light work and local inhabitants for the heavy. It was confirmed by the Admiralty College that the entire fleet was in full readiness for the beginning of the navigation season, and the War College had ordered all field regiments in St. Petersburg and Reval, as well as a company of bombardier guards, to be prepared for embarkation by ship. In this way they hoped to divide Frederick II's attention quickly, and in spring to divide his forces as well, to avoid seeking the enemy over great distances and to no purpose, nor exhaust the troops with marches, but to draw Frederick to Pomerania and force him to fight.

Todtleben, whom it was proposed to leave in Pomerania, asked to be relieved of his duties, being angered at an imperial reprimand. The reprimand was caused by the fact that Todtleben made known in Germany information about the occupation of Berlin in which he glorified himself alone and slighted others. Buturlin sent a copy of this information to St. Petersburg. From there he received a rescript that Todtleben's communiqué "was compiled with the utmost impudence, as he exaggerates his own service at the expense of almost the entire army. In particular he clearly abuses Lieutenant General Chernyshev and his corps, and reviles the Austrian general Count Lacy and his corps in a similar manner, as if he was seeking to cause hatred between the two allied forces and even coldness between our courts. Despite the fact that he praises the action of our artillery and gives it the advantage over that of the enemy, nevertheless he discredits its condition, saying that it disintegrates when facing any major action. A great deal of his effortry also consists in the fact that, without giving the commander-in-chief a similarly detailed report, nor sending one here, he dared to disclose these matters quite contrary to all military rules.

"Because we also indeed remember services rendered, and by our mercy are accustomed to consign transgressions to oblivion, we thought fit, while letting him know of our righteous anger and displeasure, to give instructions that he immediately try to make amends for his misdemeanor and once more earn our grace by the exact fulfillment of everything you command of him, and that will be entrusted to him in the future. This is provided that he renounce this written account. Otherwise our clemency is withdrawn. As a consequence, we command you to instruct him (1) To apologize to Count Chernyshev in your presence alone or before two witnesses only, and if need be even in writing. (2) To collect all copies, as many as there are of course, and to bring them to you. (3) To renounce this written account formally and in writing in the German language, adding that it naturally emanates from his enemies and from such as wish to cast suspicion on the zealousness of his service to us, and to create a coldness between two mighty allied courts. (4) To have this renunciation printed in the newspapers in Königsberg.

"Lieutenant General Count Chernyshev probably will not be content with such satisfaction. You may tell him that in forgiving the offense caused him by Count Todtleben he will give us a further example of his boundless diligence to service, and that this will be regarded by us as a merit."

When, as a consequence of this rescript Todtleben sent in his resignation, another rescript was sent to him. "We have observed with regret from the reports of Count Buturlin that the poor state of your health and a number of other circumstances have led you to ask to be released from your service. We have not been accustomed to keep anyone against his will. As the war, however, is now virtually coming to a close, we have need of your continued service more that at any other time. Your release at this time also would follow circumstances subject to a number of interpretations with respect for the honor and exalted nature of your service. In gracious memory of all your services, shown thus far to be zealous, and always distinguishing these from passing incidents, we are unable at this point to agree to give permission for the resignation you ask for (retirement). In particular, as we are certain of your laudable desire for real and significant glory and of your diligence towards us, we have commanded that not only all the light cavalry and the two infantry regiments appointed in support of them shall be put under your command in such a way that you are directly responsible only to General Field Marshal Count Buturlin, but that in addition your corps be enlarged, as much as necessary to fulfill those projects about which you will be told more extensively by him."

Todtleben remained in service, and in a letter to the Chancellor Count Vorontsov, "to his father and benefactor," swore to use the remaining days of his life to show himself worthy of the trust and favors of so august a monarch.

NEGOTIATIONS WITH AUSTRIA CONCERNING COMPENSATION

It was believed that the war was coming to a conclusion, that the campaign of the following year would be the last, and therefore there was an urgency to agree upon the conditions of a peace settlement. The Russians suggested to the Austrian court the conclusion of a new convention "by means of which we may enact those measures and instruments which at the end of the present onerous war best may serve to determine a just reward for the losses borne during its course at the expense of the enemy and the disturber of the general peace. Her imperial All Russian majesty and her majesty the empress-queen have so much greater a right to demand and to receive such a reward that in the first place they should receive back those provinces stolen by the king of Prussia. In addition we must

place proper restriction on the power of such a sovereign, whose iniqui-
tous schemes know no such limits."

In the convention it was resolved that the two powers, during the entire further duration of the war, would each have no less than eighty thousand regular troops in the field. They would continue the war with their
joint forces until the conclusion of a peace treaty by general agreement
confirmed the security of their provinces, and the just objectives of both
sides were attained. Neither power must lay down its arms until the empress-queen took assured possession of the whole of Silesia and the county
of Glatz, and until the empress of All Russia obtained possession of the
kingdom of Prussia (East Prussia), at this moment indeed already conquered by her arms. As European peace may never be established firmly
until the means to disturb it have been removed from the king of Prussia
in the manner already outlined, their imperial majesties would make every effort to render this service to mankind. To this end they must summon all the powers to this convention, in particular the king of France.
The king of Poland, the elector of Saxony, must not only be restored to
his hereditary possessions but also receive satisfaction for injury and
losses. The French language in which the convention was written must
not serve as an precedent for the future. The empress-queen would
continue to pay the empress of All Russia one million rubles a year
in subsidies.

On presentation of this convention Esterhazy replied that the problem
at present was not so much related to the conclusion of any new conventions, as was constraint of the king of Prussia by forceful and decisive
military actions. This in itself would place his court in a position whereby
it could carry out the obligations it has undertaken. These consist in hon-
oring the Russian interest as its own, acquiring everything possible for the
empress-queen, as well as the satisfaction of the Russian court for losses
incurred. Esterhazy had given reassurance with the word of the empress-
queen, and he now confirmed the same. Consequently the Russian court
must have no doubts regarding the fulfillment of these firm promises.

Esterhazy suggested that now it was more important than anything else
to keep France from signing a separate peace. Therefore it was needful
to act with caution in relation to ancient and still active prejudices. It
would not be difficult to succeed in this respect should both imperial
courts put their proposals forward by degrees and simultaneously. It was
clear that France would not sympathize very much with the acquisition

of East Prussia by Russia. Therefore any convention in which the annexation of East Prussia by Russia was mentioned would be harmful. The problem lay not with the policy itself but in the method of implementation. Instead of a convention, Esterhazy had directions from his court to make a declaration that the empress-queen would assume the most solemn undertaking sincerely to use her most earnest efforts to see that the Russian court received such rewards as it wanted for itself.

He was told in reply that a new draft of the convention had been drawn up which was made rather more acceptable, as a declaration had been attached which would absent, not only from France but also from the other courts, any fear regarding the augmentation of the Russian empire by the kingdom of Prussia. This convention suggested that the province of Prussia be granted to the Polish Commonwealth and that such measures should be taken as would serve the mutual satisfaction of both sides.

"Certainly by this," the reply went on, "it is understood that we must spare the court of France. The proposed convention will not perturb it by anything at all new. In particular, in opinion here, we must beware that if nothing is resolved now, or a general declaration is made that is concealed from the court of France, that court will either think that by its response it has removed from this side any desire to receive East Prussia, or will suspect that it is not completely trusted. Finally the empress is also well aware that the whole policy depends upon success of arms, for if the Almighty is not pleased to give His blessing not only will the new convention fail to gain the kingdom of Prussia for this court, but her majesty the empress-queen regardless of many and ancient treaties will not obtain Silesia and the county of Glatz, and this provisional convention must give way in the light of any future peace settlement, whatever it may be. On the other hand, if Providence has determined to bless humankind by curtailing the arrogant and damaging power of the king of Prussia, and the empress-queen takes possession of Silesia and the county of Glatz, it is practically impossible that the single desire of both imperial courts and the simple agreement of the French should not be obtained for the delivery of East Prussia to this court. The king of Prussia in losing Silesia, previously in his possession, will not continue the war in order to retain East Prussia, which he himself abandoned. We must be merely in agreement about this and act in the present campaign to ensure that its success is in keeping with this expectation. Therefore we ardently desire to conclude this matter once and for all, in order to give our exclusive attention to military activities alone." The convention was signed by Esterhazy on March 21.

He received a severe reprimand from Maria Theresa for doing so. The convention was immediately sent to France as, in accordance with an agreement with Versailles, Austria could not conclude any agreement without the knowledge of the court of France. A reply was received that Louis XV was unable to accede to such a convention as it mentioned only the rewards for the imperial courts, mentioning the other allies either in general terms or saying absolutely nothing about them. "The treaty of 1746," Maria Theresa wrote to Esterhazy, "stated specifically that in the event of any breach of the peace by Prussia, Silesia and the county of Glatz were to be returned to Austria, and that Russia was not to make any conquests but was to be satisfied with two million gulden. Now this solemn decree has been invalidated and a new decree is being enacted whereby Russia would receive the very same benefits as us, although Prussia has breached the peace only with ourselves and Saxony. Silesia is our ancient hereditary land, whereas East Prussia has never been part of Russian territory. We received agreement with respect to the return of Silesia from all the allies, and thus far have suffered the greatest peril and losses.

"In spite of all this we long ago reassured the empress of Russia that we are in full agreement for compensation for her losses and are as earnestly committed to her interests as to our own. As far as this question in general is concerned, whether it is necessary from our side to acknowledge the kingdom of Prussia as a conquest by Russia and in doing so to give a guarantee, then here in Vienna there is no doubt as to our own position. We firmly hope only through the generosity and great perspicacity of the empress of Russia that her majesty will by no means deign to act in opposition to our interests, to the general well-being and her own objectives, as great harm may come from the convention instead of the advantage expected."

The harm, in the opinion of the empress-queen, consisted in the fact that Austria and Russia could be abandoned by all the other allies. In order not to irritate the Russian court the following arrangement was devised in Vienna. The paragraph in which the annexation of East Prussia by Russia was mentioned was to be excluded from the convention and in its place a separate secret article was drafted having the same content, but with the addition that the promise of Austria in respect to the annexation of East Prussia by Russia was not valid if, against all expectations, Austria did not receive Silesia and the county of Glatz. The secret article must be concealed from France. Elizabeth accepted these changes.

Russia wanted to acquire East Prussia in order to exchange it for Courland or other, more strategic, Polish provinces. The court in Vienna wanted to make its own changes in respect to this also. Vienna was seriously concerned that Denmark, which had not received thus far an agreement from Russia with respect to Holstein, would take English subsidies and put its own fresh troops, consisting of twenty thousand men, at Prussia's disposal. Esterhazy received a rescript from Maria Theresa on July 27 (New Style) which expressed considerable alarm and a desire to put a stop to the Holstein irritations, "as the ever-present cause of a new and most dangerous excitation of strong emotion may lead to the outbreak of war." Maria Theresa asked Esterhazy to use his most fervent efforts to ensure that the Danish proposals not be completely rejected in St. Petersburg. An agreement must be based upon renunciation of Holstein by Grand Duke Peter Fedorovich. Instead he could take Prussia for himself. This would reassure Denmark completely, and not raise envy in the other nations at the extension of Russia power.

RELATIONS WITH DENMARK

Denmark was indeed strongly alarmed by the curtailment of talks over Holstein and by the proposals for Russia to keep East Prussia. The French ambassador, Marquis de l'Hôpital, told the chancellor of a letter from the Danish minister, Baron Bernstorff, to the French minister, Duc de Choiseul. The letter stated that should Russia acquire East Prussia, and the heir to the Russian empire not renounce his pretensions and not give up his hatred for the king of Denmark, then the Danish king would be in the most dangerous and calamitous position. It was well known in Denmark that the grand duke was constantly planning its destruction. Consequently the king was convinced that sooner or later he would have to go to war with Russia. Naturally he considered whether it would not be better to start this war now rather than when Russia had no other enemies. In his second letter to the duc de Choiseul, Bernstorff let it be known that Denmark, without wishing to break its friendship with France, would enter an agreement with England and the king of Prussia. Choiseul replied that, even so, an agreement with Prussia would be a breach of friendly relations with France.

DEATH OF MIKHAIL PETROVICH BESTUZHEV-RIUMIN

The renowned diplomat who recently had represented Russia in France, Count Mikhail Petrovich Bestuzhev-Riumin, died on February 26. Prince Dmitry Mikhailovich Golitsyn, who was in Paris to give him some support, was entrusted with the conduct of affairs on the death of Bestuzhev until the new ambassador, Senior Gentleman of the Chamber Count Peter Chernyshev, arrived. Choiseul assured Golitsyn that, in the name of the king, he once more had intimated to the Danish minister that Denmark keep quiet in St. Petersburg about its conditions in respect to the Holstein question, and that an opportunity be found later to conclude this matter amicably. France would never agree to arouse the displeasure of the Russian empress by interfering in such a matter.

DE L'HÔPITAL REPLACED BY BRETEUIL

In St. Petersburg the French ambassador also changed. L'Hôpital was sent there because there was nobody better. Louis XV had no confidence in him, but he did not conduct a correspondence with him behind the ministry's back. However L'Hôpital did not know that the king was conducting a clandestine correspondence with Empress Elizabeth, unbeknown to the ministry. The secretary at the embassy, the well-known Chevalier d'Éon,[7] was favored with this clandestine correspondence from the king. The king discovered that L'Hôpital was becoming very expensive in St. Petersburg, that he was incapable of carrying on affairs of state, was very trusting of the Russian chancellor Vorontsov. "He is given instructions," wrote the king, "to explain some matter or other, but before doing anything else lets Vorontsov know all about it."

The difficulty consisted in finding a successor. At last the successor was found, Baron de Breteuil,[8] whom the king believed capable of conducting a secret correspondence. Éon received instructions from Louis XV to let the new ambassador have any information concerning the character of the empress, her ministers and all others employed in the conduct of foreign relations. Breteuil himself was given these instructions. "To inquire in particular about the attachments and the opinions of the grand duke and the grand duchess, and to try to win their favor and trust. Marquis de l'Hôpital neglected the young court, and in particular set the grand duchess against him by the part he played in the recall of Count Poniatowski from St. Petersburg. If, and this is not open to question, the grand duchess should turn to Baron Breteuil with complaints about his predecessor's conduct, the baron must make use of this opportunity and artfully intimate that he knows the king's feelings with respect to the grand duke and the grand duchess, and he can assure her that his majesty will be very pleased to assist in fulfilling their wishes. If they would like to see Count Poniatowski once more in St. Petersburg, his majesty will not only not object, but will promote the idea that the king of Poland once again appoint him ambassador to Russia." The French court did indeed render assistance in Warsaw towards the return of Poniatowski to St. Petersburg, but soon had to stop assisting in this matter. They were frightened off by the strong negative feelings of the empress towards the prospect of seeing Poniatowski at her court for a third time.

RELATIONS WITH ENGLAND OVER RUSSIAN COMPENSATION

In London there was displeasure at the Russian reply to the British peace proposals. The duke of Newcastle mentioned this to Prince Alexander Golitsyn. "This court made the preliminary communication with respect to a peace settlement out of a desire to please, and out of particular consideration for the empress because she is not a little burdened with the prolongation of the war, spending a great deal of money upon it without hope of receiving adequate reward. Our court therefore trusted that the empress's rely would be composed in the same peaceable manner. On the contrary, your reply was expressed in a manner not suggestive of any inclination towards peace on the empress's part. Our fundamental and natural interests require that Russia and England always find themselves in positive agreement. Even now that could be so, by making peace with the king of Prussia irrespective of her allies and without disregard to Russian interests."

"The empress," Golitsyn replied, "while accepting with gratitude the preliminary report of his britannic majesty, could not give any other reply because she cannot initiate moves that might lead to the conclusion of peace without the agreement of all her allies. The current maintenance of the close alliance between England and Prussia must also serve as an example for other governments. The alliance of Russia and Austria is most natural and necessary. In contrast, the present alliance between England and Prussia has a very weak and insecure foundation, as it is based not upon the mutual advantages of the courts but only upon personal relations towards the king of Prussia. Frederick II is mortal, and consequently this alliance will end with his death. The honor, dignity and security of

Russia dictate that the empress not regret any expenditure upon such a just war, the more so as the resources necessary for the maintenance of the war may run dry more quickly for the enemies of her majesty, even if the empress has no expectation of any benefit herself. Nevertheless it is in her power to obtain that compensation which by the rules of justice no one may deny her." At this point Newcastle interrupted Golitsyn. "What do you understand by these words?" "It is clear even without my elucidation," Golitsyn replied.

After this conversation another minister, the celebrated Pitt, inquired of Golitsyn whether the empress intended to hold on to her gains in East Prussia. "I always ascribed to the Viennese court a lust for power and aspirations to extend its territory," said Pitt. "I never thought this about your court. Your sovereign took part in the war solely out of generosity, in order to defend the king of Poland, without having in mind any gain." Golitsyn replied that the empress's intentions were not known to him. Nevertheless anyone impartial must acknowledge her majesty's right to sufficient compensation for such colossal military losses in confirming the liberties and security of Germany. "At this point," wrote Golitsyn, "not only the public but even the court feel within themselves the justice and the plausible potentiality for your majesty to keep East Prussia in perpetual ownership. It already is expected here. Pitt is of this opinion. Repeating the fact that Russia and England have natural common interests, he gave me to understand that the time may soon come when the actual allies of Russia, in particular the Viennese court, will be more envious of the well-being and power of your majesty than that of England."

When, in St. Petersburg, Ivan Ivanovich Shuvalov turned to Keith to learn the opinion of the English court in respect to Russia's annexation of East Prussia, Keith replied that in such case the war would not come to an end soon, for the king of Prussia would sooner bury himself beneath the ruins of the last of his cities than agree to such humiliating conditions. The Russian annexation of East Prussia would arouse universal envy and would be a source of anxiety in Europe, as there would be a struggle at the first suitable opportunity to snatch this province from Russian hands. Shuvalov replied that he did not understand how annexation of such a small province could arouse universal envy, and if that was so, might it not be possible at least to leave East Prussia in pawn to Russia until another way could be found to obtain satisfaction. Keith replied by saying that neither the one nor the other would be possible since all governments would clearly see Russia's intention to take Baltic trade into its own hands, and through that the trade of the entire North.

PANIN RECALLED FROM STOCKHOLM

Panin was recalled from Stockholm and handed over affairs to Stakhiev, councillor at the embassy, who described in the following words the state of affairs in Sweden before the meeting of the Riksdag. "By this (the king's invitation of officials to the Riksdag) the doors now have been opened for overt political activity of the various parties and factions into which the Swedish nation is divided. Without doubt their leaders soon will unfurl their banners of various hats and caps, and will commence to work publicly to increase the number of their partisans. Here the movements of both parties, those of the court and of the Senate, are worth of particular attention. The first, being oppressed and powerless, is thus far not giving the slightest appearance of activity. The second, being dominant and the strongest, and consequently the most numerous, is plagued with numerous divisions. It is also prey to various factions, of which the two most important are concentrated about the rivalry of two senators, the first minister Baron Höpken and the steward of the royal children Baron Scheffer. Each of these two rivals is trying in particular to gain the favor of the court party, by which each hopes to increase its faction. So far neither has succeeded noticeably in this because of the immobile nature of the court and its removal from political matters.

"In discussing the outward appearance of the movement of both factions, Senator Baron Höpken seeks to link as little as possible any ideas of Swedish independence with any adherence to foreign powers. His rival Baron Scheffer on the other hand, while not tolerating any mediation, blindly obeys France and idolizes everything that he sees or hears to be of French creation. For that reason, even in the sphere of agriculture, he follows the French in everything. As the local spirit of freedom in such matters will not tolerate oppression and strong measures, even this senator, through a display of arrogance and quick temper, has clashed with a great many, and in particular with the lesser bourgeoisie, where he is not trusted in the slightest. Senator Höpken, on the contrary, makes considerable use of this fact, particularly this summer, being almost in daily contact with the lesser bourgeoisie. Consequently he has more hope in the next Riksdag of comforting himself with the patronage of office if a third faction does not take the high ground from him.

"Such a faction at present is growing in heady fashion under the leadership of Colonel Baron Pechlin, who at the last Riksdag rose with considerable distinction and served the government party, by which he became swollen with pride. Not being satisfied with the monetary reward given him at that time for his efforts, he has taken it into his head to obtain the position of manager of the governing party before the following Riksdag, for which reason he came here last year. The Senate considering him capable of carrying out only simple managerial instructions, banished him back to the army in Pomerania, for which reason he has become extremely embittered against the Senate and is now gathering his own faction. This may be called by the ancient Roman example the Censors' faction, for it believes the foundation of its activities to be curtailing the interests of the court at the last Riksdag, and in the next Riksdag setting a limit to the emerging power of the Senate.

"The fading gray hair of Senator Count Tessin finds a lot of sympathy here, both for presenting himself once again in the theater of the Riksdag, and also for overcoming the contempt he had brought upon himself from his disciples, who make up the greater part of the Senate, by the display of his feelings to them when this old man, arrayed in his infirmity, gave his blessing to the new leader and promised in the event of success to support him and show the Swedish people that he is still capable of accepting their sweet-smelling sacrifice and sacraments."

On this report Vorontsov wrote, "I must instruct Stakhiev to behave very modestly and neither to attach himself to any party, nor to interfere in any way in the domestic affairs of Sweden or the Riksdag, but to lean somewhat to the party of Senator Höpken, who by all accounts is inclined to favor us."

Another exhortation was added to the eloquent Stakhiev in the rescript. "You are advised to send us reports about everything that goes on there, and any news which deserves to be taken as reliable information by us. Do not, however, enter into the extraneous description of vices or of mankind's natural passions. Write clearly and without metaphorical and allegorical expressions, which do not serve other than to obscure the content of your reports and consequently occasion difficulty in supplying you with the necessary instructions."

OSTERMANN REPLACES PANIN

In place of Panin, Brigadier Count Ivan Ostermann was appointed as ambassador to Stockholm. On June 23 Stakhiev reported, "A certain exalted person and, in political matters, one who can get things done, a reliable friend, recently told me in extreme confidence that the dispatches received here from the Swedish ambassador in Paris are full of envious intimations from the French ministry about the Russian court. In the words of the Swedish ambassador, the French court in no way intends to permit Russia to keep the lands it has conquered from the king of Prussia." In response Vorontsov observed, "The pointed intimations to Stakhiev from a friend, who is unknown to us here, have the deliberate appearance of wishing quite skillfully to bring us into conflict with the French court." "The Austrian ambassador Count Goëss," Stakhiev's report went on to say, "told one of his acquaintances, 'France cannot give Russia support in the Swedish Riksdag. The interests of both courts constantly come into conflict in Sweden. France gives Sweden significant subsidies solely in order to alienate it from the Russian court, so as to be able to promote Russia as an object to scare Sweden if need be.' Goëss added that he could not understand why the Russian court so neglected Swedish affairs, and did not try to control them directly itself, but calmly allows France to destroy the Russian adherents completely." In response Vorontsov remarked, "We have never comforted ourselves with any hope that the French court would ever turn to our advantage our particular interests in Sweden. Moreover there has been no attempt whatsoever on our part properly to assist the French, and we will not be deceived in this of course. Nevertheless for our part we have never neglected Swedish affairs but, on the contrary, made every effort to preserve a mutual friendship. Perhaps by such neglect is understood the fact that for some time we have ceased sending many thousands of rubles from here to be squandered in the Riksdags. Had the government any spare cash at this point, perhaps it could send a few thousand rubles to attempt to turn matters successfully to its advantage, to gain the attention of many of the divided parties there and to get them to look favorably upon the views of Russia; but any success in such a venture cannot be guaranteed."

Stakhiev's report concluded in the following manner. "Goëss said that the destruction of the remaining adherents of Russia evidently will be completed at the next Riksdag unless the court in St. Petersburg sends a minister here who is a little more exalted in station, and who is a little more wealthy in his own right than Ostermann. Panin did not find himself in such straitened circumstances. Moreover by the maintenance of a good table he gained the love for himself, not only of many celebrated people of importance, but even generally of the majority of local society, which greatly regretted his departure." In response to this Vorontsov remarked, "This is a premature, very vain and rather impertinent assessment of Count Ostermann."

RELATIONS WITH POLAND AND TURKEY

Some strange news came out of Poland. Arriving one day at the residence of the Lithuanian chancellor Count Czartoryski, Voeikov found Crown Chancellor Malachowski already with him. Czartoryski immediately complained that nearly all matters relating to their duties had been taken out of the chancellors' hands. For the most part everything was being carried out by Marshal of the Court Mniszech, who with the assistance of his father-in-law Count Brühl, the Saxon first minister, distributes the offices. There has been considerable unrest and chagrin at this behavior among the lesser nobility, which sees in this a contravention of the constitution. Last year Mniszech called Crown Chancellor Malachowski to Lublin before a local tribunal because the chancellor was prosecuting him in a certain case in the Crown Assessor Courts from which there was no right of appeal. It was an example unheard of in Poland. Although a reconciliation was effected between them through the mediation of the primate and several others, it was on condition that they personally bear no malice towards each other. As satisfaction for the insult cast upon the character and office of chancellor, Mniszech was to declare in writing that everything that had taken place in the tribunal court be struck from the record. This declaration has not yet been made. Not being prepared to bear any further insults of this kind, they proposed asking the king not to let anyone assume their duties, and to order Mniszech to give satisfaction to Malachowski.

Then both chancellors begged Voeikov, as minister of the power guaranteeing the Polish constitution, to assist them in this matter and report everything about it to his court. Voeikov replied that they should have ended long ago their personal quarrels so that there might develop a sensible tractability one with another. As Czartoryski and Malachowski insisted that Voeikov intervene in their affair, he went to Brühl to discuss the chancellors' complaints. Brühl replied that the king wished for the same thing also, that all Polish affairs follow the course of law and that the chancellors work hard towards this end. Prince Czartoryski, however, had not been in Warsaw for about two years. He lived on his estates, for which reason there was delay and hiatus in his affairs because they were being carried on by correspondence. Malachowski was only in Warsaw for short periods of time. He was a kind man and did not seek quarrels or make intrigues, and would not be alarmed even now were it not for Czartoryski, a restless man, proud, fiery, indomitable, who now was inciting Malachowski. He was assisted considerably in this by a courtier, the Lithuanian court dignitary Count Poniatowski, whom Czartoryski was using in his intrigues as a man who had an extraordinarily high opinion of himself.

In his report Voeikov responded in this manner. "As much as I could make out concerning Prince Czartoryski in the short period of time he has been here, I find that the way he is presented by Count Brühl is reliable. This gentleman cannot be trusted in anything. Although he is very intelligent, he is also proud, quick-tempered and indomitable to the highest degree. On his arrival in Warsaw he was not slow in visiting the English ambassador Lord Stormont, accompanied by his brother Adam, the Russian military commander, and his nephew Count Poniatowski. They stayed for about two hours."

Chancellor Count Vorontsov sent a letter to him on this matter. "On one hand it would be desirable, necessary and useful to the honor and influence of our court were the Polish ministry restored to its proper importance through your mediation. On the other hand it can be seen clearly that Count Brühl and Mniszech, having unlimited influence with the king and being so distressed by the chancellors, are not in a position to yield to the exhortations of our court, having sufficient reservations which cannot be refuted before outsiders. Statements relating to this matter may lead to their complete alienation. Moreover would not such an attempt, purely from the point of view of the chancellors, produce a certain coldness between us and the Polish court? So in my opinion your excellency needs to act very cautiously in this matter and maintain a balance between these matadors, so that in these present particularly critical times there is a real equilibrium. The more so, as we may hardly console ourselves that the best exercise of power and advantage in Polish affairs may be acquired through the superiority of one or the other parties. It almost may be said in accordance with our proverb that 'he who is not a parson is a priest.'"

A meeting of the Sejm was approaching and Voeikov learned that complaints had been inserted into the instructions to the deputies concerning the burden to the Polish gentry of the passage of Russian troops. When Voeikov reported this to St. Petersburg, he received instructions to suggest to Brühl that this would be sensitive for Russia and harmful to the common cause. Behind the scenes Brühl must attempt by every possible means to abort the Sejm at the very start. Voeikov carried out his instruction and Brühl replied with assurances that the Sejm would certainly break up because it would not reach the point of electing a marshal. "There is only one danger," remarked Brühl, "that the English and the king of Prussia will try as hard as possible to lead the Polish gentry into a confederation, and will use considerable sums of money to bring these mercenary-minded and reckless people to the point of rebellion. Not long ago Benoît, secretary to the Prussian embassy, received a number of letters from his king for Poles and, incidentally, for the Czartoryski princes. This family, with its party, will not stop making trouble for the king, and patently threatens a confederation, bringing into it even Crown Hetman Branicki." Reporting this to his court Voeikov remarked, "It is my opinion that the Poles will not suddenly make up their minds to a confederation, seeing the proximity of the Russian army and indeed with a certain part of it already on their territory."

The Sejm did break up. After this Voeikov demanded another service of Brühl, to try to snare the Prussian couriers regularly travelling to the Prussian emissary in Constantinople and back again. Obreskov reported that the affairs of the Prussian emissaries were going badly in Constantinople. Turkey did not want war, although the khan of Crimea was trying as hard as possible to make the Porte quarrel with Russia, presenting petitions about robbery by the Zaporozhian Cossacks.

In October Obreskov made it known that the Neapolitan ambassador had received word about the appearance of a man calling himself the Russian prince Ivan, dethroned in 1741. The impostor could be about twenty-five years of age or more. He was short. His face was of a somewhat dark complexion, his hair black, his face considerably pockmarked. There was a pistol wound on his neck. He spoke Russian, French, German and to a certain extent understood Danish and Swedish. He concealed his identity beneath common surnames, observed extremely quiet behavior, was content with little until the receipt of replies or bills of exchange which he was expecting from Copenhagen, Berlin and Brunswick. He wrote three letters to the queen of Denmark and had sent them by post. In these letters he related how he escaped from Russia in 1754 from the region of Azov, and had been in a number of countries of Europe. In 1757 he had arrived incognito in St. Petersburg, from whence he left for Brandenburg and thence to Copenhagen, where he stayed over the winter of 1757-1758 until the arrival in June 1758 of the Russian fleet. In his opinion the fleet was given instructions to demand from the Danish court his return to Russia. Therefore he had set out in secret from Copenhagen to the island of Samsø, from whence he was sent packing from the kingdom in order to avoid any conflict with the Russian court. From Denmark he had made his way to Germany to Prince Ferdinand of Brunswick,[9] and was witness to the battle of Bergen.[10] In Frankfurt there was an attempt to detain him on an order of the duc de Broglie but he escaped to Switzerland, and from there to Italy. He embellished his story with circumstances serving to prove the justice of his claim, and did not in any way contradict himself. From a letter of the Danish minister Bernstorff it was clear that he was a charlatan and would have been arrested in Denmark had he not managed to escape.

FINANCIAL DIFFICULTIES

Elizabeth declared that she would continue the war stubbornly even if she had to sell half her dresses and diamonds. These words already contained a hint of how the finances of the empire were suffering from the war. At the beginning of June Chief of the Commissary Prince Yakov Shakhovskoy told the Conference that if the Main Commissary was not returned the money, which now extended to more than five million rubles, owed to it from various government bodies, and if the arrears were not made up, there was no hope that in the present year the entire sum of money requested could be sent to the army. He pointed out that military personnel were paid only for January and February but that for the other two months of the first third of the year there was nothing from which their pay could be supplied. The Conference sent this report on to the Senate, which replied that measures had been taken to collect the debts and arrears. The Chancellery of Works reported that it had a debt with the College of State Accounts of 103,876 rubles for 1757. The Chancellery of Works incurred considerable expenses related to the construction of the Winter Palace. Twenty thousand rubles were assigned to the carving in the gallery of this palace, to designs by Rastrelli.[11] This work was given to the master craftsmen Gillet, Dunker and Rolland, who undertook to maintain at their expense fifty foreign craftsmen and fifteen Russian carvers. An officer of the Guards went to the Moscow province to recruit a thousand plasterers. The Yaroslavl town council was fined for concealment of plasterers and stone masons, as were the elder and the peasants of the hereditary lands of Prince Eletsky in the Liubim district.

At the end of the year the Chancellery of Works requested 60,495 rubles for construction of the Winter Palace. The Senate ordered an inquiry and it turned out that in 1754, following an estimate, 859,555 rubles were allocated for building the palace. Later an additional sum of 372,672 rubles was allocated. Furthermore by 1759 it had given instructions to assign 143,713 rubles for internal construction. From 1759 until completion of construction it was agreed to assign, and in fact was allocated, one hundred and twenty thousand rubles a year. On the basis of this information the Senate ordered payment of the money to the Chancellery of Works to be refused. Let it be content with one hundred and twenty thousand rubles.

The Polish retinue in Paris not only did not receive wages for 1760, nor was it paid in full even the previous year. The College of Foreign Affairs was allocated 191,377 rubles a year, and an additional 29,822 rubles and thirteen hundred chervontsy in extraordinary expenses. At the Chancellery of State Accounts there was a debt of 512,713 rubles and thirteen hundred chervontsy. There were arrears of 412,562 rubles for the customs tax-farmer Shemiakin. The Senate ordered payment strictly enforced.

According to the registers for 1758, 1,478,643 pails of wine were sold and 2,731,675 rubles were collected, as against 1749, when wine was sold at various prices, and less than 154,555 pails were sold, but more than 1,465,924 rubles received. Of salt, 6,272,639 puds were sold, which was less than all previous years. Count Peter Ivanovich Shuvalov made the following suggestion. It was well known that nothing was given to innkeeper tax-collectors for costs in their taverns, such as crockery, firewood, candles, transportation of liquor and other things. Consequently they had to spend their own money on these items and could not help getting into trouble by appropriating state revenue. In the light of this there must be caution that people are not punished for what they cannot avoid. They must be given what is necessary for the upkeep of taverns. The Senate agreed. Four military governors were dismissed for insufficient surveillance of tavern dues.

The Winter Palace, St. Petersburg

Shuvalov announced that he was putting the Artillery Military School
on a proper footing. To ensure that there was no shortage of money in the
future, as had happened in the past, he suggested establishment of a bank
specifically for the artillery and engineer military schools, the capital
raised by remaking copper cannon into coin. Any copper coin remaining
after distribution following re-minting would represent significant capital should a money shortage recur. The Senate admitted that this was a
very necessary and useful measure, and placed responsibility for the establishment of the bank upon Shuvalov himself.

LOTTERY

We have seen that of methods used for increasing state revenue in other
countries a lottery was not regarded appropriate to Russia. Now it was
proposed to try this way of increasing revenue. The grand master of ceremonies, Baron Lefort, recommended a project to the Conference to reconcile a major state lottery with benefit to Treasury, avoid danger of the
lottery not being fully subscribed or that, to avoid scandal and loss of
credit, it must be made good with Treasury money. The Conference approved the lottery and appointed Baron Lefort general director under the
patronage of the Senate. It was decided to establish a cash lottery at one
ruble for a ticket in St. Petersburg, Moscow, Riga, Reval and Königsberg.

STATE OF TOWNS

In spite of the necessary attempt, because of the circumstances of the
time, to restrict expenditure as much as possible, the Senate recognized
the need to spend a substantial sum for that time to recompense a son for
a father's services. Count Peter Ivanovich Shuvalov made the following
recommendation. "In order to spur someone on to exert every effort in the
service of the fatherland, we must assure him of reward. Service is a reason for compensation. Compensation serves as a great incentive for those
enterprises that might be perilous for him who ventures upon them, but
which are of value to his sovereign and fatherland and, it appears, service
is as linked to compensation as the soul is to the body. The trust our sovereign shows us obliges us to intercede for those who have the courage
to venture upon enterprises of great service to the fatherland. The family of Ivan Kirillov is living in extreme poverty and, it may be said, is
without sustenance; but Kirillov rendered the fatherland a significant
service. Those fruits of this service which come from Orenburg and its

province may serve as proof. While serving as senior secretary of the Senate in 1734 Kirillov submitted a project for building a city on the Or river and was sent there to put it into effect. Following construction of the town, trade was established, but the revenues from this trade were not substantial. They amounted to only four thousand rubles, but now they are up to one hundred and fifty thousand a year and even more. In addition, there are now five copper foundries in which up to twenty-six thousand puds a year of copper are smelted. There are four iron foundries, in which up to one hundred and eighty thousand puds of iron are processed. Yet there is a debt of 7,591 rubles outstanding against Kirillov, the author of all this wealth, and this debt must be recovered from his son, the senior auditor of the War College." The Senate decided to present the empress with a paper requesting a grant of ten thousand rubles for Kirillov, taking the debt into account in this sum.

Ostermann's commission on commerce was set up following a suggestion by the same Shuvalov. To expand trade, merchants must be protected. The Senate ordered that all injuries caused by soldiers against the merchants of Novy Torzhok be investigated thoroughly. Conscripts robbed and beat up the merchants of whom one, Tetiukhin, died the following day from blows received.

The Senate sent an instruction to the Chancellery of Works demanding a reply from Captain Lieutenant of Guards Shuvalov, sent to recruit plasterers for the Winter Palace. He had detained members of the Chief Magistracy under guard and, without displaying any order, merely repeated that he was acting as a soldier. Yet the Chief Magistracy enjoyed the same privileges as other colleges and lay within the jurisdiction of the Senate. Only the Senate held the right to place the members of the municipal administration under arrest.

On a complaint from the Medical Chancellery the Senate issued an instruction that in those towns which by an edict of 1737 had a physician the municipal authorities be reminded as firmly as possible that salary and money for accommodation be provided by the municipal authority for these physicians every four months. There should be no deductions or withholding payment for more than three days after the lapse of any four month period, for which there can be no excuses. The Medical Chancellery wrote that a physician who did not receive his salary suffered considerable hardship. The municipal authorities, notwithstanding the edicts already confirmed, were withholding these salaries out of stubbornness.

For that reason the chancelleries of those towns were seeking to recover twice the physicians' salaries from the municipal authorities, without accepting any excuses. One half was to be sent to the military hospital, and the other sent without delay to the physicians. Until the municipal authorities paid the double salary municipal judges should be held under arrest in the municipal offices without the right to leave the building. It turned out that in Tambov the physician had not been paid any salary for five years.

Not everywhere, as in Torzhok, did merchants let themselves be beaten by conscripts. The College of Justice reported to the Senate that although Solodovnikov, a burgomaster of the Tikhvin municipal administration, denied gathering citizens of Tikhvin to beat up the officers, Captain Ivan Shuvalov, Adjutant Yakov Golenishchev-Kutuzov and the driver Vasily Ogibalov. For that reason those inhabitants of Tikhvin, with Solodovnikov, should have undergone questioning with lashes. Solodovnikov, however, was completely unmasked. He had sent messengers of the municipal authority to petition for the expulsion of traders and blacksmiths of Tikhvin for beating up these officers. Yet Shchetinin, a servant at the Tikhvin monastery, and the blacksmith Kirpichnikov gathered about thirty men for the fight and gave out cudgels in the entrance hall of the municipal chambers, in order to see the officers off and to give them something to boast about in St. Petersburg. He was not satisfied with beating up Golenishchev-Kutuzov, but ordered them to catch and beat Captain Shuvalov, who was even beaten in the town square because of his edict against the municipal authorities.

Because of its aversion to pointless bloodshed and in order to put an end to the investigation which had dragged on for no less than four years, and lest the inhabitants of Tikhvin arrested in respect to this case be deprived of their trade and business, the Bureau of Justice suggested that Solodovnikov be punished with the knout for the crime stated and other acts of impertinence. During the time of his arrest by the commission he got together with other convicts and, breaking in to the judges' chambers, shouted that he was dissatisfied with the investigation into his case and that they be taken to St. Petersburg. He also was punished for his insolent absence from the investigation, for his twice-repeated departure from the commission under guard, for beating a soldier of the guard and for threatening that he would beat to death whoever should take him, for leading the inhabitants of Tikhvin to the Great Tikhvin monastery, for breaking to pieces monastery cell doors, and for carrying off under guard the son of the servant Bykov. He was to be released but not ever again be appointed to any office. Those citizens of Tikhvin who obeyed him and beat the officers should be punished with lashes. Shchetinin also testified that citizens of Tikhvin and the blacksmiths stood up for the blacksmith Shepelev, who was beaten by Ogibalov. A fight broke out because they were taking him away. In addition, money should be exacted from Solodovnikov and the citizens of Tikhvin who beat the officers, for showing a lack of respect. The Senate ordered that Solodovnikov be punished with lashes instead of the knout.

It appeared that factories established in a number of towns under Peter the Great were now in a sorry state. For this reason the Conference decided, because of the disorder in the whole of Europe brought about by war, that now would be a most opportune time to invite skilled artisans to the empire. Any such attempt would be futile until at least one factory was brought into proper working order and satisfactory condition. Until then they must remain in their present sorry state. For example there were so many tailors in Russia for making luxuries that they were injurious to the state. Yet experience had shown that in the whole of Moscow the number of qualified tailors was scarcely worth mentioning, when there was urgent need to make uniforms for the army. The state had an abundance of good quality iron, but when special materials were put together for the army vehicles loaded with the best iron rarely reached their destination. The Senate, on receipt these opinions of the Conference, ordered the Chief Magistracy to confirm that factories were being supported, and that blacksmiths were producing goods in sufficient quantity as required by municipal regulations. It would be impossible to avoid the expenditure of a significant sum of money to bring in artisans from abroad. The Conference knew that in current circumstances there was an extreme shortage of money for even the most necessary business of government. Therefore the Senate could make no decision at this time with respect to bringing in artisans, and that the Commission on Commerce must consider the possibility of recruiting artisans without loss to the Treasury.

Could the Commission on Commerce give those in trade any security whatsoever from robbery? On August 24 the Senate received an edict from the empress herself. "It has come to the attention of her imperial majesty, to her extreme anger and displeasure, that Governors Pushkin of Voronezh and Saltykov of Belgorod are wreaking considerable havoc and even carrying out extortion and robbery. She therefore gives instructions that they be investigated most thoroughly."

For amelioration of their lot free homesteaders were released from the authority of the civil and military governors and given their own stewards. The free homesteaders of the Orlov district, however, sent a petition to the Senate. Ensign of the Guards Glazov, together with his clerk, appointed to them against their wishes, was bringing them to ruin, taking away their wives and children and holding them in prison in chains, starving them to death, beating them mercilessly with lashes and rods and giving the free homesteaders' daughters into marriage with landowners' peasants. His agents took a considerable amount of money and removed clothing, grain and other domestic goods as well as chattels when they passed through a district. They killed a two-year old child in the arms of its mother. Therefore the free homesteaders requested Glazov be removed from their district and they be placed under the jurisdiction of the Orlov provincial chancellery as before. The Senate gave orders that Glazov be dismissed immediately, and someone be appointed in his place chosen by the free homesteaders themselves.

The Senate discovered that citizens were suffering insults and unnecessary harassment from forest wardens, who were appointed even to places where there was no forest suitable for shipbuilding. It gave instructions that all such forest wardens be dismissed immediately, and asked for a report from the Admiralty College as to who appointed them, how long ago and for what reason. Finally the Senate decided to replace the military governors every five years, leaving in office only those who were meticulous and not under any suspicion, and whom landowners and citizens asked to be left in their posts.

CELEBRATED EDICT OF AUGUST 16, 1759

These orders of the Senate, made in the months of August and September, were a consequence of the famous edict of the empress of August 16. "Through love for our subjects, it is with much sorrow that we are forced to recognize that many of the laws established for the felicity and wellbeing of our state are not carried out because of notorious domestic enemies, who prefer their illegal profit to their oath, duty and honor. Equally we feel that the evil that has taken root has no limit. Our Senate, as the first institution of state, through its office and through the power invested in it, should have been required long ago to overcome the many violations of good order, increasing without hindrance to the great detriment of the state, in the institutions within its jurisdiction. Insatiable avarice has reached such a point that several institutions, established in the cause of justice, have been made into bazaars. There is extortion and bias with the authority of judges, and licence and negligence through the encouragement of lawbreakers. Many matters in the state are to be found in pitiful condition. The poor, with whom we sympathize deeply, are oppressed by injustice. Our gentleness and moderation in the punishment of criminals brings such recompense to us from ingratitude.

"We enjoin this our Senate, as the true sons of the fatherland, whom we consider as our own in all matters, while expressing their duty to God, the state and the laws of the sovereign emperor our most beloved parent, to use all their strength and diligence for the restoration of people's welfare, so much desired by all. Although there are no petitions and denunciations, nevertheless because of circumstances well known to the Senate this evil must be curtailed and eradicated. Every senator by his clear conscience must know, without any difficulty, the harm being done in the state and those lawbreakers, who are known to him. Therefore he must not be tempted to extend mercy to such evildoers, and occasion wrongful injury to the innocent. As a true son of the fatherland he must remember his fear of God and his duty, in the knowledge that those elevated to be the judges of others must consider their fatherland their kin, and integrity their friend. They know which ideas to respect, which errors in institutions to correct, which judges under suspicion to replace, how to investigate, and most of all to search out the causes leading to the attainment of truth, without prolonging matters. Everyone knows of many harmful cases, such as the prolongation of legal proceedings, disintegration in many places, judges enriching themselves excessively, endless criminal investigations, the misappropriation of our interests by those appointed to safeguard them, theft in the sale of salt, in the levy of conscripts and in taxes upon the people for the essential needs of the state. All this are incontestable proofs that in themselves reveal the means to bring an end to the disorder experienced by all."

AUGMENTATION OF THE SENATE

Elizabeth did not want to limit herself to words alone. We have witnessed her angry edict in respect of governors Saltykov and Pushkin. Besides, the Senate had to be given the means to carry out those responsibilities which the empress demanded. There were not many senators, and some of them met in the Conference. Consequently they could not always be present in the Senate. New senators were appointed: Lieutenant General Kostiurin, Nepliuev the well-known governor general of Orenburg, Count Roman Larionovich Vorontsov[12] and Lieutenant General Zherebtsov. The Senate was now made up of Prince Nikita Trubetskoy, Field Marshal Buturlin, General Admiral Prince Mikhail Mikhailovich Golitsyn, Chancellor Vorontsov (who, like his predecessor Bestuzhev, never attended the Senate), Counts Alexander and Peter Shuvalov, Prince Shcherbaty, Kostiurin, Prince Alexis Dmitrievich Golitsyn, Zherebtsov, Prince Odoevsky, Count Roman Vorontsov, Nepliuev, Khitrovo and Prince Mikhail Ivanovich Shakhovskoy.

PRINCE SHAKHOVSKOY APPOINTED PROCURATOR GENERAL

The policy of augmenting the Senate would not have yielded any significant results had the former procurator general, the extremely senile Prince Nikita Yurievich Trubetskoy, remained in office. He was relieved of his burdensome duties and in his place was appointed a man well-known for his active public work, his probity and incorruptibility, Chief of the Commissary Prince Yakov Petrovich Shakhovskoy. The chief procurator of the Senate, Glebov,[13] was appointed in his place to the post of chief of the commissary and Count Ivan Grigorievich Chernyshev was appointed chief procurator.[14]

SHAKHOVSKOY'S CONFLICTS WITH COUNT PETER SHUVALOV

It was clear that Ivan Ivanovich Shuvalov particularly promoted the appointment of Shakhovskoy as procurator general. At least he was the first to reveal Elizabeth's intention to appoint him to this post. Shakhovskoy, in his words, replied that "this would be to his great misfortune." When Shuvalov persuaded him to take the appointment, which was such a great mark of empress's confidence, Shakhovskoy told him straight that in this new office he would have two major scoundrels to deal with, Count Peter Ivanovich Shuvalov, who was accustomed, without looking too closely at his methods, to drive through his ideas come what may, and Prince Nikita Trubetskoy, who would be replaced against his wishes. Shuvalov pointed out in this regard that Shakhovskoy would find support in all crucial matters from the empress herself and that "as for my brother, I assure you that he will not be an obstacle to the execution of your duties."

Conflicts between Peter Shuvalov and Shakhovskoy nevertheless were inevitable. Shuvalov, like many well-intentioned men, did not want in any

way to hinder the work of those similarly well-intentioned in the "execution of their duties," and had no intention whatsoever of interfering in the
work of the procurator general when he endeavored to introduce order,
speed and justice into the courts, to observe sound economic principles
in government expenditure, *so long as* he did not touch the departments
controlled by Shuvalov, and did not extend his surveillance to them. The
new procurator general found that many departments were not sending
information and reports to the Senate. The senior secretary told him that
it was impossible to ask for accounts from some institutions, such as the
Bureau of Money or from the department responsible for minting copper
coinage, both under the control of Count Peter Ivanovich Shuvalov. Shakhovskoy found that he could and should demand accounts from even these
institutions and sent for them. Shuvalov, outraged, went to the Senate. "I
never expected," he said, "such demands from my own benevolent colleagues, neither from the procurator general, nor from the gentlemen senators. If through any doubts you might have you did indeed want to look
over the register of cash in hand, you could have asked me privately and
I would have instructed it be shown you." "The Bureau of Money," said
Shakhovskoy, "in common with all other colleges and chancelleries, is
answerable to the Senate. Therefore I was duty bound to ask for an account from it as well." Shuvalov changed countenance. "So it was you,
sir, who gave the order," he said. "It was I," Shakhovskoy replied.

Similar conflicts also took place in the Conference, of which Shakhovskoy was likewise a member. Ivan Ivanovich Shuvalov had to intervene.
He spoke courteously, affectionately to Shakhovskoy. "My brother Peter
Ivanovich complains," he said, "with tears in his eyes that you are hound-
ing him." Shakhovskoy asked for a day to be set aside for talks with Count
Peter Ivanovich in the presence of Ivan Ivanovich, which should decide
who was right and who was wrong. Ivan Ivanovich agreed. On the day
appointed the two rivals went to his residence and were sat opposite one
another. Count Peter Ivanovich, who was used, in Shakhovskoy's words,
to gain the upper hand through his eloquence in debate and the exposition of a case, spoke first, laying all blame upon Shakhovskoy. From his
own account of the proceedings Shakhovskoy claimed that Shuvalov's
eloquence greatly irritated him and perhaps he had an image in his mind
of his Moscow house full of the patients from the military hospital. Whether
that was the case or not, instead of directly answering Shuvalov's accusations and presenting each point to his own advantage, Shakhovskoy used
the childish method of abuse. "You are yourself totally without blame, of

course!" He gathered up the rumors repeated by Shuvalov's enemies, suggestions that his best, most useful plans had mercenary motives, and poured all this suddenly upon his head. All of Russia was in a state of agitation because of the shortage of salt as a consequence of an enforced monopoly by the manufacturers from Perm. Shuvalov suggested that the most simple and practical method of ameliorating this problem was to get salt from another source, from Lake Elton, and the problem would be solved. It was an incontrovertible service to all! This is how Shakhovskoy represented the matter to him. "You did this to increase your own revenues, so that all the state peasants who earned their living supplying the Perm saltworks with firewood would turn to the mining works, from which you would take the best for yourself."

Shakhovskoy would not concede, without sullying its importance, even Shuvalov's most useful work, namely the abolition of internal customs duties. "In this way," he told Shuvalov, "you have also freed your own iron ore from internal duty and, they say, on your own order merchants have presented the empress with diamonds and you with the Star of St. Andrew with diamonds." Of course Shuvalov would not lower himself to reply to these accusations, would not lower himself to reply that he could not refrain from proposing measures beneficial to the country such as the abolition of internal customs duties, simply because through this measure his iron ore would indeed be free from duty, and so on. He got up, courteously bowed to Shakhovskoy, and said, "I humbly thank you for your kind frankness with me. I can see well enough already that your excellency has a particular gift of gaining the upper hand with points of evidence, and of winning listeners over to his opinions." Shakhovskoy did not understand the irony of the last words and ingenuously described this meeting in his notes, betraying himself to Shuvalov before posterity, before whom it remains unclear just how Shuvalov resolved his conflicts with Shakhovskoy in the Senate and the Conference.

The new procurator general once again insisted that the holders of offices arrive at the times set by general regulation. The Chancellery of Confiscations reported that although it was obliged indeed to fine all military governors who did not arrive at the set times it had some doubt regarding the imposition of fines. (1) The general regulation stated that they should arrive on the shortest days at six, and on the longest days at eight in the morning. There was not in fact any precise elaboration as to how the short and the long days were to be calculated. (2) It was reported from a number of towns that the military governors were in their chancelleries but that it was not possible to say at what time they arrived and left because of an absence of clocks in those towns. (3) The military governor of the Gremiachie military chancellery was absent on many days because there were no judicial matters to be attended to or needing criminal investigation. Should a fine be imposed for such absences? It was impossible for the Chancellery of Confiscations to deal with this matter because of a shortage of secretaries and minor officials, for in the whole state, apart from the Baltic, Siberia and Orenburg provinces, there were two hundred and fifty large and small towns and districts which must send reports on this matter every four months.

The Senate gave the following instructions in response to this report. Hour glasses must be kept where there were no clocks. A fine should not be imposed where the governor was absent for lack of work. They might arrive even after the time stipulated in the regulations if the clock was in disrepair, but everyone must arrive at the same time without fail and remain on duty for the time laid down in the regulation, and if necessary even beyond the prescribed time, in order that matters not be neglected.

MOST SIGNIFICANT LEGAL DECISIONS

We should note the most significant legal decisions. We have mentioned the most important case in a series of internecine conflicts and raids amongst landowners, the case of the Lvovs and Sofonov where so many peasants were killed. A special commission was appointed to deal with this case, but the Lvovs came to a settlement with Sofonov and they asked that the commission be abolished. The Senate replied that although they had reached a settlement and Sofonov was satisfied in his suit against the Lvovs it was not possible to leave the arguments, fights and murders committed without investigation. Whosoever was found guilty by the investigation would be treated according to the law.

The College of Justice forwarded the résumé of another case. Men from the Voronezh Dragoon Regiment of Colonel Timofeev testified, after torture, that they crushed to death a member of the regiment, Poliakov, on the orders of the colonel because of his connection with the colonel's wife, who did not give her consent to this murder, committed at a time when the colonel's wife had gone to the wooden hut where Poliakov lived. When she called Poliakov's wife out of the hut she took her off to a peasant's hut at the back. The assassins took advantage of this opportunity, rushed into the wooden hut and crushed Poliakov to death. This was at midnight, which also directed suspicion on the lady. In addition she gave orders to dig Poliakov's body out of a trench and carry it off into the forest. The colonel's wife said that she called Poliakov's wife out to the peasant hut at the back for domestic reasons. When she heard about the murder, she ordered the body be dug up and given a proper funeral by the church. She did not report the incident, fearing her husband, but told her confessor in confidence. The Voronezh provincial chancellery and the College of Justice ordered the colonel's wife to be tortured, but the Senate decided that the opinion of the College of Justice about torture be set aside, as in the Code it is forbidden to believe the denunciations of serfs. The colonel's wife, Timofeeva, should be released without a fine, as she was kept under arrest for many years. She had been punished enough by being confined under arrest for the fact that, while knowing about the murder, she did not report it. Furthermore she was under no obligation to do so.

PEASANT UPRISINGS

As previously in domestic affairs peasant uprisings concerned the government most of all. The peasants were suppressed and assigned to Shuvalov's iron mills in the Kazan district. Following their petition, the Senate appointed the retired ensign Zhdanov steward for the protection of the peasants of the Kadom district, as they had been deprived of the right to speak for themselves because of their insulting language and destructive behavior. In the village of Yegorievsk in the province of Galich-in-Volhynia the peasants stopped obeying their landowner Tarakanov. A commissioner was sent to them with a detachment of troops and official witnesses. The commissioner read a published edict in church but the peasants declared that the edict was in response to a petition of their landowner, and therefore no longer would they in any way obey either him or his servants. Up to three hundred of the peasants in Yegorievsk gathered together cudgels and long knives, and sent the commissioner and his detachment packing. They would not give him permission to speak any further about the edict. In the Arzamas district the peasants of the landowner Bessonov rose in revolt.

There was much more trouble with monastery peasants. At the beginning of the year four complaints came to the Senate from peasants of a number of monasteries concerning unlawful acts, destruction and torment from monastic authorities, stewards and lay brothers. The peasants wrote that they had petitioned the bishops and the Synod but received no satisfaction. Later the Cabinet forwarded to the Senate requests from the peasants of the Kaliazin monastery in the Kashin district, the New Savior monastery in the Shatsk district, the Transfiguration monastery in the Belev district, the Savior monastery in the Yaroslavl district and the cathedral church in the Murom district. The Cabinet informed the Senate that the petitioners, elected by the peasant communes, must have raised the courage to put their petitions to the empress herself, since the offenses against them had become unbearable. Although they were prohibited from presenting their petitions to the empress herself, she would forgive them and gave orders for their complaints to be resolved. Complaints were received also from peasants of the St. Joseph monastery of Volokolamsk and others. The Senate told the Synod that the complaints of these peasants had not been investigated directly, therefore it was not possible to acknowledge their justification. Yet had they not been subject to excessive burdens, they would not have been driven to make complaints without cause. The peasants of the St. Joseph monastery begged that a special commission be set up to look into their problem. As a commission was already in existence to look into matters at the New Savior monastery, it was decided to transfer to this commission consideration of the complaints of the remaining monastery peasants as well. Four lay members were appointed to the commission and the Synod was to appoint members from its own body, as many as it thought fit.

The peasants of St. Sabbas the Guardian monastery did not limit themselves to sending petitions. Up to three hundred gathered together and arrived at the monastery with clubs. They asked the guard on duty to let them in to the almoner. The gates were, of course, locked. Then they broke them down, shouting that the clerk, the chorister and stableman should be sent out to them, threatening to beat them to death. Later, a second time, up to two thousand gathered and placed themselves along all the roads near the monastery, inspecting all passers by, looking for three peasants taken near the monastery by a military detachment sent from the Synodal office They shouted that if these peasants were not released to them, as well as the clerk, the chorister and the stableman they had previously demanded, they refused to allow the military detachment out of the monastery, and would kill them. A captain with a company of soldiers was sent against them. The Synod reported that this uprising was caused by two monks who ran away from the monastery. When these monks were caught the peasants freed them and laid siege to the monastery. The captain did not find the peasants near the monastery, but beyond the monastery settlement. They attacked the detachment, and two soldiers were wounded. The detachment had to fire bullets, then retreated to the monastery from the fury of the attacking peasants, as thirty men from the detachment were wounded. The Senate ordered that another two hundred men with a staff officer be sent to the monastery, and demanded that the Synod instruct the priests to persuade the peasants to submit.

REGULATION OF CHURCH ESTATES

The uprisings of the monastery peasants must have set in motion discussion of the difficult question of changing the administration of church property and revenues from them. On July 3 the Senate, at the express personal command of the empress, discussed the monastery peasants and the revenues collected from them, as well as establishment of housing for veterans. Prince Kozlovsky, chief procurator of the Synod, was summoned and reported that the Holy Synod intended to assign two hundred thousand rubles each year for the maintenance of veterans, and perhaps even more. Subsequently there was a conference in the Senate with the Synod on October 6. Dmitry (Sechenov), archbishop of Novgorod, Sylvester of St. Petersburg, Bishop Veniamin of Pskov and Porfiry of Kolomna came to the meeting at the Senate. The procurator general, Prince Shakhovskoy, made the point that on September 30, 1757 the empress ordered discussion of monastery and episcopal revenues but only on July 24, 1760 did a conference take place at the Senate with the Synod on this matter. No decision was sanctioned or signed. Therefore the procurator general, seeing that the empress's edict had not been observed for three years, considered it his duty to suggest to the general assembly that they carry the wishes of the empress to conclusion, finding the most expeditious means to do so. The synodal members declared that they affirmed their opinion, given on July 24, that were officers assigned to the episcopal and monastery villages for the administration and collection of revenues the greatest destruction to the villages would ensue. This would cause constant anxiety and difficulties between the officers and the monastery authorities as in the past when the villages were administered by the Monastery Office. That is why in 1720 Peter the Great returned them to the monasteries.

In recent years it had been impossible to find money for establishment of houses for invalids and maintenance of those who retired. No arrangement had been made covering all monasteries as to how many pensioners should be maintained where. Always and every year those who were retired and sent for accomodation to the monasteries were accepted. They were maintained by the monasteries. Moreover, some [monastery] revenue was sent to the bursar's office for their specified expenses. It was impossible to provide information relating to all transactions for all revenues collected and the measures taken to do so. This was because of remoteness and the distances involved. Should reckoning of accounts and investigation be made, the present authorities could not be responsible for those who had died. The retired maintained by the monasteries complained about monastery authorities, and the authorities about the retired, for their excessive demands and intemperate behavior. It was impossible for the diocesan bishops to oversee and to avert all these problems, owing to remoteness and distance.

In rebuttal the Holy Synod proposed that the retired not be maintained by the monasteries at all. Instead all episcopal and monastery peasants should be covered under the landowners' tax assessment. From this money the Holy Synod would assign annually an additional three hundred thousand rubles into government funds for approved expenses in the following manner. The Holy Synod would make a supplementary payment for the Synod, the Palestinian Rest Homes, the maintenance of the alms-houses, the military hospital and so on up to sixty thousand rubles, then from the banns and printing revenues, to satisfy these expenditures. The inherited estates, as formerly, would fall to the episcopal houses and monasteries, which would be obligated to maintain the episcopal houses with their seminaries, and all the buildings within the monasteries. Should her imperial majesty not be pleased to sanction these arrangements formally, and an imperial injunction should follow, the Holy Synod would observe without fail.

Several days after this meeting, as if on purpose, news arrived of strife between monasteries concerning ownership of hereditary estates. Retired Lieutenant Karmanov, Sergeant of Guards Sukin and two soldiers, living in the New Savior monastery, reported that they were sent from the monastery to supervise monastic peasants mowing meadows situated in the Moscow district on the Goledianka stream. After they had mown the hay they were intending to take it to the monastery stables when Markell, a representative of the Androniev monastery, gathered together many men, including the monastery servants and peasants, and attacked these officers and the peasants of the New Savior monastery without cause, breaking the arms of several, punching their heads, and stealing the hay. Karmanov, with several of his colleagues, petitioned the Synodal Office and the Moscow Consistory but their petitions were not accepted.

EVENTS IN TOBOLSK AND IRKUTSK

The matter of oppression of the Tatars and people of Bukhara by the diocesan authorities of Tobolsk was not investigated by a mixed commission of religious and laymen because the members of the commission argued amongst themselves. The Senate closed the commission and fined its members. It transferred the matter for consideration to the new metropolitan of Siberia and the provincial chancellery.

Further to the East, in Irkutsk, there was also a commission dealing with plundering by merchants of the municipal tavern dues to the sum of one hundred and fifty thousand rubles. The merchants confessed and petitioned that they would pay half of this money but could not pay the other half as, apart from their houses and belongings, they would have nothing left. The Senate decided not to recover the other half, and not to subject them to punishment. On investigation the deputy governor Major General Wulf and his colleague, Colonel Slobodskoy, excused themselves for their lack of knowledge of civil service regulations.

It was soon necessary to appoint a special commission to investigate the behavior of the chairman of this Irkutsk commission, Collegiate Assessor Krylov. The Senate was told that this Krylov invited Wulf, the deputy governor of Irkutsk, to his place, dragged him before the commission, took his dagger from him, then threw him out and proclaimed himself in control of the province. The Senate sent a courier to bring Krylov to St. Petersburg in chains. In the meantime Krylov sent in a report that he was visiting the merchant Zaitsev with Wulf, and that he pushed to one side the secretary of the Irkutsk chancellery, Brusentsov, for his impolite language. Wulf, jumping up at once, pulled his dagger from its scabbard and stabbed Krylov in the arm. Then they all left the house and Krylov demanded that Wulf accompany him to the commission, where he asked Wulf why he perpetrated such an evil crime against him, and Wulf replied that he was a Prussian. Then Krylov, afraid that Wulf might stab him to death, demanded his dagger, which Wulf did indeed hand over. The Senate did not change its decision, and we shall hear later of Krylov's other escapades.

Even in Siberia a peasant uprising could not be avoided. In Yalutorovsk district the peasants petitioned that they were refusing state plowing and gathering of grain. An ensign was sent with a detachment to exhort them. When they took the ringleaders the peasants hit the detachment with cudgels, liberating the village elder and other ringleaders defeating the whole detachment and wounding the ensign in the face with a cudgel. Moreover the peasants had guns and bayonets. The sexton of Kurgan settlement, on leaving matins, shouted so that everyone could hear that evil must be eradicated by evil. The village priest Joseph let the peasants into the belfry, declaring that it had been built by them. The Senate commanded that the peasants be told to be obedient, and asked the governor to find out whether it was better to plow the land or collect quitrent grain from the peasants. He was to beat the most prominent factory workers with lashes and send them to work in Nerchinsk, and report to the Synod about the priest and the sexton.

CONFLICT BETWEEN SENATE AND CONFERENCE

Siberia was becoming more and more important because of its subterranean riches, which excited great hopes, particularly in the difficult financial circumstances prevailing at the time as a consequence of the much-prolonged war. These circumstances forced attention toward the opposite, the Western borders, to see if it were possible to receive more than so far obtained from the Baltic provinces and Russian Finland. On this issue conflict erupted in the Senate with the Conference. The Senate received an extract from protocols of the Conference regarding the revenues from Lifland, Estland and Finland. The question was which of these provinces had carried onerous burdens under Swedish dominion in the past, and what was being received from them now. In conclusion it required the Senate to consider this matter and to offer its opinion, which should be presented to the Conference. The Senate authorized the following reply. It would send an extract from the protocol to the Conference that the necessary intelligence and information on this matter had been gathered. The State Senate discussed the matter but came to no decision, in the first place because there was lack of a quorum of Senators, but in the second place because the State Senate, the primary institution of state apart from her imperial majesty, was not obliged to give its opinion to anybody. Moreover the ministers of the Conference were all themselves members of the Senate. Consequently the issue, as a matter of state, must be decided by the entire Senate at a plenary meeting. It was signed by Nepliuev, Prince Alexis Golitsyn, Prince Odoevsky, Zherebtsov, Count Roman Vorontsov, Kostiurin and Prince Mikhail Shakhovskoy.

V

DEATH OF EMPRESS ELIZABETH, 1761

DESIRE FOR PEACE, AND NEW YEAR CELEBRATIONS

A strong desire to end the burdensome war was expressed during the celebrations of the New Year of 1761. In the first display of fireworks set off before the palace on January 1 the New Year was represented as a winged youth bringing a laurel wreath and *a branch from the Mount of Olives* as a gift. He stood on the guns, standards and flags conquered from the enemy. Before him lay the keys and arms of the royal city of Berlin, capital of Prussia and Brandenburg. "This demonstrates," stated the newspapers, "that our most gracious sovereign is using the illustrious victories gained by her arms and the honorable reputation we have acquired for one purpose only, through them to hasten and to put in place the longed-for resolution of conflict and universal peace."

FINANCIAL ESTIMATES FOR THE FORTHCOMING CAMPAIGN

Renewed efforts were necessary to procure that longed-for peace. Above all some consideration must be given to financial resources for the troops. Over the past year over three hundred thousand rubles had not been delivered to the army. It was agreed that this money be dispatched as soon as possible. The Commissary fixed a sum for pay in 1761 of 1,465,728 rubles. Buturlin had asked for 2,031,000. "Although the full amount you ask for is not available," he was told, "there will of course be sufficient, as the sum determined will be received more promptly than before. We shall try to ensure that this is so as conscientiously as possible, in particular as you have included in those two million up to three hundred thousand for extraordinary expenses which may be taken from another account so that the Commissary remains as much as possible within strict observation of its regulations."

Buturlin proposed 1,122,488 rubles for provisions for the whole army. "As you are below strength," he was told in reply, "and as prices sometimes are falling, there must be significant surpluses. We are at present basing our calculations not on the whole year, but just the campaign. There is now almost as much as will be needed, from the moment the army enters the field, in supply depots on the Vistula. There is a shortage of what is required for the maintenance of regiments earmarked for Pomerania. There is also somewhat of a deficiency on the Vistula, especially in what the troops need to take with them for a month and to keep in reserve there for another month. Nevertheless this does not amount to a significant sum and we are certain that you will overcome this problem either by appropriating provisions, issuing a receipt, or by contract and purchase using (1) two hundred thousand rubles in Königsberg recast into Prussian coins, (2) other money now with the provisions administration, (3) sixty thousand that was taken recently from Königsberg and (4) one hundred and fifty thousand thalers made on a bill of exchange from Berlin sold in Danzig. If you manage to make do with these funds until the army leaves the Vistula to take the field, there is no doubt that during the campaign there will be no shortage of cash.

"Military operations will not suffer delays and procrastination because a million rubles of subsidy here will be obtained for you in full, and the first half of it very soon. From it, first of all, you will have to take sufficient funds to procure future supplies depending on the plan of operations, and use the rest on buying other provisions. Later, from the thousand puds of silver received from us, you will have more than a million rubles of Prussian money. If we assume that the campaign lasts six months, and for each month you use twenty-five thousand chetverts of grain, and that each chetvert costs five rubles, you only need nine hundred thousand rubles. We have not taken into account the groats, oats and hay, but then grain has never become so expensive nor so much of it needed. Also no account has been taken of what may be obtained as a result of events on enemy soil. Let us say the six-month campaign will cost precisely a million for provisions and forage. You will then have another million left over for other expenses.

"As to rations for the hussars, for which you now request more than six hundred thousand rubles, our Treasury can never bear such expense.

Moreover it would be extremely unjustified to spend such sums in vain. Therefore you must always support them by requisitioning on enemy territory or see that they receive provisions from the supply depots. You should also consider whether they ought to be organized on a completely different basis, as previous budgets were based on the assumption that they were to remain at all times in Ukraine, or were to fight only on the Turkish steppes. If there is no means of feeding them at the enemy's expense nothing remains but to return them all to Ukraine, and in their place increase the number of cossacks. You need a significant sum for extraordinary expenses. For this purpose we are assigning you everything realized from the million thalers from Berlin and, moreover, all future indemnities, should the Almighty give his blessing to our forces."

Buturlin was sent a *particularly secret* rescript on January 25. "Those circumstances have now passed, or may soon pass, when we were obliged to try to preserve Prussia in good condition. Circumstances are coming when we must make sure simply that our army is supplied with everything necessary, and is a force terrifying to the king of Prussia. Therefore we instruct you (1) to gather the full number of drivers you need from the civilian population of Prussia, giving them a surety. We realize that such a roundup of drivers in 1759 did not bring much benefit to us. We were told they ran away. Because of our good supervision and management we no longer need fear such a possibility now. We know that it was not so much that they ran away as they got out of hand because of our dreadful cupidity. (2) If there are insufficient men in the regiments you may replace them from orderlies and in their place take from Prussia sons of fathers living at home, assuring both orderlies and drivers that at the conclusion of hostilities they will be released to return to their homes."

What then were those new circumstances which no longer permitted the sparing of East Prussia, that is, removed any hope of it remaining in Russia?

FRENCH PEACE PROPOSALS

On the evening of January 11 the French ambassador went to the chancellor with a dispatch from the duc de Choiseul which stated that the king of France most definitely desired peace because of the state of his domain. In respect to this matter the ambassador presented the following declaration, requesting a swift reply. "It is most certainly common knowledge that the forces of the king of Prussia are so exhausted that if England could not assist him he would be forced to render every satisfaction which his unjustified invasion gives us the right to demand.

"Even with English assistance the exhaustion of this sovereign is so evident that the powers have come together for restoration of peace and the preservation of law. So long as their alliance remains steadfast have no fear that the king of Prussia would dare to disturb the peace and imperial law with new attacks after a peace settlement. The king of France does not foresee any possibility that the next campaign can bring the allies into a better position than at present. The king cannot hide from his faithful allies that he must reduce his auxiliary forces, and that the continuation of the war seriously exhausts the revenue of his government, so that he cannot be responsible for the precise fulfillment of obligations undertaken towards the allies. The king hopes that her imperial majesty will sacrifice her own interests to this great enterprise, just as the king himself intends to sacrifice his."

NEGOTIATIONS BETWEEN ALLIES

On the following day, January 12, Esterhazy gave the chancellor a note dated January 1 from Maria Theresa relating to the French declaration, stating that it was necessary to try to conclude a peace settlement, if possible that winter. "A future peace settlement," stated the rescript of the queen-empress, "may be of three different kinds. (1) Positive, whereby we, together with our allies, receive satisfaction, as a result of which our most dangerous enemy will be brought within appropriate bounds. (2) Satisfactory, whereby we shall be satisfied only in part and the enemies' forces will be reduced only to a degree. (3) Unsatisfactory, whereby the king of Prussia will leave a war he began in a grossly audacious manner without losing territory and without paying significant damages.

"Continuation of the war is the most hopeful way of achieving peace and security for us and for our allies. It is not difficult to understand that the drift towards a peace settlement shown at present is very regrettable to us. Yet there is nothing to be done. We must also pay attention to the situation of our allies and we are ready for peace if, of course, it is to be at least a satisfactory and not an unsatisfactory peace settlement. For that reason we have given instructions that the French ambassador be informed that, with regard to present circumstances, we do not insist on obtaining the whole of Silesia and the county of Glatz, but will be satisfied with a certain portion, if by this means a peace settlement may be concluded before the opening of the campaign. Meanwhile we think a congress must be convened for the conclusion of a fair and honest peace treaty, at which an understanding may be reached rather more conveniently, not only with our enemies, but also with our friends. Besides, we may also gain considerable time."

On January 30 Baron Breteuil informed the chancellor that, with the agreement of the Austrian ambassador, the duc de Choiseul had instructed the Genoese ambassador Sobre, who was leaving for London, to convey the congratulations of his republic to the new king of England, George III, on his accession to the throne. He was to make certain cautious suggestions to the English ministry with regard to the restoration of a common peace. Breteuil added that the duc de Choiseul himself did not have much hope of success because of Sobre's lack of status, but that he would simply like to find out the views and disposition of the English court. The king had given instructions to Breteuil to ask whether her imperial majesty would be pleased to give instructions to Prince Golitsyn in London to support the peace proposals made by the duc de Choiseul to the English court, as a consequence of which the duke would apply directly by letter to Pitt, the secretary of state for foreign affairs. This letter would be delivered in the first place to Prince Golitsyn, as ambassador of a power allied to France and on friendly terms with England. Would Golitsyn, on his part, support the contents of this letter as strongly as possible, and would he try to obtain a swift reply, through which it might be possible to begin negotiations for a peace settlement?

The Russian reply followed on February 1. "Of course," it stated, "no one would dispute the fact that if we wanted a swift peace settlement we must conclude only an honorable, stable and effective peace. There is no doubt but that his majesty the king of France agrees with our point of view. If we were talking simply about a stable and honorable peace settlement, the plan would have been prepared already. The whole of Silesia and the county of Glatz would have to be delivered to the empress-queen, and Pomerania to Sweden, promised by the king of France and by Austria in the Stockholm convention of September 22, 1757. The Danish court must be confirmed in the system of the alliance with regard to the king of Prussia. It would not only be fitting to reward the king of Poland, but even to put him into a position whereby his lands, open from all sides, should not easily find themselves in the circumstances in which they are today.

"England would have to be constrained, not only to a just bargain in American matters, but also to cede the island of Minorca to France. We should also be rewarded for our losses with respect to the common enemy, as demanded by the dignity of our rank, the causes for complaint against the king of Prussia, our considerable assistance in the war, our future effective support and the security of our allies.

"In as much as we must think about the possibility and considerable difficulties that accompany full attainment of all these aims, at the very least we must also to try to ensure that the forces of the king of Prussia are significantly reduced, and that by this means England would lose much of its influence in continental affairs. At least in this respect the allies would obtain some compensation for their losses, so that they might work calmly and securely for the restoration of the well-being of their governments.

"In reality the strength of the king of Prussia is now diminished. He no longer has the armies with which he hoped to stand against everyone. Yet after the battles of Palzig and Frankfurt, after the losses at Dresden,[1] after the Maxen affair[2] and finally after spending all winter in the field under arms, it turns out that nonetheless he was in a condition, having lost the whole corps of General Fouqué at the beginning of the past campaign, not only to appear in the field but even to put his affairs in order once more. At the same time as, on the one hand, his affairs fall into an ever worse state from one day to the next, on the other hand the forces of the allies improve and have at least reached the point when frivolous opinion in respect to the invincibility of the Prussian forces has been destroyed in the last soldier. When despite all this we still meet such difficulties in the attainment of our accepted objectives, it is easy to conclude that the reduction of the king of Prussia's forces can be of short duration only and such that, even if they were not used, he would become considerably stronger than before.

"When in the midst of such a ferocious war, when in the face of the constant exercise of all his forces, when almost all of his neighbors are his enemies, he finds nevertheless that he is capable of replenishing the terrible losses in his armies with unbelievable speed, to what condition then will he bring his forces in two years of peace, if the means to do so remain in his hands? Then it will lie in his power to consider on whom of the imperial princes taking part in the present war against him to take revenge, to display all his strength and teach the empire never again to venture its contingents against him.

"The sanctity of the Treaties of Westphalia was powerless to prevent this present war. The alliance of great powers did not inspire fear in him, and now will frighten him even less. Armed and guided in the united spirit of courage and firmness, the powers could not impose sufficient limits upon him, even when brought to a state of weakness. Can they control a sovereign sacrificing everything to glory alone when France will turn all of its attention to improvement of its fleet and its affairs in America and will, perhaps, reduce its land forces; when the empress-queen will be forced to do the same, or else peace in no way will be distinguished from war; when the king of Poland can simply gather his scattered subjects, and we will have to spread our army across the full extent of our empire?

"We can honestly say that the prolongation of the war is becoming extremely difficult for us. Yet if in the present peace settlement so earnestly desired, because of haste or any other misfortune measures are not taken against the possibility of a new war which might indeed soon break out, then in a few years we will not be in a position again to lead such an army to the Oder, even if we receive substantial millions of subsidies, because an army may not always be at the ready in Lifland. When we examine the question of diminishing the strength of the king of Prussia in some detail we must confess with extreme regret that those crying out against him because of his injustice and inhumanity are his adherents and defenders. Despite his weakened position, and after making considerable mistakes, nevertheless he has become more honored than before in the opinion of those who judge him by his appearance. He has become great for the reason that he could for so long oppose such strong powers and will become incomparably more exalted if he loses nothing in the peace settlement.

"We shall not refer at all to the Danish court, and shall leave his most Christian majesty to judge in what circumstances that court will place itself, and where its inclinations must lean if the forces of king of Prussia remain in their present state. The most favorable political stance of the Ottoman Porte for the well-being of Europe, not to interfere in the affairs of the Christian powers at war between themselves, only awaits the minute for peace to be concluded in order, either immediately to reject with disdain the proposals of the king of Prussia reduced to a state of weakness or, were he to preserve all his forces and by that means acquire a new importance, to accept them with pleasure. We are driven to think of these precautions not simply because of our own unilateral interests. Our frontiers are extensive and we are surrounded by many neighbors. The situation of the frontiers, however, is such as may cause us merely a great deal of vexation and trouble, but rarely may we expect substantial danger. The position of our allies is completely the reverse, in particular that of the empress-queen. She may be exposed simultaneously to an attack in the very heart of her hereditary possessions from two directions, and may not receive any swift assistance from anywhere. So it is only the substantial interests of our allies that compel us to speak with such fervor about the reduction of the forces of the king of Prussia.

"France is in a completely different situation to us. However much England sacrifices to maintain the king of Prussia, it can always obtain more than it loses. However well and decisively matters in America and other parts of the world are concluded, should England maintain its influence on the continent of Europe and not fear for its German possessions and for its allies, it will find sufficient pretexts to bring about the collapse of the much improved French fleet, its distant colonies and trade in general. In this way the stability of the future peace settlement and the security of all the allies depends upon reducing substantially the strength of the king of Prussia. This must be the first and most important basis of a peace settlement. Yet how can such a reduction of strength be achieved?

"The empress-queen will not insist on acquiring everything to which she has an indisputable right. As she has already made several gains in Silesia, and may hope that in the coming campaign she will make even more, her enemies, if they sincerely desire peace, cannot avoid making concessions to her there. Also we may be so bold as to hope that if a peace settlement came to a stalemate because of some trifle her majesty would give it up quickly rather than resolve to continue the war. The king of Poland, as elector of Saxony, suffered such an unjustified attack, and his lands have been so inhumanely ravaged, that the antagonists themselves cannot but acknowledge the need to offer him proper compensation. This compensation cannot consist in money alone, the more so as it is impossible to guarantee that the money will be paid, especially if it is a substantial amount. For that reason, in addition to the principality of Magdeburg and the Prussian possessions in Lusatia, the king of Poland must be granted everything that can be obtained through the fervent and unanimous efforts of all the courts. Sweden must acquire something in Pomerania, gaining better rounded borders there.

"For our part we believe that the best that could be gained from this war would be if the forces of the king of Prussia were reduced substantially, and that we would be in a position to rely upon the fact that war would not break out again soon, that we would be at peace for several years, not needing to render what is for us such onerous assistance to our allies, and what is for them sometimes belated assistance. We have already declared previously that we want to acquire the province of East Prussia, having full rights to it. It has been conquered by us from an antagonist who declared war upon us. Furthermore it does not belong to the Holy Roman empire. We certainly do not want to acquire this province in order to expand the borders of our empire, which are extensive enough without it, and not as compensation for losses, since the possession of East Prussia would be a burden upon us, but solely in order the more reliably to confirm the peace. Later, by ceding it to Poland, we may conclude thereby the many mutual claims which are inconsistent with our earnest desire to preserve this Commonwealth without violation of peace and with all of its rights and freedoms. Such a desire cannot be declined, the more so as even this province, covered with lakes and marshes, will not make a great deal of difference to the power of the king of Prussia.

"One objection may be raised, that the king of Prussia, through his own stubbornness, would sooner bring himself to any extremity than agree to its concession. We are not obliged to respond to his stubbornness with an ever-ready indulgence. Nevertheless if the peace procedure goes according to our desires and the main aim, a substantial reduction in the strength of the king of Prussia, can be achieved, and if in this respect it turns out that our acquisition of East Prussia is extremely difficult, and if we see that in sacrificing our rights to East Prussia we can improve the conditions for peace for all the allies, and in particular for France, we will give it up. Then our faithful allies, of course, must furnish us with an equivalent compensation."

The College of Foreign Affairs was told to give a copy of this declaration to Count Esterhazy, attaching to it the following note. "The empress-queen, through her sense of justice, is pleased to recognize that our present behavior scarcely corresponds to our customary candor. We have never set in motion with France any matter whatsoever about which we have not reached an agreement in advance with the empress-queen, and which we have not for the most part left completely to her direction and good offices, despite the fact that everything comes to us not only already agreed beforehand with France, but often at such a time and in such a manner that there is no time to take any other decision. The close proximity of the courts is conducive to this. The novelty of political and intimate alliances with France commits the two countries to many *ménagements* of which we are not in any way envious.

"Matters that relate to us in the very same degree as they relate to France could, at the very least, be mentioned at the same time to us as well. It is enough that because of the distances involved we hear later and make decisions later. Even if the rejected proposals of the Prussian Colonel Schwerin mean nothing, nevertheless they were communicated to the court at Versailles a month earlier. As to the actual proposals for a peace settlement, we would never have expected that not only were they concealed from us at the time but even now, when the matter has almost come to a conclusion, only some incomplete pieces of information have been offered us, which served only to confuse us, and could not facilitate real and most useful decisions by the empress-queen.

"No evidence will oblige us to believe that the main points have not already been agreed without us, or that it is hoped to bring us to a peace settlement prepared beforehand. Should this happen against all our expectations, we want to make clear in advance that, even if the very best terms for us were to be inserted, such as could only be desired, we will never agree to such a peace settlement, will refuse any benefits, and will find occasion to conclude a separate peace with the king of Prussia. Let only the glory remain to us. As former victors, we will be content with our triumphs. We will have given the gift of peace to the vanquished, but will not have not accepted the honors due.

"Our empire, thank God, is in such state that it cannot greatly fear the vengeance of the king of Prussia and he, of course, would be the first to seek our friendship. On the other hand if the peace proposal proceeds in a proper manner, and in accordance with the dignity of the allies, and they act with us with the very same sincerity with which we act ourselves, the empress-queen may indeed count upon us sharing everything, whether dangers, losses or gains."

On February 3, the day after receiving these two papers, Esterhazy went to the chancellor with a clarification relating to them. He began with an expression of the greatest pleasure over the Russian reply to the French proposal. The answer, in his words, was based upon the rules of sound politics and in full accord both with the dignity of the empress herself and also with that of all her allies. After this the envoy changed his countenance, giving it a sorrowful expression, and declared that to the extent he was overjoyed by the reply, he was equally saddened by the note addressed to his court. There the empress-queen obviously was being reproached, as if for her part incomplete frankness was shown the Russian court and clandestine decisions were made with France without giving Russia prior notice. The note even concluded with a threat that the empress would be forced, while abandoning any expected benefits from the war and the alliance, to think of other measures. Esterhazy had in his hands incontrovertible evidence of the friendship of his sovereign for her imperial majesty, as a consequence of which she had never hidden and would never hide from such a true ally not only any deeds, but even her views. On the powerful assistance of the All-Russian empress his sovereign places every hope for the future peace settlement and the well-being of her subjects.

As proof of the innocence of his court in the actions attributed to it by the Russian note, Esterhazy read two memoranda presented in Vienna by the French ambassador, as well as a copy of instructions sent in regard to this matter to Count Starhemberg in Paris. The first French memorandum explained why it was safer and more beneficial to conduct peace negotiations at two congresses, in Paris and in London, outlining the reasons why these important matters could not be entrusted to any one of the allied courts. Saxony demanded for itself an excessively large measure of satisfaction and, because of its misfortunes, was not in a position to add any appropriate pressure to the negotiations. Sweden was incapable by virtue of its government.

Russia was far distant, and above all these matters related to two wars, of which Russia was participating only in one. Moreover, having an English ambassador in St. Petersburg and a trade agreement with England, Russia could not undertake to support the interests of France against the British court, not to mention the fact valuable time would be wasted in explaining to the Russian minister the mutual claims of England and France in both the Indies. The Austrian court, like the Russian, was taking part solely in the German war and England was taking part only in the war at sea.

In view of this, France declared its readiness to undertake negotiations independently. The first proposal to the adversaries could be based upon leaving matters in their present position. The Swedes, as an arrogant nation, may comfort themselves with the honor of fulfilling the guarantee of the Treaties of Westphalia. France could grant subsidies for the restoration of credit in the bank of Stockholm. This would end the main criticism of the Senate, that proceeded not so much from the unfortunate war as such, as from the drain upon government resources. Russia could keep control of its conquests, and to remove its readiness to seek English subsidies the king of France would offer Russia his own subsidies. He would also guarantee that Russia would not be troubled for debts contracted in Poland during the present war, and that the demarcation of frontiers in respect to the Ukraine would not be acted upon.

France would make a general effort in the peace settlement on behalf of the king of Poland, stipulating in advance that Saxony would be cleared of the enemy immediately, and be given the duchy of Cleves as compensation. Together with the house of Austria, France would strike a bargain relating to the exchange of the territories of Hesse and the county of Hanau, leaving matters in Silesia unchanged. France would sacrifice to the general cause everything already lost.

The empress was satisfied with Esterhazy's explanation. The irritation subsided, especially when it could be seen that Russia, in the peace settlement projected by France, would be placed in an advantageous position. As Esterhazy begged for retraction of the note, by which the empress-queen would only be deeply saddened without any advantage to the general cause, instructions were given that the note be taken from him and that he be given another "in which, while preserving all the good reason of the former (note), only those words were retracted which the ambassador suggested might have offended the empress-queen to no purpose." "We consider it necessary," the new note stated, "that our ministers together with those of the empress-queen at present in Paris not only be in close accord, but together try not to permit the court of France coming to a precipitate settlement. With every means at their disposal they shall maintain the alliance in the recognized system. It may easily be foreseen that this important matter will not be concluded without significant changes in the positions taken already. As the empress-queen is closer to knowing everything touching upon a peace settlement and common matters, as well as foreseeing matters through consideration of the circumstances, naturally her majesty will recognize the necessity, for her own and for our interests, to inform us about everything well in advance.

"We reassure you with our immutable word that we shall keep all communications a close secret. For our part we now confess to her majesty in total trust that if, against every expectation, it should happen that France desires to conclude a peace settlement to which only allies could accede, we will never accede to such a peace treaty, even should conditions be inserted most advantageous and desired on our part. We are certain that the empress-queen will agree with us that it is better to abandon all benefits and, being the victors, to be satisfied with victories alone rather than accept honors to which we are not entitled."

It was agreed with Breteuil that, before the main congress, negotiations should begin between France and England by a letter from the duc de Choiseul to Pitt, conveyed by Prince Golitsyn. Instructions were given to write to Golitsyn that the empress would consider it the summit of his diligence to his service and the art of diplomacy could he find the means by whatever mediation might be necessary, only in such a way as would be unremarkable, to bring England to make tentative proposals for peace to the Russian court. In this England would deliver into his hands the determination of the peace negotiations, as evidently France was seeking to appropriate this honor.

On February 21 Baron Breteuil told the chancellor he had received new instructions from his court to seek an assurance without fail from the Russian court that the draft declaration regarding the peaceable intent of the allies, proposed by his court, was accepted in all parts, and in particular the last point relating to a demarcated or non-demarcated armistice, depending upon the choice of the adversaries.

The draft consisted of two points. According to the first the city of Augsburg was nominated for the general congress. It was left to the courts of London and Berlin as to whether there should be a general congress, or whether there should be two congresses, the later to decide whether to conclude peace negotiations or simply prepare the preliminaries, leaving the most important business again to a general congress. The second point offered an armistice, and once more left it to England and Prussia whether there would be an armistice, and whether to prescribe a time period.

Breteuil explained to Vorontsov that an armistice was becoming necessary to France to preserve what was left of its trade, in both the Indies and the colonies. Breteuil was told that the empress was in agreement to the choice of Augsburg as a site for the congress. She agreed that a declaration to this effect should be made in London through the Russian envoy Prince Golitsyn, but with the proviso that the declaration be put together in Paris by the ministers of the king, together with the Russian envoy. She was also in agreement with two congresses, but that a congress carrying only a general title initially be put forward.

In respect to an armistice, the empress agreed solely out of friendship for the king of France, as proof that she often gave preference to the interests of the allies above her own. She believed herself that an early start to the campaign and vigorous operations in the field were the only ways of achieving an honorable and lasting peace. Any armistice was useful only to an enemy conducting war in his own territory. Any armistice could have harmful consequences for the entire alliance if on its expiry nothing were resolved in respect of a peace settlement, and it became necessary to commence the war anew. Should the king of Prussia be allowed undisturbed to suck the life blood out of Saxony during the entire period of the armistice, apart from the fact that he would thus become stronger, it would be difficult to find a justification before the world for such an armistice.

If we were to enter negotiations about an armistice, these would also be as difficult as negotiations over a peace settlement itself. At the very least the king of Prussia would demand that our army not move from the Vistula or approach his territories. In this way he would gain as much as by holding Saxony, for we must beware of the fact that forage for our army on the Vistula was short during the summer, and that consequently for the winter we would have to abandon the great part of Prussia. The number of horses with our army could not be lessened in any way. Their maintenance was different from that in other armies. Naturally it was possible, in exchange for vast sums of money, to find forage in Poland, but it was impossible to transport almost anything using Polish horses and roads.

It was clearly evident that the interests of the allies were divided. France considered an armistice necessary for itself in respect of its overseas possessions. Russia believed an armistice extremely harmful for the alliance and extraordinarily advantageous for the king of Prussia. Naturally Austria would have to agree to it. Russia insisted on an early opening of the campaign and vigorous action in the field. France, to cool the bellicose ardor of Russia, was of the opinion that there would be no success in the forthcoming campaign. Austria was not in condition to act vigorously.

On March 31 Baron Breteuil secretly passed to the chancellor information sent from Vienna by the French ambassador. Count Kaunitz, the initiator of the war, was trying to continue it by every means possible, and for that reason was placing every hindrance in the way of a peace settlement. Maria Theresa herself, on the contrary, very much wanted a peace settlement because not only the treasury, but every single source of income and support was completely exhausted. Provincial authorities were refusing to pay taxes and furnish soldiers. Because of lack of money the army could be brought up to one hundred and ten thousand men only. For that reason Field Marshal Count Daun flatly declared on his departure that he was in no position to act aggressively against the king of Prussia. Besides, his generals and soldiers would not dare or had no desire to fight the Prussians.

Breteuil knew for certain that Count Kaunitz was not in agreement with Count Esterhazy on the matter of abrogation of the treaty of 1746, which was replaced by a new agreement signed by Esterhazy without authority or any order. Therefore Count Esterhazy no longer was privy to any secrets of the cabinet in Vienna, and moreover Count Kaunitz would not remain a minister for long. On April 11 Breteuil again requested the chancellor to authorize the Russian ambassador in Paris to agree to an armistice. Vorontsov repeated his previous reply, that it was quite inopportune to suggest an armistice at this time.

France gave way. An armistice was not mentioned in the declaration it sent to England. In response the empress instructed a letter be sent to the Russian ambassador in Paris asking him to express her pleasure to the court there at its silence on this matter. He was to say that the king had done everything in his power to accelerate a peace settlement, and now must show invincible determination in any measures taken to conclude nothing less than an honorable and lasting peace settlement with the king of Prussia, and to give the aggrieved parties adequate compensation. For this the present campaign must be continued with the very same determination as before. No mention was to be made of any armistice whatsoever, especially as circumstances never had promised a better campaign. The Russian ambassador in Paris was instructed secretly that in the most extreme event, should France absolutely insist on an armistice, he should not hurry to agree to it. Without refusing outright and without promising anything he was to continue friendly representations against an armistice, while awaiting information from Count Keyserling in Vienna. He was also to direct Keyserling to persuade Kaunitz not to agree to an armistice. Nevertheless the empress-queen could judge better whether they could hold France firm to this or, in losing her assistance, be exposed to danger.

The request of the Cabinet in St. Petersburg was met. The ambassadors of the allied courts in Paris decided to set the period of the congress between July 1 and 15 (New Style) and to commence military operations from all sides as soon and as vigorously as possible. As a consequence the College of Foreign Affairs was directed to assemble a plan and instructions to the Russian ambassadors in London, Paris and Vienna. These instructions were to include the following. "We wish the congress to take place soon, not so that a peace settlement in actuality should follow immediately (as in such a mélange of interests there is the danger that a swift peace settlement would not be the most advantageous peace or that the war, coming to a temporary halt, might flare up with even greater ferocity), but in order to see the more quickly the real inclinations and opinions of the courts in London and Berlin, and to take necessary measures with greater precision. We intend to act with extreme intensity in this campaign in order to increase the enemy's compliance and allow no possibility for delay in negotiations that may be advantageous to him.

"It seems to us that one thing remains to the French court. Having temporarily abandoned Asia and America, it should make as much use as possible of its present advantages in Germany. By setting its affairs and those of its allies straight in Germany, it would bind those allies to France and thus make the glorious alliance permanent. In reducing the power of the king of Prussia it also would lessen the authority of England because the king of Prussia, left with his present military strength, would not permit the allies to render each other mutual assistance. England, with support on the continent, would not wait until the French fleet was once more in a flourishing condition before commencing a naval war. To refute this view you could put forward the single fact that the major asset of the house of Brandenburg consists in the person of the present king of Prussia. It is true that he is quite capable of devising projects harmful to his neighbors and of carrying them out. Yet everybody knows that all stratagems leading to his present extraordinary power were prepared by his forebears. He has merely made use of circumstances, while following a political plan put together in this house somewhat before the time of Frederick II. The administration he has introduced in the provinces, completely martial and not civil, cannot be appropriate for a long-lasting peace settlement.

"We are almost certain that France will not delay sending its minister to London. We even hope that he will succeed in concluding a separate peace with England, thus detaching this power from the king of Prussia. This will leave France free to act against him, at the very least on the basis of the Treaty of Versailles of 1758 with the empress-queen.[3] England, in concluding a peace settlement with France would be bound, neither in a direct nor in an indirect manner, not to render assistance to the king of Prussia. The resolution of matters with him would be left to ourselves and Austria. A number of courts may experience apprehension that this negotiation, at first very limited, will spread perceptibly further and lead to a peace settlement similar to that at Aachen.[4]

"Although we cannot oppose directly the dispatch of a French ambassador to London, we may suggest that in the present change of ministries in England State Secretary Pitt, a great champion of the interests of the king of Prussia, might think it necessary to make allowances for the aspirations of his people, which has become proud of its military successes. He may therefore try to take negotiations into his own hands, and by prolonging them and the war, extend his own importance. His authority may diminish if matters do not proceed through the Southern but through the Northern Department, through the hands of the new state secretary, the earl of Bute.[5] Therefore Pitt has even said that he does not think there may be a need for our good offices. We are not annoyed by this, and do not want to thrust our good offices forward. We offered them simply out of friendship towards the king of France. It would not be harmful to our interests and to those of our allies to suggest to the earl of Bute, in a skillful way, that if separate negotiations with France were extended for some time, only his colleague Pitt would receive all the honor and glory.

"This step must be coordinated with great caution. In a very similar manner all the victories of Prince Eugene[6] and the duke of Marlborough[7] were turned to nought and France, despite its parlous state, achieved an advantageous peace settlement. Is there any reason why this may not happen even now, that English zeal towards the king of Prussia may suddenly cool and he will find himself abandoned at a time when more than anything he hoped for English support? The skill displayed before now in such matters by our envoy Prince Golitsyn and his earnest endeavors in our service give us confidence that at the very least he will do everything possible, without compromising himself and us. It must be insisted that France give instructions to any ambassador sent to London not to conceal anything from Prince Golitsyn and to be subordinate to him, at least acting in concert with him in everything."

BUTURLIN'S UNSUCCESSFUL OPERATIONS

As Russia insisted on the fact that an honorable peace settlement must depend exclusively upon vigorous operations of the allies against the king of Prussia it was natural to expect that its military dispositions be in keeping with this policy. At first this plan of campaign was put together. First, to occupy the fortress of Kolberg and establish a major depot there, then to move the army towards the Oder and make a diversion to the enemy by the siege of some important fortress. Now this plan was changed. Buturlin was instructed to march into Silesia, join there with the Austrian army under the command of Field Marshal Baron Loudon and advance upon the enemy in full strength. This *generous* intention gave cause for great joy in Vienna. "We, together with the empress of All Russia," wrote Maria Theresa, "have no deficiencies in the armed forces destined to curb a dangerous enemy. It is simply a matter of using these forces at the proper time and in complete cooperation."

"It is an incontrovertible principle," stated the rescript from the empress to Field Marshal Buturlin, "that if we do not conduct operations in the present campaign from all directions with extreme earnestness we must fear the most harmful consequences. Conversely, by strong and swift actions, all dangers may be averted, and we may expect the most beneficial rewards from the present war. We need not enter into detailed considerations with you how to accelerate your campaign and how to make your operations as significant as possible. We are confident that you will not let slip a single hour. As General Loudon, in view of his present difficult position, naturally is awaiting the good news of your approach with great impatience, we cannot but advise you once again to hasten as much as possible your march towards Silesia and to keep him regularly in touch. Your approach will give Loudon courage and the king of Prussia will see what he must expect from you. He already has experienced the bravery of our forces. Now we must inspire in him a respect for your own person."

Before the campaign commenced Todtleben once more requested to be relieved of his duties. It was thought that he was dissatisfied by the fact that he had remained a major general for so long, and on April 19 a rescript was sent to Buturlin. "The request of Major General Count Todtleben to be released from our service cannot be accepted by us, particularly as it has been reiterated many times already. This time it is reiterated before the very start of the campaign, at the very time when nobody can be permitted to ask to be released. You do well to deflect him from such an intention. You may reassure him that at the first round of promotions he will not be passed over. In this respect suggest to him, as sensitively as possible, that we desire to show him our favor but that the frequent reminder and importunate solicitation, even the demand to be released, simply delays any mark of favor. You have done well to permit Count

Todtleben to see the Prussian lieutenant general Werner. We are almost certain that if it comes to a meeting Werner either will suggest talking about a peace settlement or will attempt to spread suspicions of our allies. You must hear everything out. Without replying positively to anything at all, report to us anything concerning a peace settlement; to the second possibility you may respond immediately that we are completely assured of the steadfastness and sincerity of our allies. Even if it were not so, we would rather consent to be deceived than to harbor suspicions about them and not stand firm in present circumstances. Any act of insincerity will serve merely to continue this wasteful war. There is but one way to attain a peace settlement, that is to propose one directly, and to demonstrate actual readiness to satisfy the aggrieved parties."

Werner did not propose a peace settlement to Todtleben, merely an armistice for one month. At the same time Todtleben sent Buturlin a letter from his friend in Berlin stating that peace already was concluded between England and France. In response a rescript was sent to Buturlin on April 30. "It is not difficult to conclude that they were simply trying to learn how great is the resolution and zeal on our part. Had they received agreement to an armistice, they would have trumpeted this news with embellishments in the Austrian and French armies. The letter that Todtleben received from Berlin served merely as preparation, so that Werner's suggestions might have the fullest impact. Therefore inform Count Todtleben that he must beware of similar suggestions and not believe them. We trust that there are not at present any impediments to your campaign. We shall expect shortly pleasant news concerning the successful commencement of the campaign."

Buturlin entered the field to join up with Loudon, to whom a separate corps was given at the insistence of the Russian court. Maria Theresa acceded to this against her will, as her favorite was Field Marshal Daun; but Daun was disliked in Petersburg, with good reason. Frederick II was in Silesia with fifty thousand troops. A Prussian corps, contained by Daun, was in Saxony under the command of Prince Henry. In Pomerania Rumiantsev's corps was on its way to lay siege to Kolberg. It is easy to understand with what impatience news was awaited in St. Petersburg from Buturlin that he had joined Loudon in Silesia, that the united Austro-Russian army had overwhelmed Frederick II and so brought this burdensome war to an end, preparing the ground for a simple matter for the diplomats, the conclusion in Augsburg of an *honorable* peace settlement, as this was understood in St. Petersburg and Vienna. It was easy to understand the irritation occasioned by Buturlin's reports which cruelly deceived these expectations.

In this mood of irritation a rescript was penned by the empress and sent to the commander-in-chief on August 14. "However much we examined every trifling detail with you at the commencement of the present campaign and during the drafting of the plan of military operations; however much we were satisfied with your exposition of the main aspects and objectives, leaving the rest to your good management and zeal for the cause, we tried simply to express to you in a forthright manner the great and indisputable fundamental facts as to why we wanted the present campaign to be decisive. That is why throughout the campaign we have reminded you only of those very same fundamental facts. We have been awaiting with impatience some good news from you, such as we have been promising ourselves stemming from your fervor for the cause, from the excellent condition of the army to which you have attested yourself, from the well-known bravery of our troops and from the very circumstances which many times have been advantageous to you. We have been awaiting accounts of those firm decisions taken by you by which we ourselves in St. Petersburg might calculate your movements and consequently be in a position to direct you on the basis of authentic knowledge. Yet not once have you furnished us with precise expression of your affairs and circumstances by which we could make any calculation with any degree of conviction as to how, for example, this edict may find you. Although your reports have been received sufficiently frequently, they rarely if ever describe the direct whereabouts of the enemy and General Loudon. As far as the army itself is concerned we either see a new objective in each report, when the previous one has still not been achieved, and it is always contrary to the previous one, or even, ultimately, an expectation that in a few days time yet a different decision will be taken.

"Everything you did during the past winter to bring the army into readiness for the campaign, in many cases the prudently supervised administration, in particular the timely march to Poznan and the consequent arrival of all the army there as early as May, earlier than at any time previously, earned our complete approval. By doing this you fulfilled an important point of the plan and reassured everybody that your operations naturally would correspond to the assurances we gave our allies. In this way you made sure that the court in Vienna reinforced and empowered the young and foreign General Loudon, and all its attention was turned upon you both. You must have perceived clearly that everything would depend upon the speed of your march into Silesia, that more than anything else you had to destroy the prejudices of the allies and the enemy about the slow movement of our army. It is because of these prejudices the allies have been unable to rely firmly upon our promises, and the enemy has been able to turn all his forces boldly in another direction.

"Naturally out of an abundance of zeal for the cause and wanting instead of doing one thing to do two, you have divided your attention. On your arrival in Poznan you were about to take the decision to march into Pomerania, hoping to drive the enemy out of there, to hasten the capture of Kolberg and to be in good time to march into Silesia. You reported this to us as if it were a matter of certainty. You have not paid respect to the fact that, however praiseworthy and splendid it is to embrace numerous matters all at once and to carry them out with singular success, you always must attend to what is most important. Moreover you did not even perceive that although the taking of Kolberg lies very close to our heart, we in no way connected this with your operations. Naturally there was some waste of time in pursuing this objective which was not in accordance with the plan, and raised doubts in Baron Loudon's mind, which was extremely harmful at the commencement of the campaign, particularly when it was still necessary to destroy previous prejudices.

"Had you then stuck with this objective and carried it out swiftly, perhaps something decisive would have resulted. At the very least General Zieten[8] would now be in Pomerania, Loudon would not have made his diversion into Moravia and the supply depots prepared for you would not have been broken up. The king of Prussia would not have been so powerful against Loudon, who would have known what he could expect from you, and what measures of his own he would need to take.

"You cancelled your intention of marching into Pomerania, as it did not conform with the plan. Unfortunately you did not turn all at once to the main matter, that is to the march into Silesia and directly to Breslau, but wanted first of all to make an attempt against Glogau. For this you requested Loudon to send siege artillery, provisions and some troops there for you. It would have been easy to foresee that Loudon was not in a position to do this once the king of Prussia turned all his attention towards him and came into Silesia with a not inconsiderable force, being himself covered by his fortresses and covering them in return. Your objective and request must have renewed earlier prejudices in Loudon, thereby causing us such profound regret. We repeat what we emphasized to your predecessor, in no way should you ask for what cannot be possible, as this gives rise to distrust and disagreement between allies and wastes a lot of time.

"At last we had considerable pleasure when, abandoning your attempt upon Glogau, you conceived the idea of marching straight on Breslau by way of Militsch, giving formal reassurance to Loudon of this and consequently taking upon yourself a new obligation. When the forces of the king of Prussia were so modest that he was able only out of necessity to hold back Baron Loudon it would have been easy to imagine into how many parts he would have had to divide his forces had you brought upon him the need to do so by your move against Breslau by way of Militsch. He needed to defend this important city, the depot of all his military requirements, and to guard against the possibility that you might cross the Oder, and at the same time that Loudon did not approach this river from any other direction.

"General Zieten had scarcely began to march against you towards Kostiani when you, as always conforming in your zeal to the cause and wishing to do two things at once, adopted the objective of stealing a few days' march upon him, cutting him off from Silesia, and in order to do so to march to Wartenberg instead of Militsch. In addition you believed that there would still be sufficient time for the main operations in Silesia. Now, of course, you regretted that you did not even attack Zieten immediately, thus removing the conceit of the king of Prussia and the allies that our army never attacks. By marching on Wartenberg you made it necessary to try to join up with Loudon only in the vicinity of Brieg.

"In your letter to Baron Loudon you remark quite justifiably about his complaints that the king of Prussia knew even beforehand of your desire to join the Austrian army. We made no great secret of this ourselves. The fact is that the enemy did not know where the meeting place would be. You would have joined up with Loudon if you had you headed directly for Breslau, even if the king then placed General Zieten before Breslau to defend the city against you. In 1757 Prince Bevern under the guns of this very city dug in to strongly entrenched positions and lost a considerable army.[9] You could have done the very same thing with Zieten, and even had you not succeeded in doing this, yet with your superior forces, while keeping Zieten occupied with a small corps and in that way masking your departure from Breslau, you could have crossed the Oder immediately where the king least would have expected it. Then Zieten would have been obliged to escape through Breslau and our forces would have been able to enter the city on his heels. The king, despite all his inventiveness, would have been obliged either to permit your unimpeded meeting with Loudon or to attack such forces as were assured of victory.

"From your communiqué of July 25 we saw that, despite the occupation by our forces of the heights about Breslau, despite the insignificant garrison and the absence of other enemy forces in the vicinity, despite the fact that your light cavalry was entering the suburbs freely to the very gates of the city and that there was no fear of unintentional approach by the enemy as Brigadier Krasnoshchekov was on the other side of the Oder, despite all this you held a military council at which all the difficulties of an attempt upon Breslau were presented. The military council, while agreeing with you about the nature of the difficulties, left everything to your discretion. You decided immediately to go directly to Leubus and cross the Oder there or somewhere more suitable. If the possibility presented itself, you were to make an attempt on Breslau and try to join up with Loudon, as long as the expected transport with provisions and money from Poland was not delayed on the other side. At this point, where the matter demanded firm resolution, you did not particularly have to enlarge in the council on the difficulties and dangers entailed in the enterprise on Breslau, and by doing so weaken the enthusiasm for it. Moreover it was shameful on the part of members of the council that not one of them thought, in exaggerating the difficulties, that you were trying to find out who would find the courage to overcome them.

"To tell the truth, there was no need whatsoever at this point to bring the matter up in the military council. Even from here without further consideration we know that a formal siege of Breslau could not have been undertaken, owing to lack of siege artillery. Even had there been sufficient artillery it would have been dangerous, having crossed the Oder, to become locked between Breslau and the entire forces of the king of Prussia. The city would have to be taken by assault, which would have demanded not advice but direction and resolution. The more extensive the city, the easier it would have been to take it by assault. Fortresses somewhat stronger have been taken in this way. Anyone who, with a free hand before Breslau nevertheless did nothing, would be unable to threaten Glogau or Liegnitz by a march towards Leubus. At a first glance at the map of Silesia it is clear that by a march towards Leubus you would make crossing the Oder more difficult, not easier. Leubus lies opposite Liegnitz itself.

General Knobloch naturally would hurry to place himself before this city. Had you not managed to defeat Knobloch immediately on your crossing, and then could not take Liegnitz, you could not have moved anywhere from where you could cross the Oder, and it would be even less possible for General Loudon to get to you past Schweidnitz.

"It is strange that not one of the generals pointed out that the most convenient place to cross the Oder is below where it is joined by the Weide. Leaving a small detachment on this river you could have covered your rear and supply lines to the depots in Poland and, crossing the Oder somewhat higher up than Leubus, would not have been exposed to these impediments but would have been nearer, both to the enterprise on Breslau and to meeting Loudon and the provisions from the counties of Glatz and Bohemia as promised by the court in Vienna.

"The need for our arms to distinguish themselves in the present campaign by a significant and advantageous exploit vital to the common cause has now reached the point where the court in Vienna, waiting to see which way the campaign goes, does not know what instructions to give its ministers with respect to the congress. Our ambassadors, having orders to act with firmness, to spur on our allies to act in like manner and to support their interests, will find themselves in a difficult position if our arms do not perform in keeping with our intentions. With the loss of Pondicherry[10] France has lost all its possessions in the East Indies but in Germany, having managed to repulse an attack, now is forced to suffer the entire pride and arrogance of the English ministry. The Danish court is vacillating between the two sides and its conduct depends upon conclusion of the campaign. If nothing of consequence is achieved in the present campaign it will be hard for us once more to bring an army to the Oder in the next campaign, and find quickly the money necessary to do so. You will recall that in the third year, after gaining unprecedented victories, we did not make use of these most favorable circumstances. Last summer we did not even seek any opportunity to that end and our army is passing this summer also without having sight of the enemy. Obviously its importance, which has been preserved up to this point in peace negotiations, will diminish. Our most incontrovertible demonstration [of importance] will lose its value and our allies, no longer considering our assistance essential, will act merely in conformity to their own interests. The king of Prussia will be certain that he gave battle recklessly to our forces which cannot themselves do him any harm. He will turn all his forces against the house of Austria and, becoming stronger than before, will exclude us from general European activity, having no doubt that even without his asking East Prussia soon will return to him of itself.

"Your retreat from Breslau even when the garrison there was small and the enemy not in the vicinity, and when General Knobloch, coming to the city's assistance, could not stand up to our light cavalry, must of necessity have the following effect in these conditions. The king of Prussia will be even less inclined to seek battle with you and he may even less expect or fear that you will attack him or any corps of his or take any of his middle-strength fortresses. Therefore it must be expected that he will reduce his garrisons in a number of places and, reinforcing his army as much as possible, direct it against Baron Loudon. Such a point of view on the part of the enemy will not be very flattering to our arms. Yet every cloud has a silver lining, and you have more of an opportunity now to gain the upper hand over the king, the more so as he is confident of his advantages over you. When such an opportunity arises you must demonstrate actively to the general staff and to the entire army how the enemy's disdain is a disgrace to its image, and how in addition the glory of our nation demands that vengeance be taken upon him through defeat for such disdain.

"Your correspondence with Baron Loudon was the cause of some coldness, although this has also been brought to an end swiftly. As you have not fulfilled any of his requests since then and have not managed to render him any assistance through any diversion, we must fear that dissatisfaction on Loudon's part will be renewed and even reinforced. His court may suspect that our instructions to you have not been the same as were communicated to him for information. At any other time we might not have paid a great deal of attention to this, but now general negotiations have begun, Prussia has made overtures to the Porte and we have insisted that the court in Vienna entrust its main forces to Loudon. So far in all fairness we cannot say that he has not carried out what was asked of him. Therefore now most of all we must make sure that there is not the slightest distance and disagreement. We must demonstrate by some distinguished enterprise that our instructions in reality have been those communicated to the court in Vienna."

BUTURLIN RETREATS

Dissatisfaction with Buturlin receded when he reported on August 3 that he had crossed the Oder safely with the entire army, occupied Liegnitz, met Loudon and taken the firm decision to advance still further. Frederick II, not being in any condition to hinder the joining of Buturlin and Loudon, and even less to attack them, built himself a fortified encampment almost under the guns of Schweidnitz. Here he determined to await the attack of the enemy or to hold him in inactivity until such time as lack of provisions compelled him to retreat. On August 21 Buturlin told St. Petersburg that on the twenty-third he would attack the enemy without fail. On August 22 he wrote that the attack was abandoned and instead he decided to advance upon Schweidnitz to compel Frederick II to give up his advantageous position between Seidlitz and Würben. On the very same day he sent another communiqué that he was dissuaded by Baron Loudon even from the advance on Schweidnitz, and therefore he decided to leave Count Chernyshev's corps with Loudon until the end of the campaign. Buturlin himself would cross the Oder and move towards Glogau or "somewhere."

CHERNYSHEV TO ACT WITH LOUDON

He received the following rescript in reply to his communiqué. "We shall not hide from you that we have been more saddened by this news than had some misfortune befallen our forces. We shall not now analyze in detail how many contradictions there are in your communiqués, how few of the circumstances known to us are in agreement with them and with news reaching us from other quarters, nor the arguments and commentary that will follow both from friends and enemies. All of this you may easily imagine for yourself.

"We cannot leave without comment that when already so much time has been lost during various delays in the march from Poznan you absolutely should not have crossed beyond the Oder but sought possible operations on this side. Alternatively, having crossed the Oder and joined up with Loudon, you should have taken advantage immediately of this conjunction, of your superiority of forces and most of all of the confusion of the enemy, to make up for the lost time and not to waste it again on fruitless and endless seeking of advice. We have no words to express how the crown of glory was hanging above you and how you have lost it irrevocably. We have no words to set the past right or to dismiss the general opinion of Europe at this time that throughout the entire present campaign our sole intention was to play for time and, doing nothing, to return home. Still less can we explain with decorum to our allies why we coerced the court in Vienna to take the command from Count Daun and entrust it to Baron Loudon, why we coerced the Austrians to suffer considerable losses and to establish supply depots for our army, why we exhausted their provisions, which they could have used for themselves. There may have been a simple explanation for all this, namely that you wanted to attack the enemy, but that there was no opportunity or possibility of doing so. Yet simply by checking the circumstances and in the light of your own reports we are assured of the opposite. Our allies not only have indubitable witnesses but also written proof in your memorandum in response to Baron Loudon that it was not the strengthening of the fortifications of the enemy's camp that stopped you from attacking him. At that time there was not yet any strengthening of the fortifications. When you had covered twelve versts you requested a protracted rest. After the enemy strengthened the fortifications the Russian and Austrian general staff were summoned and told that it was possible to attack, and that not only the day but even the hour was appointed. As all of this now serves no purpose, we want to get down to the matter in hand.

"We instruct you not to make a vain attempt on the fortress of Glogau and so waste time, but to advance swiftly towards Frankfurt take Berlin immediately following the example of last year with the only difference that you take a larger indemnity from the Berliners for their ingratitude and make use of everything as you may. Should Prince Henry send a corps against you for the defense of Berlin, attack him immediately without careful study and seeking of advice. There has been so much fruitless advice in the present campaign that the very word 'advice' ultimately has become loathsome. To say that our forces may not be capable of attack may come only from those envious of the glory of our arms, and therefore we instruct you most strongly that should anyone dare say that our forces are incapable of any attack not only should he be arrested there and then, but should even sent here in chains like a scoundrel. It may be hoped that by your march towards Frankfurt the Prussian forces in Pomerania will be obliged to vacate that province. You must endeavor not to let this corps slip from your grasp either. You must destroy it and concern yourself most of all about taking up winter quarters in Pomerania. As regards Count Chernyshev and his corps, we fear only that the decision taken in this case will be changed because of some unforeseen adventure, and he will not be left with the Austrian army, as in fact there is no other way now to set right what has happened and to show the world that, despite poor operational coordination, both courts are nevertheless in the closest agreement."

SCHWEIDNITZ CAPTURED BY LOUDON WITH RUSSIAN HELP

Buturlin's further movements were also subject to reprimands, whereas pleasant news was received from Count Chernyshev, who gave notice that Schweidnitz had been taken by the Austro-Russian forces. On this event a rescript to Buturlin from the empress followed. "Little use was made of our forces in this valiant enterprise, only four companies of grenadiers. Nevertheless we are delighted that it demonstrated the offensive capability of our forces. The Austrian general staff and our enemy have given them incomparable praise. They climbed the walls like lions and, entering the city, formed themselves up so quickly that they might have been brought there for a parade."

Chernyshev's success showed Buturlin in a poor light. Rumiantsev, sent to lay siege to Kolberg, also alarmed Buturlin by his distinction. Buturlin was ordered to put under Rumiantsev's command as many troops as he requested, to supply him with everything and not to make it difficult for him in any way, certainly not to confuse him with orders, "for we are fully satisfied with his service and endeavor, and with every direction of his in the present campaign." Buturlin replied that should he send the larger part of his forces, he would have very few left himself. He received a rescript in reply. "We observe with great regret that you are demonstrating a certain *jealousy* towards that trust with which we have favored Count Rumiantsev. This can be perceived more clearly than anything from your short and dry order to him and from your communiqué, as if by reinforcing him the entire army will consist of only ten regiments. Our favor is founded merely upon his merits and virtue, and by no means as a consequence of the lessening of it to another. You remain his commander-in-chief. Your rank and our personal favor towards you cannot give any cause for jealousy towards a subordinate."

TODTLEBEN'S TREACHERY

It was hoped that in taking Kolberg Rumiantsev in some way would set right a situation frustrated by Buturlin. A contemporary (Bolotov) stated that they did not expect anything else of Buturlin in the army. "The character of this great landowner, advanced in years, was too well-known to all the government. Everybody knew that he was incapable of commanding not only the army but even two or three regiments. His only habit, to take a drop too much liquor and even sometimes to drink in company with the most ignoble people, made everybody distressed and filled them with the greatest indignation. Above all, as he was an ignoramus and completely unknowledgeable in all matters. Everyone was in despair and did not expect the slightest success in the forthcoming campaign in which, indeed, they were not at all deceived."

To the sad outcome of the campaign was also added the treachery of a general whose name was mentioned very often in the journal of military operations of the Russian army and was mentioned usually in respect of successful operations, namely Todtleben, the head of the light cavalry. As far back as June 21 Buturlin informed the empress of a strange occurrence.[11] During his march to the army in Pomerania, in a camp near Berstein, on the general advice of all the regimental commanders of the corps under his command, Major General Todtleben was arrested on June 19 for open correspondence with the enemy which was harmful to his service. The causes which gave rise to his arrest were as follows. Lieutenant Colonel Asch, working under Todtleben's command in chancellery matters, caught a Jew sent by Todtleben to Küstrin. In this Jew's boot was found an exact German translation from a secret order of the commander-in-chief, as well as of the army's route from Poznan to Silesia sent to Todtleben from Buturlin, and a note written in Todtleben's hand in cipher. All these papers were in an unsigned envelope, but with Todtleben's seal. A passport was found on the Jew, issued by Todtleben. Captain Fafius received a handwritten order from Todtleben to send the Jew to Küstrin with a group of cossacks. On Todtleben was found a letter of his, sealed but not as yet dispatched, to the banker Gotzkowsky in Berlin.[12] The Jew confessed that he carried letters to and from the Prussian Prince Henry to Todtleben. He was to give the packet found in his boot either to the commandant, to Prince Henry or to the king of Prussia himself. On the evidence of Todtleben, his correspondence with Prince Henry dealt with the prince's request that he not permit his corps to ravage the king's domains. Todtleben replied that if Prussian officials produced the provisions and forage requested nothing would be heard of pillage by soldiers. "As for myself," Todtleben added in a letter to the prince, "the prince may be assured that I do not tolerate any robbery but discourage it as much as possible. I do not wish for any reward but for the prince, as an old friend, to plead on my behalf for the return of my only son. As a child of eleven he was taken by force and enrolled as a soldier. I also ask for the return of my villages which have either been taken away completely or sequestrated."

About three weeks later the Jew Zabadko[13] appeared and gave him a sealed letter from the king. The letter stated that the king ordered all local government officials and heads of districts tend to their posts and organize supplies for the Russian army. In exchange Todtleben must keep good order in his forces and spare Prussian lands. When a peace settlement was concluded the king would not forget Todtleben's request relating to his son and his villages. Todtleben sent the Jew off with a reply that there would be no complaints whatsoever of destruction by Russian force, and he asked that his son be discharged to continue his studies. Three weeks later the Jew returned, bringing news of the discharge of Todtleben's son and a letter to his father. The king reassured him of every favor if he would discontinue the devastation carried out by his detachment.

"For the last three years," Todtleben further testified, " I have been thinking how to capture the king in some way. I thought the best time of all would be when the king confided completely in the Jew Zabadko. Then it could be possible to persuade the king to come to a meeting or to find out when and where he would be on reconnaissance with only a few men. Then the Jew Zabadko arrived a third time with two sealed envelopes. In one there was a cipher code and in the other a letter from the king. The letter stated that the leader was overjoyed that a friend gave such reassurances regarding clemency to his lands. He hoped that the friend would serve this campaign further for the relief the leader's subjects. He asked him to let him know whether the Russian army would operate this year in a defensive or offensive mode, whether a corps would be sent to Loudon and whether the friend was in any way envious that there was a new claimant for the hand of Kolberg (Rumiantsev). I replied that the friend had received the letter from the leader and would reply at the first opportunity. I gave instructions to the Jew Zabadko to tell the king I would very much like to speak with him. Zabadko came back once more with a letter from the king, full of kind reassurances and with a request that I write a response to his previous questions. In order to evade a reply I wrote to the king about my new appointment and alluded to the enclosures I sent him. These enclosures consisted of the orders and route I received from the field marshal.

"If, I had undertaken anything dangerous and contrary to my oath of allegiance," continued Todtleben, "I would have sent the order and route earlier, not when the order was no longer a secret and already carried out. As soon as I received the ciphers in the sealed envelope I showed them to Lieutenant Colonel Asch, saying that this is what a Jew had brought me, even ciphers from the king's cabinet! Asch was astonished as to where he could have got them. I told him in reply that the Jew, of course, was himself in the king's cabinet. With God's help I shall take the king directly this year and the field marshal shall have these ciphers. Asch, if he still has a spark of honesty and Christian virtue, must acknowledge the truth of this testimony as I have often said publicly that I hope to inflict a direct blow this year. Gotzkowsky, when he was with me, inquired to whom in St. Petersburg he should address himself in order to incline the court towards the king's favor. The king was growing tired of war and willingly would have employed a million or two. I replied that I was quite unfamiliar with those in St. Petersburg, but that if a written offer were sent, I would discuss this with the field marshal."

Todtleben was sent to St. Petersburg[14] after which yet another letter to him from Frederick II was seized. The king wrote that he could not give him the estates he requested (the Militsch squirearchy) but promised to give him another comparable to it. He also declined his request to divorce him from his wife, who was living in Silesia, declaring that for this to happen she must forward a petition herself.

The unsuccessful outcome of the campaign was particularly burdensome to the Russian government because it rejected an armistice more strongly than anyone else and insisted on vigorous operations in the field as the only possible way to force Frederick II towards an *honorable* peace settlement for the allies. We have observed how the difficult position of Russia in respect to its principal ally, Austria, was emphasized in the rescripts to Buturlin. Keyserling, the Russian ambassador in Vienna, was appointed plenipotentiary to the Augsburg congress. Prince Dmitry Mikhailovich Golitsyn was appointed to his position in Vienna. Until such time as he should arrive a nephew of the chancellor, Count Alexander Romanovich Vorontsov,[15] was appointed chargé d'affaires. Corresponding to this change Esterhazy was recalled from St. Petersburg because of, or under the pretext of, his illness and Count Mercy d'Argenteau[16] was appointed in his place.

On July 21 the young Vorontsov wrote to his uncle from Vienna about a conversation with Kaunitz. "Count Kaunitz spoke with me for a long time and did not hide the fact that they were not a little astonished by the slow progress of Field Marshal Buturlin. Kaunitz argued that often by being merely twenty-four hours late you may deprive yourself of all the successes of an entire campaign." Vorontsov also wrote to his uncle that incidently he heard that Loudon was beginning to despair of any successes in the campaign in the light of the slow progress of the Russian army.

On August 14 Vorontsov again wrote about Kaunitz's displeasure at the operations of Russian forces in Silesia. He argued that after crossing the Oder a great deal might have been achieved, but that time had slipped away. Kaunitz was afraid that through procrastination the Russian army would be forced to march to winter quarters on the Vistula and the campaign would have been to no purpose. According to Kaunitz, Loudon asked Buturlin whether he wanted to attack the king himself or would leave the attack to the Austrians, with the proviso that each support the attack with twenty thousand troops. This suggestion did not produce any action. On August 25 Vorontsov wrote that Kaunitz was seriously concerned at the inactivity of the forces, the more so as a lack of success in the campaign would stir up all the supporters of Field Marshal Daun against him. It was well known that the empress-queen, almost against her will, had yielded to Kaunitz's request to put the greater part of the army under Loudon's command. In Vienna all the blame was laid upon Fermor, who apparently for some time had not concealed his ill-will towards the house of Austria, demonstrating this dislike to the officers sent to the Russian army from Vienna at every opportunity, and complaining that it was thanks to the court in Vienna that he had been deprived of the main command.

Vorontsov's news of the impression made on Maria Theresa by the occupation of Schweidnitz was interesting. "The empress," Vorontsov wrote, "herself plays down the importance of this operation, and believes it is impossible to hold Schweidnitz through the winter. Her majesty has been very miserable every day recently, and the reason for this is her partiality towards Field Marshal Daun. The emperor has exasperated her by making use of the capture of Schweidnitz to extol Loudon at the expense of Daun. The empress stood up for her favorite in a fury, and from that time belittled the importance of Loudon's action. At a reception at court, in conversation with one of the foreign ambassadors, she expressed the opinion that she found great difficulties in stationing troops in winter quarters in Silesia, and all those who had business with her that day said that they had never seen her so angry."

In Vienna there was great concern at the siege of Kolberg. There were fears that if this city were not taken and the Russian army left for winter quarters on the Vistula, Prussian forces would move out of Pomerania into Saxony and there hinder the operations of the Austrian forces.

ANGLO-FRENCH PEACE TALKS BREAK DOWN

At the same time as there was talk about the sad outcome of the campaign in Vienna, from Paris and London the Russian ambassadors reported the sad outcome of the peace negotiations between France and England. The successor to Mikhail Petrovich Bestuzhev at the French court, Count Peter Grigorievich Chernyshev, reported on August 31 that the duc de Choiseul held a conference with all ambassadors of the allied courts. After speaking in detail about the entire progress of peace talks between France and England, Choiseul asked the ambassadors, in the name of the king, to report to their courts that France conducted these talks with the assent of all the allies and by general agreement, that is without confusing its particular war with the German war, the cessation of which was left to be conducted by talks at the Augsburg congress. Particular tractability was shown from the French side in order to reach a specific peace settlement with England. Everything possible had been sacrificed, but England was intemperate and displayed unwillingness for a peace settlement by absurdly and intentionally confused demands and replies. The king therefore had taken the decision to break off these fruitless negotiations and instructed him to assure all his allies that he firmly intended to remain in the alliance with them, solemnly observing his obligations.

Chernyshev reported that the lack of success in Silesia and the parting of Buturlin from Loudon would not have any influence upon the decision of the French court, although he pointed out that the duc de Choiseul responded to these events with great distress; in particular the opinion was expressed that the expenses involved in the movement of the army were not in keeping with its success. Chernyshev replied that even though two French armies had combined they also did nothing to the enemy and were forced to separate without achieving anything.

The conversation concluded that the present campaign must be considered unsuccessful for all sides and, in order to improve matters, measures must be taken for the success of the forthcoming campaign. The chancellor made an interesting observation for the empress on this report. "Large sums of money are required for the continuation of the present war and the strong measures necessary for organizing the next campaign are simply not in the Treasury at present. If your imperial majesty will not deign to provide gracious instructions on the papers forwarded from the Conference and the Senate, I really do not understand how we can be committed with any advantage even to a commencement of the next campaign."

FAVORABLE CHANGES IN THE ENGLISH MINISTRY

In the spring Prince Alexander Mikhailovich Golitsyn reported from London that the court in England sincerely wanted to bring the German war to an end, as it was incurring considerable losses, but it was by no means as concerned about a separate peace settlement with France. Therefore in England the greatest concern was that the allies' proposal concerning a peace settlement was not merely an attempt at gaining time. Golitsyn described his conversation with the famous Pitt, who assured him that England sincerely wanted peace but could not abandon the king of Prussia. "He tried to prove to me," wrote Golitsyn, "through his crafty and eloquent language, as is his habit, the necessity for England to remain inseparably and fervently with the aforesaid monarch. I merely tried to contradict him in a few words, affirming that when eventually this haughty and insolent sovereign again regroups his forces, drained of effectiveness and resources in the present war, he will not fail once again to disturb any peace that might be restored unless England were the guarantor against any attempts by this monarch to disturb that peace. In his reply Mr. Pitt tried to give me to understand that it was impossible to place much reliance upon such guarantees and that, in his opinion, a superiority of forces such as Russia possessed would serve as sufficient guarantee. The king of Prussia would not dare to disturb its peace and consequently the empress, without any cause to fear the actions of this monarch, whose forces were exhausted by war, has no reason to wish to destroy his realm." Pitt also told Golitsyn that in England there was a feeling of obligation to the empress for the fact that arrangements for a peace settlement, so helpful and pleasing to God, were begun and based in London through the Russian ambassador.

"I am sure," said Pitt, "that the restoration of peace in Europe, partly or even completely, depends upon your sovereign. In my opinion the conclusion of a German peace settlement is liable to meet great difficulties, as the agreement of so many great powers, who must conclude peace not through compulsion but simply out of magnanimity and a love of peace, will be difficult. On the contrary, a separate peace settlement between England and France may be concluded swiftly. France is so exhausted that it cannot prolong the war with England. Consequently England must use these favorable circumstances and demand a very advantageous peace settlement from its enemy. Those powers which do not have fleets or colonies in other parts of the world do not have any cause to take any part whatsoever in this war. It does not concern them in any way." "In my opinion," replied Golitsyn, "European sovereigns must pay as much attention to colonies as to European possessions, following the example of England which, although having no possessions in Germany, nevertheless continually interferes in its affairs." "France," Pitt continued, "must not comfort itself with the hope that Hanover will serve as a road to America or India."

In respect to Russia's immediate interests, St. Petersburg wanted to take advantage of a change in the ministry in England, the departure of the earl of Holderness and his replacement by the earl of Bute, a favorite of the new king George III. In connection with this event Vorontsov sent the following letter to Golitsyn. "As a new state secretary has been appointed in place of the earl of Holderness, he will naturally wish to make his mark at the commencement of his ministry. Your excellency must try earnestly, while contriving to promote towards yourself the friendship and confidence of the present minister, to suggest to him as skillfully as possible that an alliance and friendship between her imperial majesty and the king his sovereign, being always natural, may be hindered only by (the English) alliance with the king of Prussia, of whom they have always been justifiably apprehensive. Now their resources are being used simply to no purpose, or they are receiving deceptive assistance. Her imperial majesty is firm and unshakable in the fulfillment of her obligations. You are far from advising any irregular behavior to the English court, and there can be not the slightest reproach in the delicacy of his britannic majesty in the observation of his obligations. If more respect were paid to his own interests the resolve and usefulness of former allies and their natural conjunction of interests once more would be placed in justified comparison to the mercenary aspects of such an ally who, in exchange for the strong support rendered him and the diligence of the whole British nation, is merely grateful for this favor. In laying before it now his natural dispositions, England can see that they would be so incompatible that it would be impossible to take comfort merely in goodwill. Because it transpires that France really wanted to take all peace negotiations into its own hands on account of its war with England, with greater justice here in St. Petersburg we would now wish, in a skillful manner, to reach the point whereby France may communicate with England only about its particular peace settlement while the congress is coming together or continues its work. In the meantime England could discuss a peace settlement with the king of Prussia with the court in St. Petersburg, in a preliminary manner, which may lead to a decision at some future congress. For this reason your excellency may wish to make a particular effort in your introduction of ideas to lead matters imperceptibly in this direction."

To begin the process in St. Petersburg, the English envoy Keith was handed a note in which it was pointed out that as the empress would never revoke her intention to seek for herself and for her sublime allies a durable, honorable and satisfactory peace settlement, and as her allies were of the same mind, it now depended upon his britannic majesty to promote a just peace settlement between England and France, and to incline the king of Prussia to the just satisfaction of the aggrieved parties.

On July 21 Golitsyn told his court of the impression this note made in England. Both ministers, the earl of Bute and the duke of Newcastle, responded in the same manner, that it was not at all easy for them, and it was almost impossible to incline the king of Prussia to this point of view. Later they relayed an instruction of Frederick II to his ministers in London, in which he stated that he had made a firm decision not to cede an inch of territory to his enemies, and that he agreed to make peace on one condition, that each state remained in possession of what it held in 1756. "Such obstinacy and injustice from this sovereign," wrote Golitsyn, "somewhat alarmed the ministry here, which is convinced that without any just recompense to the aggrieved parties peace cannot be expected in Germany. This year's campaign must signify the intentions both of this and of the Prussian court with respect to a German peace settlement." Against these words Chancellor Vorontsov made the following note. "To our considerable regret the present campaign gives no hope from any quarter for the successful conclusion of this accursed war."

On September 7 Golitsyn reported the breakdown of peace negotiations between France and England. On September 25 he notified St. Petersburg that Pitt had left the ministry, and of his conversation with the earl of Bute about this. "Although it is impossible not to regret," said Bute, "that this unusually gifted minister who has rendered great service to his king and nation, has left his service in such critical circumstances, nevertheless this was unavoidable because of his extreme ambition and lust for power, to his habit over five years of giving orders to everyone and having his way without the slightest contradiction. When I entered the ministry I tried to agree with him in every way possible. Finally, in the most recent circumstances, I was obliged not only to differ with him in my opinions but even to maintain my own opinions with extreme firmness. Seeing that the remaining ministers were not in agreement with him, and counting on few friends in parliament, Pitt thought fit to leave the ministry."

Reporting this conversation Golitsyn wrote, "Pitt's departure from the ministry must be attributed to the earl of Bute alone. He has looked with impatience and not a little envy upon Pitt's lust for power and brilliant qualities. All Pitt's enemies continually fanned the flames of disagreement between them. By virtue of the imperial instructions given me I have tried, with extreme diligence, to assist in this, intimating to the earl of Bute that while Pitt remained in his ministerial offices all the honor and glory for the happy events for England would belong to him alone as a reproach to other ministers. For some time I could see the positive success of my intimations, yet I never could have expected the change to take place so swiftly. This change is important and useful to our general policy because, in the first place, Pitt's successor, the earl of Egremont,[17] does not have any of the merits of his predecessor. In the second place Pitt's well-known enthusiasm for the interests of the king of Prussia, and his overwhelming hatred for France and for everyone who wishes it well in the present circumstances, cannot be discerned in the earl of Egremont. In the third place, without Pitt, opposition to the ministry in parliament can be expected. Demands for money for the war and for subsidies will meet considerable obstacles."

At the beginning of December, while informing his court of the impending war between England and Spain,[18] Golitsyn expressed "servile joy" that, thanks to this new war, England no longer would pay a great deal of attention to the war in Germany, and the king of Prussia would not receive strong support.

SWEDEN'S DESIRE FOR PEACE

In St. Petersburg, in addition to England, care was taken that the closest powers, Sweden, Poland, Turkey and Denmark, rendered no assistance to the king of Prussia. Count Ostermann began the year with reports concerning the Swedish Riksdag. According to these reports it seemed that there was no need to fear the departure of Sweden from the alliance. There was no need either to fear the restoration of autocracy in Sweden, although members of the party opposed to the Senate were saying that in the last Riksdag the king's power was so undermined that the Senate thought of nothing else than the transformation of the monarchy to an aristocratic form of government. This tendency would bring terrible harm to Sweden, and in the present Riksdag it was intended to oppose it by every means possible. There would be attempts to bring the Senate within prescribed limits.

When the French ambassador told Ostermann about the peace proposals made by France to the allies, including Sweden, Ostermann asked Höpken whether any hints were made about actual conditions for peace. Höpken replied that as yet none had been made, but later a secret verbal message was conveyed to him that if Sweden would agree to a peace settlement the ambassador was authorized to forward a memorandum in which it would be suggested that Sweden might think fit to renounce its formerly promised territorial compensation and be satisfied with payment for all military losses.

It is interesting to note that, according to Ostermann's report, in the highest circles in Stockholm precisely those conditions for peace were being spoken about on which consequently peace was indeed concluded by all the warring powers, that is that Prussian possessions remain untouched, as they were before the outbreak of war. How the French proposal would be accepted, in what form a reply would be given, all of course depended on the relationship between the parties. There were four of these. The first, the Senate party, was faithful to France. The second was the party of Colonel Pechlin who broke away from the first party. He united about him all those who experienced some dissatisfaction or other with the government. Pechlin was a cunning man and, because he was used in the previous Riksdag by the French party for the distribution of money, knew all the intrigues going on at that time. He was using this knowledge now against the French party. The third, the old Russian party, was known as the Caps. The fourth was faithful to the court. The last three parties were united in the Riksdag because all of them acted equally against the Senate, and when they came together made up a majority, although in all other respects they were in complete disagreement with each other. The Swedish reply to the French declaration stated that Sweden would be very pleased to enter into peace negotiations. The king wanted a swift peace settlement if he could conclude it in accord with his dignity and that faithfulness with which he always kept his obligations to his allies.

In the meantime Senator Höpken, as a consequence of strong displeasure with him in the Riksdag, had to relinquish management of foreign affairs. This was very unfortunate for Ostermann, who hoped to learn a great deal through him, whereas his successor Count Ekeblad[19] was entirely dependent upon the French ambassador. Ostermann once more had to reassure his court in respect of rumors about the restoration of autocracy in Sweden. These rumors came to St. Petersburg from Korff in Copenhagen. Ostermann wrote that it was a most unlikely event, in particular because the king did not enjoy the love of the people and the queen, by her manner, even less so. Everybody knew the king obeyed the queen in all matters. The rumor had been started on purpose by d'Havrincourt, the French ambassador in Stockholm, and [Joakim Otto von] Schack-Rathlou, the Danish ambassador, who together used every means to save their friends, the members of the Senate party, and disseminated information that the court party was organizing something counter to Swedish liberties.

When the Russian reply to the French declaration concerning peace was delivered in Stockholm the king charged his minister in St. Petersburg, Baron Posse, to reassure the Russian government that Sweden would do nothing about a peace settlement without a general agreement, and would not fail to ask for the empress's advice. Ostermann, however, told his court that no significant action from Sweden could be expected in the forthcoming campaign because of lack of money, irregularity of the payment of French subsidies, the obvious displeasure of the people, and a strong desire to bring to an end this war, which was a drain on all resources. Before the beginning of the war the army consisted of thirty-two thousand men, but now there were no more than eighteen thousand in Pomerania, including those who were sick. Although a levy of conscripts was decided upon and they were assembled, without money they could not be outfitted with uniforms or transported to Pomerania.

At the end of July Ostermann reported reinforcement of the French party, which earlier had managed to incline Pechlin to their side with the use of money. Pechlin remained excluded from the assembly at court, in spite of every effort and monetary payments by the French party. Disputes with Pechlin almost led to fighting. "For my part," reported Ostermann, "in such critical circumstances in my conversations, without entering into their irritations, I try to suggest they remain calm and come to a mutual understanding." To this Vorontsov remarked "that he should utilize a judicious caution in similar Swedish domestic affairs, and not get involved in them under any circumstances." In spite of this Ostermann suggested to his court a pension and the promise of protection in order to draw Senator Höpken to their side. He was a very influential man because of the quality of his mind.

On December 21 Ostermann gave notice that Ekeblad told him, on behalf of the king, that the war was becoming terribly onerous for Sweden, and the king wanted to redouble every effort for the renewal of general peace negotiations. Ostermann added that the Swedish people were tired of the war to such a degree that Russia must not give the appearance, at least in written declarations, that it wanted to force Sweden to continue the war; otherwise France would turn all the hatred of the Swedes against Russia.

STRENGTHENING OF FRENCH INFLUENCE IN POLAND

In Poland the Russian envoy Voeikov tried, as before, to hinder any dealings between Prussia and Turkey. In January he wrote that once again he asked Count Brühl whether it were possible, in some covert way, to seize the Prussian courier. Brühl, as before, reassured him that they were making use of every method to this end, but that his son-in-law Count Mniszech had told him, "We have trustworthy information that the Prussian couriers are disguised now in Polish, now in Wallachian dress, and are sent on their way through our lands, which reach the very frontiers of Moldavia, by the castellan of Cracow, Count Poniatowski, and the Russian commander Prince Czartoryski." Voeikov told Brühl that he had one thousand chervontsy allocated for the interception of the Prussian couriers. Brühl replied that it was difficult to do anything with the money because those grandees devoted to the king of Prussia send considerable detachments of troops to accompany the couriers. Would it not be better to make use of Russian detachments under the leadership of a skillful officer, who might appear in Poland under the pretext of purchasing provisions for the army? This method was acknowledged, from the Russian point of view, to be even more difficult.

In regard to Polish affairs themselves Voeikov reported an interesting conversation with Bishop Soltyk of Cracow,[20] who told him that he was leaving Warsaw and would not return for some time, thanks to the French ambassador Marquis de Pomy, who was interfering in all matters and carrying on a strong campaign of sedition. Count Brühl stood up to him at first, but later the cunning Frenchman, with the help of Brühl's daughter Countess Mniszech, managed to master Brühl so completely that he obeyed him in everything in spite of the warnings of his son-in-law Mniszech and the bishop. This, said Soltyk, later would be very harmful to the Commonwealth, in view of the king's advanced age. The French wanted to reinforce their party in order to give the crown to Prince Xaver, the second son of King August,[21] who was completely devoted to France. Count Brühl supported Prince Xaver because the eldest son of the king, the hereditary prince of Saxony, was ill-disposed towards him. In a friendly conversation with Voeikov Count Mniszech also expressed his displeasure with the French ambassador, who managed to deceive his father-in-law Count Brühl. In connection with this matter Voeikov told his court that the French ambassador was going to Pulawy, the Czartoryski estate, for a meeting with the prince. The Danish envoy Osten was going also.

TREATY BETWEEN TURKEY AND PRUSSIA

The alarm of the Russian court over the Prussian couriers may be explained by news from Obreskov in Constantinople that a treaty of friendship and trade was concluded between Prussia and the Porte on March 20. In spite of the character of the treaty it made a very bad impression in St. Petersburg because it could give reassurance to the subjects of the king of Prussia, make him more demanding during peace negotiations and give him the opportunity to maintain his ambassador in Constantinople openly. Obreskov advised his court to remain completely indifferent to the matter as, if any representations were made from the Russian side, the Porte might make a strong response which could lead to the breakdown of good relations between the two countries. Complete silence would be more in keeping with the dignity and might of the Russian empire than any representations, from which the Porte might conclude that its treaty with Prussia had considerable significance in the empress's eyes. This would only increase its Asiatic pride and sense of power. The advice was taken, and the consequences demonstrated its benefit.

DANISH COURT ACTS OVER THE HOLSTEIN AFFAIR

The threat of war came not from the South but from the North, and from where it least might have been expected. On July 11 at nine in the morning the Danish envoy extraordinary Count Haxthausen visited the chancellor and declared that he was ordered by his king to make a verbal and friendly suggestion to the Russian court. His majesty of Denmark was obliged to notice with regret that the All Russian grand duke and duke of Schleswig-Holstein was demonstrating little inclination towards the amicable settlement of his disputes with the Danish crown, and was continuing to maintain his former malevolence towards Denmark. Consequently Denmark feared for its future security. Therefore out of necessity his majesty was making a final appeal for a swift and categorical reply to his representations, otherwise his envoy was entrusted to declare formally that his majesty of Denmark must consider the grand duke his manifest enemy, and therefore take measures against his highness, as well as against the Russian empire. The chancellor replied that these threats were used quite inopportunely, and that the Russian court was not frightened.

Indeed the College of Foreign Affairs received the following rescript. "The Danish court is mistaken if by its threats it expects to bring about the action desired. It is mistaken not because we consider these threats merely empty words, by no means! We assume, on the contrary, that perhaps Denmark has indeed the courage to do as it proposes. We imagine that it has entered a close alliance with our enemies, has at last the courage to put its forces to the test which it has been parading for so many years and with which it has now enticed its friends and neighbors, now baited them. We do not hold its forces in contempt; yet the more significant and the more important the danger, the more we look to our glory and the more we shall find the means to defend the persecuted innocence, the honor and name of our empire.

"As a great deal already has been sacrificed by us for establishment of peace in the North, so even now we cannot be content with those efforts which have been used by us up until now for the preservation of friendship with the Danish court, and consequently also peace in the North. We want, for our part, to do everything either to avert a rift with Denmark or unquestionably demonstrate to the world that it is not up to us to prevent a calamity in those circumstances where passion overcomes justice and common sense. Therefore we have advised his highness the grand duke that he give priority to the well-being of his lands over his justified indignation, and should not only not break off negotiations with the Danish court, but as far as possible even facilitate them.

"We ourselves have every intention, making use of our position as mediators, to make every effort to reconcile as many of the different interests as possible and, through the just satisfaction of both sides, to turn distrust and suspicion into agreeable harmony. Therefore we console ourselves once more with the hope that this matter will not lead to any regrettable extreme measures. In order not to lull ourselves with hope, we give orders through our College of Foreign Affairs to instruct Korff, our minister in Copenhagen, to communicate the contents of this rescript to the court. He should read it, as it were, as an extract from a dispatch, adding that although the expressions of the rescript are not very affectionate, they in fact directly express our intention; besides, the Danish court was not very moderate in the expressions it used.

"Further it should be pointed out that should the Danish court begin in any way to put its threats into operation or break its present neutrality and give the slightest assistance to our enemies, Korff has in reserve an instruction to leave the court in Copenhagen immediately. He should make his way slowly to Hamburg and there await our further instructions. We give these orders in the expectation that Denmark already has commenced initial steps towards the measures it intends to take, and therefore however firmly he speaks, it is impossible to alter these in any way. It may turn out contrary to our expectations, namely that the Danish court already regrets the threats it has made, or as a consequence of any happy event for the allies has adopted a different point of view. In that case Korff must be instructed not to read this edict to the Danish court, but to state that as, from our point of view, the king of Denmark was not given the slightest occasion for complaint, we do not see by what right the king of Denmark could deem the grand duke his manifest enemy, except perhaps that the grand duke unwillingly would have ceded that land which belongs to him by all rights. Therefore we cannot be at all convinced that the instructions given to Count Haxthausen were really such as he presented them, in which case we do not want to answer them at all in detail."

The Danish court expressed moderation and merely petitioned the allies of Russia to mediate an amicable resolution of the Holstein affair. The allies, naturally, stood by Russia and did not want to complicate their relations with the Holstein question. England explicitly declared it would not take part in this affair.

FREDERICK II'S DESPERATE PLIGHT

The shot was fired in vain, because Russia was not frightened. The Danish court could not make up its mind at the time to use its threat when the only sovereign capable of assisting Denmark, Frederick II, was in a desperate position, having been abandoned by England, his only ally. The hopes which Prince Golitsyn linked with the departure of Pitt from the ministry proved justified. The earl of Bute openly acted against Prussian interests. Frederick II could not recover after Kunersdorf. He was forced to change an aggressive into a defensive war, but did not have sufficient resources even for this. The country was laid waste, his forces were demoralized, the best officers were killed or taken prisoner. Frederick said himself that his forces were no longer in the condition they were at the beginning of the war, being fit only to frighten the enemy from a distance. Frederick clearly saw that his enemies, albeit slowly, were achieving their goals, that the struggle was becoming impossible for him, but how could he bring it to an end? The peace settlement they were demanding, honorable for them and shameful for him, could be agreed only by the complete breakup of all that had been acquired, brought together through such effort, the loss of Silesia, Pomerania, East Prussia itself, that territory through which he was king.[22] From being the king of Prussia, was he to become again merely the elector of Brandenburg? With this thought, of course, Frederick could not reconcile himself, and another thought, to flee from disgrace by violent death, imprinted itself deeper and deeper in his mind.

Frederick's plight was becoming so perilous that it was impossible to rely upon the sluggish progress of the Russian army the following year and the incoherence of the actions of the last commander-in-chief Buturlin. This was the fourth commander-in-chief in five years of the war, and all four were distinguished by a certain character and identical method of operation. All four achieved significant military rank *in the line*, all four were lacking the abilities of a commander-in-chief. They moved slowly on the leading strings of the Conference, acting within fixed directives. They would meet the enemy, withstand his onslaught, defend themselves, and sometimes would realize after an engagement that they had gained a great victory, smashing the enemy completely. This did not change their attitude towards their obligations, did not change in any way their operations in the field, did not give them the abilities to take the initiative. They would not take a step in order to exploit their victory, to finish off the enemy conclusively. As before they would await an edict with a detailed plan of action.

There was one more temptation. The Austrians with their Daun-Given-to-Cautious-Tactics![23] We fought and defeated the enemy, but what about the Austrians? Let them fight the enemy now. Let them even deal the final blow to the enemy. We will not envy them. We need to rest, to concern ourselves with the most important thing, the preservation of her imperial majesty's victorious army, the preservation of the glory won by her arms. As soon as the usual news arrives that there is a threat of a shortage of provisions and forage, move back to the cherished banks of the Vistula, to the supply depots, and begin again.

That is why a historian studying attentively the entire progress of the Prussian war would not repeat the rumor emanating from the French ambassador in St. Petersburg that Apraksin retreated to the frontiers after his victory because he received from Bestuzhev news of the empress's illness. Did all his successors do the same on the instructions of similar letters? In that case there was not even the shadow of military art, of military competence and understanding. The war was carried out in a primitive manner. The forces entered enemy territory, fought with the enemy they happened to come across there, and in the autumn withdrew. In the Conference in St. Petersburg this was well understood and they wrote, "The first art of a general consists in taking such measures which neither time, circumstances, nor the movements of the enemy can impede." It was not possible, however, for Apraksin, Fermor, Saltykov or Buturlin to learn this skill from the rescripts they were sent.

RUMIANTSEV CAPTURES KOLBERG

In St. Petersburg the traditions of Peter the Great yet remained. His views on war were remembered as a living practical school, in which the best of all military talents were allowed to develop. The present war was compared in St. Petersburg with the most skillful period of the military leader in the war against Karl XII. The same results were expected, and they were not to be disappointed. Good students began to emerge from this school. At the very beginning of the war a foreigner,[24] having discredited all Russian generals, stopped with respect before the young Count Rumiantsev, as a man who had taken considerable trouble to make himself competent for service, acquiring a wide theoretical knowledge.

To this theoretical knowledge the five years of war also had added practice. Rumiantsev stood out from the other generals and was entrusted with setting right the campaign of 1761 by taking Kolberg, before which city Russian forces had suffered a lack of success for the past two years. The foreigner found one deficiency in Rumiantsev, namely his impulsiveness. Thus far senior Russian generals had been so distinguished by such excessive caution that the contrary quality may be regarded as a necessary antidote. Frederick II made every effort to defend Kolberg, but on December 1 Rumiantsev finally beat off Duke Eugene of Würtemberg, who attempted to revictual Kolberg, after which the fortress was obliged to surrender.

Sending the keys of Kolberg to St. Petersburg Rumiantsev wrote to the empress, "My happiness in this matter is all the greater because of its timing. I believe I have made this the first gift for the solemn birthday of your imperial majesty, offering up heartfelt prayers to the Most High for the safety of your inestimable good health, for the longevity of your reign and the continuous increase of glory to the authority of your imperial majesty, crowned by countless victories." Rumiantsev's report of the latest operation of the Russian forces in the Seven Years War was published on December 25, the last day of Elizabeth's life.

ELIZABETH'S ILLNESS AND DEMISE

At the start of the year we begin to come across material relating to the poor health of the empress, who listened to reports lying on her bed. Elizabeth very much wanted to live for a time in the new Winter Palace, and on June 19 the procurator general, following her edict, asked the Senate to make every effort to see that her winter home, being newly rebuilt, at least that part in which her imperial majesty had her own apartment, be completed as swiftly as possible. The apartment was not finished. Rastrelli asked for three hundred and eighty thousand rubles for the complete decoration of the whole winter home, and for one hundred thousand in the first instance.

In the meantime a number of major calamities took place. On June 29 fire destroyed eighty-three warehouses with hemp and flax in five blocks along the Lesser Neva, as well as a great number of wooden barges on the river. The merchants lost more than one million rubles. The empress instructed the Senate to think quickly of means to assist those who lost their possessions in the fire. They turned to the Merchants' Bank. It only had 729,539 rubles, but the Senate decided to use two hundred and eighty thousand rubles to assist the victims of the fire. The allocation of the grant was handed over to the Commerce Commission.

The efforts being made by France for a peace settlement and an armistice were very disturbing. When that danger disappeared, news began arriving of the sad progress of a campaign upon which so many hopes were placed. A new campaign must be prepared under extremely difficult financial circumstances. Buturlin turned out to be completely incapable of commanding the forces. The procurator general Prince Shakhovskoy applied to be relieved of his post, saying that he was exhausted by the burden of affairs. Count Mikhail Larionovich Vorontsov, grand chancellor since the end of 1758, found Bestuzhev's legacy too much for him. He constantly complained of ill health, applied to be relieved of his post or asked that Prince Alexander Mikhailovich Golitsyn, formerly ambassador in London, be appointed to him as an assistant, thus soliciting the advice of a skillful diplomat from that most important posting. Count Peter Ivanovich Shuvalov was almost always and dangerously ill.

On November 17 Elizabeth suffered a bout of fever but completely recovered on taking medication, and become occupied once more with matters of state. On December 3 the Cabinet Secretary Olsufiev came to the Senate and informed them of an imperial command. The empress told the Senate of her anger about the extreme disagreements that were taking place over political matters and the fulfillment of edicts emanating from her. There were long delays in coming to decisions, which meant either that they did not want to, or could not, make decisions on matters of state. A few months earlier the appointment of Brigadier Suvorov as manger of the Nerchinsk manufactories was confirmed, but he had yet to be sent. Grand Master of Ceremonies Baron Lefort continually attended the Senate meetings but no decision had been made about his affairs, whereas it would have been more fitting to arrest Rubanovsky, who had informed against him. This matter could be resolved very quickly, without procrastination, in order not to lose face before foreigners and that the standing of the government not be damaged. The empress long ago gave instructions to appoint the merchant Gerasimov as sorter of hemp and flax within the port of St. Petersburg, but so far this instruction was not acted upon. A number of petitions sent from the Cabinet to the Senate remained undecided. Her imperial majesty was aware that not all senators came to meetings, some rarely and others almost never, which was why there were such delays in carrying out its business. If someone did not attend, his absence must be reported to the empress. There was an instruction of her imperial majesty concerning assistance to the victims of the latest major fire (June 29), but so far nothing had been done.

On December 12 Elizabeth again felt ill. She began to vomit blood and phlegm violently. The doctors Moisey, Schilling and Cruz decided to let blood. They were very frightened when they observed the rapid worsening of her condition. In spite of this the empress seemed to recover within a few days. On December 17 Olsufiev came to the Senate once more and relayed an edict from the empress herself. Those under arrest throughout the whole state for bootlegging were to be released, the cases against them quashed and those banished were to return. The Senate was to find a way with diligence and dispatch to replace the revenue from salt, because it had been collected with great damage to the people, and those appointed to this task were abusing their powers.

On December 20 Elizabeth felt particularly well. Two days later, on the twenty-second at ten in the evening, severe vomiting with blood and phlegm began again. The doctors also noted other symptoms because of which they considered it their duty to announce that the empress's health was in danger. When she heard this diagnosis on the twenty-third Elizabeth made her confession and communion. On the twenty-fourth she took extreme unction. The illness became so severe that in the evening Elizabeth made them twice read the prayers for the dying, repeating them herself after the priest. The agony was prolonged overnight and for the greater half of the following day. The grand duke and grand duchess were constantly by the bedside of the dying woman.

At four in the afternoon the doors of the bedroom were opened into the reception chamber, where the highest dignitaries and courtiers were gathered. Everyone knew what this meant. The senior senator, Prince Nikita Yurievich Trubetskoy, came out and declared that Empress Elizabeth Petrovna had died and the new sovereign was his majesty the emperor Peter III. This was met by weeping and moaning throughout the palace. The new emperor went off to his own part of the palace. The empress Catherine Alekseevna remained with the body of the late empress.

SIGNIFICANCE OF ELIZABETH'S REIGN

In the absence of a careful study of Russian history of the eighteenth century it has been customary to repeat that the period from the death of Peter the Great until the accession of Catherine II was wretched, unworthy of study, a period highlighted by intrigues, palace revolutions, the supremacy of foreigners. With the progress of historical scholarship in general and with the more attentive study of Russian history, such views can be repeated no longer. We know that in our ancient history Ivan III was not the creator of Russia's greatness, but that this greatness was prepared before him in the sad period of princely internecine strife and the struggle with the Tatars. We know that Peter the Great did not lead Russia from non-existence to existence, that such so-called transformation was a natural and necessary phenomenon of national growth, of national development. Peter's major significance consisted in the fact that through the power of his genius he helped his people effect an important transition, attended with all manner of dangers. Scholarship does not permit us likewise to make a leap from the time of Peter the Great to that of Catherine II. It compels us with particular interest to delve into a study of the intermediate epoch, to see how Russia continued to live that new life after Peter the Great, how it came to understand the material of transformation without the assistance of the brilliant emperor, how it found itself in its new situation with its light and its dark sides, for in the life of a man and in the life of nations there is no age in which there is not both the one and the other.

In the West, where many were alarmed at the sudden appearance of a new mighty power in the East of Europe, they consoled themselves with the fact that this appearance was transitory, that it depended for its existence on the will of a strong man, and would come to an end together with his life. This expectation was not justified precisely because this new life of the Russian people was not the creation of one man. It was not possible to turn back, as no individual, no nation as a whole may turn back from youth to childhood and from maturity to youth. It was possible to make, and there had to be made, particular retreats from the plan of transformation as a consequence of the absence of a single strong will, as a consequence of the weakness of the sovereign and the selfish aspirations of individual strong personalities. So a certain opposition to Petrine initiatives emerged in the intensification of personal management in the provinces, in the building of an extra level above the Senate, now under the name of the Supreme Privy Council, now under the name of the Cabinet. A sadder consequence was the digression from the idea of Peter the Great in respect to foreigners.

The strongest danger in the transformation of the Russian people from its ancient history to the new, from the age of feeling into the age of thought and knowledge, from a domestic, enclosed life to the public life of nations, the great danger consisted in the relationship with foreign peoples who outstripped them in the sphere of knowledge, from whom, for this reason, it was necessary to learn. In this position, as a student with respect to contemporary foreign nations, lay the very danger to the strength and independence of the Russian people. How do you combine the position of student with freedom and independence in relation to the teacher? How

do you avoid in these circumstances subordination, imitation? The extreme subordination of the people of Western Europe to their teachers, the
Greeks and the Romans, served as an example, when in the period of the
Renaissance they completed the very same transition the Russians completed in the period of reform, but with the difference that the danger of
subordination was diminished for the West by the fact that they subordinated themselves to those long dead, whereas the Russians had to learn
from living teachers. In this respect Peter the Great rendered a great service to his people, reducing the period of study, forcing them to pass
swiftly through a practical school, not leaving the Russian people for long
in the painful position of students, making use of incredible efforts in
order, at least in respect of domestic resources, not only to make his people
equal with his educated neighbors but even to give them superiority. This
was certainly the case with building up the forces and the fleet, through
brilliant victories and important acquisitions, as this suddenly gave the
Russian people a respected place in Europe, raised its spirit, delivered it
from harmful disparagement from those deemed to be civilized. Peter
kept constantly to the rule to entrust to Russians the highest positions of
military and civilian administration. Only secondary positions might be
occupied by foreigners.

On the death of Peter this important rule was put aside. His fledglings
introduced internecine strife, ousted one other, thinned out their ranks.
Foreigners took advantage and forced their way into the highest positions.
The unfortunate attempt of 1730 inflicted a heavy blow on Russian families standing in the highest positions, and the reign of Anna was marked
by the ascendancy of Biron. However many attempts are made in particular individual respects to play down the calamities of this period, it will
remain forever the darkest period of our history in the eighteenth century,
as it was not about personal misfortune or material privation. The spirit
of the people suffered. There was a sense of betrayal to the basic, essential rule of the great reformer. There was experience of the darkest side
of the new life. The yoke from the West was felt more heavily than that
previous yoke from the East, the Tatar yoke. The victor of Poltava was
humbled, made a slave to Biron, who would say, "You, Russians...."[25]

The daughter of Peter the Great delivered Russia from this yoke. Russia *came to its senses*. Russians once again appeared in the highest posts,
and when a foreigner was appointed to a secondary position Elizabeth
asked whether there really was no Russian who could carry out the task.

A foreigner was appointed only when there was no capable Russian. The activity of the people was freed from constraint by the abolition of internal customs. Banks appeared to assist landowner and merchant. The energetic exploitation of mineral resources began in the East. Trade with Central Asia took on wider dimensions. The southern steppes received population from abroad, a population homogeneous with the main population, therefore easily assimilated by them and not alien or incapable of being digested by the body of the people. A general land survey was introduced. The question of monastery landholding was prepared for solution in close connection with charitable establishments. The people, coming to its senses, began to speak on behalf of itself and about itself. Literature appeared. A language was developed worthy of a people expressing itself. Writers came to the fore who remain alive in the memory and mind of posterity. A folk theater appeared, a newspaper. A university was founded in Old Moscow. Man, who formerly perished under the axe of the executioner, became a useful worker in a country which, more than any other, had need of a worker's strength. Torture was deliberately suspended at the first opportunity, and in this way its abolition was prepared in practice. For some future time a new generation was prepared, brought up on other rules and habits than those which held sway in previous reigns. Serried ranks of active people were educated and fitted to make the reign of Catherine II renowned.

In speaking of her reign, we must not forget the character of Elizabeth herself. Merry, carefree, passionate for the pleasures of life in her youth, Elizabeth had to pass through the difficult school of experience but passed through it to her advantage. Extreme caution, restraint, attention, an ability to make her way between people pushing one another about but without pushing them about, these qualities were acquired by Elizabeth in the reign of Anna, when her security and freedom constantly hung by a thread. These qualities Elizabeth also brought to the throne without losing her good nature, tolerance, so-called patriarchal habits, a love for sincerity, for simplicity in personal relations. Inheriting from her father the ability to select and keep about her talented people, she called into service a new generation of Russians, celebrated in her reign and after. She was able to moderate their behavior, to keep Peter Shuvalov close to her and at the same time elevate Shakhovskoy. In this, of course, her caution was of considerable service, allowing her to decide policies, not suddenly according to the suggestion of someone or other, but by listening to others, considering their opinions, thinking and thinking for a long time. "I think for a long time," said Elizabeth, "but once I have made up my mind to anything I never let the matter rest until I have pursued it to the very end." This slowness was also the principal accusation against Elizabeth. Yet it may be asked, who was the accuser?

For a long time we were badly served by our history of the eighteenth century. Thanks to extensive historical endeavors, exclusively embracing ancient Russian history, we were able to discover details concerning Grand Prince Iziaslav Mstislavich, and yet remained in complete ignorance about personalities and events of the eighteenth century. In the first place, anecdotes served as the main source, constantly perverted as they went from mouth to mouth and giving a mistaken idea about people and actions because of their fragmentary nature and biased point of view, whichever side they took, good or bad. In second place was information from foreigners, and in particular ambassadors' reports, which were read avidly precisely because of an absence of any of our own.

Why should we not believe such sources? An ambassador occupies an important position. He deals with sovereigns and ministers. He knows everything precisely as it took place. He must know because he was obliged to communicate reliable information to his court. Indeed it is a significant source. We may find extraordinarily interesting information and details in such material. Still we must treat this information, these details with particular caution! There is no witness who would be less impartial and from whom, in the majority of cases, attempts would be made to hide the truth more than a foreign ambassador. If he gives a compliment, whom is he complimenting? He who gives in to him, often by violating the interests of his native country. As soon as the same person shows less compliance the ambassador, without remembering previous service, will abuse him. If the ambassador meets obstacles in carrying through some matter for his court, these obstacles, in his words, are not due to the fact that this matter, in whole or in part, is not in accord with the interests of the country; no, they certainly proceed from the intrigues of disloyal people. We know now where the slowness of Elizabeth in deciding of important matters came from. Yet foreign ambassadors, who needed to decide a particular policy as quickly as possible, reported to their courts in great irritation that this dilatoriness proceeded from Elizabeth's lack of concern, from her passion to concern herself with trifles while important matters were not advanced. This is how even Williams viewed matters, when consumed with impatience to complete as quickly as possible the treaty on subsidies. We know Elizabeth's justification in delaying ratification of this treaty. Apart from the natural desire of every ambassador to explain obstacles to his affairs through the bad motives of others, to praise favorites and to censure enemies, he was himself deceived by the stories of these favorites, by their explanations of the causes of failure.

In face of this, of course, everything was set down to the intrigues of enemies and the lack of concern of the empress, to whom there was no admittance to talk of such serious matters. What did Bestuzhev not talk about at length to Williams in justifying his failure? The natural and necessary rapprochement of Russia and France, in his own words, proceeded from the fact that Ivan Ivanovich Shuvalov liked reading French books. Was not this very like saying that the Austro-French alliance proceeded as a consequence of a flattering letter from Maria Theresa to Madame Pompadour, as if the alliance did not have to follow after the change in existing relations thanks to Frederick II, and as if the alliance of England with Prussia did not lead inevitably and immediately to an alliance between France and Austria?

Moreover the participation of Russia in the Seven Years War was explained by the personal irritation of Elizabeth with Frederick II, who allowed himself to ridicule her! We need not resort to such trivial explanations. We know that the foundations of foreign policy were simple in those days. They consisted in the preservation of the political balance in Europe, particularly if that balance were upset nearby. At the beginning and in the middle of the eighteenth century, and at the beginning of the nineteenth century, Europe conducted the most bloody wars for the maintenance of this principle of political equilibrium. It kept Louis XIV in check with the War of Spanish Succession. It kept Frederick II in check with the Seven Years War, just as at the beginning of the present century it overcame the ambitions of Napoleon I. In the last two conflicts Russia played a most major role and with an identical right, although even during the Napoleonic wars there were those in Russia who said, "Why should we fight France? It is so far from us!" The burning of Moscow demonstrated to those gentlemen just how far France was from Russia. Probably even during the Seven Years War there were those who asked why Russia should meddle in such a long and wasteful war for the sake of Austria and Saxony.

The daughter of Peter the Great did not think this way. For her the upstart king of Prussia, not fastidious over means to expand his kingdom, was Russia's most dangerous enemy. Elizabeth could not set her mind at rest in respect to the East until the ships built by the English for Persia on the Caspian Sea were destroyed by fire. In precisely the same way she could not set her mind at rest in respect to the West until the powers of the king of Prussia were reduced, as he completely justified the view of him held by the Russian court by his attack upon Saxony. The powers of the king of Prussia were reduced thanks to the firmness and energy of Elizabeth, and if they were not reduced as much as she would have wished, they were reduced sufficiently to the point where, subsequently, Catherine II did not find them a hindrance to the attainment of her goals. Apart from this important consequence of the Seven Years War for Russia, it was also a school from which Russian commanders emerged who made the reign of Catherine II so brilliant in military terms. In this way, while giving our due to Catherine II, we must not forget how much, both within Russia and without, was prepared for her by Elizabeth.

DOMESTIC AFFAIRS IN THE LAST YEAR OF ELIZABETH'S REIGN

In conclusion we should glance at domestic government in the last year of Elizabeth's reign. At the very beginning of the year the Senate replied to the Conference which had requested 16,700 rubles and six hundred chervontsy for various items of expenditure. "There is a deficit every year in the College of State Accounts from statutory revenues. For this reason many items of expenditure cannot be paid, and this is a debt against the College of State Accounts. At present there is a very considerable shortage of money and the Senate cannot hope to carry out the requests of the Conference. The College of State Accounts cannot release even the sum prescribed for the maintenance of the court. Although the Senate has responsibility for providing the College of State Accounts with revenues, so far it has yet to find the means to do so. The College of State Accounts has borrowed 8,147,924 rubles." After this the College of State Accounts issued a report. In the ensuing four-month period, beginning January, it had to pay their highnesses for the maintenance of the imperial court and the Life Guards Company 144,897 rubles for the four-month period beginning September of the previous year, but there was no money whatsoever in the College of State Accounts. Approximately 221 puds and three funts of efimoks of farmed-out customs duties for October, November and December had not been received. The Commission on Commerce stated that the 43,738 rubles it received from Shemiakin for October were being kept for payment into the empress's chamber. The Senate gave orders that this money allocated for the chamber of the empress be handed over to the College of State Accounts, and the remainder recovered from Shemiakin within seven days. The Senate ordered the Commissary to deliver as soon as possible the sum that had not been sent to the army for wages for 1760, more than three hundred thousand rubles, as well as the 1,465,728 rubles for 1761. A million rubles were assigned from the Salt Bureau to the empress's chamber, and already arrears of 2,115,043 had accumulated. Besides this the Salt Bureau was obliged to pay 1,089,823 rubles towards military expenses. The bureau asked whether the sum for military expenditure could not be reduced in order to pay off the arrears into the empress's chamber. The Senate replied that this was not possible. In the month of August the College of State Accounts reported it needed 2,119,135 rubles for the most urgent expenses, including the debts of the College amounting to 2,686,831. At present there were 50,162 rubles on hand in the College of State Accounts. It should receive 61,394 rubles for the efimoks handed over to the Mint, and there were 10,087 rubles in the Moscow Treasury, making 121,644 rubles in all and leaving a shortfall of 1,997,490 rubles, which together with the debts came to 2,565,186 rubles.

We have seen that a lottery was established. The revenues from this were to go to the maintenance of retired and wounded senior and junior officers and rank and file. A lottery consisted of fifty thousand tickets out of which there were 37,500 winning tickets divided into four classes. Each ticket was set at eleven rubles for all classes.

In June the procurator general stated that the empress had instructed him to propose to the Senate the establishment of a house to support widows and orphans, the daughters of meritorious people who were poor and without patronage and sustenance. For this purpose her majesty would grant a certain sum from her own revenues. The Senate sent a request to Synod to set aside the St. John convent in Moscow for the widows and orphans, or another similar to it, with a sufficient number of rooms and a stone boundary wall. As far as regulations were concerned it was to inquire in the library of the Academy of Sciences how such houses were maintained in foreign countries and to collect information through the College of Foreign Affairs from the ambassadors appointed to foreign courts.

The Commission on the Code of Laws, on which sat the two Senators Count Roman Larionovich Vorontsov and Prince Mikhail Ivanovich Shakhovskoy, completed two parts of the Code, the judicial and the criminal.

The Senate issued the following order in March. "As the above-mentioned composition of the Code is very necessary for the management of civil matters in the entire state, it follows that the labor of the whole society should be used in our councils to this end. Therefore it is the duty of every son of the fatherland to assist in this matter with advice or by deed, and to try to assist its conclusion with fervent diligence. Similarly the Governing Senate trusts that everyone of whatever rank or title, when chosen to work with the Commission, will not refuse to do so but, ignoring all difficulties and expenses, will try willingly to make themselves useful, hoping first to leave an indelible memorial of themselves for future generations and, above all, to receive recognition for work beyond the call of duty. To this end, on the request of the Commission of the New Code, two men must be sent from each province to a hearing of the Code chosen from staff and senior officers, from the gentry and the exalted nobility, from the cities of every province (with the exception of the newly conquered provinces, that is the Baltic, Siberian, Astrakhan and Kiev provinces), not excluding even those permanently retired from all duties who are nevertheless suitable for this business, after an election of all the gentry of these cities. If they wish to elect someone to the aforementioned hearing from those who are in St. Petersburg on state business, they have the right to do so. Later, after a similar election, the merchants should send to St. Petersburg one member of the merchant community by next January 1, 1762."

In respect to Ukraine the Senate declared, "The hetman of Ukraine shall appoint designated but competent men to examine the Lithuanian Statute, supplement any insufficiencies, delete what is unnecessary and send such material to the Senate with a delegate able to give a detailed explanation of it all."

Apart from the election of delegates to the Commission on the Code of Laws, the nobility were to take part in other elections. On June 5 the Senate granted landowners the right to elect military governors from among their number who had villages near a city and could maintain themselves by revenues from them. In addition the Senate considered raising the salary of officials from the nobility as well as that of the military governors. Presidents and members of colleges, governors and governor's assistants from the Russian nobility, for the most part from those meriting such appointment but who were not wealthy, had received up to that time in St. Petersburg half the salary of those on the army scales, and in other cities half of the St. Petersburg scales. The governor and deputy governors in the Baltic provinces received two-thirds and in the interior provinces half of the Baltic scales. With such a small salary, the Senate suggested, they were quite unable to support themselves without extreme indigence, given the present state of affairs, and for that reason the salaries of civil and military officers must be equalized. Presidents [chairmen] shall receive two thousand four hundred rubles, a high procurator three thousand, a general master of petitions and a master of heraldry two thousand five hundred, vice presidents one thousand eight hundred, councillors one thousand two hundred, court councillors eight hundred, assessors six hundred. In all provinces the governors shall receive two thousand five hundred, deputy governors two thousand, assistants eight hundred, provincial military governors eight hundred, their assistants three hundred, the military governors of subordinate towns four hundred, and suburban military governor two hundred. Two copecks should be levied on each pail of wine, beer and honey, on deeds of purchase twenty-five copecks, on certification of land for proprietors three copecks for every quarter, and from every legal action three copecks for every ruble in order to cover these new payments.

News coming in from the provinces persuaded the authorities that they must certainly take measures against the abuses of provincial administrations. For example the Senate became aware that in the vicinity of the city of Tsaritsyn a number of officials were taking significant bribes from those passing along the Volga. In the Senate the procurator general read a letter to him from Major General Lachinov from Tambov. On July 8 Lachinov was at the Kazan horse fair at the Verkholomov monastery. There is steppeland near the town of Verkhny Lomov known as Durovskaia, on which a number of robbers always gathered at about the time of the fair and committed numerous robberies and murders. The year 1761 was no exception but a steward of the nobleman Semeonov, gathering together his peasants and some strangers, carried out a search for the robbers and found them. He killed their leader with eleven others but brought two of them alive to the chancellery of the military governor,. where they told of their escapades, saying that during the attack on their gang the notorious robber Topkin seized the stolen money from their band and made off. The military governor sent a detachment in pursuit, and the robber was caught. Lachinov, who visited the military governor, saw the robber but noticed that he was rather insecurely confined, not as a villain, but in conditions appropriate to a minor offender. Later Lachinov heard that the robber was even going about the market on a string of carts and, finally, he heard that the military governor had let him go. The Senate ordered the Tambov provincial chancellery to find out whether Bologovsky, the military governor in Verkhny Lomov, indeed had confined the robber Topkin insecurely and released him. The Tambov chancellery replied that there was no such person as Bologovsky as military governor in Verkhny Lomov. Ensign Vysheslavtsev held the office of military governor but by what authority and from where, the chancellery of the Tambov military governor had no knowledge.

The Senate gave orders to the Tambov military governor's chancellery to conclude an enquiry regarding Bologovsky as soon as possible. Their report demonstrated their ignorance of the whereabouts of Bologovsky and by what authority Vysheslavtsev was carrying out the duties of military governor. Such ignorance could be attributed only to their poor management, for the chancellory must always know of the absence of a subordinate military commander and his replacement. In future it must not make any such unfounded statements whatsoever to the Senate. At last the missing military governor was run to earth and made a statement to the Senate that he was given leave for two months by the provincial chancellery, about which he had let the military governor in Tambov know. As regards Topkin, he was confined, and not allowed to go anywhere, but disappeared one night because of a sentry's negligence. He slandered the military governor in Tambov for being on friendly terms with Lachinov. The case was passed to the chancellery of the Voronezh government.

The troubles of the free homesteaders continued. To alleviate their plight they were removed from the Department of the Military Governors and given their own elected managers. The electoral principle just as in ancient, so too in the new Russia, did not bring the expected advantages, thanks to insufficiency in society of cohesion and authority by which it could restrain its elected officials. The new free homesteader managers became more onerous than the military governor. Therefore the Senate now dismissed all free homesteader managers, and the free homesteaders once more were placed under the department of the provincial and military governors' chancelleries. Instructions were given that for their good order there were to be selected among them men invested with authority over a hundred, over fifty and over ten, and that they elect middlemen from their number, learned men of good conscience, to deal with matters between them. It was made abundantly clear to civil and military governors that they were responsible for the free homesteaders and were to protect them from injury, as the Senate would inspect vigilantly and send couriers to gather intelligence as to how assiduously the civil and military governors looked after free homesteaders.

As far as the general survey of the land was concerned, the Senate gave orders that surveying in the Moscow district and province be completed, also in the districts of Novgorod, Veliky Ustiug and Viatka, but that other places in the governments of Moscow and Novgorod be left for the duration of the present military campaign, owing to a lack of money in the Treasury.

In respect to life in the towns, we notice a report of the town council of Karachev about the merchant Moriakin. The local merchant community did not wish to have him amongst them because of his dishonorable conduct. The merchants of the city of Viazma petitioned that last year it requested that Yudichev, then burgomaster on the Viazma town council, be removed for his dishonorable conduct and brought to trial. They also asked that there be only three officials on the Viazma town council, following the example of other towns, with a change every two years. Presently there were six members on the Viazma town council, two burgomasters and four aldermen, an unnecessary and purposeless burden for the merchant community. Later the Senate gave orders for Yudichev to be dismissed and that the merchant community elect another in his place. It was for the Chief Magistracy to recommend to the Senate how many members there should be on a town council, and after how many years they should be changed. Although Yudichev was indeed dismissed, consideration of his dishonorable conduct did not follow, neither was a decision taken either to lower the number of members of the town council or to reduce their period of service, whereas the Chief Magistracy itself lowered the number of members in the government and other councils of Moscow and Kaluga, and permitted several to change. The Senate gave instructions to the Chief Magistracy to resolve this matter as soon as possible.

There has been mention previously of the conflict between the two authorities in the cities, the military governor and the police. The police in Kolomna reported that the local military governor, Ivan Orlov, went to the office of the chief of police with a large number of horsemen and fired the pistols he had in both hands into the office. On the same day the military governor, while riding along the most crowded streets with the landowner Kriukov, together with his hunting dog, fired his pistols.

With respect to life in the villages we come across information relating to the murder of the landowner Captain Isakov, with his wife and three children, by his peasants. A fourth infant was spared at the plea of the nurse. News was received from Kazan province of a revolt of peasants in Simbirsk against the landowner Turgenev. The Senate could not but observe that it was the monastery peasants and those attached to mills and factories who were principally in a state of unrest. Yevdokim Demidov presented a petition relating to the workmen at his Avziano-Petrovsk factory who all stopped work because of false information that an edict had arrived about their release from factory work. Peasants also rose in revolt at the factories of Nikita Demidov,[26] in Orenburg province at the copper-smelting plant of Count Sievers, and in the Penza district at the dyeworks of Count Andrei Shuvalov. While carrying out the usual process of first admonishing the peasants to submit and then putting them down with a military detachment in the event of stubbornness, the Senate gave orders that special, well-disposed and reliable men should be sent to gather information as to why the peasants were in revolt. Was there some offense against them, some oppression? In addition a study must be drawn up about attachment of peasants to private factories that might once and for all make a fundamental determination relating to all factories and the peasants attached to them, and in that way to eliminate all the difficulties.

In respect to *immigrants* throughout eastern Ukraine and the province of Orenburg the Senate resolved to deport to their former place of habitation only those who had not yet acquired a home of their own, in particular the runaways, and to leave those who had set up a home and were engaged in arable farming.

The well-known case of Assessor Krylov[27] served as an example as to how far bureaucratic willfulness might go in the far-flung corners of the empire, especially in distant Siberia. The following events took place in addition to his other deeds. There was a two-headed eagle on the municipal tower in Irkutsk with St. George on the breast, as is normal. Instead of the eagle Krylov gave instructions that a sheet of tin be set up with the superscription "Set up in the month of September 1760 in the days of Collegiate Assessor Krylov, administrator in Irkutsk." Beaten out above the superscription was a coronet of nobility framed with laurel leaves. The senators decided that Krylov be tried by a special commission. Only one senator, Zherebtsov, did not agree, saying that a special commission was unnecessary, that Krylov should be tried by the College of Justice and that the action in respect of the coat of arms should be sent to the Privy Chancellery. On this matter there was serious disagreement. The other senators took offense. Why, in their opinion, had Zherebtsov put forward so many decrees? It was as if they, the senators, were opposed to decrees. Then the procurator general stated that he was stopping the proceedings in order to report to the empress. Elizabeth gave instructions to try Krylov by a special commission so that those offended by him receive satisfaction as quickly as possible, and that conscientious and impartial men be appointed to the commission. With such a scoundrel the matter must be acted upon by order of her majesty, whatever anyone might say.

NOTES

Additional information on personalities and topics found in the text and notes is available in George N. Rhyne and Joseph L. Wieczynski, ed., *The Modern Encyclopedia of Russian, Soviet and Eurasian History* (MERSEH), (formerly *The Modern Encyclopedia of Russian and Soviet History*); George Guetsche and Harry B. Weber, ed., *The Modern Encyclopedia of Russian and Soviet Literatures* (*Including Non-Russian and Émigré Literatures*) (MERSL) *The Modern Encyclopedia of Russian and Soviet Literatures* (*Including Non-Russian and Émigré Literatures*) (MERSL); Paul D. Stevens, ed., *The Modern Encyclopedia of Religions in Russia and Eurasia* (MERRE), (formerly *The Modern Encyclopedia of Religions in Russia and the Soviet Union* (MERRSU); and David R. Jones, ed., *The Military-Naval Encyclopedia of Russia and the Soviet Union.*

CHAPTER I

1. The treaty of May 1746 was part of the elaborate development of a coalition embarked upon by Chancellor Bestuzhev-Riumin, who saw Prussia as the greatest threat to Russian interests in the Baltic, to contain Prussian expansion.

2. These territories were seized from Austria by Prussia during the War of Austrian Succession.

3. August III, king of Poland, was also elector of Saxony. This territory was occupied by Frederick the Great in 1756. It was this act which set off the series of events known as the Seven Years War.

4. Count Alexis Petrovich Bestuzhev-Riumin (1693-1766), chancellor of Russia, 1744-1758.

5. Count Mikhail [Il]larionovich Vorontsov (1714-1767), vice chancellor of Russia and Bestuzhev-Riumin's deputy, 1744-1758. He was chancellor, 1758-1762. Vorontsov was a francophile opposed to the anti-French policies of Chancellor Bestuzhev-Riumin.

6. Count Nicholas Esterhazy was the Austrian ambassador to Russia.

7. Grand Duke Peter Fedorovich, Karl Peter Ulrich (1728-1762), duke of Holstein and grandson of Peter the Great, was made heir to the throne of Russia by Empress Elizabeth in 1742. He was an ardent admirer of Frederick II of Prussia and therefore opposed to the main thrust of Russia's foreign policy.

8. Prince Wenzel von Kaunitz-Rietburg (1711-1794), Austrian chancellor, 1753-1792. Kaunitz was the Austrian advocate behind the alliance between France, Austria and Russia against Prussia.

9. Courland, a duchy under nominal Polish suzerainty, with its capital at Mitau, covered present-day Latvia south of the Dvina river, with a coastline extending from Riga to East Prussia. It became part of the Russian sphere of influence after 1717.

10. Fedor Dmitrievich Bekhteev was a diplomat under the patronage of Vorontsov, the vice chancellor. Bekhteev was one of the agents sent incognito to France in 1756 to reopen diplomatic relations with Louis XV. He was responsible in Paris for negotiating Russian accession to the Treaty of Versailles. At the end of 1756 he was made Russian chargé d'affaires in Paris, awaiting the appointment of a full ambassador.

11. Russia wanted to include a secret clause in the treaty invoking French assistance should Russia find itself at war with Turkey. France was opposed to such a clause, fearing it would undermine the good relations it assiduously developed with the Porte in order to protect French trade in the Middle East.

12. Antoine-Louis Rouillé de Coudray, comte de Joury (c. 1689-1761), French secretary of state for foreign affairs. French foreign policy also was pursued directly by Louis XV independently of, and sometimes in direct opposition to, the ministry. The king's private foreign policy was conducted through "the King's Secret," directed by his cousin Louis François de Bourbon, prince de Conti. The King's Secret was particularly active in the affairs of Eastern Europe and Russia.

13. Alexander Mackenzie Douglas, a pro-Stuart Scotsman, was agent for the King's Secret in Russia in 1755 and 1756-1757, posing as a surveyor of mines in Eastern Europe and Russia. Douglas was responsible for agreeing to the inclusion of a secret clause in Russia's accession to the Treaty of Versailles regarding French support of Russia in the event of war with Turkey. Douglas was reprimanded by Paris for his encouragement of Elizabeth in this matter. The draft of the treaty was destroyed in Douglas's presence, and he was recalled to Paris.

14. Prince Georg-Adam Starhemberg (1724-1807) was Austrian ambassador in Paris in 1754-1766. He was described by Horace Walpole as "German and French, vain, gallant and insignificant: would be very troublesome to everybody that knows him, if he did not know everybody." The surname is sometimes spelled Stahremberg.

15. The Czartoryskis were known as "The Family" and exercised considerable power in northern Poland and Lithuania. The leaders of "The Family" in the mid-eighteenth century were Michal, chancellor of Lithuania and August, military governor of Ruthenia.

16. Sir Charles Hanbury Williams, British ambassador to Russia in 1755-1757. He formerly served both in Berlin and at the Saxon court. He was a confidant of Grand Duchess Catherine, later Catherine II, and energetically opposed the reconciliation of Russia and France.

17. Stanislaw-August Poniatowski (1732-98). His mother Konstancja was a member of the Czartoryski family. Poniatowski traveled to St. Petersburg in 1755 as secretary to Hanbury Williams. There he became a lover of Grand Duchess Catherine. He was also Polish-Saxon plenipotentiary in St. Petersburg, 1755-1758. He later became king of Poland, 1764-1795.

18. August III (1696-1763). He was styled Friedrich August II as elector of Saxony, and August III, as king of Poland 1733-1763. He had received Russian support in his bid for the Polish throne in exchange for his recognition of Russia's claim to Courland.

19. Bekhteev here refers to the "new system." On the eve of the Seven Years War a diplomatic revolution took place whereby the "old system" of alliances between Britain, Austria and Russia against France and Prussia was replaced by the "new system" of Russia, France and Austria against Britain and Prussia. The new alliance between France and Austria was established by the Treaty of Versailles of 1756, to which Russia adhered in 1757.

20. A confederation was an armed league of citizens sworn to pursue a grievance until justice, from their point of view, had been obtained. It could be formed by the king or formed against him. In the eighteenth century confederations were almost as frequent as sessions of the Sejm. In effect a confederation was a legalized form of civil war and a recognized part of that constitutional chaos that characterized Polish domestic politics.

21. Samogitia (in Russian Zhmud) is situated in northwestern Lithuania.

22. Count Charles-François de Broglie (1719-1781) was French ambassador to Saxony-Poland and a highly placed member of the King's Secret. He was vehemently anti-Russian.

23. Jeanne, marquise de Pompadour (1721-1764), was the mistress of Louis XV. She was a friend of Belle-Isle and Bernis and an advocate of the alliance with Austria.

24. Charles Fouquet (1684-1761), comte de Belle-Isle, duc de Gisors and a marshal of France, was French minister of war, 1757-1760.

25. François-Joachim de Bernis (1715-1794), cardinal and French secretary for foreign affairs, 1757-1758.

26. As a result of the Treaty of Westphalia (1648) Sweden acquired Western Pomerania, the islands of Rügen, Usedom and Wollin, Wismar, the archbishopric of Bremen and the bishopric of Verden as fiefs of the German empire. It thus

obtained control of the Baltic and a footing in the North Sea as well as three deliberative voices in the Imperial Diet.

27. Count Mikhail Petrovich Bestuzhev-Riumin (1688-1760) was the elder brother of the chancellor. He was a very experienced diplomat, having served in Stockholm, London, Berlin, Warsaw and Vienna. He was Russian ambassador in Paris, 1755-1760.

28. Heinrich Gross (died 1765) was Russian minister in France, 1744-1749, to Prussia, 1748-1750 and ambassador to Saxony-Poland in 1752-1758. He was used by Brühl as a conduit for anti-Prussian propaganda. Gross later served in Holland (1761-1762) and Great Britain (1765).

29. Count Heinrich von Brühl (1700-1763), prime minister of Saxony, 1746-1763.

30. Gédéon de Benoît, formerly Prussian secretary in Dresden and since 1758 Prussian resident in Warsaw, was the conduit for information from Russian, Polish and Saxon sources, through a network of informers, to Frederick II.

31. Jan Sobieski (1624-1696), king of Poland from 1674, is famous for defeating the Turks under the walls of Vienna in 1683.

32. Anna Gavrilovna Yaguzhinskaia was implicated in a bogus conspiracy by Count Armand Lestocq and the French chargé d'affaires, the marquis de Bonacd'Allion, after which she was publicly whipped, had her tongue severely damaged and was banished to Siberia. See Volume 37 of this series.

33. Paul-François de Gallucio, marquis de l'Hôpital (1697-1776), French ambassador to Russia, 1757-1761. Horace Walpole notes that "the French were so determined to secure the Czarina that they chose about seven of their handsomest young men to accompany their ambassador." *Horace Walpole's Correspondence* (London, 1937-1983), Vol. 21, p. 53.

34. Field Marshal Count Stepan Fedorovich Apraksin (1702-1758) distinguished himself in the war with Turkey, 1737-1739. He was Russian ambassador to Persia in 1742. Apraksin was particularly close to Grand Duchess Catherine and Alexis Bestuzhev.

35. General Christoph von Manstein (1711-1757), a Baltic German who was born in St. Petersburg, at one time served in the Russian army, becoming adjutant to Field Marshal Münnich. In 1740 he played an active part in the downfall of Ernst Biron, duke of Courland. In 1745 he entered Prussian service. His *Memoirs of Russia*, a valuable source of Russian military history in the eighteenth century, were published in London in English translation in 1790.

36. James Keith (1696-1758), a Scottish soldier, served with distinction in the Russian army, but in 1747 joined Frederick II of Prussia as a field marshal. He was killed fighting the Austrians at the battle of Hochkirch in 1758. His manservant was from the Russian empire and known as Stefan the Kalmyk.

37. General Hans Karl von Winterfeldt (1707-1757) was described by Carlyle as "the most shining figure in the Prussian Army, except its chief." In the 1730s he helped train the Russian army on Prussian lines. In Russia he married Fräulein

von Maltzahn, step-daughter of Field Marshal Münnich. He was killed at the battle of Moys, 1757. Thomas Carlyle, *Frederick the Great* (London, 1858-1865), Bk. XVIII.

38. Ivan VI (1740-1764), grandson of Empress Anna's sister, was made emperor when only eight weeks old. He first was placed under the regency of Biron and then of his mother Anna Leopoldovna, princess of Brunswick-Bevern, holding the throne from October 1740 until December 1741, when he was deposed by Elizabeth. He was banished with his family to Kholmogory in the Northern Russia, 1744-1756, and then placed in solitary confinement in the Schlüsselberg fortress until his murder in 1764.

39. Anna Leopoldovna (1718-1746), princess of Brunswick-Bevern and mother of Ivan VI. After the coup by Elizabeth she was exiled with her husband and family to Kholmogory in Northern Russia, where she died in childbirth in 1746.

40. Count Ernst Johann Bühren (1690-1772), who later adopted the French name Biron, duke of Courland, the lover of Empress Anna and her chief of government. He was exiled by Elizabeth to Pelym in Siberia in 1741.

41. Field Marshal Count Burkhard von Münnich (1683-1767) was born in Oldenburg, later serving in both France and Saxony before entering the Russian army, where he had a distinguished career fighting the Turks. He was the political rival of Biron, whom he brought down in 1740, to become first minister. He was sent to Siberia by Elizabeth in 1741, but was released in 1762.

42. Field Marshal Count Alexis Razumovsky (1709-1771) was born a cossack shepherd, Alexis Razum. He became Elizabeth's lover in 1732 and may even have married her in 1742. Unwillingly he was made a field marshal observing, when the honor was conferred upon him, that "Your majesty may create me a field marshal if you like, but I defy you or anybody else to make a decent captain of me."

43. Prince Nikita Trubetskoy (1699-1767), procurator general and therefore chairman of the Senate.

44. Grand Duchess Catherine Alekseevna, later the empress Catherine II (1729-1796), was born a princess of Anhalt-Zerbst. She was brought to St. Petersburg by Empress Elizabeth and married Grand Duke Peter, heir to the throne, in 1745. Their son Paul was born in 1754.

45. Ivan Ivanovich Weymarn, chief of staff to Apraksin, has left a much less flattering account of this campaign than is to be found in Soloviev, "Über den ersten Feldzug des Russischen Kriegsheeres gegen die Preußen im Jahr 1757 (Concerning the First Campaign of the Russian Armed Forces against the Prussians in the Year 1757)," *Neue Nordische Miscellaneen* (New Nordic Miscellanies) (Riga, 1794).

46. Count Peter Alexandrovich Rumiantsev (1725-1796) came to prominence as a military commander during the Seven Years War. He distinguished himself at Gross-Jägersdorf in 1757, at Kunersdorf in 1759 and the siege and capture of Kolberg in 1761. He later had an extensive military career under Catherine II.

47. General Wilhelm Fermor (1702-1771) was descended from an English family which joined the Russian service. He had a career in the Russian army in Poland and Turkey. He was made commander-in-chief, 1757-1759, despite his closeness to and support of Apraksin, largely because he was willing to act directly on the instructions of the Conference. He was later a member of the Russian Senate, 1764-1768.

48. From March 1756 Elizabeth left much of the day-to-day development of government policy, in particular the management of foreign, military and naval affairs, to a small advisory council of ten members known as the *Konferents* or Conference of the Imperial Court, sometimes also referred to as the Council of State or the Cabinet. Count Esterhazy later claimed that he originally suggested the idea of the Conference to Elizabeth as a way of curbing the power of Chancellor Bestuzhev. Bestuzhev also claimed the institution as his own idea to "alleviate" the commander- in-chief in the field by providing him with a coordinated infrastructure of support. The Conference originally was established to deal with fundamental questions of state policy but soon extended its brief to more particular matters of administration of the war effort down to the purchase of caftans for Kalmyks. Though Bestuzhev himself chaired the first meetings, it was headed regularly by Count Peter Shuvalov, who was effectively in control of domestic affairs for most of Elizabeth's reign. Decisions of the Conference had to be accommodated by the Senate, the body responsible for the administration of the machinery of government.

49. Field Marshal Count Alexander Borisovich Buturlin (1694-1767) fought in many of the campaigns of Peter I. He became chief administrator of Ukraine under Elizabeth, a senator and later governor of Moscow. He was appointed a field marshal in 1756.

50. Prince Mikhail Mikhailovich Golitsyn (1681-1764) was trained in the navy and became an admiral of the fleet. He was president of the College of Justice in 1727-1732, Russian ambassador in Persia, 1745-1748 and commander-in-chief of the Russian navy, 1748-1761.

51. Peter Ivanovich Panin (1721-1789) had extensive experience in steppe warfare and in the war with Sweden, 1741-1743. He was promoted general in 1755. For his distinguished part in the battle of Gross-Jägersdorf he was awarded the Order of Alexander Nevsky. He was wounded at the battle of Zorndorf in 1758, when he was promoted lieutenant general. He took part in the seizure of Berlin in 1762, after which he became commander of the Russian forces in Prussia. In 1774-1775 he was put in charge of the suppression of the Pugachev uprising by Catherine II.

52. Andrei Timofeevich Bolotov (born 1738), as a company commander in the advance guard at Gross-Jägersdorf, recalled in his memoirs the complete chaos of the Russians, inexperienced at facing the Prussians, during the initial assault. Andrei Bolotov, *Zhizn'* (St. Petersburg, 1870-1873), Vol. 1, pp. 520-521.

53. Prince Nikolay Vasilievich Repnin (1734-1801) as a young officer from the highest aristocracy distinguished himself at the battles of Gross-Jägersdorf, Kunersdorf and the taking of Marienwerder. In 1759 he acted as the Russian liaison officer with the French army. He had the rank of colonel during the raid upon Berlin. In 1762 he was made major general. In the reign of Catherine II he had a distinguished career as a soldier and diplomat.

54. Franz Nadasdy (1708-1783), a brilliant Hungarian cavalry officer who later defeated Winterfeldt at Moys. He eventually attained the rank of field marshal in the Austrian army.

55. See Note 52, above.

56. Count Hermann Karl von Keyserling (1696-1765) was the Russian ambassador in Vienna throughout the Seven Years War, 1752-1761. He served formerly as ambassador to Poland 1733-1744 and to Prussia 1747-1748.

57. Prince Alexander Mikhailovich Golitsyn, (1723-1807), Russian ambassador in Great Britain and Hanover, 1755-1762. He later became vice chancellor, in charge of the College of Foreign Affairs, 1762-1775.

58. Robert D'Arcy, earl of Holderness (1718-1778), Secretary of State for the Northern Office in two successive British administrations, that of Pitt-Devonshire, 1754-1757 and of Pitt-Newcastle, 1757-March 1761, when he was replaced by the earl of Bute. He thus was responsible for relations with Russia throughout most of the Seven Years War. On his dismissal King George III is reported to have said that "he had two secretaries, one who would do nothing, and the other who could do nothing, and that he would have one who both could and would."

59. Baron Jakob Wolff was British minister-resident in St. Petersburg, 1750-1759, and thus subordinate to Williams.

60. On June 18, 1757 Frederick II was soundly beaten by the Austrians under Daun and could have been more severely so, had Daun's caution not prevented him following up his success in the field.

61. Robert Keith (died 1774) British ambassador to Vienna, 1748-1757 and to St. Petersburg, 1758-October 1762.

62. The Austrians were defeated by Frederick II on the eastern outskirts of Prague on May 6, 1757.

63. Britain conducted a careful diplomatic game with Russia, verbally supporting Frederick II, but not wishing in any way to jeopardize its very important trade with both Russia and Sweden.

64. Russia was correct in its assessment that Britain would not supply troops to Frederick II or send a fleet into the Baltic at this time. Pitt had ambitious plans for British operations in Canada, the Caribbean and on the coast of Africa. Neither ships nor troops would be available for Prussia. Britain did supply Frederick with a financial subsidy.

65. Count Nikita Ivanovich Panin (1718-1783), Russian ambassador in Denmark, 1747-1748 and in Sweden, 1748-1760. It was in Sweden that Panin developed an appreciation of the constitutional limitations on the royal prerogative

which he tried to introduce to Russia on at least two occasions after his return to St. Petersburg. He took an active part in the overthrow of Peter III in 1762.

66. Count Anders von Höpken (1712-1789). A founder of the Hats party in Sweden, he was one of the commissioners appointed to negotiate with Russia at the end of the Russo-Swedish War of 1741-1742. In order to muster popular support, the Hats took a decidedly anti-Russian stance as well as seeking specific limitations to the Swedish crown. In 1746 Höpken was created a senator and became chancery president of Sweden in 1752-1762.

67. Adolf Friedrich of Schleswig-Holstein-Gottorp (1710-1771) was bishop of Lübeck, 1727-1750. In 1743 he was elected heir to the throne of Sweden by the Hats so that they might obtain better conditions of peace from Empress Elizabeth, who showed a particular fondness for the House of Holstein, into whose family her sister Anna, with whom she was close, had married. As King Adolf Fredrik he reigned over Sweden from 1751 to 1771. He was a figurehead with real political power residing with the Riksdag. He made an abortive attempt to regain the political prerogative in 1755-1756 but the result was a diminution in royal authority. He was legal guardian of Grand Duke Peter.

68. The Lisbon earthquake that all but destroyed the city occurred on November 1, 1755. It caused Horace Walpole to write to a colleague that "there have been lately such earth-quakes and water-quakes, and rocks rent and other strange phenomena that one would think the world exceedingly out of repair." *Horace Walpole's Correspondence* (London, 1937-1983), Vol. 9, p. 179.

69. The Treaties of Westphalia, between France and the Holy Roman empire, and Sweden and the Protestant estates, were both signed in October 1648. They ended the Thirty Years War and settled the religious status of the German states. The Treaty of Versailles, between France and Austria (1756) renewed the Treaty of Westphalia. The Franco-Swedish treaty of March 1757 was also intended to guarantee the Treaty of Westphalia. As guarantors of the treaty France, Austria and Sweden assumed particular rights over any changes to the balance of power and territorial borders within the German empire.

70. Count Victor Friedrich Solms, Prussian ambassador in Stockholm until 1757, was later (1762) appointed Prussian minister in St. Petersburg, where he served for seventeen years. In Russia Solms was close to both Catherine II and Panin. It can be observed that Panin's attachment to the "old system" was always strong and was reactivated under Catherine, where his former association with Solms was useful during negotiations for the First Partition of Poland.

71. Queen Louisa Ulrika of Sweden (1720-1782) was the sister of Frederick the Great of Prussia and a woman of great intelligence and charm. When she first arrived in Sweden she associated herself and her husband Adolf Fredrik with the Hats, then led by Tessin. When her promotion of absolutist ideas came to the fore and she became leader of 'the court party,' Tessin broke with her. She was responsible for encouraging the cultural life of Sweden on the basis of French taste.

72. Count Carl Gustaf Tessin, chancery president of Sweden 1746-1752.

73. Louis de Cardevac, marquis d'Havrincourt (1707-1767). After a successful career in the army, rising to the rank of lieutenant general, he was appointed French ambassador to Sweden, 1749-1763.

74. At the battle of Rossbach in November 1757 the French were soundly defeated by the Prussians. As St. Germain put it, "The first cannon salvo decided our rout and our shame."

75. This note of Panin demonstrates his "old system" thinking. Austria and France opposed each other under that system of alliances, and Panin believed that France was not to be trusted, particularly if successful against Britain. These views were colored by Panin's experience of the French in Sweden, and lack the foresight to see that indeed it would be France which would be defeated by Britain, and that France and Austria would be pushed into an even closer alliance after the death of Louis XV. The final sentence is highly ambiguous in Russian, and the nations identified in square brackets are hypotheses rather than certain facts.

76. François-Michel Durand de Distroff (1714-1778), minister plenipotentiary of France at the Congress of Aix-la-Chapelle, chargé d'affaires in London, 1749-1751 and Holland, 1751-1752, was minister of the king of France in Warsaw in 1754-1762. In 1772 he was appointed minister plenipotentiary in St. Petersburg, where he actively opposed the partition of Poland.

77. The lands of the former Ostrogski family in Volhynia were disputed between the Czartoryskis, who had a slender claim, and their enemies led by Hetman Branicki.

78. Ivan Stepanovich Mazepa (1645-1709), hetman of the Ukraine. He negotiated with the kings of Poland and Sweden to throw off the sovereignty of Russia, joining Karl XII in the Swedish invasion of Ukraine. Both were defeated at Poltava in 1709, Mazepa fleeing to Turkey. See Volume 27 of this series.

79. Filipp Orlik (1672-1742) was elected hetman of the Ukraine in succession to Mazepa in 1710. He made a treaty with the Tatars that, with the aid of the Turks, he would recover a free cossack state astride the Dnieper, and signed "articles" recognizing Ukraine as a protectorate of Sweden in perpetuity. He lived in Sweden 1714-1720. Orlik gave his support to Stanislaw Leszczynski in his abortive attempt to regain the Polish throne in 1733-1734. Later he spent many years of exile in Turkey.

80. The Ukrainian cossacks established the Sech (camp), a fortified camp on a bend of the Dnieper river, at the end of the sixteenth century. It served as the center for the Ukrainian cossack community, the Zaporozhian Host, on both banks of the river north of the Crimean khanate.

81. The Tatars invaded the Crimea in 1239 and set up a khanate on the peninsula under Turkish suzerainty from 1475. The khanate lasted until 1774.

82. The Ingul river flowed from the estuary of the Southern Bug north to Elizavetgrad, a fortress only recently founded as administrative center of New Serbia in 1754. The Ingulets lay seventy-five kilometers further east, from the mouth of, but flowing west of the Dnieper through Krivoy Rog, a settlement of

the Zaporozhian Cossacks. To have extended the putative frontier of the Ukraine four hundred kilometers north and east would have brought it into the heartland of Southern Russia.

83. Concerning Elizavetgrad, see the preceding note.

84. Jan Klemens Branicki, grand hetman of the Crown from 1751, was a leading opponent of the Czartoryskis, organized the Court party and was an adherent of the French. He was humiliated during the Seven Years War, as guardian of the Polish frontiers, by his inability and unwillingness to stop Russia marching at will through Poland into the territory of Frederick II.

85. Count Jerzy August Mniszech (1715-1778) was married to Amelia Brühl, daughter of the Saxon prime minister and a kinsman of the Potockis. He was opposed to the Czartoryskis. He held the post of marshal of the court, 1742-1767.

86. Antoni Potocki, Palatine of Bielz, one of the leaders of the Potocki clan.

87. Prince Mikhail Nikitich Volkonsky (1713-1788) was the son of Princess Agrafena Petrovna Bestuzheva-Riumina, the sister of the chancellor. Following a military career, and with the support of his uncle, he became a diplomat serving in Poland in 1746-1749, where his task was to counteract the influence of France and Austria. In 1749-1756 he was adjutant-general to Field Marshal Lacy, governor-general of Lifland, before being appointed ambassador in Warsaw, 1757-1758. Again his task was to try to reconcile the disputing Polish factions and to counter the influence of France and Prussia. He was recalled to active service in 1758-1762, distinguishing himself at the battles of Palzig and Kunersdorf, as a result of which he was made a lieutenant general. He took an active role in the coup against Peter III, later becoming Catherine II's chief administrator in Moscow.

88. Princess Agrafena Petrovna Volkonskaia, née Bestuzheva-Riumina (died 1732), was a well-connected aristocrat who had been accused of conspiracy against the Supreme Privy Council to regulate the succession following the death of Peter the Great in 1725. She was exiled and died in obscurity.

89. According to Article IX of the Treaty of "Perpetual Peace" between Russia and Poland of 1686, the king of Poland was required not to oppress or to permit the oppression of any person professing the Greek Orthodox faith.

90. Catholics of the Slavo-Byzantine rite, originating in 1594 with the recognition by the Orthodox bishops in Poland of the authority of the Pope.

91. The Chigirin prefecture of Poland lay south of Kiev on the Dnieper river, and on the border with Russia.

92. Count Andreas Hadik von Futak (1710-1790), general of cavalry in the Austrian army. In 1757 Hadik briefly occupied Berlin, where he exacted an indemnity of three hundred thousand gulden.

93. Prince Yakov Petrovich Shakhovskoy (1705-1777). In 1740 he was appointed chief of police by Biron. He served under Elizabeth as chief procurator of the Synod, 1741-1753, before becoming chief of the commissary, and thus a minister of the Conference, throughout the period of the Seven Years War, 1753-1760. He was known for his honesty and opposition to corruption. In 1760-1761

he was procurator general of the Senate, where he blocked Shuvalov's attempt to devalue the copper coinage. Under Catherine II he served in the Senate. See Volume 42 of this series.

94. Ivan Ivanovich Shuvalov (1727-1797), a cousin of Alexander and Peter Shuvalov, was from 1749 a favorite of Elizabeth. He was a sensitive patron of the arts and science, assisting in the founding of Moscow University and the Academy of Fine Arts.

95. Count Peter Ivanovich Shuvalov (1711-1762). After the coup of 1741 which placed Elizabeth on the throne Shuvalov was made a gentleman-in-waiting to the empress. He married Elizabeth's confidante Mavra Yegorovna Shepeleva (1708-1759). He was appointed to the Senate in 1744, where he promoted economic reforms in order to raise revenue for the state by alternative, indirect taxation apart from the poll tax on the peasantry. He successfully advocated the abolition of internal customs duties in 1753, considerably opening up Russian domestic trade. He was made a member of the Conference in 1755. Peter Shuvalov was strongly pro-French and anti-Prussian.

96. General Field Marshal Count Alexander Ivanovich Shuvalov (1710-1771) headed the feared Secret Chancellery during Elizabeth's reign. He was retired by Catherine II.

97. The procurator general chaired meetings of the Senate.

98. The Secret Chancellery, sometimes called the Secret Office, was created by Peter the Great as a political police. It changed its title under Catherine II to the Secret Investigative Office, and was administered by the Senate.

99. As a consequence of the establishment of the Most Holy Governing Synod in 1721, whereby the government in effect took over the administration of the church and church lands, the income from ecclesiastical property was often called upon to support public works, particularly in the areas of public health and the relief of the poor.

100. Dmitry Vasilievich Ukhtomsky (1719-1775) was one of the first native Russians to be trained in Western architectural practice. He opened his own architectural school in 1747. His most notable project was rebuilding the Senate House in Moscow, begun in 1753.

101. The Gentry Bank, also known as the State Bank for the Nobility, was established in 1754 with the aim of extending long-term credits to landowners, often on the security of their serfs. Much of the money thus realized was used to maintain a luxurious life style rather than for productive investment.

102. The Holy Synod was established by Peter the Great in 1721 as a collegial body to supervise church affairs, following the abolition of the patriarchate. It was headed by a layman with the title of chief procurator of the Synod. See Note 99, above.

103. The residence of the Ukrainian hetman was established at Glukhov, near the Russian border, and with a resident Russian minister, after the destruction of Mazepa's headquarters at Baturin in 1708. It was the seat of the College of Little Russia, 1722-1782.

104. Ivan Ilich Skoropadsky (1646-1722), hetman of Left Bank Ukraine, 1708-1722. In 1708 Skoropadsky joined Peter I rather than Mazepa, and was rewarded with the title of hetman. He tried to protect the interests of Ukrainians, but his authority was constantly undermined by the Russian government, especially by the introduction of Russian and other non-Ukrainian Slavs as settlers in central Ukraine.

105. See p. 41.

106. New Serbia was the name given to that part of New Russia west of the Dnieper, settled by Serbian colonists in 1752-1753, and centered about the main town of Novomirgorod.

107. Ivan Ivanovich Nepliuev (1693-1773) served as Russian resident in Constantinople in 1721-1735 and headed the College of Foreign Affairs, 1735-1739. He was governor of Kiev in 1739-1741 and then administrator of Orenburg district, 1742-1758, responsible for the whole of the South Siberian and Ural steppes. He was particularly sensitive to the needs of the indigenous populations during a period of aggressive Russian expansion. He became a senator and Conference minister, 1758-1756, and supported Catherine II in the coup against her husband.

CHAPTER II

1. General George (Yury Yurievich) Browne (1698-1792) was an Irish Jacobite mercenary who took service with the Russian army in 1730. He fought successfully in a number of campaigns before being captured by the Turks. After adventures as a slave and a spy Browne eventually was restored to Russian service. In the Seven Years War he contributed to the allied victory at Kolin in 1757 and was largely responsible for the Russian success at the battle of Zorndorf. He was later promoted to the rank of field marshal and made a count of the Russian empire. His nephew Maximilian was commander of the Austrian forces in Bohemia and fell at the battle of Prague.

2. Alexander Vasilievich Suvorov (1729-1800) later became one of Russia's greatest military commanders. At this time he was serving as an orderly officer in Fermor's division with the rank of first major (1756-1758), not that of lance corporal. In 1760 he became member of the general staff with the rank of lieutenant colonel.

3. Prasse was very close to Bestuzhev. This is attested by the his reports published in Ernst Herrman, *Geschichte der europäischen Staaten, Geschichte des russischen Staats* (History of the European States. History of the Russian State) (Hamburg, 1853), Vol. 5, pp. 218 ff. (Soloviev's note).

4. Dmitry Vasilievich Volkov (1718?-1785) was a protégé of Bestuzhev in the College of Foreign Affairs. In 1756 he was appointed secretary of the Conference of the Imperial Court, in which capacity he also acted as secretary to the commission investigating his former patron. In the later years of Elizabeth's reign, because of a lack of initiative by the other ministers Volkov, according to Panin, was virtually prime minister. After Elizabeth's death he became chief adviser to

Peter III and head of the chancellery. He supported Peter during Catherine's coup. He was briefly arrested in 1762 but soon released and sent as deputy governor to Orenburg. The irony of this "promotion" would not have been lost on Volkov, as Adadurov had been "punished" by this appointment in the wake of Bestuzhev's fall.

5. Ivan Perfilevich Elagin (1725-1796). "Adjutant" Elagin was a scholar and friend of Catherine, Bestuzhev, Razumovsky and Poniatowski. In Catherine's reign he had a distinguished career as a translator from French and German.

6. Vasily Evdokimovich Adadurov (1709-1780) was appointed tutor in Russian to Catherine when she arrived in St. Petersburg as Princess Sophia of Anhalt-Zerbst. When Catherine came to the throne Adadurov was made curator of Moscow University and president of the College of Manufactures. He was made a member of the Senate in 1764.

7. *Was ich baue, das reissen die andern nieder.* Soloviev gives the original German, then translates it into Russian.

8. Grigory Nikolaevich Teplov (1717-1779). In 1743 Teplov was appointed tutor to Alexis Razumovsky's brother Kirill, in which capacity he toured Europe with his master in 1743-1746, spending time in Tübingen and Paris. He then acted as Razumovsky's assistant when his master was made Hetman of the Ukraine. He later was imprisoned by Peter III for "intemperate utterances." He took an active part in Catherine's coup, drafting her manifesto and oath of allegiance, as well as the abdication document of Peter III. He was not favored by Catherine on her accession, as he might have expected, because of the fact that Bestuzhev's examination of the notes of his trial pointed to Teplov as the traitor who informed on Catherine's correspondence with Razumovsky.

9. In using the plural Elizabeth refers not only to Catherine's officially recognized son Paul, born in 1754 (though his father may well have been Sergei Saltykov and not Grand Duke Peter), but also her daughter Anna, who was born in December 1757 and was the child of Poniatowski. Anna died in December 1758. Catherine later had three children, a boy and two girls, by Grigory Orlov.

10. The reference probably is to the first five volumes of the twenty volume *Histoire générale des Voyages* (General History of Travel), edited by Abbé Prévost d'Exiles and others and published in Paris in 1746-1770. This popular work went through a number of editions in the late eighteenth and early nineteenth centuries.

11. The initial volume of the French *Encyclopédie* was published in 1751. The first three volumes caused such controversy that only after censors had their way were later volumes published. The first seven volumes appeared by 1757. Catherine's serious reading habits, for her time, of radical and avant-garde material is emphasized by this detail.

12. In a note Soloviev states that it is his opinion that by *homme d'or* Catherine had in mind Hetman Kirill Razumovsky and by 'the motionless one' his brother Alexis, the empress's husband.

13. The reference here is to the defeat of the Franco-Imperial army at Rossbach on November 5, and of Austria at Leuthen, near Breslau on December 5, 1757.

14. General Prince Alexander Mikhailovich Golitsyn (1718-1783). He is not to be confused with a member of his family with the same name and patronymic serving as Russian ambassador in London.

15. Field Marshal Count Leopold von Daun (1705-1766) was the Austrian commander-in-chief during the Seven Years War. He was very experienced in European warfare, having fought in successive campaigns in 1734-1748. He was successful against the Prussians at Kolin in 1757, at Hochkirch in 1758 and at Maxen in 1759. He was heavily defeated and seriously wounded at Torgau in 1760.

16. These were the first cossacks Frederick II had ever seen and he inspected them with great attention after which he is reported as saying, "Just look at the kind of scum I have to fight!" J.W. Archenholz, *Geschichte des Siebenjähren Krieges in Deutschland* (History of the Seven Years War in Germany) 2 vols. (Berlin, 1840), Vol. 1, p. 164.

17. General Friedrich Wilhelm von Seydlitz-Kurzbach (1721-1773) was one of the greatest Prussian cavalry officers. He revolutionized battle strategy by bringing the heavy cavalry into the advance guard rather than maintaining them in the rear. He was placed in charge of the cavalry at the battle of Rossbach, routing the Austrians. From a Prussian perspective he was responsible for the Prussian victory at Zorndorf. He was later severely wounded at the battle of Kunersdorf.

18. J.G. Tielke's *An Account of some of the most Remarkable Transactions of the War between the Prussians, Austrians and Russians from 1756 to 1763*, 2 vols. (London, 1788), confirms most of the details reported by Soloviev. Apart from Russian sources, Soloviev followed Arnold Schaefer's *Geschichte des siebenjährigen Krieges* (History of the Seven Years War) (Berlin, 1867).

19. Rambaud, commenting on this rescript, states that "nothing gives a clearer indication of the length of the road which Elizabeth's Russia still had to travel before it deserved the title of 'European.' While the Russian armies were already capable of taking on the army of Frederick in battle, Elizabeth's pen-pushers (and indeed the empress herself) remained on the intellectual and literary level of the logothetes of Byzantium." A. Rambaud, *Russes et Prussiens. Guerre de Sept Ans* (Russians and Prussians. The Seven Years War) (Paris, 1895), p. 198.

20. This letter apparently was written by an English Captain Lambert, employed as a Prussian spy. It is to be found in the sixth volume of the *Archive* of Prince Vorontsov, published in forty volumes in Moscow, 1870-1895.

21. Literally "a soldier never has more than two *doli*." A "dolia" was the equivalent to 44 milligrams, and so two would weigh very little indeed.

22. Fedor Ivanovich Krasnoshchekov (died 1764), was campaign ataman of the cossack regiments during the Seven Years War. He was the son of a famous

leader of the Don Cossacks. Krasnoshchekov was made a brigadier in the Russian army and, before the end of the war, rose to the rank of major general. Popular songs were written about his valor and horsemanship. The empress gave him a gold medal encrusted with diamonds, and he is shown wearing this medal in a portrait by Alexis Antropov, dated 1761, in the collection of the Russian Museum, St. Petersburg. This portrait was commissioned by Hetman Razumovsky.

23. Palmenbach's expedition was a singular failure. He did not receive effective naval support, the squadron remaining so far out to sea that its fire was ineffective. The land forces had no map of the fortress, no proper siege artillery and were so short of ammunition that they had to wait for the Prussians to fire in order to pick up and reuse their cannon balls. As Tielke, a Saxon officer seconded to the Russian army reported "thus ended a siege, which may justly be called too serious for a joke and too trifling for earnest." Tielke, Vol. II, p. 361.

24. The "major losses" refers to Frederick's defeat of the Franco-German forces at the battle of Rossbach in November 1757 and the taking of Louisburg in North America by the British from the French in 1758.

25. This is probably a reference to the Treaty of Westphalia of 1648 incorporating the various historical legal codes holding the German empire together including the election of the emperor, the landholdings of the kings, princes and estates as well as the religious settlements within the more than three hundred divisions of the empire.

26. Étienne, duc de Choiseul (1719-1785), was a firm advocate of the French alliance with Austria. He advanced in political circles, after a military career, through Madame Pompadour, who obtained for him his first diplomatic post as ambassador to the Vatican, 1753-1757. He then served in Vienna, but was recalled to Paris to become minister of foreign affairs in December 1758. He held this office until October 1761. Choiseul was a foreign minister of vision and drive, and has been compared with his principal rival, William Pitt. French assistance to Austria was rapidly diminished as Choiseul recognized that Britain, not Prussia, was France's principal enemy.

27. Thomas Pelham Holles, duke of Newcastle (1693-1768), was British prime minister, 1754-1756 and 1757-1762. In his second ministry Newcastle was nominal chief executive on the understanding that real power resided in William Pitt the Elder. In 1760 Newcastle favored a separate peace with France in order to cut the cost of the war in Europe and to secure advantages gained in America, the West Indies and India.

28. There was a belief, certainly in France, that the Convention of Westminster was a Protestant league, uniting as it did Prussia, Hanover, Great Britain, Hesse and Brunswick. Such archaic ideas were never part of Frederick II's thinking. Indeed he wrote to d'Agens that "no one, not even women, any longer could be roused to fanatical enthusiasm on behalf of Calvin or Luther."

29. See Chapter I, Note 20.

30. In January 1717 Peter the Great forced the Polish Sejm, known as "the Silent Sejm," to give the Polish crown back to the elector Frederick Augustus of

Saxony. In exchange the elector, known in Poland as King Augustus II, guaranteed never again to use Saxon troops on Polish soil. Russia in acting as the protector of Polish territorial integrity thus assumed a dominating role in Polish affairs and *de facto* elector of the king of Poland.

31. Empress Elizabeth's sister Anna married the duke of Holstein and their son, Grand Duke Peter, inherited the duchy of Holstein on the death of his father in 1739. His wife, Grand Duchess Catherine, was the daughter of Peter's father's cousin. Prince Georg Ludwig was the brother of Catherine's mother and therefore, strictly speaking Catherine's uncle rather than Peter's. He was also the brother of Adolf Fredrik, the king of Sweden. This move was one further example of the constant intrigues by the Holstein-Gottorp family, still smarting from the loss of Schleswig by Peter's father to the Danes by the Treaty of Frederiksborg in 1720, to restore and consolidate their dynastic interests in the Baltic region.

32. The duchy of Courland was part of the Lithuanian-Polish republic but had been, in fact, within the domain of Russian control since the marriage in 1710 of Frederick William, duke of Courland, to the Russian Grand Duchess Anna Ivanovna, later to become empress of Russia. Anna had made her husband, Ernst Bühren (Biron), duke of Courland. Though Biron was exiled by Elizabeth in 1741 he was still titular duke of Courland.

33. Between sessions of the Sejm the Senate appointed sixteen "resident" senators, the senatus-consilium, who advised the king on the day-to-day business of government.

34. The Wettin family, the electors of Saxony and kings of Poland, were "political" Catholics, the elector Frederick Augustus having "converted" to Catholicism in order to become king of Poland.

35. Sir James Porter (1710-1786) was British ambassador to Turkey, 1746-1762.

36. Mustafa III (1717-1774) became sultan in 1757.

37. Raghib Pasha (died 1763), grand vizier under Mustafa III. He was successful in restoring Turkey's finances and putting the army into fighting order. He pursued a peaceful foreign policy, keeping Turkey out of all European wars. He signed a treaty of friendship with Frederick II in 1761.

38. Count Gavriil Ivanovich Golovkin (1660-1730) was in charge of Russian foreign affairs under Peter the Great from 1706. He was state chancellor from 1709 and from 1718 president of the College of Foreign Affairs.

39. The Economic Chancellery, also known as the College for Administering the Economy of the Synod, was established in 1726. Its function was to oversee the administration of the estates owned by the Holy Synod, the monasteries and bishops of the Orthodox church in the Russian empire and utilization of their revenues.

40. See pp. 55-56.

41. See Chapter 1, Note 101.

42. Giovanni Battista Locatelli (born 1713, died some time after 1790), Italian impresario and librettist. He founded his own opera company and ran the season

at the Prague city theater, 1744-1757. He moved that year to St. Petersburg, where he was made head of Elizabeth's operatic enterprises, introducing *opere buffe* to Russia, including an indifferent Moscow. His appointment ceased with Elizabeth's death, after which he ran a place of entertainment in St. Petersburg called *Krasnyi kabak* (Red Tavern).

43. The Merchants' Bank was established within the College of Commerce in 1754. It granted credits to enterprises engaged in foreign trade as well as to industry. It was abolished later because of the abuse of its benefits by a few.

44. Perhaps Elizabeth had in mind the Hôtel des Invalides in Paris, which was built by Louis XIV at the end of the seventeenth century to house seven thousand aged and invalid veterans.

45. Luke 7:5.

46. The "black lands" were originally that common land occupied by free peasants who paid tribute directly to a prince. From the sixteenth century onwards tracts of "black lands" were given to private land owners and the former free peasants became serfs. "Black lands" survived longest in the north of Russia where land was less coveted.

47. See p. 57.

48. In the Russian provinces civilian affairs were run by the governor and local militias and the police were in the hands of the voevoda or military governor. There were ancillary military governors in smaller towns and outer districts. The military governors were notoriously corrupt, and were often associated with the very criminals they were purportedly appointed to combat.

49. The Commission for the Composition of the Code of Laws was founded in 1754 on a suggestion by Count Peter Shuvalov due to the chaotic nature of current legal practice. The commission was told that the Code of Laws was "to be clearly worded and consist of intelligible laws suited to present-day conditions while taking into account past customs and conventions" as the empress Elizabeth claimed that "even angels would not be able to make sense of" the present legal code. She was horrified by the barbaric punishments incorporated into the first two chapters, "written not with ink but with blood." Though the commission continued its work the empress was little inclined to act on its suggestions. The commission did tackle the vexed question of serfdom and laid foundations for further developments in this area in the reign of Catherine II.

50. Free homesteaders, *odnodvortsy*, belonged to a class of citizen midway between the nobility and the peasantry. They were largely descended from armed servitors settled on the borders of Muscovy in the mid-seventeenth century. These servitors were recruited originally from the minor, landless nobility and other middle-ranking military classes. They had the right to own land and, until 1743, even serfs. They were taxed with the peasantry but had the service obligations of the nobility.

51. There were a series of Bashkir uprisings in 1755 against Russian colonial oppression during which Russia was able play the interests of the Bashkir aristocracy against nationalist and religious aspirations of other inhabitants of the Kazakh steppe.

CHAPTER III

1. Kostiurin was a brother-in-law of Alexander Shuvalov. His detailed report to Conference on the state of the Russian army in the spring of 1759 is contained in Vol. 7 of the *Archive* of Prince Vorontsov.

2. Lieutenant General Nikolay A. Korff, governor of Königsberg and hence, in effect, governor of [East] Prussia, 1758-1761. He conducted a policy of considerable restraint in East Prussia to avoid any accusation of Russian "barbarism."

3. General Count Peter Semenovich Saltykov (1698-1772) was of an ancient Moscow aristocratic family. He was sent abroad by Peter the Great to learn navigation but after twelve years manifestly failed to complete his studies. He was a cousin of Empress Anna and as such the family was advanced at court. In 1734 he led Russian troops in the War of Polish Succession with the rank of major general. He rose to the rank of lieutenant general in 1741 and was made a senator. He was on friendly terms with Grand Duchess Catherine from 1744. In the 1750s he served with the Ukrainian militia before his appointment as commander-in-chief.

4. Empress Anna's mother was Praskovia Saltykova, the grandmother of Anna Leopoldovna.

5. Lieutenant General Karl Heinrich Wedell (1712-1782) replaced Dohna as Prussian commander against the Russians in July 1759. He was given "the powers of a Roman dictator," as Frederick II expressed it in his instructions. In his private order to Wedell, dated July 20, 1759, Frederick told him to "go in upon Saltykov; attack him straightway; let us have done with this wriggling and haggling."

6. Ernst Gideon, Baron von Loudon (1717-1790) came from a family of Scottish origin that settled in Livonia before 1400. He was in Russian service in 1732-1741. Failing to gain a post with Frederick the Great, he then entered Austrian service. In 1757 he gained the rank of major general of cavalry and became commander-in- chief of the war zone in 1760.

7. Thémicoud, also known as Démicoud, Demiku and Demikof, was a Swiss mercenary in the Russian army who was given command of a "flying corps" of cossacks. He distinguished himself at the battle of Zorndorf the previous year.

8. General Count Gottlob Kurt Heinrich Todtleben was from a family of Thuringian petty nobility. He served with the Saxon, Prussian and Dutch forces before enlisting with the Russian army prior to the Seven Years War. He was promoted to the rank of major general on the strength of the part he played at the siege of Kolberg in 1758. Apraksin and Fermor put him in charge of organizing a corps of light cavalry, which was used in an auxiliary capacity in 1759-1761.

9. The "contemporary" referred to by Soloviev was Bolotov, *Zapiski*, pp. 906-907. See Chapter I, Note 52.

10. Count Karl Wilhelm Finck von Finckenstein (1714-1800), Frederick II's chief minister.

11. Probably Lübben, southwest of Lieberose.

12. William Pitt the Elder, later Earl of Chatham (1708-1778), was the effective head of government under Newcastle from 1757, with particular responsibility

to direct the British war effort around the world. Though Pitt was not interested in Europe, he wanted the French to be pinned down by Prussia and its German allies until such time as he had defeated France in the Americas. The German war, however, was unpopular with his colleagues and in the country. Pitt's position was further weakened on this issue when the chief ally for his German policy, King George II, died in October 1760.

13. The English successes included the blockade of French ports in 1758 as well as the defeat of the French fleet off Quiberon in November 1759. In North America their success was marked by the fall of Quebec in September 1759.

14. See Chapter I, Note 69.

15. The Nobles Estate, one of the four that made up the Swedish Riksdag, was divided between the adherents of the Caps and the Hats. The Caps, originally Night-Caps, were so nicknamed because of their conservative, cautious and peace-seeking policies, following the line taken by the Swedish elder statesman Count Arvid Horn. The Caps actively sought an accommodation with the Russian government. The Hats were the partisans of a more self-assertive, chauvinist political sentiment and were led by Count Carl Gustav Tessin. The Hats were in the pay of the French and were opposed to any Russian influence in Swedish affairs.

16. David Murray, Viscount Stormont (1727-1796) was a senior British diplomat, serving as envoy in Saxony, 1756-1759, Warsaw, 1760-1761, Vienna, 1763-1772 and Paris, 1772-1778. He later held a number of offices in the British government.

17. The Russian word *raznochintsy* denotes people of indeterminate class below the nobility, the offspring of petty officials, priests and freed and educated peasants.

18. Daniel Tuptalo, known as Dmitry Rostovsky (1651-1709), was a Russian divine who completed a collection of lives of the saints (1684-1705). He founded a school for the children of the clergy in Rostov. He was canonized in the mid-eighteenth century.

19. Under Peter the Great's reform of local government in 1719 the Russian empire was divided into eleven *gubernii* (major provinces), which in turn were divided into fifty *provintsii* (provincial districts).

20. See pp. 115-116, above.

CHAPTER IV

1. In January 1760 General Alexander Glebov was given command of the artillery in the field army and one of the heroes of Gross-Jägersdorf, Major Tiuchev, was put in charge of the regimental artillery. Glebov's reforms are summarized by Christopher Duffy, *Russia's Military Way to the West* (London, 1981), pp. 121-122.

2. Frederick II, unlike some of his commanders, was very unwilling to give up his prejudices concerning the merit of the Russian army. As Warnery reports, "Never had troops sold their lives as dearly as the Russians on that day. In a transport of joy Frederick asked Seydlitz the following day, 'When you come down

to it, don't you think the Russians are scum?' 'Sire,' replied the general, 'I am not sure whether you can apply this description to infantry like the Russians who fought so well and managed to repulse our own troops'" General V. Warnery, *Campagnes de Frédéric II Roi de Prusse, de 1756 `a 1762* (Campaigns of Frederick II, King of Prussia, from 1756 to 1762) (Amsterdam, 1788), p. 275.

3. General Baron Henri-Auguste de la Motte Fouqué (1698-1774). In 1760 Fouqué was governor of Glatz and in command of the so-called "drifting corps." Fouqué's task was to maintain communication between the Prussian armies in Saxony and Silesia. To do so the more effectively, Frederick asked Fouqué to take the cross-roads settlement of Landeshut. On June 23 (New Style) Fouqué was attacked by Loudon and the Prussians were defeated. Fouqué himself was captured, together with a complete edition of the secret *Instructions* Frederick drew up for his generals.

4. Soloviev adds the following note. "Buturlin's closeness to the empress is evident from his letters to her. For example, (1) 'Sovereign Mother. I forgot to write how well things are with us here. The wife of a colonel is very forward, but her husband is old. She said, "I am really better than anyone else," but I told her that she was lying! There are those who are forty times better than you... Who do you mean? What a fool she is! Should I tell her? She would die of grief to find out that you, my dear, are better than she is. I remain faithful to the grave, for ever your true friend and slave.' (2) 'Sovereign. My soul and heart and mind and desire reside in God and in you for ever until death and therefore A. Buturlin both accepts service with joy and faithfulness and with earnest desire and also calls himself your uttermost slave.'"

5. The plan for a raid on Berlin, as well as other ideas that urged a northern, a Pomeranian, rather than a southern strategy, was first suggested by marquis de Montalembert, the French representative with the Russian army, 1759-1760. A swift raid, Montalembert calculated, would force Frederick to rush to the defense of the city and in this way upset his plans in Silesia. In addition to the Russians involved, the Austrians also sent eighteen thousand troops under Lieutenant General Lacy.

6. Count Franz Moritz Lacy (1725-1801) was born in St. Petersburg, the son of an Irish soldier who served Russia with distinction. Count Lacy served with the Austrian army throughout the Seven Years War and was made an Austrian field marshal in 1766.

7. Chevalier Charles d'Éon de Beaumont (1728-1810) was a functionary of the French ministry of foreign affairs. He entered service in the King's Secret in 1756 when he was sent on his first mission to Russia and acted as secretary to Mackenzie Douglas. He was appointed secretary to the ambassador in 1757. There were rumors, which received wide circulation at the time but have since been discounted, that d'Éon went to Russia before, in the guise of a woman, Lia d'Éon, a favorite reader of Empress Elizabeth. For details see Gary Kates, *Monsieur d'Eon is a Woman. A Tale of Political Intrigue and Sexual Masquerade* (New York, 1995).

8. Baron Louis de Breteuil (1730-1807) was a career diplomat and served in Cologne before being appointed to St. Petersburg. He was later to be a close associate of Marie Antoinette and the last chief minister of Louis XVI before the fall of the Bastille.

9. Of course the genuine Ivan VI was related to the Brunswick ruling house, and so this was a natural destination for the pretender.

10. At Bergen, near Frankfurt, the French engaged the troops of Prince Ferdinand of Brunswick. Though the French later claimed victory the battle seems to have been unsatisfactory for both sides.

11. Count Bartolomeo Francisco Rastrelli (1700-1771) was the son of an Italian sculptor who came to work in Russia in 1716. He studied in Paris, Germany and Italy before returning to Russia to become the chief architect of Empress Elizabeth, creating a style of florid decoration now known as Elizabethan Rococo. He worked on the Winter Palace between 1754 and 1762.

12. Count Roman Larionovich Vorontsov (1707-1783) played a significant role in the coup of 1741. He held various offices in the Russian government most notably heading a commission of the Senate to reform the law code in 1761. He was corrupt and known as "Big Purse" because of his reputation for accepting bribes.

13. Alexander Ivanovich Glebov (1717-1790) was married to Elizabeth's niece Maria. He held a number of senior government posts under Elizabeth and later under Catherine II. He was chief procurator of the Senate, 1756-1760. He was closely associated with Peter and Alexander Shuvalov and, like them, was unscrupulous and corrupt, though an able administrator. He was bitterly opposed by Shakhovskoy.

14. A curious memorial has come down to us from the period being described reminiscent of the Lay of Daniel the Exile [an early thirteenth-century poem]. This complaint was addressed to the empress Elizabeth by an exiled Major Kolachev. "In the Senate they torment and bring good people to ruin in every possible way, the Senators assist the robbers. It cannot be said that devastation and murder of innocent people or the arbitrary and illegal powers of the senators stand on ceremony in this state, which would not be possible in a republic! Prince Nikita Trubetskoy is no custodian, but a man who tears our laws to pieces. It is not enough to describe him as a general-robber. He, a field marshal, is a robber, a pillar among robbers in the state. He should live not staked to the ground, nor attached to a stone pole but it would be merciful [to send him] to the nearest Moscow merchant's estate on Kamchatka. We, the faithful slaves of your majesty, have been exiled to that very estate through their robber's treachery. Had such thievery taken place in the time of your majesty's father they would surely have been executed, and even if it had not come to this he would have ordered them subjected to brutal interrogation. Apparently Bestuzhev's wife alone has been found guilty of robbery. That is impossible. As if her husband did not know about it! Even if he did not know, the word of the Lord must be kept—those whom God hath brought together let no man put asunder, so that he must go into

exile as well as her. It was murder and bloodshed of Volynsky and not execution. To call it an execution is a sin. We welcomed the Moscow merchant's estate of Kamchatka for our statements of the truth about their treachery but they must have a huge, first-class salary of landed gentry estates with additional bonuses as recompense...." (Soloviev's note)

CHAPTER V

1. Dresden was forced to surrender to the Austrians on September 4, 1759 (New Style).

2. In November the Prussian lieutenant general Friedrich von Finck was instructed to hold the plateau of Maxen. He was attacked by the Austrians on November 20, 1759 and forced to surrender his thirteen thousand men.

3. For the treaty of alliance in 1758 between Russia and Austria, see pp. 1-2

4. By the Treaty of Aachen (Aix-la-Chapelle) of 1748 Silesia and Glatz were guaranteed to Frederick II.

5. John Stuart, earl of Bute (1713-1792), was a favorite of the prince of Wales, later George III, and on his accession in 1760 became a privy councillor. George III was anxious to conclude peace with France, and in March 1761 Bute succeeded Lord Holderness as secretary of state for the Northern Department. His policy was to conclude peace with France, to sever England from its connections with German politics and to make the king supreme over parliament. He was very unpopular, and made more so when he secured Pitt's resignation in October 1761. In November 1761 Bute was made prime minister following the collapse of the Newcastle ministry. For an evaluation of peace prospects at this time and the relations between Pitt and Bute over this issue see A. von Ruville, *William Pitt, Earl of Chatham* (London, 1907), Vol. 2, pp. 362-367.

6. Franz-Eugen, prince of Savoy-Carignan (1663-1736), was one of the most famous generals of the eighteenth century. He fought against the Turks, 1683-1688, 1697, 1715-1718, and against France in the War of the Grand Alliance, 1689-1697 and the War of the Spanish Succession, 1701-1714. He was the teacher of Frederick the Great.

7. John Churchill, duke of Marlborough (1650-1722), was a successful general against Louis XIV during the War of the Spanish Succession, winning notable victories at Blenheim in 1704, Ramillies in 1706 and Oudenaarde in 1708.

8. General Hans Joachim von Zieten (1699-1786), the "hussar king." He came to prominence after distinguished service in the Second Silesian War (1744-1745). He also had success at the Prussian victory at Prague in 1757 but was knocked unconscious by canister shot at the Prussian defeat at Kolin in the same year. He played a very active part in the latter part of the Seven Years War. He became a favorite companion of Frederick II in their old age.

9. In the late summer of 1757 Frederick sent General the Duke of Brunswick-Bevern into Silesia to keep watch on the Austrians in the East. Bevern, however, got himself into a poor tactical position before Breslau, where he was ignominiously

defeated and then captured by the Austrians. Frederick II was furious and on Bevern's release he was made commander of the garrison at Stettin. There he recovered favor by his purposeful activities in Pomerania.

10. The French held out in Pondicherry, the last of their Indian territories, until January 1761.

11. The Russians already were warned of Todtleben's possible duplicity by the Russian resident in Danzig on intelligence received from Hamburg. Todtleben's leniency in Berlin could be attributed to his desire to lessen the damage done to the city because of his attachment to Frederick II. Todtleben was ordered to exact the greatest financial indemnity possible from the city, yet he reduced the initial demand from four million thalers to one-and-a-half million. He spared the gold and silver factories and the *Splitgerber und Daum* foundry because they were private and not public property, yet *Splitgerber und Daum* supplied all the guns for the Prussian armed forces. He did not confiscate all weapons in the city, collecting only a few hundred out-of-date pieces which were thrown into the Spree, from which subsequently they were recovered. It can also be argued from a later and lengthy rescript from Empress Elizabeth, that this leniency towards the city of Berlin was Russian government policy.

12. Johann Ernst Gotzkowsky was described by Boswell in 1764 as "a great banker... gallant German, stupid, comely, cordial." He was a major supplier of the Prussian army and made a fortune from the war. Through later misguided business ventures, however, he died poor. It was through the good offices of Todtleben and Gotzkowsky that Berlin was comparatively spared in 1760. Frederick Pottle (ed.), *Boswell on the Grand Tour. Germany and Switzerland, 1764* (London, 1953), pp. 75-76.

13. A Silesian merchant also known as Isaac Sabatky.

14. Todtleben was court-martialled and sentenced to death in 1763. This verdict was commuted to exile, and six years later Todtleben returned to Russian service.

15. Alexander Romanovich Vorontsov (1741-1805) was a very well-educated member of the powerful Vorontsov family and nephew of the Russian chancellor. In 1759 he was sent to military school in Strasbourg but spent much of his time travelling in Europe, meeting Voltaire, Diderot and Pitt. He was sent to Vienna in 1761 and later the same year appointed Russian minister to Holland. In 1762 he was sent to London as minister plenipotentiary.

16. Count Florimond-Claude-Charles Mercy d'Argenteau (1727-1794) was an Austrian diplomat accredited to Turin before being moved to St. Petersburg in 1761. In 1766 he was transferred to Paris, where he played a crucial role in cementing the alliance between Austria and France by arranging the marriage of Maria Theresa's daughter Marie Antoinette to the dauphin, later Louis XVI.

17. Charles Wyndham, earl of Egremont, 1710-1763, was appointed British representative at Augsburg in the spring of 1761. Later in the year he succeeded Pitt as secretary of state for the Northern Department.

18. In 1760-1761 Choiseul played upon Spanish suspicions of Britain and their offended pride in order to bring them into the French war against Britain. He secured Spanish backing by the Bourbon family pact in 1761. Pitt, realizing that war with Spain was inevitable, was anxious to make a preemptive strike but was not backed by his more cautious colleague and rivals, and resigned. War was declared nevertheless at the end of 1761, to the great advantage of Britain.

19. Count Claes Ekeblad was the Hats' chancery president, 1761-1765. He persuaded the Swedes of the value of potatoes as a food source following experiments on his estates. His wife Eva pioneered the use of potatoes to make *brännvin* (schnapps), for which discovery she was elected to the Swedish Royal Academy of Sciences.

20. Cajetan Soltyk, who died in 1788, was bishop of Kiev, 1749-1759, and then became bishop of Cracow, 1759-1788. He was a supporter of Mniszech and the court party. In October 1767 he was to be one of the first victims of Russian aggression under Prince Repnin in the lead-up to the First Partition when, because of his protests at Polish coercion, he was imprisoned and later abducted to Russia.

21. Prince Franz August Xaver was later "Administrator" of Saxony during the minority of his nephew.

22. Frederick was king of Prussia, a territory lying outside the Holy Roman empire, but he also held hereditary land within the empire, notably the margravate of Brandenburg. When he lost Prussia to the Russians he was, in effect, a king without a kingdom. Prussia, Brandenburg and the other Hohenzollern lands, however, were already referred to collectively as "Prussia."

23. Daun is described in Russian as "cunctator," a reference to Fabius Maximus Cunctator, a Roman general in the war against Hannibal renowned for the cautious delay of his reaction to events.

24. Soloviev probably has in mind the Prussian spy Captain Lambert. See *Arkhiv Kniazia Vorontsova* (1870-95).

25. Soloviev notes here an example of Biron's characteristic use of this disparaging phrase when the young Prince Shakhovskoy defended his uncle against Münnich's charges, "You, Russians, often dare to defend yourselves brazenly for your worst faults."

26. Nikita Demidov (1724-1789) received the smallest inheritance of the three sons of the magnate Akinfy Demidov, but continued to build factories and to enlarge the business. He was a great traveller and patron of the arts and sciences.

27. See pp. 234-235, above.

INDEX

Aachen, 252
Abrosimov, Anisim, merchant, 116
Academy of Sciences, 290
Adadurov, Vasily Evdokimovich, 69, 74, 77, 308
Admiralty College, 201, 224
Adolf Fredrik, king of Sweden, 1, 34-36, 39, 72, 211, 274-275, 303, 311
Africa, xiv, 302
Akhtuba, river, 123
Akhtyrka, 170
Albedil, Major General, 171
Aleksin district, 57
Aleshki, 41
Alle, river, 25-27
Allenburg, 23, 25, 66
Aloe, secretary to Count Malachowski, 110-111
America, xiv, 104, 157, 161, 241-242, 251, 270, 310, 314
Androniev monastery, 234
Anna, empress of Russia, xxi, 14, 81, 132, 285-286, 299, 311, 313
Anna Leopoldovna, princess of Brunswick-Bevern, 13, 132, 300, 313
Anne of Holstein, xvii, 303, 311
Apraksin, Captain Count Peter, 20, 170
Apraksin, Field Marshal Count Stepan Fedorovich, xiv, 12-15, 17-25, 27-28, 38, 43, 46, 48-49, 63-67, 71-72, 75-79, 81-82, 95, 98-99, 106, 280, 299-301
Apsheron regiment, 140
Archangel, 174
Archangel City monastery, 232
Armfeld, Major Baron, 102
Arnswalde, 198
Artillery Military School, 220
Arzamas district, 230
Asch, Lieutenant Colonel, 264, 266
Asia, 251

Assessors, 392
Astrakhan and province, 113, 123, 291
Auer, 135
Augsburg, 248, 254, 268, 318
Augustus II, king of Poland, 109, 310-311
Augustus III, king of Poland and elector of Saxony, see also Saxony, xvi, 1, 5, 56, 59-60, 73, 110-112, 156, 165-166, 200, 204, 209, 240, 242, 276, 296, 298
Austria, xii-xiv, xviii-xix, 1-4, 7-9, 12, 14, 16, 19, 28-31, 40, 46, 50, 67, 82-85, 87, 103-106, 108, 113, 135-163, 179-182, 184-187, 189-192, 194, 196, 199-200, 203-207, 209-210, 239-255, 257, 259-263, 266-268, 279-280, 288, 296-298, 302-305, 307, 309-310, 313, 315, 317-318; Orthodox Christians in Serbia and Croatia, 28-30
Avziano-Petrovsk, 61, 295
Azov, 217
Azov regiment, 140

Baden-Baden regiment, 140
Bakhchisaray, 41
Bakhteev, butler to Empress Elizabeth, 54
Balkans, xiv, 38, 149-151
Baltic provinces, xii-xiii, xvii, 229, 235, 291-292, 296
Baltic Sea, 32-33, 50, 107, 302
Banking system, Russian, see also Gentry Bank, Merchants' Bank, xxiv, 75, 117-118, 286
Baruch, Jewish contractor, see also Boruch, 101, 130
Bashkirs, 60-61, 127, 312
Bekhteev, Fedor Dmitrievich, 3-6, 11, 63, 297-298
Belev, 122, 231
Belgorod province, 298

THE EDITOR AND TRANSLATOR

Peter Stupples was born in Britain, and is a graduate from the University of Leeds, where he also completed graduate studies. He has lived in New Zealand since 1973. He was chairman of the Russian and Soviet Studies Department of the University of Otago from 1973 to 1989, since then he has been Director of Studies, Art History and Theory at the same university. He has published extensively on the history of Russian art, particularly that of the avant-garde 1870-1930, including *Pavel Kuznetsov. His Life and Art* (Cambridge, 1989). He is currently completing a book of essays on the painter Kazimir Malevich, as well as another on the social foundations of art. He was awarded the Pushkin Medal by the International Association of Teachers of Russian Language and Literature in 1988. Stupples has been a visiting professor in Slavonic Studies and Art History at the University of Texas (1985) and a visiting scholar at the Humanities Research Centre at the Australian National University, Canberra (1994).

FROM ACADEMIC INTERNATIONAL PRESS*

THE RUSSIAN SERIES Volumes in Print

2 **The Nicky-Sunny Letters, Correspondence of Nicholas and Alexandra, 1914-1917**

7 Robert J. Kerner **Bohemia in the Eighteenth Century**

14 A. Leroy-Beaulieu **Un Homme d'Etat Russe (Nicholas Miliutine)...**

15 Nicolas Berdyaev **Leontiev** (In English)

17 **Tehran Yalta Potsdam. The Soviet Protocols**

18 **The Chronicle of Novgorod**

19 Paul N. Miliukov **Outlines of Russian Culture Vol. III** Pt. 1. The Origins of Ideology

20 P.A. Zaionchkovskii **The Abolition of Serfdom in Russia**

21 V.V. Vinogradov **Russkii iazyk. Grammaticheskoe uchenie o slove**

22 P.A. Zaionchkovsky **The Russian Autocracy under Alexander III**

23 A.E. Presniakov **Emperor Nicholas I of Russia. The Apogee of Autocracy**

25 S.S. Oldenburg **Last Tsar! Nicholas II, His Reign and His Russia** (OP)

28 S.F. Platonov **Ivan the Terrible** Paper

30 A.E. Presniakov **The Tsardom of Muscovy**

32 R.G. Skrynnikov **Ivan the Terrible**

33 P.A. Zaionchkovsky **The Russian Autocracy in Crisis, 1878-1882**

34 Joseph T. Fuhrmann **Tsar Alexis. His Reign and His Russia**

36 R.G. Skrynnikov **The Time of Troubles. Russia in Crisis, 1604–1618**

38 V.V. Shulgin **Days of the Russian Revolutions. Memoirs From the Right, 1905–1907.** Cloth and Paper

40 J.L. Black **"Into the Dustbin of History"! The USSR From August Coup to Commonwealth, 1991. A Documentary Narrative**

41 E.V. Anisimov **Empress Elizabeth. Her Reign and Her Russia, 1741–1761**

44 Paul N. Miliukov **The Russian Revolution** 3 vols.

THE CENTRAL AND EAST EUROPEAN SERIES

1 Louis Eisenmann **Le Compromis Austro-Hongrois de 1867**

3 Francis Dvornik **The Making of Central and Eastern Europe** 2nd edition

4 Feodor F. Zigel **Lectures on Slavonic Law**

THE ACADEMIC INTERNATIONAL REFERENCE SERIES

The Modern Encyclopedia of Russian and Soviet History 58 vols.

The Modern Encyclopedia of Russian and Soviet Literatures 50 vols.

The Modern Encyclopedia of Religions in Russia and the Soviet Union 30 vols

Soviet Armed Forces Review Annual

Russia & Eurasia Facts & Figures Annual

Russia & Eurasia Documents Annual

USSR Calendar of Events (1987- 1991) 5 vol. set

USSR Congress of Peoples's Deputies 1989. The Stenographic Record

Documents of Soviet History 12 vols.

Documents of Soviet-American Relations

Gorbachev's Reforms. An Annotated Bibliography of Soviet Writings. Part 1 1985–1987

Military Encyclopedia of Russia and Eurasia 50 vols.

China Facts & Figures Annual

China Documents Annual

Sino-Soviet Documents Annual

Encyclopedia USA. The Encyclopedia of the United States of America Past & Present 50 vols.

Sports Encyclopedia North America 50 vols.

Sports in North America. A Documentary History

Religious Documents North America Annual

The International Military Encyclopedia 50 vols.

SPECIAL WORKS
S.M. Soloviev **History of Russia** 50 vols.
SAFRA Papers 1985-

*Request catalogs